B#1258

D0026250

TAILORING: TRADITIONAL AND CONTEMPORARY TECHNIQUES

TAILORING: TRADITIONAL AND CONTEMPORARY TECHNIQUES

N. MARIE LEDBETTER

Associate Professor Emeritus

and

LINDA THIEL LANSING

Assistant Professor

Clothing, Textiles and Related Arts
Oregon State University
Corvallis, Oregon

Illustrations by
Loy E. Walton

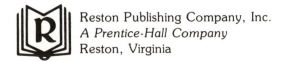

Reston Publishing Company, Inc.
A Prentice-Hall Company
Reston, Virginia

Library of Congress Cataloging in Publication Data

Ledbetter, N Marie.
    Tailoring, traditional and contemporary techniques.

    Includes index.
    1.   Tailoring (Women's).   2.   Tailoring.
I.   Lansing, Linda Thiel, joint author.   II.   Title.
TT519.5.L42   646.4′04   80-13266
ISBN 0-8359-7534-7

© 1981 by
Reston Publishing Company, Inc.
A Prentice-Hall Company
Reston, Virginia   22090

All rights reserved. No part of this book may be reproduced
in any way, or by any means, without permission in writing
from the publisher.

10   9   8   7   6   5   4   3   2   1

Printed in the United States of America

To our many tailoring students who encouraged the writing of this book.

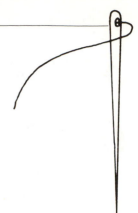

CONTENTS

PREFACE

This book facilitates decision-making in the selection of fabrics and design and in the construction of a tailored garment, using the traditional method, a contemporary method, or a combination of the two. The ramifications of various fabric and design choices are discussed as well as the implications these choices have on the construction process. Advantages and disadvantages of both traditional and contemporary methods of construction are presented, including such factors as time and skills required, design and fabric considerations, and the influence of the choice of techniques on the finished garment. Thus, by following a suggested procedural outline for each method, an individual can construct a tailored garment according to the selected choices.

This book is written and illustrated primarily for women's garments. Additional information is included so that men's garments may be constructed. However, strict, traditional men's tailoring techniques, such as a melton undercollar, hand-set collar, and chest piece, are not included.

Alternative construction techniques make this book a valuable adjunct to the pattern guide sheet or, for a basic tailored garment, it may replace the pattern guide. The book also provides assistance to the person who wishes to change some design details of the garment.

Basic concepts important to tailoring, applicable to women's and men's garments, are emphasized throughout the book. These concepts include compatibility, stability, fitting, shaping, and bulk reduction.

The techniques presented in this book are designed for the college or adult education student and for the serious home sewer who has basic sewing knowledge and skills. For the person who has had previous tailoring experience this reference can be utilized as a valuable source of some of the newer methods of construction. This book may be used similarly to a programmed text since it includes: (1) information needed to make decisions about alternative techniques, (2) detailed instructions for each technique, and (3) a means of critiquing at specific points. Each individual can progress at his or her own rate depending on the complexity of the design, the fabric chosen, and the individual's abilities.

We wish to gratefully acknowledge the influence of the late Gertrude Strickland and her book, *A Tailoring Manual,* on the traditional techniques presented in this book. We are especially grateful to Ruth A. Moser, Associate Professor Emeritus at Oregon State University, for her advice and expertise in the production of some of the materials used in this publication. We also wish to express appreciation to Kristin Stelljes for her assistance, to other tailoring students for their suggestions and encouragement, and to the faculty in the Department of Clothing, Textiles and Related Arts at Oregon State University for their interest and support.

N.M.L.
L.T.L.

TAILORING:
TRADITIONAL
AND
CONTEMPORARY
TECHNIQUES

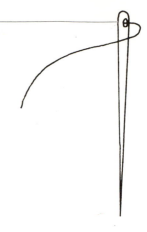

Tailoring Defined

Tailoring is the process by which the garment design lines are defined and the garment is given a permanent shape and structure of its own. Design lines, such as collars and lapels, are defined by sharp edges, and all lines within the garment should be smoothly curved or perfectly straight. The garment is molded to the desired shape, and this shape and the design lines must remain constant through extensive wear and cleaning.

Men's and women's coats, suits, and jackets are usually constructed by the tailored method. They may be made of any fabric which is relatively firm, in styles that vary from the closely fit suit to the loose coat that fits only in the shoulders. The garment must be well fit for the wearer's freedom of movement and for a professional appearance.

Tailoring demands exactness and special techniques to produce the crisp details, durability, and smooth lines that are characteristic of a well-tailored garment.

Types of Tailoring

Historically a tailored garment was made by a professional tailor who spent hours making tiny hand stitches to shape the garment. These hand methods still produce excellent results, but modern technology and current styles have given us other alternatives. Faster methods do not necessarily mean that we will have inferior and less desirable products. Examination of couture or designer-tailored apparel reveals that they too utilize the faster methods whereby a minimum of handwork is involved in producing top-quality garments. Thus, it may be more realistic to use these garments as our standard rather than the tailored garments of the past.

INTRODUCTION

1

Traditional tailoring will be used in this book to indicate the use of those techniques which have been used for many years and usually involve extensive handwork.

Contemporary tailoring will include those techniques that incorporate the use of new materials, such as fusibles, or the use of traditional materials with new techniques, such as the replacement of hand stitching with machine stitching.

Custom tailoring is sometimes used as a substitute term for traditional tailoring, but suggests that a garment is made for a specific individual. In the latter context it could apply to either type of tailoring.

Types of Tailored Garments

Fashion and personal preference usually suggest whether a garment is hard tailored or soft tailored.

The *hard-tailored* garment is constructed of fabric that is quite firm to somewhat stiff in nature, has very crisp, formed details, and extensive built-in shaping. It is often associated with men's suits and coats, and when used in women's wear, gives a mannish appearance.

The *soft-tailored* garment is made of softer fabrics and while details are crisp, they are not as rigid. The garment conforms more to the body because there is more subtle shaping. Soft-tailored garments have been traditionally considered more feminine, but fashion has also produced a softer, less structured look in menswear.

While some references associate hard tailoring with traditional techniques and soft tailoring with contemporary techniques, each may be accomplished by either method. The determining factors are more the choice of fashion fabric, supporting fabrics, and the design than the technique used. Also, some steps in construction may be omitted in soft tailoring.

The "unstructured" tailored garment will not be considered as a separate category, because usually it incorporates dressmaking techniques rather than tailoring techniques. An unstructured garment will be the result if many of the tailoring techniques are omitted.

Tailoring Concepts

The following concepts are important in determining the choices of materials and techniques that are used in tailoring.

1. *Compatibility* is a broad concept that indicates a positive relationship between two or more components. Compatibility is of major importance in selecting the garment design, materials, and the best construction techniques. Compatibility of the fabric and design with the wearer, compatibility of the components with each other and with the design, as well as compatibility with the individual's skills, personal preference, and money and time available must be considered.

2. *Fitting* requires that a garment conform to the natural contours of the wearer's body. Since a commercial pattern is designed for the "average" body, usually it will need to be adjusted for each individual to achieve a perfect fit.

3. *Shaping* forms a flat fabric to the configuration of the three-dimensional form, and details, such as collars, to the form dictated by the garment design. In tailored garments this must be done in a manner that will cause the shape to remain through countless wearings and cleanings. Shaping is accomplished by (a) cutting and sewing the fabric, (b) attaching two layers of fabric together so that a curved surface is produced (collar and lapels), and (c) steaming and pressing.

4. *Stabilizing* keeps the fabric from changing shape, especially from stretching. The total fabric may be stabilized or only certain areas. Stabilizing is accomplished by (a) underlining the total area, (b) interfacing a section, often adjacent to an edge, and (c) using a stay such as tape along an edge or seam.

5. *Reducing bulk* and defining edges is a major challenge in tailoring because medium to heavy fabrics and/or multiple layers of fabrics are often used. The bulk is reduced and flat seams and edges obtained by (a) trimming seams and beveling edges, (b) grading seams, (c) pressing, steaming, and pounding, and (d) understitching or topstitching.

Criteria for a Well-Tailored Garment

The following are general criteria for the well-tailored garment which will result in a professional appearance. More specific criteria or standards will be found in the text and the critiques in the Appendices.

1. Collar and lapels that are firm, roll smoothly, have sharp edges without the seam around the outer edge being obvious, and are identical on both sides.

2. Lapel roll line is firm, stable, and conforms to the body, does not gape or stand away. Front edge is firm, straight, and perpendicular to the floor.

3. Buttonholes are identical, firm, flat, have straight edges, square corners (except rounded keyhole), and show no signs of raveling.

4. Pockets are firm and have crisp edges, straight lines are straight and/or curves are smooth and even, and they are smooth when worn.

5. Shoulders are firm enough to be smooth and to allow ease of movement without stress on the fabric.

6. The sleeve hangs straight, and the sleeve cap is smoothly rounded without any wrinkles.

7. The sleeve and bottom hems are invisible from the right side and are smooth, firm, and flat.

8. Vents are straight, smooth, and firm, and have no obvious seams along the edges.

9. Lining fits smoothly, conceals inner construction, and gives an attractive appearance to the inside of the garment.

10. Fits to perfection.

11. Well pressed with no areas overpressed.

You will note that the concepts and criteria for a well-tailored garment are interrelated. They are important as a basis for understanding the consequences of the decisions you make regarding choice of materials and techniques. These decisions will determine the appearance, durability, and your satisfaction with your completed garment.

Decisions in Tailoring

A number of factors should be considered in choosing your design and materials and in deciding which techniques are best for you. The relative importance of each of these factors will vary with the individual and the type of decision to be made.

1. *Personal skills* and *experience* are important considerations in all decisions regarding design, materials, and techniques. The more experienced seamstress can choose more complicated designs, difficult fabrics, and challenging techniques than the person whose skills are more limited.

2. *Time available* is a definite factor in choosing techniques since traditional techniques are usually more time consuming than contemporary techniques. A complex design will be more time consuming than a simple one, and some fabrics will require more stabilizing or may not adapt to the faster contemporary techniques such as fusing.

3. *Personal preference* often dictates or limits one's choice of design and fabric. By all means, choose a design and fashion fabric that you like, one that fits into your wardrobe and way of life and one that you will wear. If you dislike handwork, choose methods that involve a minimum amount of this technique.

4. *Money available* is often a limiting factor in the choice of fabric and sometimes a pattern. Generally, try to choose the best quality fabric you can afford. Similar styles may be found in patterns that vary widely in price. Usually an expensive pattern for a tailored garment gives much more instruction in tailoring procedures than a less expensive one. As your first tailoring project you may wish to make a jacket rather than a coat or suit to reduce the amount of fabric, and thus the cost.

Plan of Work

This book is arranged so you can follow a logical sequence for the construction of a tailored garment regardless of the construction techniques chosen. Some decisions will need to be made in advance, but you will be alerted to this and given adequate information to make the decision.

Guide sheets with commercial patterns vary greatly in the extensiveness of instructions given and in the sequence followed in construction. Because you may be using different techniques than those shown in your guide sheet, your plan of work can usually follow the sequence of chapters in the Table of Contents. For your convenience a pro-

cedural outline is included in the Appendices, which will be useful in planning the sequence for the construction of your garment.

Evaluation

Standards for the fit and construction of the well-tailored garment are given in the text, and critiques, a unique feature to this book, are included in the Appendices. They have been devised to aid you in evaluating your own work. You will be alerted as to the appropriate time to refer to a particular sheet. By checking the points on the critique, you can evaluate your individual work against standards of professional tailors and determine whether or not you are ready to proceed to the next phase of construction. Checking at specific points can help you identify and correct problems that could not be corrected later in the construction sequence.

Each garment you make involves new learning experiences and different decisions. In addition to periodic evaluation during construction, a final evaluation is important for maximum learning from your tailoring experience. A critique of the final garment is also included in the Appendices. However, some factors are difficult to evaluate, especially those that involve the choice of garment design and fashion fabric as they relate to you, the wearer.

Your satisfaction with your completed garment will be the most important factor in your evaluation. Only when the garment is completed and worn can you determine if you made the best choices for yourself and your garment.

Modern concepts of clothing construction demand that tailored garments made at home have a professional appearance. The first step in achieving this effect is the recognition of the place that proper sewing tools play in the final appearance of a product. Since this initial aspect of construction is so vital, this chapter deals with the selection of the various pieces of equipment with suggestions for their use and maintenance. Even though most of these articles (except the sewing machine) are relatively inexpensive, proper selection and care will extend their efficiency and in the end will result in economy of time as well as of money.

Cutting Equipment

No pieces of equipment are of greater importance than good shears and scissors. With proper care they are considered a lifetime investment so it is well to buy the best you can afford. If funds are limited, a pair of 18-cm to 20.5-cm (7'' to 8'') shears will provide cutting and trimming capability.

Dressmaker's shears are generally 15 cm (6'') or more in length, with the average being 18 cm to 20.5 cm (7'' to 8''). There is one small ring handle for the thumb and a larger handle for two or three fingers. The handles may be either bent or straight. The bent handles are more popular because the blades will slide along closer to the table and in this manner, the fabric and pattern are allowed to remain almost flat during the cutting process (Figure 1–1). One shear blade has a sharp point while the other blade has a blunt point. The latter provides greater durability for cutting heavyweight fabrics.

Special knife-edge shears are available for use on *all* fabric weights, but they are especially good for synthetics. Synthetic fibers do have a greater dulling effect on the blade than do natural fibers, and the knife edge

1
EQUIPMENT— SELECTION, USE, AND CARE

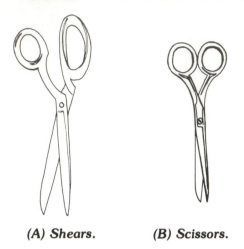

(A) Shears.   **(B) Scissors.**

FIGURE 1-1

is much more successful than the regular blade in this instance. (Natural fibers include leather and suede.) The newer lightweight designs using plastic handles and stainless steel blades resist corrosion, whereas scissors and shears of hot-drop forged carbon and steel (more easily identified by their solid steel frame and no plastic handles) are susceptible to corrosion and rust. However, because of their sturdiness, they are often the preferred scissor or shear by many teachers and industrial users. (Shears are available for the left-handed person.)

Scissors are designed for lighter or more

intricate cutting than shears and range in length from 7.5 cm to 15 cm (3'' to 6''). For general use at the machine the 15-cm (6'') length is generally preferred. The ring handles are of equal size, each just large enough for one finger, and may be plain or somewhat contoured. The long, slender blades are of uneven width with the narrow blade having a sharp point for slashing openings and the wider blade having a blunt point for extra strength and safety (Figure 1-1). Scissors are useful for trimming, grading, and notching seams and wherever careful clipping into corners is required.

Embroidery and buttonhole scissors are convenient adjuncts but are not essential items in the equipment box. Thread clip scissors have become popular for clipping threads at the machine. Some find that these are indispensable but only after one becomes accustomed to using them (Figure 1-2).

Pinking shears are not as important as good cutting shears and are usually more expensive. However, they are time savers for seam finishing on many fabrics and are well worth the cost. They should not be used for the initial cutting of your fabric. Available lengths range from 14 cm to 25.5 cm (5½'' to 10'') with 19 cm (7½'') being the most popular. Pinking shears should be returned to the manufacturer for sharpening.

Selection of Shears and Scissors

When purchasing shears remember that:

1. A solid steel frame indicates hot-drop forged construction, and this will provide long lasting keenness of edge.

2. A genuine screw instead of a rivet will help to retain perfect adjustment of blades, because it is adjustable and can be tightened.

3. Uniformly ground blade edges that are slightly beveled will aid in cutting along the entire edge.

FIGURE 1-2
Thread Clip Scissors.

4. A smooth, highly polished finish will help to prevent grinding of the edges.

5. Thin steel at the points will aid in precision cutting.

6. Testing on scraps of fabrics ranging in weight from sheer to heavy will help you to determine whether they can do the following: cut sharply from near the back of the blades to the tip of point without pulling on the fabric; fit the hand comfortably; operate easily without being too loose or too tight.

Care of Shears and Scissors

1. Use shears for the work intended. Keep an old pair available for cutting paper.

2. Keep the blades clean and free of lint by wiping them frequently with your fingers. The natural oil from your fingers, as well as the removal of lint, will help to make your shears and scissors operate more smoothly.

3. Keep free of moisture. In damp climates lint on the blades may collect moisture and cause spot rusting. Finger wiping the blades after use will help to prevent this problem.

4. Place a drop of oil at the screw occasionally to facilitate ease of use. Carefully wipe off any excess with a soft cloth or with a cleansing tissue.

5. Handle carefully. Dropping may blunt the blade tips as well as distort their precision alignment.

6. Do not force a cut by cutting through too many layers at one time. This causes spreading of the blades and possible permanent damage to the cutting edge. If the fabric appears too heavy, cut one layer at a time.

Measuring Equipment

There are many measuring devices on the market at present. The ones listed are con-

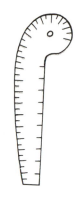

FIGURE 1–3
Curved Ruler.

sidered the most essential; others may be added as your interest and ability increase.

1. A *tape measure* of a durable fabric, 152 cm (60'') in length, and reversible with numbers beginning at opposite ends of each side is generally preferred. However, you may discover that a tape may have measurements in centimeters on one side and inches on the other. Plastic tape measures, preferred by some, are stiff and do not allow for the penetration of pins for certain types of measurements. However, because fabric tape measures may shrink or stretch with use, check the accuracy frequently against a calibrated meter or yardstick.

2. A *flexible ruler* of transparent plastic allows for more precise measuring and marking in certain areas. A 30.5-cm (12'') ruler is useful in measuring curved lines accurately and in providing a good edge for some kinds of marking. A 15-cm (6'') length is also a convenient size.

3. A *curved ruler* provides an accurate way to measure and mark curved lines (e.g., hiplines). They are available in either metal or wood (Figure 1–3).

4. A *French curve* is also helpful in redrawing lines where neckline, armholes, and bust

FIGURE 1–4
French Curve.

area curves are involved. They are available in plastic or metal (Figure 1-4).

5. An *adjustable metal* seam gauge is useful for measuring hem widths, seam allowances, buttonholes, and so forth.

6. *A hem marker* that sets on a base is useful for measuring skirt lengths. Markers with holes for insertion of pins give a line easy to follow on any colored fabric and is the most exact. However, it does require a helper to do the marking. For one person, chalk markers are fairly easy to use if the lines show up well on the garment being measured. Care should be taken that this type of marker be held close to the fabric to prevent blurring or spreading of the chalk as it is expelled from the marker. It may not be as accurate in marking as the pin marker. Be sure to buy a marker that can be adjusted to all fashion lengths.

7. A *yardstick* or *meter stick* is desirable for drawing long, straight lines. With the help of a second person it may also be used for marking hems. Both are available in metal as well as wood. Unless the wood is a hardwood, it may tend to warp, and frequent checking may be necessary to determine its accuracy. All edges must be smooth and even.

8. An *L square or T square* has true right angles and is helpful in checking accurate

grainlines. Either one can also be used for measuring hems with the aid of your helper. They are available in metal or wood.

Marking Equipment

Tailor's chalk may be used for transferring pattern marks directly to the fabric. Two kinds are available: waxy (for wool) and chalky (for all other fibers). The waxy type may be removed from the wool in pressing, while on lining fabrics it may leave grease marks. Both types are available in white and in colors. It is well to try any colored chalk on a scrap of your fabric before actually marking with it. Press over the marking to determine the effect of a hot iron. Also, a worn-down piece of hand soap is effective for fabric marking. Its marking is stable during construction but is easily removed by pressing or washing.

Colored marking pencils may be used on firm fabrics and on interfacings. Also available are water-soluble fabric marking pens that permit the easy removal of a mark by application of a bit of moisture.

A tracing wheel with dressmaker's tracing paper may be used to transfer darts and seamlines from pattern to fabric. In tailoring, its primary use is in marking the muslin test garment. It may also be employed on fabrics to be used on the inside of the garment (e.g., interfacings and underlinings). Be sure to test the tracing paper before using it on fashion fabric because it is not easily removed. Often it will not mark if the fabric is heavy, and the pattern may be torn if the fabric is spongy. Use the tracing paper with care on linings as the wheel may mark the fabric, and/or the mark may be visible on the right side.

Three kinds of tracing wheels are available: sawtooth (probably the most popular), needle point (fine points), and smooth edged. The *sawtooth* wheel makes a more conspicuous marking than the needle point. The *needle point* (if available) is more frequently used for marking paper by those who do considerable work with pattern making. The *smooth-edged* wheel gives the same kind of marking that is achieved by using a dull-bladed object. A dull blade (e.g., butter knife or letter opener) may be used in place of a tracing wheel. However, care must be exercised to avoid shifting the fabric. If your fabric is of a plain color and is firmly woven as are many linings, a tracing wheel marking may be satisfactory *without* the use of tracing paper.

Darning cotton in several different colors is useful as a quick method of making tailor's tacks to mark important pattern details. Its use is explained in Chapter 6.

Hand-Sewing Equipment

Needles

Needles for hand sewing are of many kinds and are made for specific purposes. They differ as to eye shape (round or long), length, and point (sharp, blunt, ballpoint or wedge). There are three types of needles generally used for dressmaking purposes and tailoring.

Sharps are all-purpose needles of medium length with round eyes. *Crewel,* or *embroidery,* are similar to the sharps in length but are designed with long eyes for easy threading and for carrying multiple strands. *Betweens* are very short, round-eyed needles commonly used by tailors to aid in producing short, invisible stitches. Needles may be purchased in packages of assorted sizes (sizes 5 through 10) or in packages of one size. Sizes 7, 8, and 9 are the sizes in common use.

Another type of needle often found useful in tailoring is the *tapestry* needle. It is heavy and blunt pointed with a long, oval eye designed to carry yarn through porous fabric. Even though this needle was designed for needlepoint and tapestry work it is useful in drawing yarn through corded buttonholes where a rounded effect is desired and in doing trapunto, a feature often used in decorating lining in tailored garments. Sizes range from 13 to 26.

When selecting needles remember that the larger the number of the needle, the finer the needle will be.

The needle to use must be decided by the fabric, the size of the thread to be used, and the kind of stitch to be made. Larger needles (smaller numbers) may be used on sturdy fabrics; finer needles (larger numbers) must be used on thinner materials. The yarns of the fabric should not be broken by a needle that is too large as it is inserted for a stitch. Large needles are also difficult to guide through fabric.

The size of the thread should be compatible with the size of the needle. The eye should accommodate the thread easily. The hole produced in the fabric by the needle should be filled by the thread as the needle carries it through.

The shorter the stitch being made, the shorter and finer the needle should be.

Use the following rules for the care of needles:

1. Needles remain in better condition if kept in the black rust-resistant paper in which they are packaged.

2. Dulled points may be sharpened by pushing the tip of the needle into an emery bag (often found attached to pin cushions).

3. Do not leave needles in the emery as they will rust easily in this medium.

Pins

Pins are categorized in two ways—by length and by diameter. By length, pins are measured in terms of sixteenths of an inch with number 16 being 16/16 or 1 inch long; number 17 is 1 1/16 inch long; number 14 is

7/8 inch. By diameter, pins are classified as silk (slender pin with a fine point), dressmaker (pin of medium diameter, most commonly used), bank (heavy utility pin, not for dress fabrics), color-headed (easy to see, slender and sharp) and ball point (for knits).

Pins may be purchased in boxes or in paper packages. Regardless of the manner in which they are bought, the following suggestions should be considered:

1. Pins should have smoothly tapered points with slender shanks to prevent holes from being punched into fabrics. Discard any that are blunted or rough.

2. Heads should be smooth to prevent the catching of threads.

3. Brass pins are rustproof and are often preferred for this reason.

4. Slender steel pins with colored heads are preferred by some because the heads are easy to see and the pins are easily inserted into fabric. The overall length is 1 1/4 inches.

5. Ball-point pins are suggested for use in knit fabrics, but for tightly knit fabrics fine sharp pins are better. T-shaped pins work well for pinning heavy or high pile fabrics. They are longer than ordinary pins.

6. Sizes 16 and 17 are general choices for most sewing. *Note:* Fine needles (numbers 9 and 10) may be used in place of pins on fabrics that mark easily.

7. Keep a number of pins in a *wrist pin cushion* for the sake of convenience. Additional pins should be kept in the container in which they were purchased.

Thimbles

A thimble is an indispensable aid in efficient hand sewing. It is often difficult to convince students of this fact but persistent effort on the student's part will eventually prove this point. The effectiveness of a thimble will depend upon the depth of the exterior depressions. Lightweight metal thimbles are more deeply indented and are generally preferred over the bulkier plastic variety. Regardless of the kind of thimble, it must fit the middle finger of the sewing hand comfortably without being too tight or too loose. Sizes range from 5 (smallest) to 12 (largest). Two styles are made—the closed top and the open top which tailors prefer.

A variation of the standard thimble is the leather thimble which is soft and molds to the finger. It also has a slit to accommodate a long fingernail. Some seamstresses who dislike hard thimbles find the leather thimble a comfortable alternative.

Miscellaneous Equipment

Many sewing gadgets are to be found on a notion counter. The following have been found to be useful adjuncts to many sewing projects.

1. *Beeswax* helps to strengthen threads for hand sewing and to prevent tangling. It may be purchased in a convenient plastic container which helps to keep the wax clean.

2. *Point-turner* is a flat wooden or plastic instrument for turning corners on enclosed seams.

3. *Rubber cement* is useful for pattern alterations because it leaves the pattern tissue in a smooth condition.

4. *Fusible web* is convenient at times for holding hems and facings in place permanently.

5. A *glue stick* is handy for altering patterns and on many fabrics can be used as a basting aid in holding interfacings, underlinings, zippers, and so forth, in place temporarily. Do not place *on* a stitching line when using.

6. *Magic transparent tape* (1.3 cm or 1/2'') wide is useful as a stitching guide along zippers, as well as a means of holding seams more closely where matching is desired. Do not sew over this kind of tape because it may cause the needle to become sticky. It may be used also for holding pattern pieces when altering. A heavy dispenser for the tape is very helpful; it requires only one hand to tear off a piece.

7. *Basting tape,* narrow double-faced ''sticky'' tape, is useful in place of the glue stick to hold zippers in place and is invaluable when matching plaids.

8. *Seam ripper* is an inexpensive time saver useful for removing unwanted stitching. When purchasing a seam ripper, look for one with a fine, sharp point.

9. *Tweezers* are helpful in getting hold of ''hard to pull'' bastings and other unwanted threads.

10. A *bodkin* is useful to open small darts when pressing.

11. A very fine *crochet hook* (size 12) is helpful to pull the ends of topstitching threads to the inside of the garment.

12. *Padded hanger* is useful in maintaining the shape of the garment as soon as it is basted and ready for fitting.

13. A *small box* for holding small equipment is convenient in either a classroom or home situation.

Pressing Equipment

See Chapter 8 for selection, use, and care of pressing equipment.

Sewing Machine

To construct tailored garments you need only a basic straight stitch sewing machine

that has a well-balanced stitch. A zigzag feature will be useful for finishing seams, and a serpentine or multiple zigzag[1] stitch is desirable for machine pad stitching, but neither of these features are necessary. New, sharp sewing machine needles are imperative. Sewing machine needles are sized from 9 to 16 for domestic needles and 70 to 110 for imported needles, with the smallest numbers denoting the smallest needles. A medium size needle, number 11 or 80, will be suitable for most fabrics. For topstitching with heavier thread, a larger needle (14 to 16 or 100 to 110) will be needed. Ballpoint needles are recommended for stitching knits.

If you have problems with dropped or skipped stitches, a scarf (yellow band) needle may help on many machines since it places the thread closer to the hook. However, check with your dealer before using the yellow band needle as it may not be needed on some makes of machines.

An easy and less expensive method to handle one cause of skipped stitches (especially when sewing on nylon knit or other thin fabrics) is to apply a small piece of woven adhesive tape over the needle hole. This allows the needle to make its own size hole and will prevent the fabric from being ''punched'' into the needle hole. Masking tape may also be used but it is less durable.

Your sewing machine must be treated like any expensive piece of equipment. Because wool fabrics may lint more than other fabrics previously used, clean your machine often. Refer to your owner's manual for specific instructions regarding its care.

---

[1] Three or four straight stitches repeated in a zigzag pattern.

2

SELECTION OF GARMENT COMPONENTS

The finished garment can be of no higher quality than the quality of the fabric and findings. A professional tailor cannot make a professional looking suit or coat out of poor quality fabric. Remember that the investment of time and energy will be the same regardless of the fabric used, so choose the best quality fabric your budget will allow.

How does one distinguish between a high quality fabric and a fabric of lesser quality? Quality and price are usually, but not always, synonymous. Fabric quality and price is determined by the type of fiber, the quality of the fiber, the fabric construction, and the finishing processes. Price may also be influenced by current fashion and the availability of the fiber and fabric. For example, camel's hair and cashmere are very expensive because they are in short supply. Thus, price can be used only as one guideline in judging quality.

Fabric names identify the type of fabric construction, but they are not an indication of the quality of construction. Generally speaking, high quality wool fabrics for tailoring, either knit or woven, are firm but not necessarily heavy. They are closely woven unless purposefully made with an open weave. The better quality will have more resilience than the inferior quality and thus will wrinkle less.

Judging quality requires experience. Examine many fabrics in different price ranges in different stores and compare like fabrics. For example, compare wool flannels in different price ranges with each other, and with wool and synthetic, or wool and cotton blends.

The characteristics of high quality and inferior quality are given for each of the traditional types of fabrics in the following section. However, since it is difficult to visualize fabrics, you should look for these characteristics as you see and feel actual fabrics and attempt to make value judgments.

Components of the Tailored Garment

The tailored coat or suit is stabilized, shaped or molded, and finished by the use of a variety of fabrics. The outer layer, or fashion fabric, is visible as is the inner layer, or lining. However, inner components which include underlining, interfacings, interlining, and various notions such as stay tape and shoulder shapes are not seen once the garment is completed but are equally important to the overall appearance of the garment.

Fashion Fabrics

Fashion fabrics suitable for tailored garments vary as to fiber content, construction, weight, and visual appearance. Thus, some fabrics will be much easier to tailor than others and produce a more professional looking garment.

Wool. A natural fiber that has traditionally been used in tailoring because it possesses body and strength for durability and can be eased and molded and will hold the shape imparted to it. Being a resilient fiber, it resists wrinkling, and since it is a natural fiber and very absorptive, it breathes and is comfortable to wear. Another advantage is that an all-wool fabric that has not had a special finish can be straightened if, during the finishing process, it was tentered[1] or finished off-grain.[2]

The fiber information on the bolt on which the fabric is rolled will list the fibers

---

[1] Tenter—a process by which fabric is stretched and dried to its finished width.

[2] Off-grain—lengthwise and crosswise yarns are not at right angles.

by percentage. *Virgin wool* indicates that it is made of new wool but does not indicate the quality of wool. If other than new wool is included, the tag will include the words *reprocessed* or *reused.* Reprocessed wool is made from new cuttings or scraps; reused wool has been recycled from used items. Both categories of wool have been returned to the fiber state and then spun and made into cloth. These fibers are not as strong as new fibers but will be warm and satisfactory especially when blended with other fibers.

Wool fabrics can be divided into two categories—worsteds and woolens—with each having special characteristics. *Worsteds* are made of long wool fibers that are tightly twisted and then woven or knitted into a firmly constructed fabric. They have a smooth, hard surface that resists wrinkles and they are durable; but eventually, because of these characteristics, they may become shiny from prolonged wear. Because worsteds are firm, they do not ease and mold as readily as woolens and are more difficult to press. Design details are easily seen due to the smooth surface, as are imperfect construction techniques. Wool gabardine and crepe are examples of worsted fabrics.

Wool gabardine of the highest quality will be very closely woven of fine, soft, long staple yarns giving the fabric a soft, drapeable hand and a hard surface with a dull sheen. Gabardine may be very lightweight or quite heavy—the thickness does not influence the quality. A poorer quality is often made of coarser yarn, is less tightly woven, and will feel more harsh and stiff. If it is made of short staple fibers, it will be a bit rough.

Crepe has a plain weave with highly twisted worsted yarns that give a grainy or crinkled appearance. Wool crepe may be very lightweight or a heavyweight suitable for suits and lightweight coats. The finest quality will be closely woven, resilient, and firm but flexible.

Woolens are made from shorter fibers that are less tightly twisted than worsteds and thus are generally softer to the touch. They are soft when made of fine, high quality yarns and somewhat rough if made of lower quality, or less finished yarns, such as in some tweeds. Woolens may be closely woven to produce a very firm fabric, such as a high quality flannel, or they may be loosely constructed for an open, lacy effect. Fiber ends of woolens can be easily brought to the surface to form a soft nap as found in a fleece. Woolens ease and shape readily, but they are usually not as durable as worsteds. Napped[3] surfaces will especially show wear along garment edges and in elbows, buttonholes, and pockets. Thick woolens are more difficult to tailor than thin ones because of the additional bulk in seams and design areas. Wool flannel, fleece coating, and tweeds are examples of woolen fabrics.

Fine quality *wool flannel* will be closely woven, firm but supple, and not excessively napped. A loosely woven flannel may feel soft but will be difficult to tailor because it will show press marks and be unstable. If the weave is not readily visible, hold the fabric to the light to determine the closeness of the weave.

Fleece coating is a thick fabric made of loosely twisted yarns that have been woven and then brushed to form a napped surface, but to determine quality look at the back of the fabric. The back should be closely woven and firm. Compress the fabric—the nap should spring back when it is released if the fibers are resilient.

Tweeds may be an exception to the guideline that a high quality fabric should be soft and closely woven. They may be, but often the characteristic texture of the tweed requires that the yarns be less refined and

thus they may be more harsh to the touch. The fabric should still be stable.

The care of woolens and worsteds is similar. Both usually require dry cleaning but medium to dark colors tend to conceal overall soil and can be successfully spot cleaned. Some washable wool fabrics are available but they often are not of the highest quality and generally the pretreatment and finishes cause them to be less resilient and more harsh to the touch. Even though they may be dimensionally stable to washing, the surface texture usually changes to some degree. Laundering a tailored wool garment is usually not recommended as it is difficult to reshape and to press all components satisfactorily.

Wool Blends. A combination of wool with another fiber to reduce cost, to add strength, or to give a particular effect. The blend may be a synthetic (i.e., nylon, acrilan, polyester) or a natural fiber (silk or cotton). Blends may be found in both worsted and woolens, and result in a fabric that has the properties of both fibers with the percentage of each determining the expected performance. With a high percentage of wool, the fabric will possess more desirable wool characteristics.

Wool and cotton blends are usually lightweight and suitable only for soft-tailored garments. Wool combined with silk is a luxury fabric which is often found in dressy suitings. In both blends, the higher the percentage of wool the more resilient resistant and more pliable the fabric will be.

A synthetic adds strength to fragile fibers such as cashmere as well as to short staple and lower quality fibers. But a synthetic in a blend may create some problems. For example, if the fabric has been tentered and finished off-grain the fabric cannot usually be straightened. Therefore, it is especially important that you check the fabric for straightness of grain before purchasing.

---

[3] Napped fibers have been raised on the face of the fabric to give a soft surface.

A synthetic blended with wool in a napped fabric may also present additional problems in pressing. The heat and pressure necessary to press the wool may cause the nap to flatten and be difficult to raise because the synthetic tends to heat set.[4] Again, since woven synthetics do not ease and mold well, the higher the percentage of wool in a blend the easier it will be to handle.

Cotton. A natural fiber that, in a woven suit weight and/or in a blend, is a good choice for summer suits, but to be appropriate for tailoring, the cotton must be firmly woven. This means it will also be difficult to shape and ease. A patterned fabric, either a woven-in or a printed design will help to conceal irregularities and inaccurate construction.

Cotton corduroy, velvet, and velveteen are examples of cotton pile fabrics, and like the napped wool, should have a very closely woven backing with a close and dense surface pile. The highest quality pile fabrics will be made of fine, long staple cotton that has a silky feel, is more wrinkle resistant and drapeable, and retains its original appearance. Lesser qualities will feel more harsh and stiff. The pile on velvet stands upright and after being compressed should return to its upright state when released. The pile on corduroy and velveteen lies in one direction but also should have some resiliency.

Linen. A natural fiber that is cool and crisp for summer but does wrinkle and is somewhat difficult to tailor because of its rigidity. When purchasing, look for a crease-resistant label. A variety of fabrics that resemble linen are available, but the most successful to tailor are those that are medium weight and closely woven. The lighter weight, more loosely woven fabrics may require underlining.

Silk. A natural fiber that may be made of very light or quite heavy yarns. Raw silk, made of rough, coarse yarns, usually has adequate body and weight to be used for tailored garments. It will be more durable when both lengthwise and crosswise yarns are the same weight than when lengthwise yarns are lighter than crosswise. Silk suiting, such as shantung, is suitable for dressy suits. Silk of this type is more expensive and more fragile than raw silk. Although silk is generally considered to be washable, a tailored garment will require dry cleaning to retain its original appearance.

Synthetic Fibers. May be used alone or in a wide variety of blends for tailoring weight fabrics. *Polyester doubleknits* reached a peak in popularity in the early 1970s and are still preferred by many for their stabilized strength, durability, and easy care. The most satisfactory doubleknit for tailoring is one that is closely knit of fine yarns similar to fabrics used in better menswear. These doubleknits generally wear well, but more loosely knitted fabrics may tend to catch and pull easily. Another disadvantage of some of the doubleknits is that they may become shiny with wear. Doubleknits of acrylic are usually not as satisfactory as other synthetics because they tend to stretch and ''bag'' at the elbows and knees. Because of the knit structure, doubleknits ease and mold somewhat, but they are difficult to press. Also, it is difficult to ensure flat, sharp edges. Topstitching is recommended to control edges.

Woven polyesters, acrylics, and *blends* are popular for lightweight suits and coats because they are less expensive than wool and can be washed. A major problem with some of these fabrics is that the fibers catch on rough objects and will pull. However, the

---

[4] Heat set—fibers remain in the position in which they were pressed.

stretch-woven polyester twills are less likely to pull since the yarns are crimped. Following the trend to natural fibers in the mid 1970s, woven synthetics have become more like the "naturals" in appearance. This is done by using short staple fibers or by blending with a small amount of wool to create a wool-like hand. Although a small amount of wool may change the visual appearance, it will do little to increase the fabric's easing and molding property.

Blends of various synthetics and/or of natural fibers appear to be the wave of the future. To determine the acceptability of any blend of fiber for tailoring, remember that the fabric will react in direct proportion to the percentage of each fiber used. Although many generic classifications of synthetics have come into being in recent years, high quality wool still sets the standard for fine-tailored garments.

Supporting Fabrics

Supporting fabrics include all those fabrics that are placed between the fashion fabric and lining to give shape, stability, and sometimes warmth to the total garment or to specific areas. The garment design and fashion fabric dictate the supporting fabrics to be used. Unstructured or softly tailored garments use fewer supporting fabrics than structured, shaped garments. The underlining lies directly beneath the fashion fabric followed by the interfacing, the interlining, (if used) and finally, the lining.

Underlining. A layer of fabric that is sewed as one with the fashion fabric to provide opaqueness, to prevent the fashion fabric from stretching, and/or to give additional body. The underlining can serve as a "hanger" on which to attach hems, interfacings, and other interior components as well as to serve as a cushion for edges of seams, darts, facings, and pockets. Because it does provide another layer of fabric, it will con-

tribute some additional warmth to the garment.

Two factors must be considered when determining the need for an underlining—garment design and fabric construction. They are so closely related that one cannot be appraised without the other. Consider the following points when determining need:

1. Firm, opaque fabrics of medium or heavy weight usually do not require underlinings, while fabrics that are very lightweight, stretchy, loosely woven, or sheer may need the additional layer.

2. If a soft fabric is made in a design that stands away from the body, a firm underlining will be needed; if the same fabric is used in a softly belted garment, underlining would add unnecessary bulk.

3. Smooth-surfaced fabrics that show press marks may be enhanced by the use of a lightweight underlining to shield the exterior from the inner construction.

4. Not all components of a suit may require underlining. To illustrate, a soft flannel used in a jacket may need underlining as will the pants, but a vest and a soft, full skirt will not. An underlining is desirable for skirts, which may stretch in the seat, and pants, which may bag in the knees, but the same underlining will hinder the drape of a fuller garment.

5. For warmth in a windy climate, a loosely woven fashion fabric may be underlined with a very firmly woven fabric, such as muslin, to act as a shield against air movement.

An underlining must be compatible in appearance, hand, function, and care with the fashion fabric.

1. Check for visual change. To test their compatibility, hold the two fabrics together as they will be worn. Examine them at various angles and against the light to deter-mine whether the underfabric has any in-fluence on the color. An opaque fabric may use any harmonizing color for an underlin-ing, while a more open fabric will require a matching color.

2. Evaluate the hand of the paired fabrics. The underlining should usually be lighter in weight than the fashion fabric so it will not be the dominating fabric. If the purpose is to give stability, the lightest weight stable fabric will do the job. *Silk organza* is the lightest weight fabric, gives support, and adds only a minimum amount of bulk. Do not use a crisp fabric, such as organdy, unless crispness is desired. *Nylon organza* is much more slippery and difficult to handle than silk and may have yarn slippage in the seams. *Nylon tulle* may be used if a little crispness is desired. Silk organza and nylon tulle are also excellent for stabilizing small areas such as buttonholes.

3. Check for strength and probability of seam slippage. A cotton or polyester-cotton blend batiste is quite lightweight and stable. It is excellent for underlining in pants because it is strong and will resist seam slip-page. Lightweight synthetic underlinings such as SiBonne® and Siri® work well but are a little more slippery. Most fabrics suitable for linings are not recommended for underlining because they are too slippery. This makes them difficult to work with, and yarn slippage at the seams is more likely to result where there is stress.

4. Check for wrinkle resistance. A perma-nent press fabric provides the advantage of being wrinkle resistant, but because of this factor may be more difficult to press flat in the seams. Muslin is inexpensive and is available in a variety of weights from medium to heavy. It was traditionally used by French couturiers, but for today's tailored garments it is too heavy and it is not crease resistant.

5. Determine the desirability of fused underlinings. An underlining that is fused to the fabric produces a fabric similar to a bonded material. Most fusible interfacings are too stiff to be used in the total garment as an underlining and may not wear well when the garment is flexed. A fusible nylon knit is considered by many to be the best choice if a fusible is desired for overall stability. The knit will be more flexible and generally will not abrade with wear. The knit should be preshrunk and completely fused according to the fabric instructions.

Interfacings. The choice of interfac-ings can be an important factor in the ap-pearance of the finished garment. An inter-facing that is too stiff will make interfaced areas appear different from the rest of the garment. An interfacing that is too soft will result in a limp, shapeless effect. Frequently it is desirable to use different weights and different types of interfacings in various parts of the garment to give the desired result. The collar and lapels may require a heavier interfacing, detail areas a lighter one, and hems still a lighter one.

One must analyze the function of inter-facing for each area of the garment. Inter-facings are used to:

1. Mold or roll an area, such as lapels and collar.

2. Give added body, as in a jacket front or coat front.

3. Give a crisp, defined look to a design detail such as a pocket flap.

4. Reinforce an edge, such as the front opening or hem.

5. Give stability to keep the fashion fabric from stretching, as in the back shoulder area.

6. Support the fashion fabric across a body hollow, as in the front shoulder area.

There are two categories of interfacings that are used in tailored garments: *nonfusible* and *fusible.* Both are available in woven and nonwoven constructions and in a variety of fiber combinations.

Hair canvas, a nonfusible interfacing traditionally used for the fronts and collars, is the only interfacing that is used exclusively for tailored garments. It is a woven interfacing containing a percentage of animal hair which gives the fabric resiliency. The hair tends to cling to wool, thus making the fashion fabric and the interfacing feel as one fabric. The best quality of hair canvas contains some wool which increases resiliency and shapeability. Hair canvas is available in several weights and in a variety of fiber contents to be compatible with various weights of fashion fabrics.

Woven or nonwoven fabrics of synthetic, cotton, or blends of various fibers may be used, especially if the fashion fabric is not wool or where support, not moldability, is desired. Nonwoven interfacings will not mold as well as woven ones, but they give stability and do not ravel; thus, they are excellent for reinforcing a slashed pocket or a design area. Interfacing for hems may not need to be as heavy as that used in the garment fronts, so a lighter weight woven fabric cut on the bias for flexibility is often used. Woven, all-cotton wigan is traditional for back shoulder interfacing. Since its main function is to provide stability, other lightweight, firmly woven fabrics (e.g., muslin) may be used equally as well. All cotton or cotton blends are strong and will resist stress more than slippery fabrics.

Fusible interfacings are available in the same fiber combinations as nonfusibles with the exception of hair cloth. At this writing only one fusible, fusible Arco®, has a small hair content. This is the heaviest and firmest fusible interfacing available and is appropriate for medium and heavy weight wool or other fabrics where more body is needed.

Fusible interfacings can be divided into three types, determined by their construction: *woven, nonwoven,* and *knit.*

1. Woven fusible interfacings are available in various weights and should be cut following the same grain as a conventional interfacing.

2. Nonwoven fusible interfacings may be nondirectional, or they may be stable in length but stretch crosswise. The nondirectional ones are good stabilizers but do not shape well. The latter type (crosswise stretch) is cut as a woven, but any piece to be cut on the bias, such as the collar interfacing, is better placed on the crosswise grain since maximum stretch is in that direction. The nonwoven interfacings, which feel spongy and have many parallel fibers on the surface, tend to abrade with use more than those that feel smooth or have a netlike appearance as a result of being needlepunched[5] during their construction.

3. The fusible knit interfacing is compatible with knits and may also be suitable as a lightweight interfacing in wovens. It is stable lengthwise and stretches on the crosswise grain. A variation of the knitted construction is the weft-inserted fusible interfacing which has a knitted warp and a straight filling. It is fairly stable in both directions and has the most stretch on the bias, much like a woven.

One must remember that fusible interfacings produce a fabric that is much firmer and stiffer after being fused, so always fuse a sample following the manufacturer's instructions. Then check the fused sample to determine if mark-off occurs (visibility of the edge of the interfacing from the right side).

---

[5] Needle punch—a technique used in manufacturing to create a nonwoven fabric by uniting fibers in a web.

[6] Sawtoothing—notches about 1 cm to 1.3 cm (3/8'' to 1/2'') deep (like large pinking) along the inner edge of the interfacing.

This will not be a problem if all edges of the fusible interfacing end at a seam. Otherwise, pinking or sawtoothing[6] the edge of the interfacing can help to prevent mark-off. Also, compare the fused sample with the original fabric to determine if there is any change in the surface texture.

Before selecting the interfacing, determine where the garment will require interfacing and how much support and/or flexibility is needed for each area. The collar and/or lapels will almost always need to be interfaced. If the collar and lapels roll, the interfacing will need to be moldable. Garment fronts will need support at least along the front edge and perhaps for a larger area depending on the firmness desired. If the garment has a smooth shoulder line, interfacing across the front shoulder will give a smoother appearance. Detail areas such as pockets, cuffs, bands or yokes, and belts will require interfacing for sharp edges and crispness. Edges of the garment, including hems, will wear better and have more body if interfaced. The soft-tailored garment may omit interfacing in hems and front interfacings may be narrower, but usually the soft effect will be best achieved by using a lighter weight and more supple interfacing in the other areas.

Refer to Chapter 9, which explains methods of application, to decide if you wish to use traditional or fusible interfacings or a combination in the front, lapel and collar area. This decision must be based upon the fabric (i.e., will fusibles be satisfactory), the desired appearance, personal skills, and time available. For small detail areas, such as pockets and bands, fusibles work well if the appearance of the fashion fabric will not be changed by fusing. Mark-off is an important consideration in deciding whether to use fusible interfacings in hems.

To select the best interfacing within the category you have chosen, place the nonfusible interfacing between two layers of fashion fabric, then feel the weight and body. Roll it over your hand to determine the flexibility, then fold the layers and curve them to simulate a collar. A moldable fabric will form a soft roll without creating sharp points as it curves.

Ask the salesperson if there are any samples of the interfacings they stock which have been fused to various weights of fabrics. If not, purchase a small amount of the interfacings that appear to be possibilities (a light and a heavier weight) and fuse to your fashion fabric according to the manufacturer's instructions. Test the fused sample for flexibility and moldability in the same manner as nonfusible interfacings. Look for mark-off and compare the fused area to the nonfused fabric to determine if there is any surface change.

Most interfacings are available only in neutral colors which are acceptable since most tailoring fabrics are opaque. However, if your fabric is light colored or has an open weave, place the interfacing behind part of the fashion fabric and hold the fabrics vertically to determine if there is any color change where the interfacing is positioned. If the garment is to be underlined, the underlining may be placed between the interfacing and fashion fabric if necessary, but this may create extra bulk, especially in the collar and other detail areas. It will also destroy the effect of the hair canvas adhering to a wool if a wool fabric is being used. If possible, it is preferable to choose a colored interfacing that blends with the fabric and/or underlining. In extreme cases it is even possible to dye an interfacing to get the desired color to blend with a pastel.

Interlining. A layer of fabric placed between the lining and the other components of the garment to provide additional warmth. This layer of fabric may be attached to the seams of the outer garment or sewn to the lining. Or it may be a separate layer that zips in. A garment to be interlined will require more ease to provide space for the additional bulk.

Occasionally, an interlining fabric may be treated as an underlining and sewed as one with the fashion fabric. This is done when more bulk is desired in the fashion fabric both for the design and for warmth.

The climate, the amount the jacket or coat will be worn outside, and the thickness of the fashion fabrics and the other garments that will be worn under it determine the need for an interlining. Fewer coats are interlined today because many people do not live in extreme climates and those who do often are not outside for extended periods. A lightweight sweater is frequently worn to give added warmth to a coat without benefit of an interlining.

The interlining fabric needs to be soft, supple, and warm. For warmth, a fabric is used that can trap air and create dead air spaces for insulation. A loosely woven wool provides the greatest warmth while cotton flannel will provide extra weight but not as much warmth. A zip-in interlining may be made of napped flannel or synthetic pile fabric.

Lining. Makes the garment easier to slip on and off over other clothing and protects the fashion fabric and inner construction from abrasion and perspiration. Esthetically, the lining adds opaqueness and body, conceals the inner construction, and makes the inside visually attractive. Depending on the fabric it may give the garment the appearance of luxury.

A lining fabric should be slippery (or have a smooth surface), opaque, pliable or supple, air permeable, colorfast, durable, and resistant to wrinkles, perspiration, and yarn slippage in the seams.

The fiber and the weave determine the visual and functional qualities of the lining. Manufactured fibers are most commonly used for lining fabrics because they are

smooth and durable. Rayon and acetate, being cellulasic fibers, are more air permeable and thus may be more comfortable to wear than polyester and nylon. Silk is a luxury lining that feels soft to the touch but, depending upon its construction, may not be durable for a garment that receives heavy wear. Cotton linings are generally unsatisfactory because they are not slippery and tend to wrinkle.

The type and closeness of the weave are important to the durability of a lining. A satin weave provides the most slippery lining, but to be durable the satin must have short float threads and be firmly woven. Crepe is not quite as slippery as satin but smooth enough to slide easily and will usually wear better than satin. Taffeta makes a crisp lining suitable only for garments that do not mold closely to the body. Be prepared for an audio sensation because taffeta rustles as one moves. Unless very firmly woven, taffeta is subject to seam slippage in areas of stress. A twill lining is very durable and thus often used in men's as well as women's jackets and coats. Plain weaves made of smooth yarns are the most likely to have yarn slippage in stress areas, an important consideration in skirt and pant linings.

In order for knit garments to retain their stretch, a knit lining should be used. Polyester blouse and lightweight dress knits may be used, or nylon tricot works well. Test the fabric for its crosswise stretch to be sure it is compatible with the stretch of the fashion fabric. A crepe lining cut on the bias is satisfactory in sleeves (in knits) where there may be strain.

Synthetic linings may be backed with a metallic, reflective finish to provide additional warmth by reflecting the body's heat back to the body. This backing makes the lining stiffer, and it will usually not wear as well as the noncoated lining. One complaint is that the metallic backing cuts down air circulation and body evaporation, but lack of air permeability can be an advantage in a windy climate.

Another fabric that adds warmth is a satin lining backed with napped wool or cotton, laminated foam, or a quilted batting. If a pile or other warm fabric is used to line the body of the coat, a slippery lining such as the napped-back satin should be used in the sleeves. Like the interlining, the thicker linings will take up additional space within the garment; thus, the garment must have more ease.

When *selecting* the lining fabric, hold the lining and fashion fabrics together to see how they drape and fall. The lining should be lighter in weight than the fashion fabric. Garments that mold or are held closely to the body will need lighter weight and more flexible linings than those garments that stand away from the body. Thus, a taffeta or heavy satin would be suitable for a loose coat but not for a softly belted one.

To determine if yarn slippage will occur, run your fingernail firmly over the fabric near the cut end. If the yarns separate, the fabric will not be very stable. To determine wrinkle resistance, squeeze a handful of fabric and release it. Do the wrinkles stay in or do they disappear?

Some fabrics that are designed specifically for linings are treated for perspiration resistance which is particularly important for acetate fabrics. Look on the bolt for this information. For heavier weight linings, it is often necessary to look for fabrics designed specifically as lining fabrics. For lighter weight linings, polyester dress and blouse fabrics, such as crepes and satins, are very satisfactory.

The choice of color for a lining is a personal decision; however, the coat or jacket will be most versatile if a one-color lining that blends with the garment color is used. A one-color woven jacquard gives interest without limiting the garment's versatility. In multicolor designs, stripes or geometrics tend to be less limiting than florals. A variety of simple trims may be used to add interest to a plain lining.

The same lining need not be used in the skirt or pants as is used for the jacket. For example, a heavier, more expensive satin or jacquard lining may be used in the jacket and a lighter weight crepe for the skirt or pants.

Notions

Sewing thread used in tailoring has traditionally been of silk because it is fine and has resilience similar to wool; however, it has become increasingly expensive and difficult to find in many areas. A fine, long staple, spun polyester thread has elastic properties similar to silk and will perform very well on wool as well as other fabrics. Choose thread that matches in color or is a shade darker in value.

Basting thread is used for temporary and permanent hand basting. Tailor's basting thread is a strong cotton thread; if not available, quilting thread works well as does mercerized sewing thread. A cotton thread is preferred because it is easier to remove and does not twist and knot as easily as the synthetic. However, a fine silk or polyester thread may be used for basting any fabric that mars easily with pressing. This is especially important where bastings are used to indicate interior lines (center front, grainlines, and so forth).

Darning cotton or *cotton embroidery floss* in various colors is useful for tailor tacking.

Topstitching thread or *buttonhole twist* is used for decorative hand or machine topstitching, hand-worked keyhole buttonholes, and for sewing on buttons. Buttonhole twist or topstitching thread is available in silk which is sold in small spools containing 9.15 m (10 yds.) of thread. Polyester topstitching thread is comparable in size to silk, is less expensive, and has more thread on larger spools. Both have a sheen with silk having the greater amount. Polyester thread is available in a wide range of colors. A double strand of sewing silk or polyester may be substituted for a topstitching thread if a good color match is unavailable in the twist. Topstitching thread may match or contrast with the fashion fabric. Inconspicuous topstitching may be done with regular sewing thread.

Buttons are usually decorative as well as functional and can completely change the appearance of a garment. The pattern envelope indicates the number and size of buttons required. If the number of buttons, spacing, or size is changed, adjustments may need to be made in the garment. The wise person buys an extra button or two so there will be a spare in case one eventually is lost.

Buttons are of two basic types: the *sew-through* and the *self-shank*. Sew-through buttons are a better choice for a double-breasted garment since shank buttons tend to droop when they are sewed on and not buttoned. Sew-through buttons usually have two or four holes (occasionally three) and are generally sporty in appearance.

Buttons vary in thickness and visual weight. A lightweight fabric calls for a more delicate button than does a very heavy or coarse fabric.

For a garment requiring frequent buttoning, look for a very smooth round button. Square buttons and rough unevenly shaped buttons will wear on the buttonholes.

Buttons that match or blend with the garment will make a more versatile garment. Decorative or contrasting colored buttons tend to be more distinctive and may limit the choice of other accessories. Simply styled buttons on a basic coat allow the coat to be worn for both dressy and casual occasions.

Self-fabric buttons are unobtrusive, but often a textural contrast is needed. Professionally covered buttons cost little more, will have stronger backs, and can be much more interesting than the typical forms that are available to cover your own. Many sizes and shapes are available with self-fabric rims, two-fabric combinations (a leather rim and self-fabric center is striking), or with a delicate gold or silver edging or filigree overlay for a special dressy button. Covered belts and buckles are also available. Unusual buttons may be made from the fashion fabric by methods other than covering a commercial form. Some ideas are given in Chapter 22.

Backing buttons are sometimes used behind the button. Buttons that take a great deal of stress and those that are on delicate fabrics will be stronger and less likely to tear the fabric if they are sewed through tiny buttons on the inside of the garment. Backing buttons that match or blend with the fashion fabric and are about 6 mm (1/4'') in diameter, two or four hole, and very flat should be used. On a double-breasted garment there may be lining behind the button; thus, the backing button should match the lining.

Tailor's tape, traditionally of linen but now only available in cotton, is a plain woven, flat tape 6 mm to 1 cm (1/4'' to 3/8'') in width. It should be lightweight and thin but very firm. If regular tailor's tape is not available, a synthetic straight hem tape may be used. Polyester twill tape may be too bulky for some fabrics.

Tape is used to shape and stay the front and lapel edges and the lower armhole, and to keep the roll line from stretching. Depending on the fabric and interfacing, tape may not be necessary in short jackets when a fusible interfacing is used except to stay the roll line.

Shoulder shapes or pads are used to smooth the shoulder area and/or alter the shoulder line. When the natural shoulder look is fashionable, nothing or a thin shoulder shape may be used. When fashion decrees a broader shoulder look or a more square look, the shoulder pad is used. At any time one may use shoulder pads to give a more natural look to shoulders that are very sloping and/or narrow, rounded, bony, or uneven in height or width.

Shoulder shapes or pads may be purchased or made to fit the individual's specific needs. Good shapes or pads for tailored garments are often difficult to find. They should be large enough to cover the entire shoulder area and not just be a triangle that perches on top of the shoulder. There are two types of shoulder pads: those for regulation set-in sleeves and those that give a rounded line to a raglan, kimono, or cut-in sleeve. If suitable commercial shapes or pads are not available, you can use the instructions in the Appendix to construct your own from hair canvas or other firm interfacing and layers of nonwoven interfacing or polyester fleece or cotton felt.

Weights are sometimes used in the hem of a jacket or coat to control the hang of the garment. Lead weights are available in a variety of sizes; either covered or uncovered. Chain weights come in different widths and weights and are attached by hand after the garment is completed.

Zippers for skirts and pants are commonly 18 cm (7'') long but may be 23 cm (9''). Choose a lightweight, flexible zipper in a color that matches the fashion fabric as closely as possible.

Hooks and eyes for the waistband of pants and skirts should be of the large solid type that are extra sturdy. They are available in nickel or black finish. Commercial or self-covered large hook and eye sets may be used on a coat or jacket.

Snaps are usually covered when used for closures on coats and jackets. They may be purchased covered or may be self-covered, and are usually a large size (2–4) in nickel or black finish.

Grosgrain ribbon is useful for staying or backing a waistband. Choose the width of your finished waistband and a color that matches your fashion fabric.

Waistband stiffenings give rigidity to waistbands. Professional waistbanding, a nonroll, heat-set stiffener can be used in place of interfacing. Men's waistbanding, a preassembled waistband, finishes the inside of men's pants.

Seam binding is a straight tape frequently used to finish hem edges. Woven binding is firm and may also be used as a stay tape. Lace binding has stretch and is suitable for knits.

Double-fold bias tape, preferably of a synthetic, may be used to encase seams in unlined garments or may be opened to use for a Hong Kong finish.

Compatibility of Components

A beautiful design, plus high quality fabric and construction by an expert tailor can still produce a failure if all of these components are not compatible with each other. Likewise a beautiful garment should enhance the individual who wears it.

Compatibility of Fabric and Design with Personal Skills

Before choosing a fabric and pattern each person should assess his or her skill level. What types of garments have you constructed and what types of fabrics have you used? A person who has made many garments with details such as collars, cuffs, and pockets will be more experienced than a person who has made a similar number of very simple garments. Since tailored garments are usually made of heavier fabrics, handling the added bulk in the seams is one of the major differences between tailoring and dressmaking. Shaping or molding the fabric to conform to the body and the garment design involves tailoring techniques that are more easily done with moldable fabrics. If you have not sewed with wool, you will be delighted to find how it eases and shapes.

Do you like to do detailed sewing and are you particular that corners are square and seams roll under? If not, choose a design with few details. It is important to choose a fabric and a pattern that are compatible with your skills so that you can produce a garment that is satisfying to you. After classifying yourself as an intermediate or advanced sewer, consider the fabric and design characteristics you wish to avoid or choose.

Easy Fabrics and Designs. Easiest to tailor are fabrics of 100 percent wool that are light to medium weight, firmly woven but supple, and with surface texture or an all over pattern such as tweeds or heather flannels. Designs that have patch or inseam pockets, a minimum number of buttonholes or none, no jacket or sleeve vents, cuffs, or details, such as complicated seaming, will be the easiest. However, choose a design with a collar and/or lapels and preferably set-in sleeves so that you can learn these basic tailoring techniques.

Difficult Fabrics and Designs. Very rigid, hard-finished fabrics in any weight and fiber will show imperfections of construction, are more difficult to press, and will not ease and mold easily.

Fabrics with a distinctive pattern in the weave or a pattern created by combining colored yarns, such as plaids, require matching if the pattern is repeated at regular intervals. Small or faint stripes or plaids are as difficult, if not more so, to match than bolder patterns. A pin stripe requires that the yarn of the pin stripe be matched. If it does not match, it will be very noticeable. With a wider stripe, if matching is a yarn off, it is not as noticeable because the major part of the stripe carries the eye. Vertical patterns require less matching than do horizontal patterns. Plaids require both vertical and horizontal matching.

Loosely woven fabrics ravel more easily, usually are not opaque, and are ordinarily stretchy and thus not dimensionally stable enough to tailor unless they are underlined.

Very thick fabrics are more difficult to press. Also, the bulk in the seams is more difficult to handle. However, some thick fabrics can be compressed with steam, heat, and pressure to reduce thickness. This requires more care and time in pressing, but bulk in seams is easier to reduce by this method.

More garment ease will also be required for a garment made of a thick fabric rather than a thin one, creating more problems in fitting.

For your first tailoring project, choose a fabric that will present a minimum of difficulties. As your skill increases, choose the more challenging fabrics and designs.

Compatibility of Fabric with Garment Design

The pattern envelope will list suitable fabrics for the design, but often the listing is so simplified that one still has major decisions to make. For example, gabardine may be listed, but did the designer have in mind a very soft, lightweight gabardine or a heavier, firmer one? Each fabric will create a very different effect. What effect do you wish to achieve?

The following design features require special consideration when selecting the fabric:

1. Small design features such as epaulets, intricate shapes on pockets or yokes, straps on sleeves, or narrow belts require lightweight, firm fabrics.

2. Gathers are best in a lightweight, flexible fabric, and if the gathers are quite full, the fabric should be soft and very supple.

3. Fitted jackets or coats are most successful in light to medium weight fabrics that are firm, moldable, and hold their shape. Softer fabrics may be underlined to give the required body.

4. Voluminous styles require lightweight, nonbulky fabrics, especially if the coat or jacket is belted or the skirt is full.

5. Unlined jackets or coats are difficult to slip into easily, thus the sleeves should be full, or one may choose a fabric that slides easily.

6. A set-in sleeve that is wide at the wrist requires fabric with body to hold the shape rather than allowing it to fall in folds.

7. Softly rolled collars need a flexible, moldable fabric that will roll rather than crease.

8. Dress-length coats will hang better if made of a slightly heavier fabric with more body than a short jacket of the same style because of the added weight of the longer skirt.

Design Limitations Imposed by Fabric. _Patterned fabrics_ will be easier to construct and more pleasing to the eye if the garment design is carefully chosen to complement the pattern of the fabric. A pattern with a minimum number of pieces reduces the amount of matching required. For a lengthwise stripe, usually the fewer horizontal seams, such as waistline and yokes, the better. For horizontal patterns, the fewer the number of vertical seams the better. For example, a one-piece sleeve requires less attention than a two-piece sleeve, a one-piece front less than a seamed front, and skirts with a minimum number of gores less than multiple ones.

Bold designs, such as wide stripes, require that the pattern placement on the body and the relationship to the design lines of the garment be considered. This is not an important consideration for small or blending patterns.

Details such as pocket flaps and epaulets should be matched if a patterned fabric is being used. A pattern with many details such as these creates a major task of matching, and the details will be lost in the pattern of the fabric unless you cut the small pieces on the bias (or crosswise if a stripe) to create a decorative effect.

Plaids may be balanced or unbalanced. Test by folding through the center of a repeat in both the crosswise and the lengthwise directions. The _balanced plaid_ or _stripe_ is exactly the same on each side of the center of the repeat (Figure 2–1). A perfectly balanced square plaid is exactly the same in both the lengthwise and crosswise directions (Figure 2–2). If the plaid is rectangular rather than square, the lengthwise and crosswise plaids will be different though each by itself may be balanced (Figure 2–3).

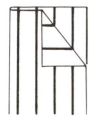

FIGURE 2–1
Balanced Stripe.

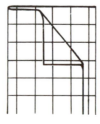

FIGURE 2–2
Balanced Square Plaid.

FIGURE 2–3
Balanced Rectangular Plaid.

Unbalanced plaids have some part of the plaid that does not repeat evenly when the plaid is folded through the center of the repeat. Look carefully—sometimes only a single thread or line is different (Figure 2–4). Examine both lengthwise and crosswise repeats; the plaid may be balanced in one direction and unbalanced in the other, though more generally it will be the same in both directions.

Balanced or *even plaids* are the easiest to work with and are suitable for garments with center front and/or back seams or bias

FIGURE 2–4
Unbalanced Stripe.

FIGURE 2–5
*Appearance of Diagonal Weave on
Collar or Lapels.*

seams, since the plaid can match in both directions.

A plaid that is uneven crosswise requires that all pattern pieces be laid in one direction. A plaid that is uneven lengthwise must also be laid in one direction but it presents added problems with such designs as kimono sleeves and full, gored skirts. Generally, for all plaids choose designs with as few seams as possible.

Stripes can be analyzed in the same manner, but you have only one direction with which to be concerned. Any fabric with a pattern repeat will require considerations similar to those just mentioned with respect to plaids.

Subtle diagonal weaves, such as gabardine, may be treated as a solid color, but obvious diagonals require special consideration. Do not choose a pattern that designates "not suitable for obvious diagonal fabrics" or that has lapels (Figure 2–5), a shawl collar with center back seam (Figure 2–6), long kimono sleeves, or bias seams such as gored skirt sections. The fabric with no right or wrong sides is an exception since the fabric may be reversed in half the garment to produce a chevron effect.

Heavy, thick fabrics dictate narrow, simple silhouettes. Semifitted styles are appropriate but not closely fitted ones. The waist will have added bulk if the garment is cut straight and belted. Only the tall, slender person can wear a full coat of heavy fabric without being overpowered. Single-breasted designs are preferable, but if a double-breasted design is used, plan to bring the facing only to the center front so there will be only three thicknesses of fashion fabric across the front instead of four.

FIGURE 2–6
Back of Shawl Collar.

Small collars or details are very difficult to construct in thick fabrics and are usually bulky looking. Self-fabric buttonholes may be very difficult or impossible in some thick, rigid fabrics. Solutions to this problem may be to make the buttonhole lips of matching (or possibly contrasting) lighter weight fabric, hand-worked buttonholes, fabric or cord loops, inseam buttonholes, or toggles. A design without fasteners may also be a choice.

Compatibility of Inner Components with Fabric and Garment Design

As a general rule, the quality of the inner components should parallel the quality of the fashion fabric. Any fashion fabric will shape better with a good quality interfacing, but do not splurge on expensive hair cloth for low quality fashion fabric. All inner fabrics must be compatible with the fashion fabric in the care required. All inner fabrics, with the exception of lining and some fusible interfacings, should be preshrunk. As previously discussed, in choosing inner components consider weight, thickness, flexibility, moldability, stability, and body of each component in relation to the fashion fabric and the garment design.

Compatibility of Fashion Fabric and Garment Design with the Wearer

The authors assume that the readers have a basic background in the selection of clothing to enhance body size and shape, personal coloring and other personal attributes, to coordinate with the wardrobe, and to meet the person's psychological and social needs. The following discussion is intended to serve as a quick review.

Color and Value. A coat or suit is often a basic item that will be worn with many other garments in the wardrobe. If the garment is to serve this function, choose a color that is wearable with the other colors in the wardrobe. It need not be your most flattering color, but it should be becoming. Will there be another color such as a blouse or scarf between the face and garment? If so, the relationship of the garment color to skin tones will not be as important, perhaps, as the relationship of hair color since the hair and garment are always viewed together from the back. Remember that light values and bright intensities tend to enlarge the figure, and medium to dark values and duller intensities make the figure recede. This may be an important consideration for the large or small person since a coat or suit covers a large area of the body. If upkeep is important, choose a medium to dark color that will conceal soil and require less dry cleaning.

Line, Scale, and Proportion. The silhouette and design lines of the garment can give a lengthened or shortened appearance to the figure. A garment that skims the figure and has dominant vertical lines, such as a single line of buttons or princess seams, will increase apparent height. Full styles, big sleeves, horizontal yokes, pockets, and belts, draw the eye across the figure and visually increase width. The size of details such as collars, cuffs, and pockets needs to be in scale with the size of the wearer. Big collars will overpower the small person, and tiny details will be out of scale on the large person. Certain lines emphasize figure irregularities. Raglan and kimono or dolman sleeves usually increase the slope of rounded or sloping shoulders, and raglan sleeves are also difficult to fit on the square-shouldered person. A set-in sleeve is usually the best camouflage for shoulder irregularities.

Large hips will be minimized by skirts with vertical seams or pleats that lead the eye up and down rather than across as a yoke will do.

The acceptable length of the jacket or coat is determined by fashion, but the individual also needs to be considered. Generally, a longer jacket that covers the derriere is flattering with pants on women who have heavy hips. Men's jackets usually come just below the seat but may be adjusted slightly up or down to achieve a better proportion of jacket length to pant length, as may women's also. The fashionable skirt length will influence the length of the jacket. The proportion is more pleasing if the jacket is not the same length as the exposed length of the skirt; thus, shorter jackets are often worn when skirts are long and longer jackets when skirts are short.

Skirt and coat length should be chosen within curent fashion to be most flattering to the wearer. When skirts are long, the short person will want to stay on the short side of fashion for better proportion. If skirts are relatively short, leave as large a hem as possible in a coat or skirt. Wool fabrics (except those with very hard finishes) can usually be lengthened without showing the old hemline.

Texture. Fabric texture was discussed in relation to the design, but the relationship to the body is also important. Thick fabrics add width to the silhouette and/or may tend to overpower a frail, slender person. Thick fabrics combined with a full silhouette will not only increase apparent size greatly, but will also produce a very weighty garment. A heavy coat can become physically tiring to wear.

Dull or moderately rough surfaces do not enlarge the figure as much as smooth shiny ones. Since wool is not a shiny fiber, this would be a more important consideration when choosing a synthetic.

Textural contrasts within the garment may also be desirable. Smooth buttons are pleasing on a napped fabric, and suede piping is a nice textural contrast to a smooth fabric such as gabardine.

Commercial Pattern Selection

Tailored garments vary greatly in style, but all tailored garments will include some or most of the following components. Special tailoring techniques are associated with each.

1. Rolled collar and lapel in which the interfacing is attached to the fashion fabric.

2. Tape to stabilize the front edge and roll line on the lapel.

3. Fabric buttonholes or worked keyhole buttonholes.

4. Pockets.

5. Shaped shoulders.

6. Set-in sleeve with shaped cap.

7. Interfaced hems.

8. Vents at the hem of sleeve or in the back or sides at the lower edge of garment.

9. Lining.

For maximum experience choose a pattern incorporating as many of these features as possible.

A wider variety of styles are usually available in suit or jacket patterns than in coat patterns for both men and women. After analyzing your physical proportions and other requirements, you often can not find a pattern that is just what you want. Some design adjustments, such as pockets and other details, are easily changed, so choose a pattern that has the neckline, shoulder style, and basic seamlines you wish. Dart and seam placement may be changed unless they involve complicated design lines. A wise choice is the classic style which will enable you to wear the garment longer and still be in style.

For the man or woman who chooses a fitted jacket and who has a large difference between the chest or bust and waist measurements, a design with as many vertical darts or seams through the waistline as possible will facilitate fitting. A large-busted woman should have a vertical seam or dart that points to or crosses the fullest bust—two darts or a seam and dart are most beneficial. For the woman who has an hourglass–type curve from the front view, a jacket with a side seam rather than a side panel should be chosen. A four- or six-gore skirt will be more flattering and easier to fit for the woman with large hips or prominent front thighs than a two-piece skirt. Set-in sleeves are traditional in tailored garments, but are difficult to fit a full-busted woman with a large upper arm and narrow, sloping shoulders. A raglan or a kimono sleeve may be more comfortable and may present fewer fitting problems.

Note the way in which the pattern is illustrated. A jacket or coat will be shown over the type of garment for which ease has been allowed. For example, a coat shown over a soft dress will not have enough ease to wear over a jacket. The description on the back of the pattern envelope may also give similar information.

Generally, you should buy the same size pattern you would use for a dress because additional ease has been added by the designer. If in doubt about the size of pattern to buy, take your bust, waist, and hip measurements (see Chapter 3). Coats and jackets are usually purchased according to chest size for men and bust size for women. If the woman wears larger than a B cup bra, then a size smaller pattern may be needed and a bust alteration made. Try to *fit the shoulder* and purchase the pattern that previous experience shows fits best in this area. Skirts and pants patterns are purchased by hip measurement, and the waistline adjusted as necessary.

Purchasing Garment Components

Your pattern envelope indicates the amount of fabrics and specific notions required; however, these amounts may need to be adjusted for your fabric, design changes, or construction techniques. Consider any of the following points that may be applicable.

Fashion Fabric

Fabric with Nap. As previously defined, a napped fabric is one in which the fibers of the fabric have been raised to form a smooth surface that may or may not have a smoothness running one direction. The term *with nap* indicates a specific layout on your pattern guide sheet. Any fabric that has (1) the raised fibers lying in one direction, (2) a pile weave, such as corduroy, velvet, or velveteen, or (3) a woven or printed design that has an up and down, such as unbalanced stripes and plaids, must be laid so the pattern pieces all lie in the same direction. This layout often requires more fabric than a *without nap* layout in which pattern pieces may be placed in either direction.

Patterned Fabrics. Refer to Chapter 6 for specific information. Follow these guidelines when buying plaids or other patterned fabrics.

1. The size of the design repeat dictates the amount of additional yardage needed for matching. A general guideline is to purchase one additional repeat for each major pattern piece (i.e., front, back, sleeve). Width of fabric and number of small pieces to be matched are also considerations.

2. Unbalanced designs require more allowance than balanced designs since a one-way (with nap) layout must be followed.

Design Changes. Your garment may be lengthened, shortened, widened or narrowed. You may want to add pockets, cuffs, belts, or other added design features. Eliminating these features usually does *not decrease* yardage requirement.

Interfacing

Changing the shape of the interfacing pattern to stabilize the shoulders and bust or chest area will require additional fabric. Twice the length from shoulder to hemline will usually be the maximum required, but size of collar, pattern size, and fabric width must be considered. *Option:* You may wish to delay purchasing the interfacing until the requirements for that fabric are determined.

Underlining

Purchase the same amount of underlining as specified for the lining if sleeves are to be underlined. If not, check the lining layout to determine if the yardage can be decreased.

Lining

If the pattern does not include a lining, a general guide is to purchase two body lengths (including hem) for a narrow jacket or two body lengths plus a sleeve length for a coat or fuller garment of 114.5-cm (45'') fabric. For 152-cm (60'') fabric, two body lengths will usually be adequate for most garments.

Tape

Estimate the amount of tape needed by measuring from the hemline to the shoulder and from the top button to the shoulder (for garment with lapel) and doubling the measurements. An extra 46 cm (18'') may be needed for other areas.

Conclusion

A successful garment does not just happen; much thought and planning are required before the first cut or stitch is taken. Choosing garment design, fashion fabric, and inner components of the tailored garment requires an understanding of the concept of compatibility as well as textile knowledge and design appreciation. Choose the best quality fabric available within your price range that is compatible with your body type, personal needs, and sewing ability. The garment design should be chosen with these same factors in mind. The inner components are dictated by the fashion fabric, garment design, and methods of construction chosen. Compatibility is the key word in their selection, as it is in the selection of the fashion fabric and garment design.

Perfect fit is the hallmark of any custom-made garment, and it is even more important to the tailored coat or suit than to less structured clothing. Since most people must adjust a commercial pattern to fit them, several steps should be followed to determine what type and amount of adjustments need to be made. Accurate measurements for both the figure and the pattern can be compared to determine where differences exist. Measuring a garment that fits you and comparing these measurements with your pattern is also helpful. Major differences should be rectified before pin fitting the paper pattern. Then you must decide whether a muslin test garment should be made. If the garment is not closely fitted, if few adjustments were necessary, and/or the altered pattern appears to fit well, a muslin test garment should not be essential. However, if in doubt, make a test garment.

Body Measurements

Current, accurate body measurements are the first step in obtaining a well-fitted garment. Enlist the aid of a friend to take your measurements as it is very difficult to measure yourself. Gather the following supplies to help in taking the measurements.

1. Six mm (1/4'') wide masking tape or water-soluble fabric-marking pen, or soft lead pencil.

2. Tape measure.

3. Grosgrain or other firm ribbon 1.3 cm to 2 cm (1/2'' to 3/4'') wide.

4. Plumb line (string with weight attached to the end) about 1 meter (3' long).

5. String about 20 cm (8'') longer than hip size.

6. Measurement chart (*see* Appendices).

Wear a full-length slip and the undergarments you will normally wear with

3

MEASUREMENTS AND PATTERN ADJUSTMENTS

your garment. (A body suit or leotard may be worn.) Take men's measurements over undershirt and shorts.

While marking and measuring the body, note any specific irregularities such as rounded shoulders, square or sloped shoulder, prominent abdomen, flat or full derriere, forward shoulder.

Marking the Body

Since several measurements are taken from the same point at the neckline and shoulders, the *neckline, top of shoulder,* and *armhole location* should be marked for the duration of measurement taking. This may be done with narrow masking tape which is very easy to position and remove, with a water-soluble fabric-marking pen (can be removed easily with a damp cloth), or with a soft lead (#2) pencil (more difficult to

FIGURE 3–1
Body Marked for Measuring.

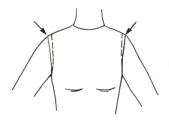

FIGURE 3–2
Armhole Seam Position.

remove). With masking tape, the center of the tape will be the exact line. Mark the body as follows (Figure 3–1):

1. Around the base of the neck across the two bones above the hollow in front, above the prominent vertebrae in back and where the neck bends at the side.

2. Across the top of the shoulder so the line bisects the shoulder and ends at the center of the upper arm. Unless one has a forward head, the line begins slightly back of the ear. To locate the beginning of the line, place a pencil at this point on the shoulder to the center of the arm. When sighting directly across the shoulder, this line should not be apparent from either the front or back, but especially the front. It may be necessary to move the shoulder point back 6 mm to 1.3 cm (1–4'' to 1–2'') to accomplish this.

3. Around the armhole, beginning in front where the arm joins the body (the arm break) to the tip of the shoulder. Find this point by marking a point on the shoulder which is perpendicular to the floor directly above the arm break, then move 1.3 cm to 1.5 cm (1–2'' to 3–4'') toward the end of the shoulder (Figure 3–2). Continue marking to the point where the arm joins the body in back. Keep the line straight across the top of the shoulder.

Taking the Measurements

The person being measured should stand comfortably tall with feet slightly apart and in a normal standing position. The person doing the measuring should strive to take all measurements with tape taut but not tight. The style of your garment will determine which body measurements you will use. However, you will find it will be helpful to have a full set of body measurements for other garments you may make. Before proceeding, place the bottom edge of the ribbon at the waistline and fasten it snugly in place. Tie the string around the widest hip. Hold a plumb line under the arm so that it falls perpendicular to the floor and visually divides the body equally from front to back. Mark at underarm, waist, and hip on both sides of the body. *Note:* The underarm division may not follow the plumb line on some bodies. In this case, adjust the plumb line for the waist and hip. Mark the underarm so the torso is divided evenly from front to back. Take the following body measurements and record them in column #1 on the measurement chart found in the Appendices. (See Figure 3–3 for the location of measurements.) Variations for men's measurements are noted in the text.

1. *Neck circumference*—place the lower edge of the tape measure on neckline mark to measure neck circumference. Note distance between shoulder marks around back of neck. (See Figure 3–3 #1a.)

2. *Shoulder width*—shoulder point to shoulder point across the back.

3. *Shoulder length*—neckline to shoulder tip (where shoulder and armhole lines intersect.)

4. *Back width*—arm break to arm break across the shoulder blades.

5. *Extended back width*—bring elbows in front of the body, measure from arm break to arm break across the shoulder blades.

6. *Chest width*—place end of tape on armhole mark halfway between tip of shoulder and the arm break; measure across chest to same position on other armhole mark.

7. *Bust (or chest for men) circumference*—with tape parellel to the floor, measure around the body at the fullest part of the bust (or chest). Do not let tape drop in the back.

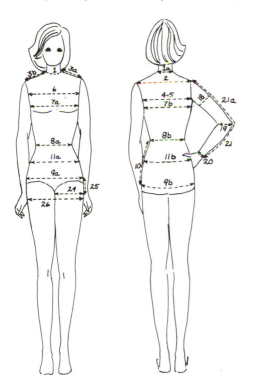
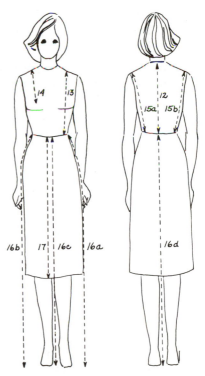

FIGURE 3–3
Locations for Body Measurements.

7a.   *Front bust (or chest) width*—across fullest bust between side seam marks.

b.   *Back bust (or chest) width*—#7 minus #7a.

8.   *Waist circumference*—place tape around waist, parallel to the floor. If waist location is questionable, bend to the side—the waist is where the body bends. Place center front and back level with sides. For men, measure around area where waist seam of shorts rests.

8a.   *Front waist width*—waistline between side seam marks.

8b.   *Back waist width*—#8 minus #8a.

9.   *Hip circumference*—place tape over string at widest hip; be sure tape is parallel to the floor.

9a.   *Front hip width*—across widest hip between side seam marks.

9b.   *Back hip width*—#9 minus #9a.

10.   *Hip depth*—bottom of waistline tape to string placed at widest hip.

11.   *High hip circumference*—measure the body circumference halfway between the waist and widest hip.

11a.   *Front high hip width*—width between side seam marks halfway between the waist and full hip.

11b.   *Back high hip width*—#11 minus #11a.

12.   *Back length*—center back neck mark to bottom of tape at waistline.

13.   *Front waist length*—center of the shoulder over the fullest bust (or chest for men) to the bottom of the waist tape.

14.   *Bust depth*—(women only) measure from the center of the shoulder to the point of bust (most prominent area of bust).

15.   *Upper back side length*—on both sides of the back, measure from the tip of the shoulder to the bottom of the waist tape. These measurements tell you if you have uneven shoulders.

16a-d.   *Floor to waist*—bottom of waist tape to floor on each side, the center front and the center back.

17.   *Skirt length*—at center front bottom of waist tape to the desired skirt length.

18.   *Upper arm circumference*—the right upper arm about 2.5 cm to 5 cm (1'' to 2'') below the arm break. (Measure left arm, if left-handed.)

19.   *Elbow circumference*—place tape around elbow, bend arm, and measure over point of elbow.

20.   *Wrist circumference*—over wrist bone.

21.   *Shoulder to wrist length*—clasp hands about waist level, measure from shoulder tip to center of wrist bone.

21a.   *Shoulder to elbow length*—clasp hands about waist level, measure from shoulder tip to point of elbow.

21b.   *Elbow to wrist length*—#21 minus #21a.

Additional measurements for pants:

22.   *Crotch depth*—sit on a hard, flat surface (chair or table); at the side seam mark, measure from the bottom of the waist tape to chair or table (Figure 3-4).

23.   *Crotch length*—from the bottom of the waist tape in front between the legs to the bottom of the waist tape in back (Figure 3-5).

FIGURE 3-4
Crotch Depth.

FIGURE 3–5
Crotch Length.

23a. _Front crotch length_—while tape is in place for crotch length, have the person being measured locate the center of his/her leg and grasp the tape at this point. Remove the tape and record the distance from the front waist. (Plumb line may be held at inside of leg to determine center of leg.)

23b. _Back crotch length_—#23 minus #23a.

24. _Thigh circumference_—measure both thighs at the largest area and record only the larger.

25. Record the distance below the widest hip where thigh measurement is taken.

26. _Note:_ For person with large thighs measure the front width from side seam to side seam at the point where the thigh is largest.

If a heavy garment is to be worn under the jacket or coat, you will be better able to determine the amount of ease required for comfort if you take additional measurements over this garment. Circumference measurements (bust, waist, hips, and arm) are particularly important.

Allowance for Ease

Garment ease is the difference between the body measurements and the pattern measurements. The amount of ease that is desirable will depend upon the type of garment, the individual's figure type, the weight and type of fabric, the purpose for which the garment is intended, the prevailing fashion, and the individual's preference for ease.

Minimum ease allowances for jackets, coats, skirts, and pants are given on the measurement sheet. You may wish additional ease (1) if the garment is to be worn for physical activity, such as bicycling; (2) if the fabric is thick and bulky; (3) if the garment is to be interlined; (4) if you wear a larger than average pattern; or (5) if you prefer your clothes to fit loosely. If the style does not fit closely to the body in a particular area, such as the waistline or hipline, do not bother to compare measurements for that area. On the measurement sheet add the amount of ease you desire (column #2) to each body measurement (column #1) to obtain the total measurement (column #3) to be compared to the pattern.

Pattern Measurements

Since designers for different commercial pattern companies vary in their interpretation of ease, each pattern used should be carefully measured and checked against body measurements to ensure correct size and fit. This should be done before any adjustments are attempted.

Note: All body measurements were taken for the full circumference of the body or for a total front or back width. Since a pattern represents only one-half of the body, circumference or width measurements made on the pattern will need to be doubled before

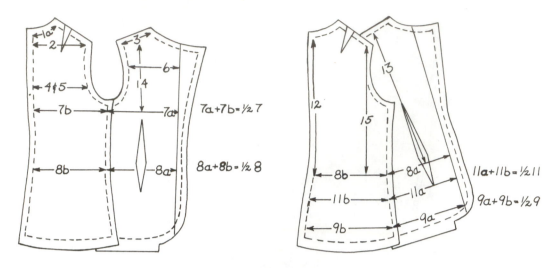

FIGURE 3-6
Measuring the Pattern.

they are recorded on the measurement sheet and compared to body measurements. Length measurements may be recorded as they are taken on the pattern.

Measuring the Pattern

Stack pattern pieces and press before beginning to take measurements. Extend all grainlines and center front the full length of the pattern. Put your name on each pattern piece. If a cork surface or cutting board is available, work on this as the pins can be stuck straight in to hold the pattern pieces. When one or both of the seams are curved, overlap seam allowances so stitching lines match and secure only the area where you will be measuring so the pattern will lie as flat as possible. Pin darts only where you will be measuring across them or between them. Remember to measure only the area between seam allowances. Take width measurements at a right angle to the lengthwise grain.

Jacket or Coat Body (Figure 3-6). Measure all possible and applicable width

and length measurements (numbers 1-17 on the measurement chart). Do not measure neck circumference unless the garment has a high neckline. If the garment is full below the bustline, waist and hip measurements are not necessary unless you would like to know just how full it is. If garment has no indentation at waistline, omit these length measurements. If garment has ease across the back shoulders rather than darts, pin the back and front shoulder seams together before measuring the shoulder width.

Sleeve (Figure 3-7). Measure the pattern according to the diagrams for either the one- or two-piece sleeve, recording measurements for numbers 18 to 21. If pattern has a raglan or dolman sleeve, measure from neckline to wrist and compare with the total of numbers 3 and 21. Or, add one-half of back shoulder width (#4) to sleeve length (#21) to obtain center back neck to wrist measurement.

Skirt (Figure 3-8). Measure and record numbers 8-8b, 9-11b, and 17, remembering to omit pleats, tucks, or darts.

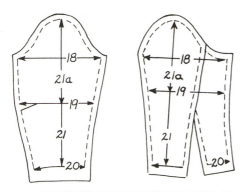

FIGURE 3–7
Measuring the Sleeve Pattern.

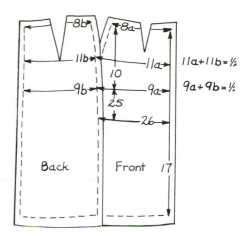

FIGURE 3–8
Measuring the Skirt Pattern.

Include number 26 if figure has prominent front thighs.

Pants (Figure 3-9). Numbers 8-8b, 9-11b, 16a, and 22-24 should be measured and recorded for pants. Depending on the shape of the hips and thighs you may find that the lines indicating widest hip, crotch depth, and thigh circumference are either closer together or farther apart than the illustration.

Comparison of Body and Pattern Measurements

After all necessary pattern measurements have been recorded (column #4), find the difference between this measurement and the total in column #3 (body measurement plus the desired amount of ease). Record as a plus if the pattern is larger and a minus if the pattern is smaller.

You cannot expect these two measurements to be the same for several reasons. First, few people are the "average" that the pattern is designed to fit; second, the amount of ease you desire may not be the same amount that is used for the pattern; and third, the designer may have perceived this garment to fit differently than you do.

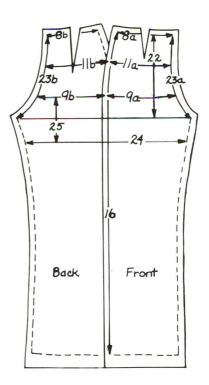

FIGURE 3–9
Measuring the Pants Pattern.

Key Areas

Compare your body measurements to the bust, waist, hip, and back length measurements given on the pattern envelope. The difference is the amount you would have to alter for the garment to fit with the ease intended by the designer.

Check your body measurements plus ease with the pattern measurements (column #4) in these six key areas. Special points to consider have been included to help you decide if you should alter the pattern, and if so, how much.

1. *Bust or chest circumference* (#7) may be correct and yet the front bust or chest width (#7a) and back bust or chest width (7b) may not be if the person has a narrow or wide back or a full chest (for men) or a large or small bust (larger or smaller than a B cup bra). Check the front waist length measurement (#15) before making any adjustment on the front pattern piece. Garment design is an important consideration in determining ease. A fitted blazer that will usually be worn open will require less ease through the front bust than one which will usually be worn closed. More ease should be allowed across the back than in the front for ease of movement.

2. *Waist circumference* (#8) for jackets and coats will vary greatly depending on the design of the garment. For a straight design the waist measurement will be the same as the bust measurement and need not be taken. For a fitted blazer, check closely if your waist measurement is large in comparison to bust, and be sure the pattern has at least the minimum amount of ease indicated on the measurement sheet. Be sure to check both front (#8a) and back (#8b) waist measurements to determine where adjustment is needed.

3. *High hip circumference* (#11) is an especially important measurement for the person whose hips begin to round at the waistline or

who has a protruding abdomen. Check the front (#11a) and back (#11b) measurements because the total measurement could be correct and still not fit your body. This measurement is used to determine the length of darts and the curve of the side seam in skirts and pants as well as fitted jackets.

4. *Full hip circumference* (#9), like the high hip measurement, should be checked for the front (#9a) and back (#9b) as well as the total measurement. A prominent derriere will increase the back measurement. The figure with a protruding abdomen may measure less across the front at the low hip than at the high hip. If so, use the front high hip mesurement in place of the front full hip measurement so the garment will hang straight.

5. *Back waist length* (#12) is important only for garments that have some fit at the waistline, or for garments with pockets if the waist length varies more than about 1.3 cm (½''). If one is short or long waisted the pockets may be too high or too low. The waist length will also influence the length of the garment.

6. *Upper arm circumference* (#18) is the most important of the arm circumference measurements. Additional ease, unless excessive, is usually not a problem but too little ease definitely is. The sleeve circumference should be adjusted according to the measurement sheet prior to checking the pattern. Elbow circumference (#19) is usually enlarged when the upper arm circumference is increased, but wrist circumference usually is not unless your measurements indicate this is desirable.

If major variations occur in the key areas, the pattern will need to be altered before it can be checked on the body. However, since one alteration may influence another, it is advisable to compare your other measurements with the pattern measurements, even though some alterations may not be made until the paper pattern has been checked on the body.

Other Areas

1. *Shoulder lengths* (#3) for left and right shoulders may not be the same in your personal measurements; however, unless they are drastically different your garment will appear more balanced if it is made to fit the minimum measurement for the wide shoulder, and a larger shoulder shape or pad is used to support the narrow shoulder.

2. *Back width* (#4) and extended back width (#5) measurements are used together to determine if there is adequate reach room in the garment. The pattern measurement should be wider than your back width (#4) measurement, but may be slightly less than your extended measurement (#5) since the ease in the sleeve will also provide some of this reach room. A person with a narrow back will have excess in this area as well as in the back bust, and both areas can be corrected with one pattern adjustment.

3. *Front waist length* (#13) may vary if you are short or long waisted, in which case, this measurement will vary by the same amount as the back waist length (#12), and the same adjustment will be made on the front and back. Excessive length in the front pattern measurement may be the result of round shoulders or a small bust. The round-shouldered person will usually find that the back waist length (#12) is too short, and a round shoulder alteration will be needed to lengthen the back and shorten the front. If a longer front pattern measurement is due to a small bust, usually the front bust width pattern measurement (#7a) will also be large, and both can be corrected by a small bust alteration. A too short pattern front waist length is usually accompanied by a too narrow front bust pattern measurement, which a large bust alteration will correct.

4. *Bust depth* (#14) indicates if a woman is high or low busted. Determine the bust point on the pattern in the following manner:

a. If garment has a vertical waistline and an underarm or armhole dart, the point at which these two darts would meet is point of bust.

b. For a princess-seamed garment, point of bust is located where the front

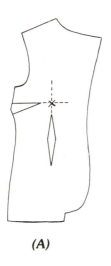 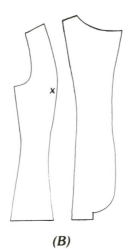 

(A)	*(B)*	*(C)*

FIGURE 3–10
Location of Bust Point.

underarm section reaches maximum width.

c.   If garment has only a waistline dart, point of bust will be 2 cm to 2.5 cm (3/4'' to 1'') above end of dart (Figure 3–10).

Do not make this adjustment until the pattern has been checked on the body since slight variation of the shoulder seam placement can change it.

5.   *Upper back side length* (#15a–b) gives an indication of shoulder slope and height. If the two *body measurements vary,* one shoulder is higher and/or thicker than the other. Check shoulder height by visual measurement. On tailored garments the low and/or thin shoulder can have additional padding, and little or no pattern adjustment is needed. Remember to fit the pattern on the side with the high shoulder. If *body and pattern measurements vary,* it may be an indication that the individual has sloping or square shoulders. Do not adjust the pattern until the pattern has been checked on the body. When pinning the pattern together for fitting, if the measurement is less on the pattern than the body measurement, pin the shoulder seams together only at the neckline so the shoulder seam can be adjusted.

6.   *Floor to waist side measurements* (#16 a–b) indicate hip height. If the left and right body measurements are not the same, one hip is higher than the other, and the skirt or pants will need to be adjusted accordingly. This measurement is also used to determine pant length. Subtract the distance you want your pants from the floor to obtain your pant length.

7.   *Sleeve length* (#21, #21a) can vary with the placement of the armhole seam and the amount of ease in the sleeve cap. Therefore, if these measurements do not vary more than 1.3 cm (½'') do not make adjustments in the pattern. If they vary more, make the appropriate adjustment above or below the

elbow (note #21a and #21b). The sleeve length may be checked by comparing the center back neck to wrist measurements (one-half of #4 added to #21).

8.   *Crotch depth* (#22) determines whether pants will be long enough to reach the waistline or will hang long in the crotch. Adjust pattern according to measurement before making any other adjustments.

9.   *Crotch length* (#23) is influenced by both crotch depth and the thickness of the body. If total measurement is correct, front (#23a) and back (#23b), lengths may vary by 1.3 cm (½'') without causing a serious problem. The amount of ease varies with body configuration and personal preference. A fuller figure usually needs more ease than a small one. A person with a protruding abdomen will need more ease in front so the pants do not pull in under the abdomen.

10.   *Thigh circumference* (#24) is used only for pants and is of primary importance to those who have large thighs, particularly in front. Adequate ease in the right area is important. Visually determine if the thigh extends beyond the widest hip at the side or if in profile the front thigh is prominent, so the adjustment can be made in the correct area.

11.   *Front width across the thighs* (#26) is considered only if this measurement is larger than the front hip width (#9a). If so, the side hip curve will need to extend past this point, or additional fullness will need to be allowed across the front depending on whether the thigh is prominent in the front or at the side. Both front and back pattern pieces will need to be adjusted if the fullness is at the side, and only the front piece if it is in the front.

Comparison of the body and pattern measurements indicates where you vary from the average figure for whom the pattern was designed or where your desired ease allowances vary from those allowed by the designer. You may elect to accept more ease than the total of your body measurement plus ease, but you should seldom accept less. By analyzing the measurements and understanding why your measurements differ from the pattern, you will be better able to make the pattern adjustments.

Pattern Adjustments

The four basic types of pattern adjustments are length, width, slope, and body bulges. Length adjustments are necessary if one has a longer or shorter trunk, arms, or legs than the average. An increase or decrease in width is reflected in the circumference measurements of the chest, bust, waist, hip, thigh, or arm. Square or sloping shoulders and a high hip are areas where the pattern must be adjusted for slope. Any area where the body curves outward is considered a body bulge, the most prominent of which is the woman's bust. But also requiring consideration are round shoulders, protruding abdomen, derriere, or hip. Identifying the type of adjustment helps one to understand how the adjustment will be made.

Checking the Adjustments

The key adjustments (bust [especially large bust], waist, hip and sleeve circumference, waist length) as indicated by comparing the body-plus-ease and pattern measurements should be made before the pattern is pinned together and checked on the body. While a paper pattern does not fit like fabric it will give you indications of where further adjustments should be made. However, pants are usually not fit in the paper pattern because the paper will not conform to the crotch shape.

Preparing the Pattern

1. Trim away excess tissue beyond cutting line on curved seams (i.e., neckline, armhole).

2. Lap seams, seamline over seamline, and pin. Place pins so points go downward when on the body to keep them from falling out.

3. Pin up all hems.

4. Clip neckline and armhole to stitching line to prevent pattern from tearing.

5. Do not attach collar or pin set-in sleeves to body of pattern. Do not pin lower armhole of raglan or kimono sleeves.

6. Pin skirt to the outside of the fitting band. Match center front, center back, and side seams. Place pins parallel to the edge of the fitting band. *Note:* Make fitting band as follows:

    a. Use a 2-cm to 2.5-cm (3/4'' to 1'') piece of grosgrain ribbon or a firm strip of fabric about 5 cm to 7.5 cm (2'' to 3'') longer than waist measurement (#8 on chart).

    b. Mark the band the length of your waist measure or size of finished waistband.

    c. Determine where garment will open—front, back, or side.

    d. Using measurement chart, front waist #8a and back waist #8b, mark waistband to correspond with this division of the waistline. (Front waist measurement is approximately 3.8 cm (1 ½'') longer than back waist measurement.)

Procedure for Fitting the Paper Pattern

1. Place jacket, coat, or skirt paper pattern on body over the same weight of garment which will be worn with it. Position center front and center back and tape or pin to hold in place.

2. Position shoulder shapes if they are to be used. Place thickest edge of pad even with the cutting line of the armhole.

3. Follow this order in checking fit of jackets and coats: neck and back shoulders, front shoulders and bust or chest area, underarm seams, waist and hips. When the body of the garment has been fitted, pin underarm seam of the sleeve from underarm to elbow and slip sleeve over arm. Match sleeve to garment at underarm and hold in place.

4. Use *critique #1* (*see* Appendices) to check fitting points. Remember, fine fitting cannot be done in the paper pattern but will be done in the test garment and/or the actual garment.

5. Especially note these points for jackets and coats:

a. Check circumference for adequate ease. The paper pattern will appear to have less ease than will fabric. *Note:* If you wear a bra with a cup size larger than a B, a large bust adjustment which increases length and width of the front will usually need to be made. When this occurs, the pattern will be too tight across the front, and the front waist length will be short, but back bodice length and width may be correct.

b. Check length of garment and/or specific areas such as waist length and sleeve.

c. Note dart placement. Darts should point to body bulge but end 2 cm to 2.5 cm (3/4'' to 1'') from largest area.

d. Shoulder slope. If pattern sets high at neckline, release the seam from the shoulder tip to let neckline sit in normal position. Make adjustment for square shoulder. If there is excess pattern at shoulder, adjust for sloping shoulder.

e. Neckline shape. The pattern neckline usually conforms to the neck shape. If neckline appears too wide, collar will set away from the neck on the shoulders. Refer to adjustment for neckline shape.

Adjusting the Paper Pattern

After checking the paper pattern on the body, make further adjustments as needed. At this point determine if it is necessary to make a test garment. If the garment is quite loose fitting and the shoulders appear to fit, or if you seldom require adjustments and the pattern appears to fit, a test garment will not be necessary. If you decide it is not required, proceed to Chapter 4 for further points to check and instruction for pattern preparation.

The following supplies will be needed to adjust your pattern:

1. Rubber cement or glue stick.

2. Tissue paper.

3. Felt-tip marking pen.

4. Ruler (clear plastic is easiest to use).

5. Tape measure.

6. Pins.

7. French curve (helpful but not a necessity).

Some general guidelines for adjusting the paper pattern (applicable to all pattern adjustments) are as follows:

1. The altered pattern must lie perfectly flat.

2. The altered pattern must have the same basic shape as the original.

3. If the length of a seam is changed, the seam that joins it must be changed by the same amount.

4. Darts or tucks must be folded before the edge can be redrawn or trued.[1] (Figure 3–11).

---

[1] Trued—to correct stitching and cutting lines after making a pattern adjustment.

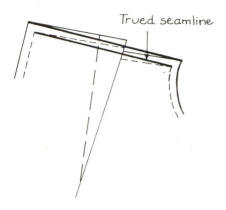

Trued seamline

FIGURE 3–11
Trueing Seamline with Dart.

FIGURE 3–12
Trueing Adjusted Seamline.

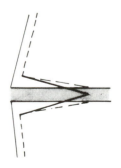

FIGURE 3–13
Redrawing Dart Line.

5. To rejoin construction lines which have been interrupted by the adjustment, join the two ends of the line keeping the original curve or straightness of the line. (Figure 3–12).

6. When an adjustment has been made through the center of a dart, redraw the stitching lines as illustrated (Figure 3–13).

7. Measure the pattern when the alteration has been completed to be sure that the amount of alteration is correct.

8. Use tissue paper to fill in areas where pattern is spread or addition is made on the perimeter.

Length Adjustment Guidelines:

1. Be sure the lengthwise grainline extends the length of the pattern. After pattern is slashed or folded, lay a ruler along this line to realign the pattern pieces.

2. Make adjustments by folding or slashing and separating an even amount along the lines indicated on the pattern.

3. Make adjustments on both the front and back pattern pieces.

4. Treat adjustment needed *on front only* as an adjustment for body bulge.

Width Adjustment Guidelines:

1. Mark a line across the width of the pattern at a right angle to the grainline. After the pattern is slashed apart or folded, lay a ruler along this line to realign the pattern pieces.

2. For a two-piece front, back, or sleeve, pin the pieces together at the widest areas (i.e., bust and hip) and treat as one pattern piece in which the seamed areas are darts.

3. Remember, width measurements represent the front or back of the body (or total circumference) and the pattern only represents one side; thus half the required front or back width adjustment is made on each half of the pattern (or one-fourth the total measurement).

4. Width adjustments may be made on either the front or back or both pattern pieces.

Slope Adjustment Guidelines:

1. Slope adjustments are basically uneven length adjustments; therefore, the point toward the center of the body usually remains unchanged while the outer edge is adjusted the desired amount.

2. Slope adjustments are generally made on both the front and back pattern pieces.

Body Bulge Adjustment Guidelines:

1. The larger the body bulge the larger the area required to cover it, thus the increased perimeter of the pattern must be reduced by darts, seams, tucks, or gathers.

2. Darts point to, but stop short of, the largest area of a body bulge.

3. The greater the degree of curve, as in an armhole or waistline, the greater the amount of fullness that can radiate from it when it is placed on the body.

4. Body bulge adjustments are usually made on only one pattern piece unless that piece has a seam, as in a princess line, or the bulge occurs on the side of the body (i.e., the hip).

Dart Transfer:

To achieve a better fit or change a design line, it is often advantageous to move a dart from one position to another position—often in the bust or shoulder areas. To move a dart that points toward the bust (Figure 3–14):

1. Mark point of bust on pattern.

2. Slash the pattern from the edge to point of bust where new dart is desired.

3. Fold old dart along stitching lines except fold to point of bust so pattern will lie flat.

4. Glue old dart permanently closed.

5. Place tissue under opening for new dart. Glue in place.

6. Make a new dart point 1.3 cm to 3.8 cm (1/2'' to 1½'') from point of bust. (Distance depends on body shape and dart placement.)

7. Draw stitching line from point to seamline on each side of dart.

Note: Darts may be converted to a seam by cutting darts along stitching lines to separate the two pieces, then adding seam allowances to each stitching line (Figure 3–15).

To shift a dart to a new position that points to the center of a body bulge, such as the back shoulder, the procedure is similar

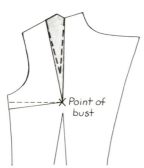

FIGURE 3–14
Transferring Dart from Underarm to Shoulder.

FIGURE 3–15
Converting Shoulder and Waistline Darts to a Seam.

FIGURE 3–16
Transferring Back Shoulder Dart to Neckline.

except that in addition to a slash for the new dart, a slash must be made through the old dart and between the points of the old and new darts (Figure 3–16). Slide this section (a) so that the old dart is closed at the seamline. Redraw the new dart.

Adjusting the Paper Pattern

Refer to your measurement sheet to determine which adjustments should be made in your paper pattern before checking the fit. Do length and width adjustments first unless the adjustment is necessitated by a body bulge or variation in slope. Some of the adjustments presented here will be made in the test garment. Thus, some include a drawing that shows how the problem will appear in the garment.

Key to pattern adjustment illustrations:

— — — — —	original seamline
- - - - - - - - - - - - -	overlap or foldout area
————————	new stitching or cutting lines
▭	filler added where pattern is spread

Jacket or coat

- _Objective:_ To increase or decrease length.

  Indication: Body length measurement is longer or shorter than pattern length in the waist length (#12), upper arm (#21a) or lower arm length (#21b).

  Procedure: Slash or fold pattern along adjustment lines marked on the pattern and spread or fold out the desired amount evenly across the front and back of the sleeve. Secure or fold and redraw cutting line as indicated. (See Figure 3–17.)

- _Objective:_ To increase front length.

  Indication: If the body front waist length (#13) is longer than the pattern (front bust width [#7a] is correct) or the pattern is designed without a dart or other fullness to shape the bustline, wrinkles will radiate from the bust to side seam giving the appearance that the side seam is too long.

  Procedure: The pattern must be slashed horizontally and spread to give more length to the front. (See Figure 3–18.) If a dart points toward the bust, the added fullness may be incorporated into it. (Note crosswise slash through underarm dart on full bust alteration [Figure 3–19].) For the dartless front, incorporate a dart to reduce the underarm seam to its original length (B). A vertical seam, such as a modified princess line, will spread equally at the seam (A).

- _Objective:_ To increase for large bust.

  Indication: The individual wears larger than a B cup bra for which the pattern was designed. Usually the pattern front bust width (#7a) is too narrow and front waist length (#13) is too short.

  Procedure: When both additional length and width are needed, the pattern must

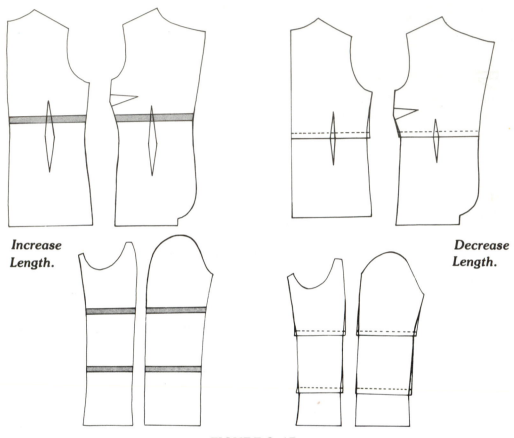

Increase Length.

Decrease Length.

FIGURE 3–17

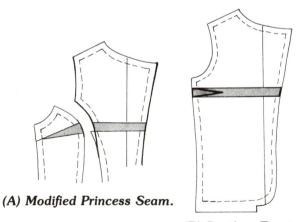

(A) Modified Princess Seam.

(B) Dartless Front.

FIGURE 3–18
Increase Front Length.

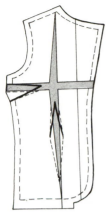

(A) Added Chest Width.

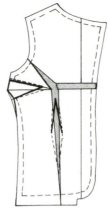

(B) Chest Width Unchanged.

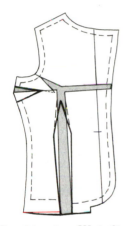

(C) Combination Waistline
Dart and Seam.

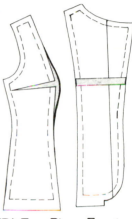

(D) Two-Piece Front.

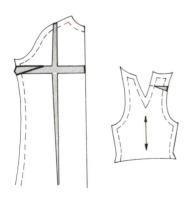

(E) Raglan.

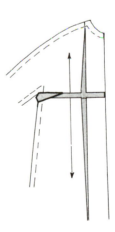

(F) Kimono.

FIGURE 3–19
Increase for Large Bust.

47

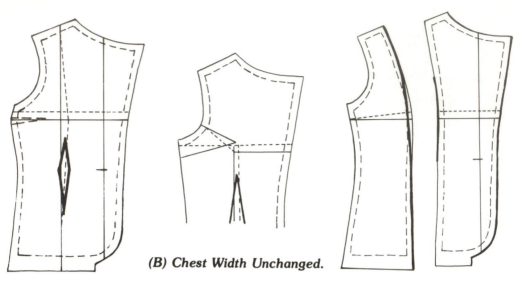

(A) Chest Width Decreased.

(B) Chest Width Unchanged.

(C) Two-Piece Front.

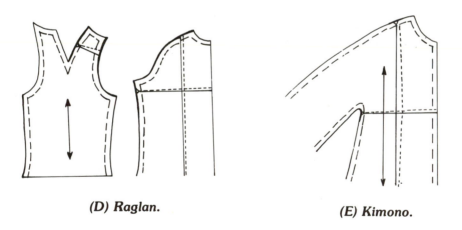

(D) Raglan.

(E) Kimono.

FIGURE 3–20
Decrease for Small Bust.

be slashed both lengthwise and crosswise (See Figure 3–19.) Slash to the shoulder as in (A) if additional width is needed in the chest (#6). If chest width is correct, slash from point of bust to arm break (B). Spread desired amount in both length and width at bustline. Size of the

waist dart is increased some, but the underarm dart is increased the most to allow for added length in front. The side seam remains at its original length. If alteration is large, underarm dart becomes too large. It is advisable to convert the waistline dart into a combination dart and seam (C). If the center section of the two-piece front extends to the point of bust, all width is added to the side section (D). If not, the center section may need to be adjusted also, but be careful not to distort the design line of the garment. The side section will not need to be spread as much as the center section when all width is added to the side because the increased curve adds length also. The raglan and kimono designs are adjusted in a similar manner, (E) and (F).

- _Objective:_ To decrease for small bust .

Indication: The individual wears smaller than a B cup bra for which the pattern was designed. Usually the pattern front bust width (#7a) is too wide and front waist length (#13) is too long.

Procedure: When both length and width must be reduced, the pattern is slashed both lengthwise and crosswise. (See Figure 3–20.) Slash to the shoulder as in (A) if less width is needed in the chest (#6). If chest width is correct, slash from point of bust to arm break (B). Lap desired amount in both length and width at bustline. Size of waistline and underarm darts are reduced, and underarm dart may be completely folded out. If only a very tiny dart remains, this fullness may be eased to the back side seam. If the center section of the two-piece front is a pleasing width, all reduction of width is made on the side section by decreasing the curve over the bustline (C). The raglan and kimono designs are adjusted in the same manner (D) and (E).

- _Objective:_ To increase or decrease front bust width (chest width for men) when length is correct.
Indication: Body front bust or chest width (#7a) is larger or smaller than pattern front bust or chest due to large or small rib cage.

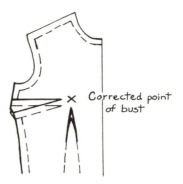

(A) One-Piece Front.

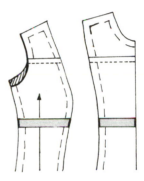

(B) Two-Piece Front.

FIGURE 3–21
High Bust.

Procedure: Follow instructions for large or small bust adjustment, omitting the crosswise slash.

- _Objective:_ To accommodate a high bust.

Indication: The body bust depth measurement (#18) is less than the pattern measurement, and when pattern or garment is fitted, the garment fullness is lower than the point of bust.

Procedure: For _one-piece_ front, mark corrected point of bust. (See Figure 3–21.) Redraw underarm dart so end of dart is level with point of bust and extend waistline dart the same amount the

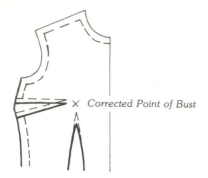

X *Corrected Point of Bust*

(A) One-Piece Front.

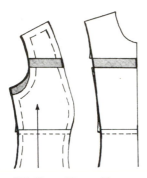

(B) Two-Piece Front.

FIGURE 3–22
Low Bust.

point of bust was raised. For *two-piece* front, above the bustline fold out amount necessary to raise point of bust. Slash and spread below the bustline the same amount as was folded out to return front to the original length (B).

• *Objective:* To accomodate a low bust.

Indication: The body bust depth (#18) is greater than the pattern measurement, and when the pattern or garment is fitted, the garment fullness is higher than the point of bust.

Procedure: Mark corrected point of bust. (See Figure 3–22.) For *one-piece* front, redraw underarm dart so end of dart is level with point of bust. Reduce

length of waistline dart the same amount the point of bust was lowered (A). For *two-piece* front, slash above bustline and spread the amount necessary to lower the point of bust. Fold out the same amount below the bust as was spread above the bust to return the front to the original length. Redraw armhole to original size and shape (B).

• *Objective:* To increase waist width.

Indication: The body front waist width (#8a) and/or back waist width (#8b) are greater than the pattern measurement.

Procedure: Reduce the amount of curve on vertical seams and/or reduce the size of darts as shown. (See Figure 3–23.) If the body has little indentation at the side, make the adjustment in the side seam, or if the body is straighter in the front or back, make the adjustment in that area.

• *Objective:* To decrease waist width.

Indication: The body front waist width (#8a) and/or back waist width (#8b) are less than the pattern measurement.

Procedure: Increase the amount of curve on vertical seams and/or increase the size of darts. (See Figure 3–24.) If the body has a pronounced curve at the side, make the adjustment in the side seam, or if the body curves more in the front or back, make the adjustment in that area.

• *Objective:* To increase back width.

Indication: Body back width (#4), extended back width (#5), and back bust or chest width (#7b) are wider than pattern back width.

Procedure: (See Figure 3–25.) Slash the pattern lengthwise through the shoulder or neckline dart and waistline darts if these are present (A). Spread desired amount at arm break and back bust or chest line. Slash horizontally to

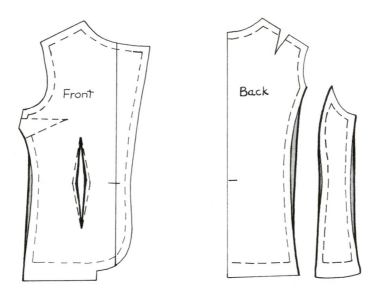

FIGURE 3-23
Increase Waist Width.

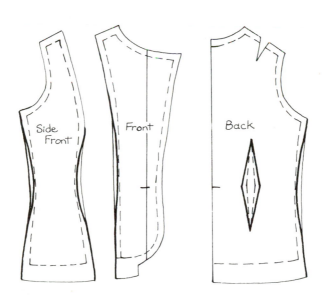

FIGURE 3-24
Decrease Waist Width.

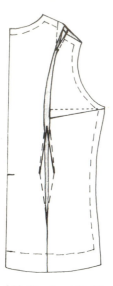

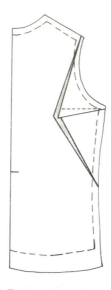

(A) Back with Darts.   **(B) Back without Darts.**   **(C) Two-Piece Back with Shoulder Dart.**

FIGURE 3–25
Increase Back Width.

lower armhole to allow pattern to lie flat. The shoulder dart and shoulder line will require adjustment and the waistline dart will be enlarged. If there are no back darts, slash as shown in (B) and spread the appropriate amount. For a two-piece back, slash and spread center piece as shown (C).

- *Objective:* To decrease back width.

Indication: Body back width (#4), extended back width (#5), and back bust or chest width (#7b) are narrower than pattern back width.

Procedure: (See Figure 3–26.) Slash the pattern lengthwise through the shoulder or neckline dart and waistline darts if these are present (A). Lap desired amount at arm break and at back bust or chest line. Slash horizontally to lower armhole if necessary for pattern to lie flat. The shoulder dart will be decreased

in size and may be completely omitted, and the waistline dart will also be smaller. For modified princess line adjust along seamline as shown (B). If there are no back darts, slash as shown in (C) and lap the appropriate amount.

- *Objective:* To increase shoulder width.

Indication: Body shoulder width (#2) is longer than pattern shoulder width.

Procedure: Slash the front and back pattern from arm break to shoulder; spread the required amount at the seamline on the shoulder, tapering to nothing at the arm break. Fold seam allowance to lie flat. Secure slash; redraw shoulder line from tip of shoulder to neckline. (See Figure 3–27.) Make same adjustment on back and front.

- *Objective:* To decrease shoulder width.

Indication: Body shoulder width (#2) is shorter than pattern shoulder width.

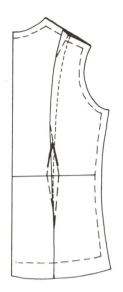 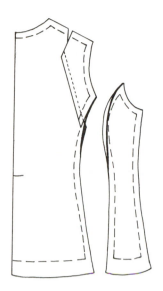 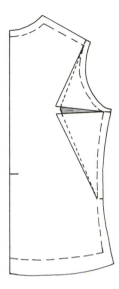

(A) Back with Darts.   *(B) Two-Piece Back with Shoulder Dart.*   *(C) Back without Darts.*

FIGURE 3–26
Decrease Back Width.

Procedure: Fold pattern as indicated from arm break to shoulder; fold out the required amount at the seamline on the shoulder, tapering to nothing at the arm break. Clip seam allowance at arm break to allow pattern to lie flat. Secure fold; redraw shoulder line from tip of shoulder to neckline. (See Figure 3–28.) Make the same adjustment on the back and front.

- *Objective:* <u>To increase extended back width.</u>

Indication: Pattern does not allow adequate ease across the back when arms are brought forward (#5). Back bust (or chest) measurement is correct.

Procedure: (See Figure 3–29.) If back armhole is quite curved as is common with a shoulder dart, reduce curve of armhole (A). If back armhole is quite straight and there is no shoulder dart,

slash and spread and make a shoulder dart. If more width is required for garment with shoulder dart than possible with (A), use adjustment (B) and increase depth of dart.

- *Objective:* <u>To adjust for swayback.</u>

Indication: The swayback causes the garment to wrinkle across the back below the waistline.

Procedure: Keeping the grain level at bust and hips determines the amounts of excess at the center back. (See Figure 3–30.) Fold out needed amount at center back, tapering fold to nothing at side seam (A). Darts will become shorter and center back seam of jacket will curve in at waist. Straighten center back if on the fold and increase darts to return waistline to original size. For skirt or pants, center back length is reduced by needed amount (B).

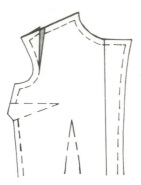

Standard Front.

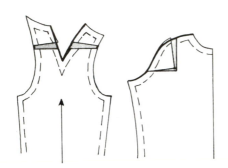

Raglan.

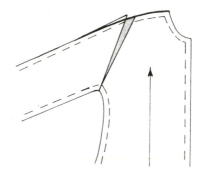

Kimono.

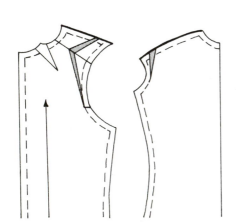

Extended Shoulders.

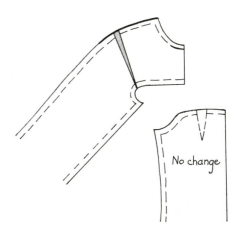

Yoke with Sleeve.

FIGURE 3–27
Increase Shoulder Width.

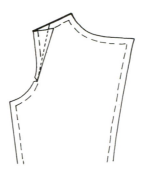

Standard Front.

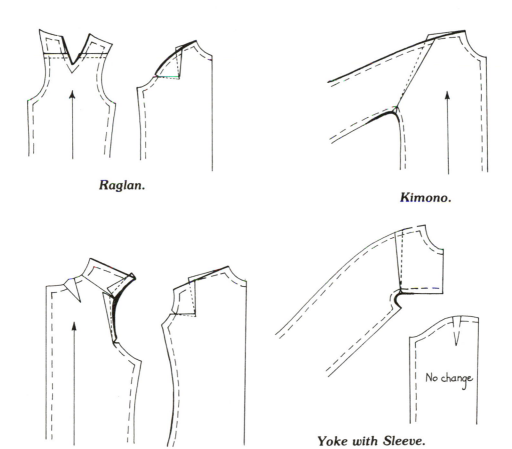

Raglan.

Kimono.

No change

Yoke with Sleeve.

Extended Shoulder.

FIGURE 3–28
Decrease Shoulder Width.

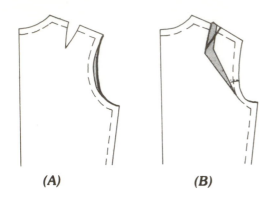

(A)   **(B)**

FIGURE 3–29
Increase Extended Back Width.

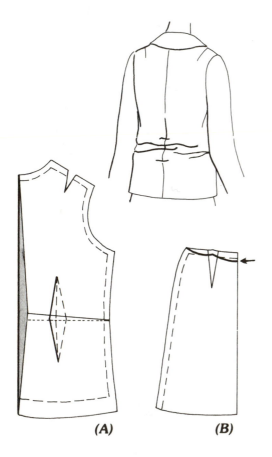

(A)   **(B)**

FIGURE 3–30
Swayback.

- *Objective:* To adjust for erect back.

  Indication: Very erect posture causes excess fabric length at shoulder blades.

  Procedure: (See Figure 3–31.) Slash across upper back and vertically through shoulder dart (A). Keeping the grain at chest or bust line and center back straight, lap to shorten the center back the needed amount. Redraw the shoulder seam. For garment with neckline dart, fold out excess at center back tapering to nothing at armhole (B). Straighten center back and reduce dart by the amount the neckline is decreased at center back. (Dart may be completely omitted.)

- *Objective:* To increase upper arm circumference.

(A) Shoulder Dart.   **(B) Neckline Dart.**

FIGURE 3–31
Erect Back.

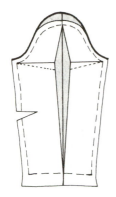

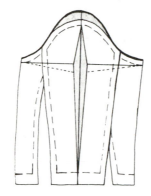

(A) One-Piece Sleeve.

(B) Two-Piece Sleeve.

(C) Raglan.

Indication: Body upper arm circumference (#18) is greater than pattern measurement.

Procedure: (See Figure 3–32.) To increase the circumference of the sleeve without unduly increasing the perimeter of the sleeve cap, trace the cutting line of the sleeve cap on a separate piece of paper. Also trace the lengthwise grain. Slash lengthwise and crosswise as shown on the pattern. Spread the lengthwise slash the desired amount allowing the crosswise slash to lap (A). Lay on traced drawing matching level of lower armhole and grainlines.

For two-piece sleeve, slash underarm section from underarm mark through lower edge of sleeve (B). Lap seam allowances of upper sleeve and under sleeve, then complete adjustment as for one-piece sleeve. When adjustment is completed, separate upper and under sleeve pieces and tape two pieces of under sleeve back together.

• *Objective:* To decrease upper arm circumference.

Indication: Body upper arm circumference (#18) is less than pattern measurement.

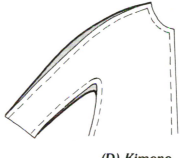

(D) Kimono.

FIGURE 3–32
Increase Upper Arm Circumference.

Procedure: (See Figure 3–33.) To decrease the circumference of the sleeve without unduly decreasing the perimeter of the sleeve cap, trace the cutting line of the sleeve cap on a separate piece of paper. Also trace the lengthwise and crosswise grainlines. Then slash lengthwise and crosswise on the pattern as shown (A). Lap the lengthwise slash the

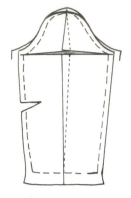

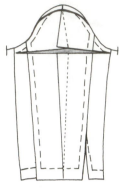

FIGURE 3–33
Decrease Upper
Arm Circumference.

(A) One-Piece Sleeve.   **(B) Two-Piece Sleeve.**

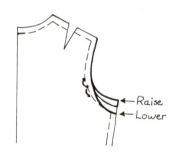

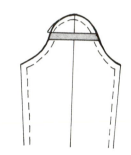

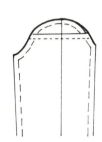

→ Raise
→ Lower

(A) Adjusting Armhole Depth.   **(B) Cap Height Increased.**   **(C) Cap Height**
                                                                    Decreased.

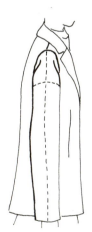

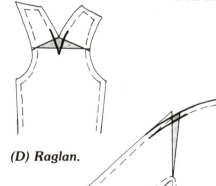

(D) Raglan.

Cap Too Short.   Cap Too Long.

FIGURE 3–34
Increase or Decrease Height of Sleeve Cap.   **(E) Kimono.**

58

desired amount allowing the crosswise slash to spread. Lay on traced drawing matching level of lower armhole and grainlines.

For two-piece sleeve, slash underarm section from underarm mark through lower edge of sleeve (B). Lap seam allowances of upper sleeve and under sleeve, then complete adjustment as for one-piece sleeve. When adjustment is completed, separate upper and under sleeve pieces and tape two pieces of under sleeve back together.

- *Objective:* <u>To increase or decrease height of sleeve cap.</u>

Indication: Grainline at lower armhole is not parallel to the floor but pulls up in the center. Diagonal wrinkles appear from top of cap, or grain drops in center and there is excess fabric in upper cap.

Procedure: Check to see that the armhole depth is correct (see Figure 3–36.) If it is too high or too low (see Figure 3–34), raise or lower the whole sleeve and remark front and back armhole shape and matching points (A). Ease in sleeve cap will be increased or decreased. If lower armhole is correct, slash across top of cap and raise upper section (B) or lap lower section (C) to adjust height of cap. If raised to increase cap height there will be more ease than originally allowed in the cap; if lowered the cap will have less ease.

- *Objective:* <u>To adjust for gaping armhole.</u>

Indication: The armhole is too large in front causing it to gape. Often this is due to a large bust or an incorrect shoulder slope.

Procedure: Check bust length and width first; if these are correct, proceed with one of these alterations. (Figure 3–35.)

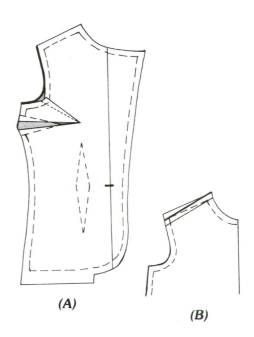

(A)

(B)

FIGURE 3–35
Gaping Armhole.

Note grain at chest level. If grain is level at chest, dart the excess out of the armhole and increase another dart (or fold to seam near bust point) to make pattern lie flat (A). If grain is curving downward at the chest (#6), make a sloped shoulder alteration only on the front (B). Sleeve will not require alteration if not more than 1.3 cm (½″) is removed from armhole, but sleeve may need to be rotated slightly to the back. If more than 1.3 cm (½″) is removed, adjust sleeve during fitting.

- *Objective:* <u>To raise or lower the armhole.</u>

Indication: The armhole is too high under the arm or too low which will make raising the arms difficult.

Procedure: Redraw the lower armhole on the front, back, and sleeve, raising or

Armhole Too Low.

Armhole Too Tight.

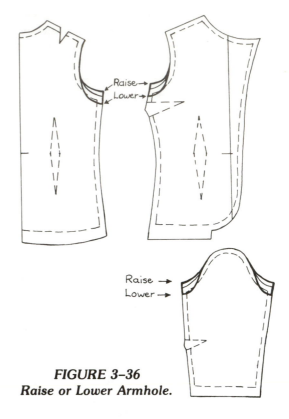

FIGURE 3–36
Raise or Lower Armhole.

lowering each the same amount (Figure 3–36).

- *Objective:* To adjust for sloping shoulders.

Indication: When viewing the body from the front, the shoulders appear more sloping than average and the back side length measurement (#15) is less than the pattern. In fitting, wrinkles appear around and below the armhole.

Procedure: With shoulder shapes in place, raise the shoulder seam until fit is smooth. Adjust so shoulder seam is in proper location even though front and back shoulder adjustments may differ. Mark new shoulder seam. Trace original armhole on another piece of paper and lay it under pattern matching shoulder point to adjusted shoulder seam. Trace the armhole on the pattern so armhole is lowered the same amount the shoulder is lowered. Adjust both front and back pattern pieces. (See Figure 3–37.)

- *Objective:* To adjust for square shoulders.

Indication: When viewing the body from the front, the shoulders appear to be close to the same height at the shoulder point as at the neckline, and the side length measurement (#15) is more than the pattern. In fitting, the shoulder points seem to be supporting the garment and the neckline appears to be loose.

Procedure: With shoulder shapes in place, if any are to be used, release the shoulder seam and allow the shoulder point to drop until the neckline and shoulders fit smoothly. Check shoulder seam position (front and back shoulder seams may differ) and mark new seamline. Trace original armhole on another piece of paper and lay it under the pattern matching shoulder point to adjusted shoulder seam. Trace the armhole on the

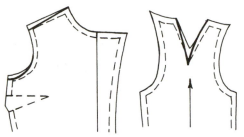

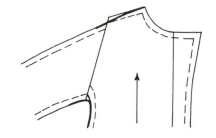

Standard.   Raglan.

Kimono.

FIGURE 3–37
Sloping Shoulders.

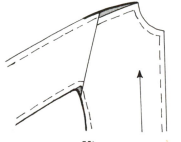

Standard.   Raglan.

Kimono.

FIGURE 3–38
Square Shoulders.

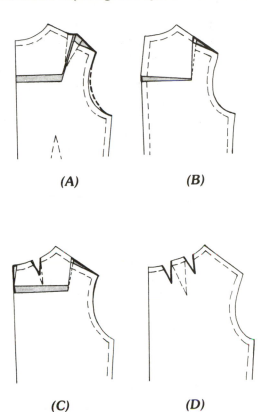

(A)   *(B)*

(C)   *(D)*

FIGURE 3–39
Round Shoulders or Dowager's Hump.

pattern so the armhole is raised the same amount the shoulder point is raised. Adjust both front and back pattern pieces. (See Figure 3–38.)

- *Objective:* To adjust for round shoulders and/or dowager's hump.

Indication: When viewed from the side, the upper back appears rounded and the head is forward from the usual position. This rounding causes the body back waist length (#12) to be longer and sometimes the front waist length to be shorter than the pattern.

Procedure: Slash horizontally across upper back and vertically through the shoulder dart. (See Figure 3–39.) Spread vertically for the needed back length keeping center back straight if it is cut on a fold (A). (If there is a center back seam, the center back may curve *slightly* (6mm or ¼ ") inward at the neckline.) Often back width (#4) will also need to be increased as noted by dotted line at armhole. (Also see alteration for increasing extended back width which gives additional width by increasing the size of the shoulder dart.)

If garment has no shoulder or neckline dart but a center back seam, as is common in men's jackets, spread vertically for needed length at center back and lap shoulder seam slightly to retain the same length on the shoulder seam (B). The center back seam will curve inward to the neckline. If garment has no center back seam or darts, reduce length of back shoulder seam by easing to front or incorporating a small shoulder dart.

The dowager's hump requires fullness directly below the back neck, thus a neckline dart fits better than a shoulder dart. (Note directions for transferring darts.) Adjust as in (B) except straighten center back seam to neckline and increase the size of darts to accommodate added width or ease to collar (C). Two small darts will fit better than one large dart (D). Darts will also need to be shorter.

- *Objective:* To change the neckline shape.

Indication: Individuals' necks may be round, or oval from side to side, or oval front to back, thus the neckline circumference may be correct but the neckline may not fit. Also a forward head will make the neckline too high in front.

Procedure: Redraw the neckline to conform to the shape of the neck. If cir-

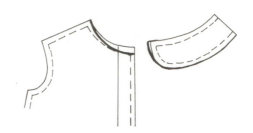

(A) Forward Head

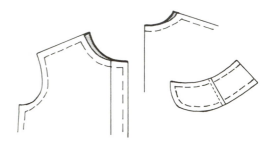

(B) Small Neck

FIGURE 3–40
Neckline Shape.

cumference is changed, adjust collar the same amount at the point where the addition or subtraction has been made on the neckline. (Figure 3–40) For a forward head, lower front neckline and add necessary length to collar at front edge (A). For a small neck (narrow side to side), extend shoulder toward the neck, fold out amount of adjustment at shoulder marking on collar (B).

- *Objective:* To increase hip width.

Indication: The body front hip (#9a) and/or back hip (#9b) are larger than the pattern.

Procedure: If the *front view* shows the body to be appreciably wider at the hipline than at the waistline, additional fullness will need to be added at the sides. (See Figure 3–41.) Use the high hip measurement, front (#11a) or back (#11b), to

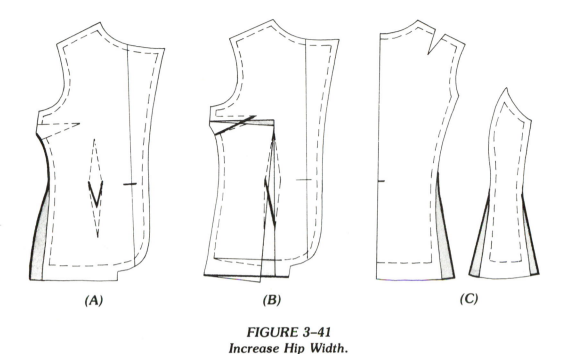

(A)   **(B)**   **(C)**

FIGURE 3–41
Increase Hip Width.

determine the degree of curvature between waist and hip. If high hip measurement is greater than pattern, curve seam out below waist (A).

If the _profile_ shows the back hip or front thigh to be prominent, increase at front or back darts or seams (C). Larger high hip will necessitate sharper curve and shorter dart (A). For pattern with dart, slash and spread as shown (B). The dart becomes deeper to place more fullness in front or back. Some figures may require added fullness in each of these areas.

- _Objective:_ To decrease hip width.

Indication: The body front hip (#9a) and/or back hip (#9b) are smaller than the pattern.

Procedure: If the _front view_ shows the body to be quite straight below the waistline, fullness will need to be removed at the sides. (See Figure 3–42.) Use the high hip measurement (front #11a or back #11b) to determine the degree of curvature between waist and hip. If high hip measurement is similar to full hip measurement, make necessary adjustment for high hip and then straighten seam. Darts may be lengthened to smooth out fullness at end of dart, but there will be little width reduction (A). Be careful not to distort design lines.

If the _profile_ reveals a very flat front or derriere, decrease at front or back seams or darts (B). For pattern with darts, slash and lap as shown in (C). The dart will become smaller reducing the amount of fullness at the end of the dart.

Some figures may require a reduction of fullness in each of these areas, but do not make hipline of garment smaller than waistline even if body hip measurement is less.

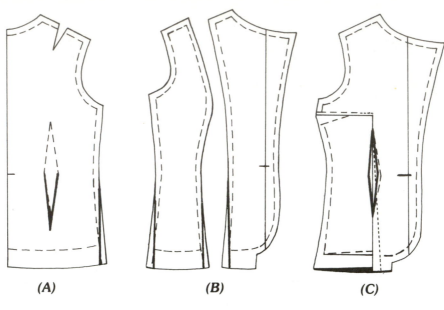

FIGURE 3–42
Decrease Hip Width.

Pants and skirts

- *Objective:* To increase or decrease length of skirt or pants.

  Indication: Desired skirt length (#17) or pants length determined by floor to waist measurement (#16) is longer or shorter than the pattern measurement.

  Procedure: To retain the design lines of either skirt or pants, add or subtract length within the garment rather than at the bottom. If garment is straight or a skirt with more flare is desired, add at the bottom. Shorten at the bottom for less flare. Slash and evenly spread or fold out the same amount on both front and back pieces. Pants may be adjusted both above and below the knee so length can be added or subtracted where it is needed. (See Figure 3–43.)

- *Objective:* To increase waist width.

  Indication: The body front waist width (#8a) and/or back waist width (#8b) are larger than the pattern measurement.

  Procedure: If the body has little indentation at the side waist, make the adjustment in the side seam, or if the body is straighter in the front or back, make the adjustment in that area by reducing size of darts. Adjust front and/or back as needed. (See Figure 3–44.)

- *Objective:* To decrease waist width.

  Indication: The body front waist width (#8a) and/or back waist width (#8b) are less than the pattern measurement.

  Procedure: If the body has a pronounced curve at the side, make the adjustment in the side seam, or if the body curves more in the front or back make the adjustment in that area by taking deeper darts. (See Figure 3–45.) Adjust front and/or back as needed. The center back crotch seam of pants may serve as an adjustment area, but front crotch seam should remain on straight of grain, especially with a fly front opening.

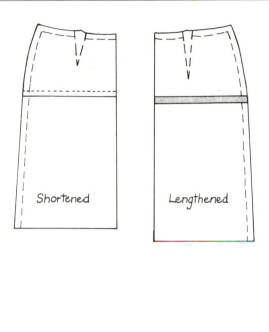

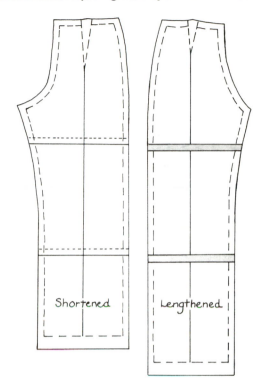

FIGURE 3-43
Increase or Decrease Length.

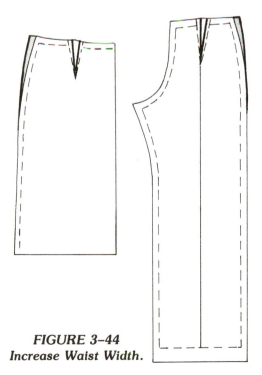

FIGURE 3-44
Increase Waist Width.

• *Objective:* To increase hip width.

Indication: The body front hip (#9a) and/or back hip (#9b) are larger than the pattern.

Procedure: (See Figure 3–46.) To add 5 cm (2'') or less in total circumference, increase width at the side seams (A). Use the high hip measurement (front #11a or back #11b) to determine the degree of curvature between waist and hip. If body high hip measurement is greater than pattern, curve seam out rapidly below waist.

If the *profile* shows the back hip or front thigh to be prominent, slash lengthwise through dart and spread needed amount (B). The dart will become deeper to place more fullness in front or back. A larger high hip will necessitate a sharper curve and shorter dart; a large thigh, a longer dart.

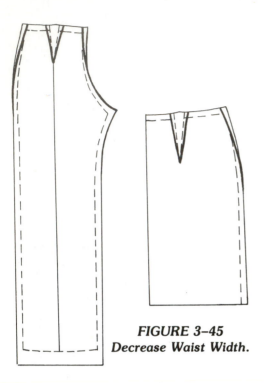

FIGURE 3–45
Decrease Waist Width.

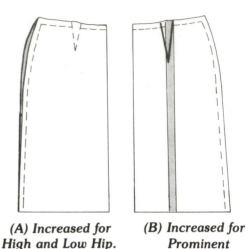

(A) Increased for High and Low Hip.

(B) Increased for Prominent Back Hip.

Some figures may require added fullness in each of these areas; however, if pants pattern was purchased by hip measurement, hip width adjustment should be minimal.

- *Objective:* To decrease hip width.

Indication: The body front hip (#9a) and/or back hip (#9b) are smaller than the pattern.

Procedure: To reduce 5 cm (2'') or less in total circumference, decrease width at the side seams. (See Figure 3–47.) Use the high hip measurement (front #11a or back #11b) to determine the degree of curvature between waist and hip. If high hip measurement is similar to full hip measurement, make necessary adjustment for high hip and then straighten seam (A). Pants may be narrowed the entire length of the leg if a narrower leg is desired.

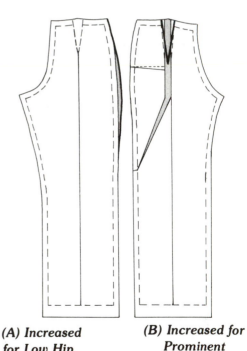

(A) Increased for Low Hip.

(B) Increased for Prominent Front Thigh.

FIGURE 3–46
Increase Hip Width.

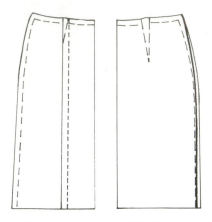

(A) Decreased for Low Hip.   **(B) Decreased for Flat Front.**

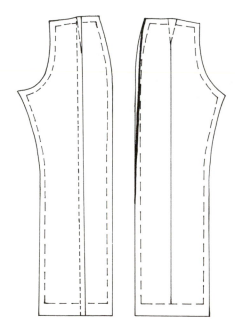

(A) Decreased for High and Low Hip.   **(B) Decreased for Flat Derriere.**

FIGURE 3–47
Decrease Hip Width.

If the *profile* reveals a flat derriere or front, decrease at front or back darts by folding out the necessary amount through the dart, thus reducing the size of the dart (B). The dart may be eliminated entirely, or a smaller one can be retained.

Some figures may require a reduction of fullness in each of these areas, but do not make hipline of garment smaller than waistline even if body hip measurement is less. If pants pattern was purchased by hip measurement, hip width adjustment should be minimal.

- *Objective:* To increase or decrease crotch depth.

   Indication: Body crotch depth (#22) is less or greater than the pattern measurement. If greater, the pants will bind in the crotch and not reach the waist.

   Procedure: Fold or slash the front and back patterns on the adjustment lines and evenly spread or fold out the amount indicated by the crotch depth (#22) measurements. Secure pattern and redraw cutting lines (Figure 3–48).

- *Objective:* To increase the crotch length.

   Indication: The crotch depth measurement (#22) is correct or has been adjusted, but the body total crotch length (#23) is greater than the pattern crotch length. Front (#23a) and back (#23b) crotch lengths indicate whether the discrepancy is in front and/or back. This variation may be due to the thickness of the body, to a protruding abdomen, or to a full derriere.

   Procedure: If abdomen or derriere is the problem, increase crotch length at center front or back but not at the side seam (Figure 3–49). Slash horizontally through crotch seam and to side seam. Spread only at crotch seam (A).

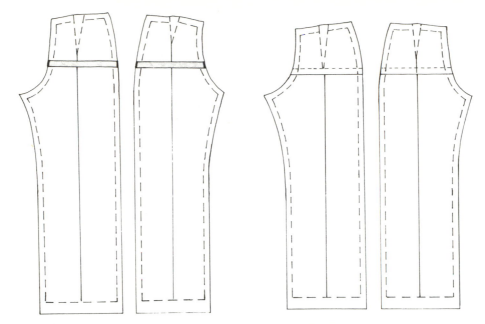

Increased Crotch Depth.   Decreased Crotch Depth.

FIGURE 3–48

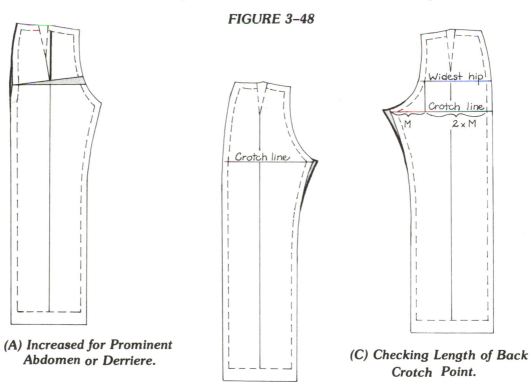

(A) Increased for Prominent
Abdomen or Derriere.

(C) Checking Length of Back
Crotch Point.

(B) Increased for Body Thickness.

FIGURE 3–49
Increase Crotch Length.

If body thickness requires a longer crotch length, draw a crotchline at right angles to the grainline and extend at the crotch point the amount needed (B). This adjustment also increases the width of the pants leg at the top of the thigh, and thus the thigh circumference (#24) is increased. Checking this measurement will be helpful in determining amount of adjustment. The back crotch point will always be longer than the front. One guideline for checking the length of the back crotch point is as follows:[2] (1) measure down the back crotch from the waist to the fullest hip (#10) and draw a line perpendicular to the crotchline; (2) measure from this point along the crotchline to the side seam; (3) divide this measurement in half, and this should be the distance from the perpendicular line to the crotch point (C).

For a full figure both adjustments may be necessary.

- *Objective:* To decrease the crotch length.

Indication: The crotch depth measurement (#22) is correct or has been adjusted, but the body total crotch length (#23) is less than the pattern crotch length. Front (#23a) and back (#23b) crotch lengths indicate whether the discrepancy is in front and/or back. This variation may be due to the thickness of the body or to a flat abdomen or derriere.

Procedure: (See Figure 3–50.) If one has a very flat abdomen or derriere, decrease the crotch length at center front or back but not at the side seams. Slash horizontally through the crotch seam and to the side seam. Lap only at crotch seam (A).

If body is thin from front to back,

draw a crotchline at right angles to the grainline as shown and shorten the crotch point the amount needed. This adjustment also decreases the width of the pants leg at the top of the thigh, and thus the thigh circumference (#24) is decreased. Checking this measurement will be helpful in determining the amount of adjustment. Refer to adjustment for increasing crotch length for guideline to check the length of the back crotch point.

Some figures that are flat front to back may require both adjustments.

- *Objective:* To adjust for large derriere or protruding abdomen.

Indication: Pants or skirt is too tight across derriere or abdomen causing side seam to pull and garment to be too short in the back or front length.

Procedure: Slash lengthwise through dart from waist to knee or skirt hem and crosswise at hipline (Figure 3–51). Spread needed amount (slash at knee for pants pattern to lie flat). Straighten side seam. Incorporate one or two darts to return waist to original size. This adjustment is applicable to either front or back.

- *Objective:* To adjust for flat derriere or very flat abdomen.

Indication: Skirt or pants are too loose in back or front only. Grainline sags at center back or center front, skirt hem may be too long at centerback or center front, and pants sag in seat or front crotch.

Procedure: Take uneven fold across hipline to reduce needed amount at center back or center front. Fold out excess vertically through darts, thus reducing the size of darts or sometimes eliminating them. Slash pants horizontally at knee to allow pattern to lie flat.

---

[2]Adapted from Jan Minott, *Pants and Skirts Fit for Your Shape,* 2nd Ed. (Minneapolis, Minn.: Burgess Publishing Co., 1974), p. 82.

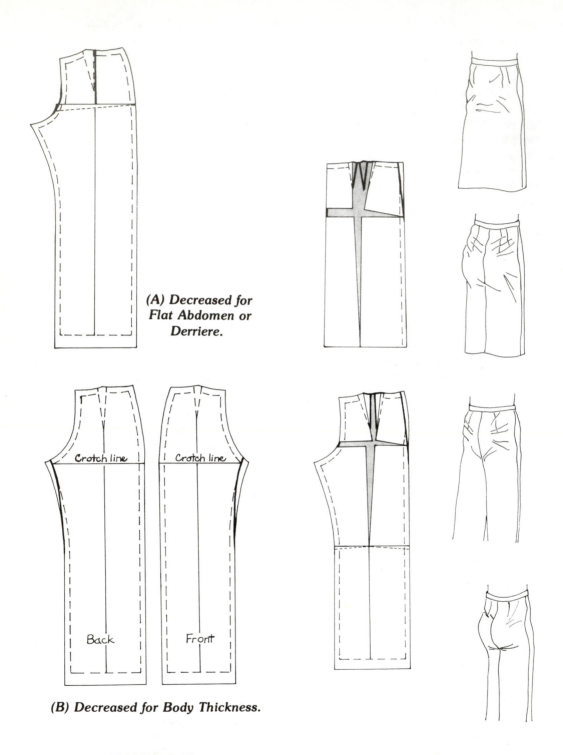

(A) Decreased for Flat Abdomen or Derriere.

(B) Decreased for Body Thickness.

Crotch line   Crotch line

Back   Front

FIGURE 3–50
Decrease Crotch Length.

FIGURE 3–51
Large Derriere or Protruding Abdomen.

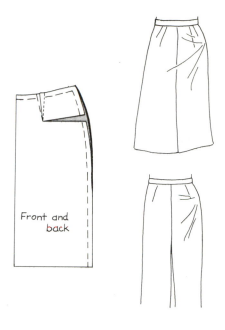

Front and back

FIGURE 3–53
High Hip.

FIGURE 3–52
Flat Derriere or Abdomen.

Straighten center back or center front seam and redraw side seam to retain waistline size (Figure 3–52). This adjustment is applicable to either front or back.

- *Objective:* To adjust for a high hip.

Indication: Side floor to waist measurements (#16a and #16b) differ. This causes skirt or pants to pull on one side of body. The other side fits correctly.

Procedure: Side seam that pulls must be lengthened by slashing pattern from side seam to dart, spreading needed amount at side seam and folding unevenly through dart (Figure 3–53).

Additional width may be added at side seam if needed. Adjust both front and back for high side. *Note:* When cutting fabric, return pattern to original height for low side.

To eliminate any possible hazards during construction, it is wise to make a test garment of the jacket or coat to be tailored before cutting into the fashion fabric. Skirts and pants may also be tested in fabric. Although testing extends the initial construction time, it saves time in fitting later. It also may save expense, and for the following reasons the dividends are well worth the effort and money involved.

1. It provides a means of testing the correct fit of the pattern and/or any pattern adjustments which may have been made.

2. It allows you to visualize the overall effect of the design. Changes in pocket design or placement, shape and size of collar, and location of buttonholes can be determined at this time. A test garment may even show the inappropriateness of the design to your figure. Thus, the design may be altered or a new pattern can be selected.

3. It helps to determine the appropriateness of the design to the fashion fabric you have selected. For example, a heavily crosswise ribbed fabric may not lend itself to a curved design line. By drawing lines on the muslin like those in the fashion fabric, the total effect can be easily visualized.

4. It allows you to become acquainted with construction sequence and details.

5. It permits you to have a relaxed and confident feeling when it is time to cut your chosen fabric. This, in itself, is a big step toward satisfaction in the end product.

Fabric for Test Garment

Heavy, unbleached muslin or fabric of similar weight is used for the test garment. While the muslin can only approximate the weight of the fashion fabric, it can assume the general shaping of your garment fabric. Lightweight fabrics may require a soft

4
THE TEST GARMENT

muslin. In this case an old muslin sheet can be used. Or, you may prefer to use an inexpensive fashion fabric for yout test garment. Unless extensive changes are required, this garment could be completed to augment your wardrobe.

A suitable fabric for a test garment for both skirts and pants is a woven check about 1.3 cm (1/2'') square (or larger). The checks are especially helpful in determining grain and correct hang in fitting. Unless extreme changes are required during fitting, this fabric may be one that you could complete as a finished garment.

Fabric Preparation

First check the straightness of the grain. The ends should be torn or cut on the crosswise grain. Pull the muslin into shape if the ends do not lie together. It is essential that the fabric for the test garment be as straight as your fashion fabric.

Next press carefully, following the lengthwise grain after checking the straightness of the grain. It is unnecessary to shrink muslin for the test garment, but if you use a fashion fabric, it should be preshrunk if it is to become a wearable garment.

Pattern Preparation

Mark seam allowances on pattern pieces using the following measurements:

Fitting seams	2.5 cm (1'')
Shoulder	
Side or underarm	
Sleeve underarm	
Side and back seams (skirts)	
Outseam and inseam (pants)	
Design seams	2 cm (3/4'')
Curved seams	1.5 cm (5/8'')
Neck	
Armhole	
Sleeve cap	
Waistline (skirt or pants)	

Hems	
Sleeves	3.8 cm (1 1/2'')
(wide sleeve requires 5 cm to 7.5 cm (2'' to 3'') depending on width)	
Jacket	3.8 cm (1 1/2'')
Coat, skirt, or pants	7.5 cm to 10 cm (3'' to 4'')

Check the angle of the front crotch seam. Straighten the cutting line if the seam is not on the straight grain. Usually a better fit results if the front seam is nearly on the straight grain. (Figure 4–1).

Sort out pieces *not needed* for testing—facings, top collar, inseam pockets. Stack all unfolded pattern pieces together and press all at once to save time. Lay the pressed pattern over a hanger or lay it flat until ready to use.

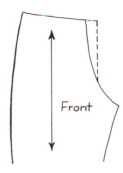

Front

FIGURE 4–1
Crotch Grain Straightened.

Cutting, Marking, and Basting

1. If a fashion fabric is used for the test garment, fold with right sides together. Muslin has no right and wrong side.

2. Lay out pattern pieces on fabric before pinning. Follow grain as carefully as if you were placing pattern on your fashion fabric. Because the fabric may be narrower than the pattern guide indicates, plan your own layout.

3. After determining correct placement, pin in place. The pins should be placed 2.5 cm (1'') inside of the seamline and at right angles to it. Since tracing carbon will be used to mark the seamlines on the muslin, placing the pins in this manner will make it possible to insert the carbon between the two muslin layers without repinning. With a fashion fabric, place the fabric *between* two layers of carbon to keep markings on the wrong side. *Note:* You may have noticed how much ''humping'' there is in fabric when pins are placed parallel to the seamline (see Figure 4–2). This is the reason why placing pins at right angles makes fabric cutting easier.

4. Cut on revised cutting lines (where additions have been made) using regular shears. Cut directionally, which is usually from wide to narrow. Cutting in this way makes cutting easier, the fabric seems to ''flow'' with the shears rather than against them. Now is a good time to get in the habit of ''cutting with the grain.'' Cut notches out instead of into the seam edge to avoid the chance of cutting too deeply into the seam allowance.

5. Transfer all pattern markings with pencil and/or tracing wheel and carbon to muslin. Use a water-erasable pen to mark on right side when fashion fabric is used. *Be accurate* in all markings.

　　a. Mark *all* lengthwise grainlines (including sleeves) and center front and center back *on the right side.* Mark crosswise grain on sleeve, chest, and hip on skirts and pants from underarm to underarm.

FIGURE 4–2
Edge Distorted by Improper Pinning.

　　b. With tracing wheel and carbon, mark darts, seamlines, buttonhole, and pocket locations on right side of muslin.
　　c. Use various colored pencils to indicate different pattern symbols as □ △ ○ ○. Match colors during construction.

6. Remove pattern and *staystitch directionally* on seamline at neck, shoulders, armholes, skirt and pant waistline, curved hipline, and any other areas that may tend to stretch during fitting. Maintain a standard stitch size, and with a slightly loosened top tension, stitch around the entire sleeve cap on the seamline, beginning and ending at the top of the sleeve cap.

7. With right sides together, match pieces and pin on the seamlines and at right angles to them. Pick up only 3 mm (1/8'') of fabric with each pin. These small ''pickups'' or ''bites'' will hold fabric more securely for basting than will large ones.

8. Hand or machine baste directionally. Do not allow stitching to pull when machine basting. If hand basting, use small 3mm to 5mm (1/8'' to 3/16'') stitches to hold the garment together firmly during fitting.

　　Jackets and Coats. Baste darts, design seams, and then shoulder and side seams. Do not baste sleeves in place until first fitting has been completed. Baste muslin under collar to garment at the time the sleeves are basted in place.

　　Skirts and Pants. For pants, press the crease lines in each leg, matching the inseam and the outseam from hem to knee. The entire length of the front crease should follow the straight of grain. The back creases may follow the grain only below the knee. Baste in this order:

1. Darts and tucks.

2. Inseam and outseam of each leg.

3. Crotch seam (place one leg inside the other with right sides together).

For skirts, baste darts and seams on specified seamlines.

Preparation for Fitting

1. Press muslin carefully following the grain. Press seams flat as basted, not open. This allows for easier letting out or taking up on seam allowances during fitting.

2. Turn up hem allowances and pin in place. Often a distracting feature in fitting is a "long look" in a garment.

3. Have your hair neat; wear appropriate shoes. Sometimes it is your general appearance that destroys the initial satisfaction with the garment.

Jackets and Coats. All fittings, including the test garment, should be constructed with shoulder shapes[1] in place if they will be used in the completed garment. However, do not feel that because you did not see the need for shoulder shapes with the test garment, the time has passed for using them. They may be added at any time that you feel they improve the appearance of your garment.

Shoulder shapes or pads may be used in tailored garments to disguise some figure discrepancies, such as one high shoulder or rounded shoulders.

The size of the shape varies with the current fashion, type of garment, and the slope of your shoulders. Generally, shapes used in tailored garments are larger than those used in dresses.

You may purchase ready-made shapes or you can make your own. Frequently ready-made ones require some "re-doing" to make them fit *your* figure. If you plan to construct your own, follow the procedure in the Appendix.

Skirt or Pants. With the fitting band on the inside of the garment, match markings of skirt or pants at center front, center back, and side seams. (If you have not already prepared a fitting band, follow instructions in Chapter 3, "Checking the Adjustments.") Since your garment will be somewhat wider than the length of the band, ease in to fit. Place the pins parallel to the edge of the band on the outside of the garment. With pins in this position, your assistant will find it easier to make adjustments than if pins were at right angles to the band, and you will be saved some possible discomfort from pin puncture.

Standards for Evaluating Fit

Correct fitting is an integral part in the success of the construction of a garment. A suit or coat may be very well made, but unless it fits well it is almost a total loss.

The following factors apply to all garments, including skirts and pants and should be considered when determining whether the garment meets the standard of a good fit.[2] All of these factors are interrelated.

1. *Grain.* At center front and center back the crosswise grain should be parallel to the floor while the lengthwise grain should be perpendicular to the floor. The grain on the left and right sides must be alike unless your garment has an asymmetrical design.

2. *Set.* Any well-fitted garment rests smoothly on the figure without any undesirable wrinkling.

---

[1] Shoulder shapes—layers of fabric that give firmness and support to the shoulder line. A shoulder pad incorporates additional thickness. The terms are often used interchangeably.

[2] Five standards are adapted from Mabel D. Erwin and Lila A. Kinchen, *Clothing for Moderns,* 5th ed.(New York: Macmillan Publishing Co., Inc., 1974), p. 214.

3. *Ease.* The garment must have enough "movability" or ease for you to move comfortably, but there should not be so much that sagging will result. The amount of ease when fitting should be determined by the style of your garment, your fabric, the activity it will be required to undergo, your size and shape, and the current fashion.

4. *Balance.* The garment hangs evenly on all sides of the body unless the design places more fullness in one area than another.

5. *Line.* The seams outline the body shape. Side seams should appear to divide the body in half when viewed from the side; the shoulder seam should lie on top of the shoulder and be invisible from front and back. Curved seams (neckline, armholes, and waistline) should follow the natural curves of your body.

Guidelines for Fitting

In fitting, the jacket should be fitted over a blouse or lightweight sweater and the coat should be fitted over the type of garment you plan to wear under it. A skirt or pants should be fitted with the type of undergarment to be worn with it.

For accuracy, fitting requires the help of a fitting partner. Your partner should stand behind you or at your side while you face a full-length mirror. This position permits both you and your partner to view the fitting process. Use *Critique #2* in the Appendices and the following guidelines:

1. If you have accurately taken measurements and adjusted your pattern accordingly, the basic length and width of the garment should require little additional attention. Adjustments for slope and body bulge will mostly be made in the test garment.

2. Diagonal drag lines indicate a fitting problem. Place finger on end of line(s) and follow to the apparent cause of trouble which may be (1) a body bulge larger or smaller than average, or (2) a body slope different from the pattern.

3. When taking up a seam (e.g., sloping shoulders) fold out the excess and pin flat along the folded edge. (Easy to do if the seam has not been pressed open.) This gives a more realistic view than if the seam is pinned so it stands away from the body. When letting out a seam, cut through the line of basting; do not remove bastings by pulling them. (Snipped bastings serve as guides in seam or dart adjustments.)

4. Fit both left and right sides. However, try to make both sides look alike. If there are major variations between the two sides, adjust each side independently. Be careful about overfitting which tends to direct attention toward an obvious body variation.

5. Do not trim off any excess part of the garment while it is on the body. After removing your garment, fold the right and left sides together and mark both sides alike unless purposefully made different.

6. After fittings are completed, test garment for ease of movement when in a sitting, bending, walking, reaching, and driving position.

Jackets and Coats

1. With the right side of the garment out, adjust the garment on the figure. Pin center fronts together through the length of the buttoned area.

2. If shoulder shapes are to be used, insert them from the armhole side (for normal set-in sleeve). The thick edge of the shape should lie flush with the cut edge of the armhole.

3. Conduct the fitting in the following order: neck and back shoulders, front shoulders and bust or chest area, underarm other with right sides together).

4. Pin and baste the undercollar to the neckline to establish the roll line (see page 209). Pin in sleeves (see page 254) after necessary adjustments have been made within the body of the garment.

Skirts and Pants

1. Since pleats are usually in addition to normal garment ease in both pants and skirts, they should not disappear at the hipline unless so intended by the design of your garment.

2. Full-length pressed pleats should remain closed when the wearer stands still.

3. Skirts and pants should hang from the waistline and not be supported by the hips. A too-snug fit at the hipline will distort the grain and often cause the garment to creep upward with body movement.

4. For pants, crotch fit is critical to comfort and appearance. Diagonal folds or drag lines radiating from the crotch usually indicate a crotch point that is too short or a crotch curve that does not simulate the body curve. Recheck your pattern for adjusting the crotch length as illustrated in Chapter 3. If problems persist that you cannot correct, refer to one of the references on fitting in the Appendix.

Analysis of Details

After the body of garment has been fitted, check the following points:

1. Buttonhole location and pocket position.

    a. Determine placement of the top buttonhole since it controls the size of the lapel. Raising the buttonhole narrows the lapel, while lowering it widens the lapel. Experiment to decide on the width best for you.

    b. Cut rounds of paper to simulate buttons and pin on the garment to help

FIGURE 4–3
Determine Button Size and Location.

determine button size as well as proper location (Figure 4–3). While the sketch in the pattern indicates the designer's choice of size and location, your own size size may dictate a change. One or two large buttons may overpower a small figure; several smaller ones may be more appropriate.

2. Distance from center front to the edge of the garment (overlap). Generally speaking, this distance should be at least equal to the button diameter. A thick button will require a wider overlap (button diameter plus thickness) to ensure that the underlap covers the buttonhole. An additional 1.3 cm (1/2'') increase may make a difference between a good overlap and a skimpy one. Topstitching will also affect the overlap because the button should not cover the topstitching.

3. Pocket size and location.
    a. Cut strips of muslin or paper in different widths and sizes and pin on your test garment.
    b. Determine correct location by the appearance of the pocket on your figure. The correct size or change in style of the pocket should be considered now. Slip your hand through the paper of fabric strip and check for ease of use as well as for the general effect. (See the introduction to Chapter 13.)

FIGURE 4–4
Check Collar Size and Shape.

4. The set of the collar as well as its shape and size.

a. Pin under the seam allowance on the outer edge of the collar to allow the collar to set well on the shoulders.

b. Determine the effect of the collar on your body. Does the shape and/or the size fit you? Does the neckline rest smoothly around the neck? Make any corrections now. (See Figure 4–4.)

5. The "hang" of the sleeve, comfortable circumference, elbow ease, and total length. (See Chapter 18.)

a. Draw in ease line slightly around cap and pin sleeve in place with pins at widths of chest and back and at top of sleeve.

b. Check location of sleeve at top of shoulder as well as at front and back. *Note:* Determining the exact hang is not necessary at this time, but it is important to see that generally there is (1) adequate ease around the cap and upper arm, (2) elbow ease at the elbow, and (3) sufficient length.

6. Roll line of the lapel and/or collar. (See page 209.) Mark this line with a pencil. Lines may change to some extent after interfacings are applied to your garment. However, this can be quickly rechecked at the time interfacings are applied. (Refer to Chapter 16.)

After final checking, remove the test garment and with a water-erasable or felt-tip pen carefully mark all changes in the *crack* of the seam. If there are variations in left and right sides, mark changes on both sides. Otherwise mark only the right-hand side and transfer these markings to the left side.

If no major changes have been made, transfer adjustments to the tissue pattern. Otherwise, use the fitted and pressed test garment as the pattern for cutting. Extreme care must be taken with the muslin if it is to be used as a pattern. So, check the outline of the fabric piece against the paper pattern to eliminate distortion possibilities. Follow this procedure:

a. Cut shell apart after marking all seam and dart changes; make any necessary adjustments (e.g., insertion of extra muslin where an increase has been made) and press carefully.

b. Use the tissue pattern for minor changes or where changes from the test garment can be easily transferred. This method is often preferred because it is helpful to be able to see through a pattern for certain identification points (e.g., as in matching checks and plaids).

c. Recheck correct grainlines in any area where grain has been affected.

d. Mark proper seam allowances where changes may have been made. (Refer to the first part of this chapter.) To insure accuracy it is advisable to mark seam allowances on the extra pattern margins, or add additional tissue.

e. Recheck to see that all necessary pattern pieces (fabric and/or tissue) are present.

Self-Fitting

You may find yourself in a situation where you do not have an assistant in fitting. A dress form made to your individual measurements is the best help in this case. However, since dress forms are expensive, many sewers do not own this piece of equipment. In this case, analyze the problem, make the adjustment, and try on the garment. Repeat until correct fit is obtained. This method can be successful if you are patient and if you have a basic understanding of what ''good fit'' means. You must have an available mirror, preferably one in which you can see your full length. A hand held mirror is helpful to observe the back fit.

A Word of Caution. While there may have been many changes made in the test garment at this time, keep in mind that as different fashion fabrics and interfacings are used, there still may be necessary adjustments. In other words, do not disregard the necessity of checking the fit at all levels of construction. You may think this is too time consuming, but as long as you are expending a considerable amount of time, energy, and money, why not make an effort to produce the best fitting garment possible?

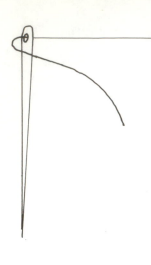

5
PREPARATION OF FABRICS AND ADJUSTMENTS IN PATTERN DESIGN

Since wool fabrics lend themselves so well to tailoring, most of the discussion in this chapter relates to wool and to wool blends. There are various reasons why wool is a popular fabric for tailored garments, but one of the principal ones is its natural tendency to shrink when subjected to heat, moisture, and pressure. This characteristic makes it a pliable fabric that can be molded into shape by proper handling. But this same tendency also makes it essential that a wool fabric be tested for possible additional shrinkage which it may undergo at an undesirable time in construction. Testing may show that the fabric is truly "ready for the needle," or it may indicate that some treatment is needed in addition to that given by the manufacturer.

Tailored garments also have fabrics other than wool utilized in their construction. Because it is necessary to shrink any material that goes inside a coat or jacket (with the exception of lining), the procedure for shrinking other fabrics will be discussed. Since summer-type fabrics (cotton, linen, and synthetics) are frequently made into tailored garments, it is necessary to understand shrinking procedures for fabrics of this nature. You must also know how to straighten any off-grain fabric. Some suggestions are also made for adjustments in your pattern design as well as directions for making a lining pattern.

Preparation of Fabric

Before anything else is done to your fabric, check it for possible flaws. To do this, hold the fabric in front of a fairly strong light to determine whether there are any visible thin places. This flaw may be found more often in napped fabrics that have been "over-napped." This simply means that too many fibers have been drawn out of the yarns at one place, thus causing a weakened or thin condition in the fabric. Other kinds of flaws that may be observed are ends of yarns, extra heavy yarn, and/or uneven yarn in a smooth fabric. (Some flaws may be easily detected in the store before the fabric is purchased, which, of course, is the best time to locate any imperfections.) When a flaw is detected:

1. Place two crossed pins in any spot where a thin place or any other flaw occurs.

2. Roughly lay out the pattern pieces on the fabric to determine whether the flaw interferes with your layout. If it is impossible to "work around" the flaw, then return the fabric to its place of purchase. A reputable store will accept a return as long as the yardage has not been cut.

Testing Fashion Fabrics

Any dry-cleanable fabric to be used as the fashion fabric should be tested for shrinkage and straightness of grain before it is cut for a garment. Any washable fabric should be washed as the garment will be washed and dried in a like manner. The following discussion deals with wool and wool blends, but the methods are applicable to any dry-cleanable fabric.

Not all wool[1] fabrics require additional shrinkage beyond that given by the manufacturer. Information secured at the time of purchase supplies some guide. For example, phrases such as *sponged and shrunk, ready for the needle,* and *London shrunk* mean only limited shrinkage control has been given the fabric. Such information does not guarantee that further shrinkage will not take place. However, it does give some clue as to the fabric shrinkability. Another hint as to what you may expect is the type of yarn as well as the fabric construction, which can influence

dimensional stability of the fabric. For example, a loosely twisted yarn or one loosely spun as well as a loosely woven fabric may tend to shrink more than those more tightly spun and woven.

The following guidelines will help you decide whether further treatment of any kind is necessary for your fabric:

1. Open-textured, loosely woven woolens usually need shrinking.

2. Closely woven, firm fabrics (e.g., gabardine and serge) rarely require additional shrinking.

3. Some wool fabrics have a sheen (e.g., broadcloth and flannel) that disappears or becomes less apparent when moisture and/or heat is applied. Test for this by pressing a corner of the fabric with a dampened press cloth. If the finish disappears and the pressed area looks dull, have the fabric pressed by a professional presser. Even though professional steaming may remove the sheen, it should produce an even, unstreaked appearance. In any case, this finish would be removed unevenly during the construction process and completely removed during the first cleaning of the garment. However, be sure to examine your fabric before taking it from the presser to be sure that the fabric appearance is as you want it.

4. Wool crepes should never be *sheet treated.* Due to the tight twist of crepe yarns, they tend to shrink when damp and are difficult to restore to their original texture by pressing. Press lightly with a steam iron or take the fabric to a professional presser.

If in doubt about the necessity of shrinking a wool fabric, test in the following manner:

1. Hand baste an area 7.5 cm (3'') square in one corner of the fabric. The square must be on the grain and at least 2.5 cm (1'') away from the cut end and the selvage.

---

[1] Since wool blends will be handled in the same manner as wool, all fabrics with wool content will subsequently be called wool in this text.

2. From the wrong side press this area using a steam iron. Measure the square to determine the amount of shrinkage.

3. Then press again using a dry iron and a damp cloth on top of a wool press cloth. Leave the iron in place about nine seconds. Measure the square as in Step 2 above. A difference of 3 mm (1/8'') on 7.5 cm (3'') will be 3.8 cm (1 1/2'') on 91.5 cm (1 yard).

4. Examine the pressed area more carefully. If there is an imprint of the iron on the wool, if a ''bubbly'' area has appeared just outside the imprint, if the measurement has changed, or if the area shows steam blotching, the fabric should be treated. *Steam blotching* refers to the wool fibers being *lifted* during the steaming process causing the fabric to appear dull wherever the steam has had contact. This effect may not be permanent and may disappear with the first dry cleaning. However, the dull surface may remain as a permanent condition as previously explained. In any case, it is well to know the effect that steam will have on your fabric before construction begins.

If a small amount of shrinkage does occur, you must decide whether the amount is sufficient to warrant the time and effort involved in further treatment of the fabric.

The next step in the preparation of your fabric is to determine whether the filling yarns are crossing the warp yarns at exact right angles. Follow these steps:

First look at the fabric to determine the straightness of the raw ends. A torn end will always be on grain, the warp ends will appear somewhat fuzzy, and in some fabrics the first crosswise yarn may be easily pulled across the entire fabric width. A *cut* end is rarely on grain unless a plaid or a prominent or pulled crosswise yarn was followed in cutting. To straighten an irregularly cut end, select a filling yarn that seems to run the entire width of the fabric. Pull the yarn until it creates a definite line in the material. Cut as far as the line extends, pull again on the

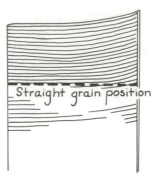

FIGURE 5–1
Skewed Fabric.

same yarn and cut. Repeat this process across the fabric width.

If the fabric permits, an unevenly cut end may be straightened by tearing. In some cases, too much loss of fabric might occur from pulling a thread or tearing to straighten the ends; if so, place a hand basting along a crosswise yarn to establish the grainline. Leave this basting in place until the garment pieces have been cut. Folding the fabric so that the basting will lie on top of basting will serve the same purpose as a torn or straightened end.

Fold the fabric lengthwise with the right side inside, matching selvages and ends. Wool and silk fabrics (and most rayons) are folded this way. Place on a flat surface with square corners. If the fabric is true grain, the selvages and raw ends will exactly fit the edges. If the fabric does not conform to the correct grain, it must be straightened.

Skewing may occur in some fabrics. The ends of the torn fabric may lie together but the selvage edges curve upward as in Figure 5–1. This condition will need straightening.

Straightening Grain

If the fabric requires shrinking, the grain may be straightened and the fabric shrunk using the sheet treatment discussed later in this chapter. The following two methods for straightening the grain apply to fabrics that *do not need* shrinking:

Method I:

1. Grasp diagonal corners and gently stretch the fabric on the true bias. Repeat this process through the entire length of fabric.

2. Check grain again. If the fabric is still off-grain it may be necessary to follow Method II or if that does not work, follow the procedure for sheet treating wool.

Method II:

1. Baste across the raw ends of the folded fabric, keeping edges even.

2. Lay the fabric on a table. If an assistant is available, pull on both cloth ends to allow the crosswise yarns of the upper layer to lie parallel with those of the under layer. If there is no one to assist, pin one end of the cloth to a table (a cork-topped table is convenient for this purpose) or place heavy objects (books) across the end to hold the fabric in place.

3. Baste (or pin) the two thicknesses of fabric together about every 45 cm to 60 cm (18'' to 24'') being sure that the crosswise grain is straight. Use long basting stitches to hold the grain in place. Pins may be used instead of basting as long as pressing does not extend over them.

4. Pin the first 45-cm to 60-cm (18'' to 24'') section to a squared, padded table or to a padded board.

5. Dampen the fabric by using a steam iron, pressing lightly on the *lengthwise grain*. If the iron does not produce sufficient moisture to alter the fabric grainlines, then use a carefully dampened piece of cheesecloth or a gauze diaper and a dry iron. To dampen the cloth, wet half and fold the dry half over it. Squeeze or wring to dampen and to evenly distribute the moisture. *Precau-*

tion: Do not press *over* the fold, basted or pinned areas, as the resulting marks or crease will be difficult to remove. *Note:* If at this point you can readily see that this method is not achieving the desired results, stop. Some firmly woven fabrics are stubborn and will require more moisture than is provided by this process. In this case, follow the procedure for sheet shrinking discussed in the next section. Some fabrics with a special finish and/or high percentage of synthetic fibers may not straighten and will have to be dealt with as they are.

6. Repeat until each marked section of the fabric has been dampened and pressed.

7. Allow the entire length of fabric to dry on a flat surface for several hours or overnight. Pin it at intervals to a firm surface, if necessary, to maintain the correct grain position while it is drying.

Shrinking Methods for Dry-Cleanable Fabrics

It should be kept in mind that there are two kinds of shrinkage in fabrics, namely *fiber shrinkage* and *relaxation shrinkage*. The latter occurs when the fabric has been under too much tension in the finishing process. In a normal shrinkage treatment some relaxation of the fabric may take place as long as tension is not applied in any way.

Measure fabric lengthwise and crosswise before treating. Jot down measurements to refer to later.

Recommended methods of shrinking follow:

Sheet Treatment for Wool:

This procedure may also be used for straightening stubborn fabric.

1. Leave the fabric folded as purchased (right sides together). Baste the crosswise ends together.

2. Wet one-half of a sheet and squeeze lightly. Open the sheet and lay the dry half

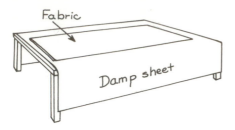

FIGURE 5–2
Sheet Shrinking.

against the wet and then wring, thus evenly distributing the moisture. There should be no dry or excessively wet areas.

3. Open the sheet and spread it over a table. Place the folded wool on it (Figure 5–2).

4. Fold the sides of the sheet over the wool. Then, from one end, fold the sheet (with enclosed fabric) over and over in deep folds of at least 30 cm (12'') as far as one-half the yardage length. Repeat from the opposite end (Figure 5–3).

5. Cover with a large towel or a piece of plastic to prevent the outside from drying too quickly.

6. Let stand several hours or overnight (the heavier the fabric the longer the time needed for complete moisture penetration).

7. Unfold and lay the wool on a flat surface, making sure that the grain of fabric is absolutely square. Smooth the fabric lightly with your hands. If fabric appears to have the same smoothness as it did originally, then allow it to dry. If it seems that wrinkles are too deep, lightly press with a dry iron.

FIGURE 5–3
Fabric Folded in Sheet.

8. If pressing is necessary, place a lightweight cotton press cloth over the damp fabric and press *lightly* with the lengthwise grain. (Be careful about shoving the top surface of the fabric with the iron.) Reverse and press the under layer, pressing only enough to remove the wrinkles. Do not press over the fold. Open the fabric to press over the fold area. Recheck the grain.

9. Allow fabric to dry completely on a flat surface before folding it for storage, if cutting is to be done later.

Steam Pressing Treatment (Noncommercial):

1. Lay folded fabric on a press board and place an evenly dampened press cloth over a section. Lightly press with a dry iron. *Do not press* over the center fold. *Do not press* until the press cloth is dry. Redampen the press cloth when necessary. Wool should feel slightly damp after pressing. Repeat until entire length of fabric has been pressed.

Note: To dampen, dip one-half of the press cloth in water, squeeze lightly, then fold wet into dry part and wring. If cloth is too wet, press with a hot iron until it is only damp.

2. Treat underside of the folded fabric in this manner, keeping the wool squared to the table edge.

3. Allow to dry thoroughly on a flat surface before folding.

Commercial Steam Treatment:

A reputable dry cleaner or a tailor will shrink the fabric, but this does not necessarily mean that the grain will be straight. If the grain is not straight after this treatment and if the operator cannot produce straight grain, then you will need to process the fabric yourself. However, be satisfied that your fabric looks evenly shrunk and pressed before accepting it from the dry cleaner. If you must straighten the grain, use the sheet treatment previously described.

Note: Few plaids are perfectly balanced so that the length and width of the plaid are exactly the same. Shrinking a woven balanced plaid can affect matching as the fabric may shrink more in one direction than the other, thus changing the shape of the plaid. Measure the plaid dimensions and then note any change after shrinking.

Treating Knits

Double-knitted fabrics are treated in much the same way as the wovens. Since knits are constructed as a tube, they are cut along one fold in order to allow the fabric to be opened for finishing processes. However, they are not always cut on a straight line. To determine straightness:

1. Hand baste a line along a wale (lenghtwise rib) near one lengthwise edge.

2. Hand baste a crosswise marking across the ends. *Note:* It may be impossible to follow a specific row of courses (crosswise loops), but you generally can get a feeling of the crosswise grain. Holding a fabric next to a windowpane or a strong light may help to define its grain.

3. Fold the fabric, matching the crosswise basted lines to determine straightness of grain.

4. Determine necessity of a shrinkage treatment. If shrinking is necessary, follow one of the three shrinkage methods previously described.

After treating, measure all fabrics both lengthwise and crosswise to determine shrinkage. Refer to original measurements.

Shrinking Interfacing and Underlining

Any supportive fabric used within a tailored garment must be shrunk. Linings used in dry-cleanable garments generally are not pretreated. A lining does not fit snugly into

FIGURE 5–4
Water Shrinking.

a garment, so if any shrinkage should occur during dry cleaning, there will still be ample fabric within the body of the garment. Linings often change appearance when they are exposed to water and it is difficult to return them to their original appearance. Straighten uneven fabric ends as explained earlier.

Both woven fusible and nonfusible interfacings (including "dry clean only" hair canvas) and underlinings may be treated in the following manner:

1. Fold the fabric lengthwise with the right sides together. Machine baste across the crosswise ends.

2. Use a large container (laundry tub, sink, or bathtub) and enough warm water to completely cover the fabric after immersion.

3. For a minimum of wrinkles, "accordion fold" the cloth and place it in the water. This method allows better water penetration than if folded in an over and over manner. (Figure 5–4). Let stand several hours or until the water is cold.

4. Drain off the water. With your hands press out as much water as possible. *Do not wring.*

5. Lay the folded fabric between two large terry towels and press out the excess moisture. Remove the towels.

6. Lay the fabric on a flat surface over a large sheet. Straighten so that the grainlines

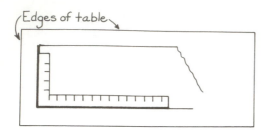

FIGURE 5–5
Squaring Grain.

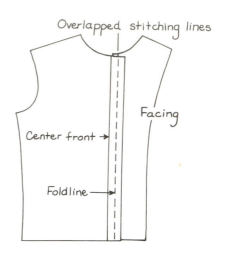

FIGURE 5–6
Eliminating Front Edge Seam.

are at right angles to each other (Figure 5–5). Smooth the cloth with your hands and allow the fabric to dry.

7. If additional steps are necessary to remove wrinkles, press *nonfusibles* on the lengthwise grain.

Note: Place tape, grosgrain, and any other woven materials used in the actual garment construction in the same water with the interfacing. Remove from the water, pull tape and grosgrain between fingers or between a folded paper towel to remove excess water. Allow to dry and then iron; pull on it as it is ironed to remove any ''give.'' Keep grain straight.

If tape is wound around a card when purchased, leave the tape on its card, bend the card so the tape may shrink, and place both in water. The card helps to eliminate wrinkling and keeps tape in order until ready to use. Stretch and press before applying to a garment.

Adjustments in Pattern Design

Changes that may improve the general appearance of the garment or facilitate construction can be made in the pattern prior to cutting. Consider the following possibilities to see if they apply to your fabric and design.

Front Edge Extension

If the front edge of a garment is on the straight of grain, the seam along the edge may be eliminated by overlapping the seamlines of the garment front and the facing and cutting the front and facing as one piece. This is a time saver in stitching, taping, and pressing and reduces bulk along the front edge (Figure 5–6).

Note: A disadvantage is that the folded edge is flatter than a seamed edge and thus would give a different appearance from the collar edge, particularly if topstitching is to be done. In case this method is used, a change will also be necessary when cutting the interfacing.

Front Edge Extension with Curved Lapel

Cut across the facing pattern at the top buttonhole level (Figure 5–7). Add a seam allowance to both cut edges and attach the lower facing section to the front by overlapping the seam allowances. The lapel edge will have a seamed edge while the remainder of

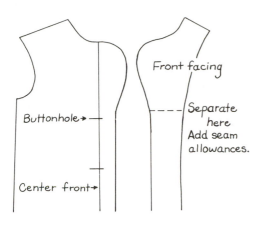

FIGURE 5–7
Making the Pattern for Partial Cut-On Facing.

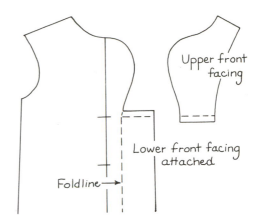

FIGURE 5–8
Pattern Redesigned for Partial Cut-On Facing.

the front will have a folded edge (Figure 5–8).

Undercollar

If the undercollar has a center back fold, replace it with a seam on the bias. A bias usually allows a collar to be more easily shaped, and the seam at the back allows the grain to follow the same direction on both collar points. Mark the new grainline on the bias and add a seam allowance at the center back. Since the interfacing and undercollar will be handled together when being shaped, also cut the interfacing on the bias with a center back seam.

Uppercollar

Lay the uppercollar pattern over the undercollar pattern with outside edges even. The uppercollar should be 6 mm (1/4'') to 2 cm (3/4'') wider than the undercollar, depending on the weight of fabric—the larger amount for heavy fabrics. Even though an uppercollar pattern is usually cut wider than the undercollar, most heavy coat fabrics will

require added width to ensure an amount that will extend over an outer curve, and some lightweight fabrics will also require an increase. If necessary, add to the neck edge of the uppercollar. If an excessive amount is added, it can be removed later.

Cuffs

One major emphasis in the construction of cuffs is the reduction of bulk. Before cutting, consider these possibilities:

1. Eliminate a seam along the lower edge of the shirt-style cuff or along the upper edge of a turnback cuff by placing the seamline on a fold.

2. Use the selvage edge (if not too heavy) as a finish on the underside of the shirt-style cuff. Thus, in cutting, eliminate one seam allowance.

3. For a straight cuff, if possible, cut the sleeve and cuff as one, or extend the facing of the cuff so that it will form the hem of the sleeve.

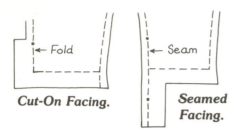

Cut-On Facing.   **Seamed Facing.**

FIGURE 5–9
Sleeve Vent Facings.

Sleeve Vents

The sleeve vent may be cut with a cut-on facing, which results in a fold along the edge of the vent, or the vent facing may be an extension of the hem so that there is a seam along the edge of the vent. The second method is not recommended for bulky fabrics, so you may wish to change the facing before you cut (See Figure 5–9).

In-Seam Pockets

An inconspicuous pocket may be preferred to a patch pocket or a welt pocket. Plan for an extension of seamlines at a location comfortable for the wearer. (See Chapter 13,

Pockets, Figures 13–64 to 70.) If fabric width permits, add the pocket shape to the back section of pattern, thus eliminating a seam. Or, extend the seam allowance to 2.5 cm (1'') to 3.8 cm (1 1/2''). If this plan is used, both upper and lower sections of the pocket can be made from the lining fabric.

Center Back Pleat in Jacket or Skirt

Extend pleat to top of garment to give support to the pleat and to eliminate any outside stitching to support the pleat. Also if possible, place the pleat edge on a fold to eliminate a seam which is difficult to manage in the hem area (Figure 5–10).

Note: To reduce bulk cut out the layer of the pleat extension that lies next to the body. Stitch a flat seam tape along the cut edge to give added support to the pleat. The same method is possible on a coat if the fabric is not too bulky. This method is not applicable if the garment has a curved back seam.

Waistband with Grosgrain Backing

Cut the waistband on the *crosswise* grain of the fabric unless a special or an unshaped band is desired. Since the band will be

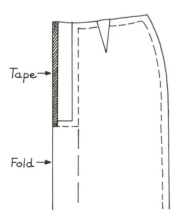

Tape→

Fold→

FIGURE 5–10
Pleat Extension.

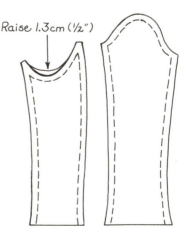

Raise 1.3cm (½")

FIGURE 5–11
Sleeve Lining Pattern.

pressed and shaped before it is applied to the garment, crosswise grain allows for easier shaping than lengthwise. Cut the waistband twice as wide as the finished band plus 6 mm (1/4'') and allow about 7.5 cm to 10 cm (3'' to 4'') in length in addition to your waist measurement.

Adjusting Armhole in Lining

Add 1.3 cm (1/2'') to the seam allowance on the lower sleeve armhole between the notches to allow the lining to cover a standing seam in the lower garment armhole (Figure 5–11).

Making a Lining Pattern

If your pattern does not include a lining pattern and you wish to line your jacket or coat, follow these instructions to make your own pattern.

Front:

1. Trace the front pattern on a piece of tissue.

2. Lay front facing under the front, trace the stitching line on the edge of facing (Figure 5–12).

3. Add 1.5-cm (5/8'') seam allowance toward center front of traced stitching line. Cut along this line for the lining.

4. If the pattern has an underarm or an armhole dart, or the two front pieces are laid together to form a dart where seams do not meet (modified princess):

   a. Slash from center of the shoulder to the point of bust.
   b. Fold out dart or close seam.
   c. Spread at the shoulder to form a shoulder pleat (Figure 5–13). Mark at seamline and 5 cm (2'') below shoulder for a shoulder tuck (A).

5. Waistline dart: mark 2.5 cm (1'') above and below waistline for tuck (B).

Back:

1. Add 3.8 cm (1 1/2'') to *center back* and

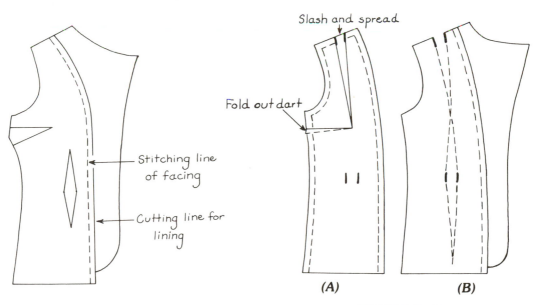

FIGURE 5–12
Front Lining Pattern.

FIGURE 5–13
Shoulder and Waistline Tucks in Lining.

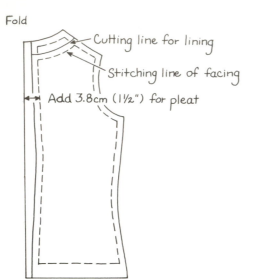

FIGURE 5–14
Back Lining Pattern.

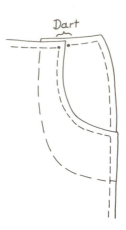

FIGURE 5–15
Lining Pattern for Garment with Pocket Underlay.

lay on fold to form an ease pleat (Figure 5–14).

    a.   Long coat: pleat may continue to hem or taper to nothing at waistline.
    b.   Vent in back of coat or jacket: allow pleat to extend through depth of hem.

Sleeve:

Cut exactly like the sleeve pattern except adjust the armhole as explained in the previous section.

Skirts and Pants:

The skirt or pants lining is usually cut like the fashion fabric with the following exceptions:

1.   *Pockets.* Inset pockets are omitted, but if a pocket underlay forms part of the garment, place the underlay on the garment pattern and cut as one piece.

    Note: Some patterns incorporate fitting into the pocket. If the two pattern pieces (garment and pocket underlay) do not fit to-gether evenly, allow the waistline to spread and incorporate this amount into a small waistline dart in the lining (Figure 5–15).

2.   *Pleats in skirts.* The lining for a pleated skirt should not interfere with the pleats and is usually cut without them. Fold out the pleats and cut the lining from the pattern. Slits may be necessary to allow for adequate movement—a center front slit for a front pleat or side slits for multiple pleated skirts. With a lightweight lining fabric, make a pleat in the lining if the function of the lining is to provide opaqueness. The lining should lie under the pleat in the fashion fabric and not distort the garment pleat.

    Note: Underlining is the best way to achieve opaqueness in simple skirts, but it is not satisfactory in skirts with many pleats.

3.   *Trouser-Style pleats.* These may appear in skirts or pants and are either loose pleats or are stitched a short distance below the waistband. Cut the lining like the fashion fabric, but stitch the pleat as a dart or as a long pleat to the hipline to reduce bulk and a ''pouchy'' look.

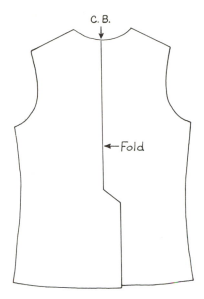

FIGURE 5-16
Usual Pattern Method for Lining with Vent.

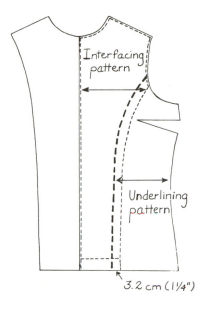

FIGURE 5-18
Cutting Front Underlining.

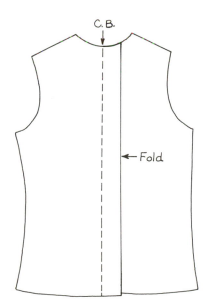

FIGURE 5-17
Revised Method for Lining with Vent.

Adjusting for Back Vent in Lining

The back vent in most patterns is cut as illustrated in Figure 5-16. An easier and stronger method is illustrated in Figure 5-17. To follow this method be sure that the back lining is _cut on the fold_ and that 3.8 cm (1 1/2'') ease pleat is allowed. With this allowance you may elect to use either method of lining the vent.

Cutting Underlining for Front

If you plan to add underlining to the front of your garment, your pattern may have instructed you to cut the underlining _exactly_ like the front. However, that method will destroy the effect of the front hair canvas interfacing because it places the underlining _between_ the fashion fabric and the interfacing. Follow the illustration in Figure 5-18 for cutting the underlining.

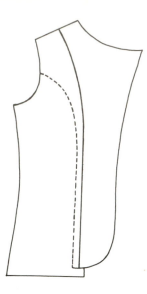

FIGURE 5–19
Facing Extended for Unlined Garment.

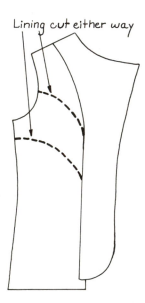

Lining cut either way

FIGURE 5–20
Partial Lining for Unlined Garment.

Adjustments for the Unlined Jacket or Coat

For the unlined garment with shoulder pads (shapes), the pads may be covered *or,* the front facing may be extended to cover the front shoulder and the pad (Figure 5–19). Also, if the fashion fabric is heavy or yardage is limited, a section of lining fabric may be joined to the regular facing across the front shoulder (Figure 5–20).

Note: For men's jackets the front section is usually entirely lined, except for sporty, casual jackets, which may have covered shoulder pads. A short lining may be used across the back to cover the pads and to give a finished appearance. Cut the short lining like the back lining pattern, including the ease pleat, and ending at mid-armhole or below the armhole.

Adding or Decreasing Pleats in Pants

Pleated pants are often fuller than desired. If so, fold out the desired amount the length of the pleat. If the crease follows the outside fold of the pleat, delete an equal amount on either side of the fold so the crease will remain centered on the front pattern piece. Retain the same waistline circumference.

To add a pleat to unpleated pants, slash the length of the crease and spread for the desired pleat size, usually 2 cm to 3.8 cm (3/4'' to 1 1/2''). Fold the pleat so outside crease is centered in the added area.

Adjusting Pant Leg Width

Current fashion varies from narrow to wide pant legs, but a pattern that fits in the waist, hip, and crotch may be easily adjusted.

1. Decide if width needs to be adjusted from hip to hem or from knee to hem. Wide bottom pants may taper outward from hip to hem or may taper in to the knee, then out. Medium width pants may be perfectly straight or taper inward at the knee. Narrow bottom pants will taper from the hip to the hem.

2. Determine the total circumference that you wish at knee and hemline.

3. Make one-fourth of the necessary adjustment on each inseam and outseam of front and back pattern pieces. For a crease to remain on straight of grain, make the adjustment the same on the inseam and the outseam.

4. If vertical seams of the pants are not on straight grain at the hem, turn up the hem and redraw it to match the slant of the inseam and outseam.

Adding Cuffs to Pants

1. Determine desired width of cuff. To the finished length, add *twice* the cuff depth plus about 3.1 cm (1 1/4'') for hem.

2. When cutting garment, mark the pant length with a clip at the seamline, add the depth of the cuff, and mark again. The latter clip designates the foldline for the hem. The first mark denotes the foldline of the cuff.

Note: If pant leg is shaped so the inseam and outseam are not on straight grain, make

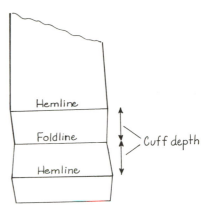

FIGURE 5–21
Adding Cuff to Pants.

cuff as follows: Add paper extension to pattern as described earlier, but allow paper to extend past the cutting line at inseam and outseam edges. Fold cuff as it will be finished. Trim cutting lines to match the inseam and outseam of the pants. When cuff is unfolded, you will notice that the edges are angled. This is necessary for the cuff to fit the pant leg (Figure 5–21).

6

PRELIMINARY STEPS IN CONSTRUCTION

Unless your pattern layout indicated otherwise, fold the fashion fabric with right sides together, selvages matching, and grain parallel and lay on a cutting table. If the tale is not long enough to accommodate the entire length of the fabric, fold the fabric at one end and place it on a chair; be careful that the grain is straight as it leaves the table. For knits or stretchy fabrics, keep the entire length on the table to prevent tension on the fabric.

Determine whether the fabric has a nap or any pattern or structural texture that will necessitate laying all pieces in the same direction. (See page 25.) A fabric may appear at first glance to have an all over texture or tweed effect, but upon closer examination it may reveal a definite repeat in the weave or the yarns. Turn back the end of the fabric so that the lengthwise grains are juxtaposed in opposite directions. Is there a difference in the way the light is reflected? Can you feel any difference when you run your hand lengthwise? Are there any dominant threads or colors, and if so, do they repeat at intervals in either the lengthwise or crosswise direction? If any of these conditions are present, then special consideration must be given when placing the pattern on the fabric.

Fabrics with Nap

Refer to Chapter 2 to determine fabrics that require a "with nap" layout (i.e., napped fabrics, pile fabrics, and fabric designs that have an up and down). Corduroy, velvet, velveteen, and brushed woolens all have a definite nap and may look quite different depending on which way the nap is placed. Generally the fabric will appear lighter in color and be smoother when the nap runs down, and it will appear richer and darker and be rougher when the nap runs up. Personal preference should dictate the direction, but if it is a color and fabric that will show creases it will be easier to brush if the nap runs down. However, if a rich color is desired, then the nap should run upward. Remember, all pattern pieces must be laid in the same direction on a napped fabric. If there is any doubt whether the fabric is directional, be safe and follow the layout for napped fabrics that is in your pattern guide sheet.

Diagonal or Twill Weave Fabric

The guidelines for choosing a pattern compatible with a diagonal or twill weave fabric were discussed on page 26. If you wish to test a pattern, draw diagonal lines on your pattern or on your test garment to simulate the diagonal pattern. Then you can see exactly how the pattern will look on each side of the body. It may be advisable to lay each test piece out singly to see how the diagonal will look.

Position of Fabric Design on the Body

Determine which part of the fabric pattern is dominant. Do this by standing away from the fabric as it is draped vertically, squinting your eyes, and seeing which area is most obvious in both the lengthwise and crosswise direction. Where do you want the most dominant areas to be placed on the body? The more dominant the pattern, the more important the decision. These general guidelines will be helpful, but they are not hard and fast rules. Usually, place the dominant line:

1. At the bottom of the jacket or skirt for visual weight.

2. Above the bustline or at the shoulder and, if possible, above or below the largest hip.

3. Either vertically at center front and

center back or placed so that a dominant area is on either side of center front and of center back.

4. Centered on the sleeve so that the vertical line meets the shoulder point.

Laying Out Fabric for Cutting

Patterned fabrics, such as plaids and stripes, may be cut in single or double layers. Cutting singly requires that the pattern be duplicated or cut once and then repositioned for the second cut. Double cutting necessitates the fabric being pinned at close intervals to keep the two layers exactly together. Single cutting is the most accurate, especially if the cut piece is laid over the second piece for exact replication, but close pinning will also make double cutting satisfactory.

When double cutting plaids, pin at the intersection of each major design for large patterns or at every other one or every third for small patterns. Place a pin through top layer of fabric, then through the same point in the under layer. Pick up only 3 mm (1/8'') of fabric and do not allow the fabric to slip as the pin is brought back through the top layer. Move pins that intersect cutting lines after the pattern is positioned on the fabric and before cutting.

After determining where you want the dominant parts of the design to fall on the body, mark these positions on your pattern. Roughly position all pattern pieces on the fabric to see your general layout, then place pieces to match the fabric design in the following order: jacket or coat front; back; collar; front facing; sleeve; then skirt (or pants) front and back. It is important that all points *match on the stitching line* — not the cut edge. The following guidelines will be helpful in placing the paper pattern so that the design will match in the adjoining pieces. Note the numbered position of matching points (Figure 6–1). Place only two pins on each pattern piece until the entire layout has been positioned.

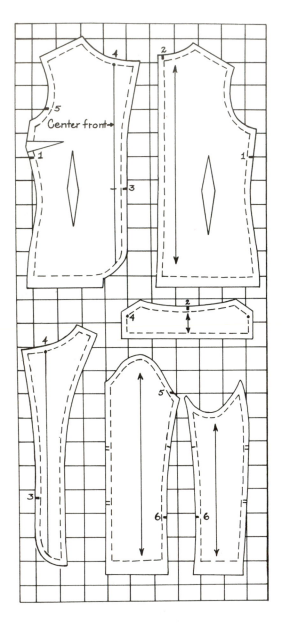

FIGURE 6–1
Layout for Plaid.

1. Place center front in the *middle* of a vertical plaid or stripe, either the dominant or subordinate part of the design. Position dominant horizontal at lower edge and bustline as desired. Examine the darts in the garment to see where they fall on the fabric design. Changing an angle or shifting a dart slightly may make it less obvious and will not unduly influence the fit. A dart is less obvious if centered in a negative space and more obvious when it cuts diagonally across a geometric pattern. Note where buttons will fall on the design repeat. Slight respacing or shifting of the pattern may be necessary to place them at the desired interval on the design repeat.

2. If garment has a two-piece front, such as a princess design, match horizontally and, if possible, also vertically so that the repeat will run consecutively across the chest and hip.

3. Place center back on the same part of the design as the center front and match at notches *below* the horizontal underarm dart, if there is one. (See Figure 6–1, notch #1.) In most cases, matching the front and back designs *below* an underarm dart will result in mismatching the upper sleeve and back. However, it is generally considered to be more essential for the lower edge of the garment to match horizontally then for the upper sleeve and back to match. The front and sleeve will match as described in Step 6. For a two-piece back, follow the same procedure as for the two-piece front.

4. Place center back of the collar on the same part of the design as the center back of the garment (#2). The pattern may be moved up and down so the crosswise design will have the most pleasing appearance on the collar front. Also consider where the collar joins the lapel (gorgeline). Depending on the shape of the collar, you may be able to match at this point, so lay out the facing, then check the collar (Figure 6–2). *Note:* You

FIGURE 6–2
Matching Lapel and Collar.

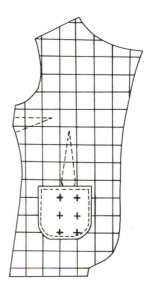

FIGURE 6–3
Matching Pocket to Garment.

may wish to change the shape of the point of a collar or lapel to better follow the line of a stripe or plaid. (See Figure 6-2, note a.)

5. Ideally, the facing is laid exactly on the same design as the garment front. The crosswise design must match, but you may shift the vertical design to achieve a better match with the collar at the gorgeline. (Figure 6-2, note b.)

6. Match the front notch of the sleeve (see Figure 6-1, #5) horizontally at the front notch of the garment unless the notch is extremely low under the arm; then match at the dot nearest the notch. Lay the sleeve with the center on the dominant vertical design unless you decided to place the center between the two dominant lines. As stated in Step 3, the sleeve and back will not usually match horizontally if an underarm dart is present.

7. For a two-piece sleeve, match horizontally at the upper and lower notches (#6) on the pattern pieces. The front seamline of the sleeve should match the entire length, but because of the elbow curve, the back may not. If possible, lay the underarm section of the sleeve so the pattern will proceed consecutively across the front of the sleeve.

8. Pockets should match the area they cover or join unless they are cut on the bias for emphasis. Lay the pocket pattern over the garment pattern and mark the dominant line of the plaid with colored pencils or pen.

This will assure an exact match (Figure 6-3). You may also wish to follow this same procedure in matching the major seamlines of the garment.

9. Instructions for matching and cutting tailored plackets and shirt-style cuffs are found in Chapter 18. Other small pattern pieces may be cut later from scraps.

10. For a suit, the skirt or pants should match the jacket.

    a. Place the center front and center back on the same position as the jacket.

    b. Place the waistline of the skirt or pant on the same horizontal design as the jacket waistline to assure continuity of design up and down.

Note: With a bold plaid or stripe, note what happens at the side seam. If two dominant designs or negative spaces will be side by side, thus forming a large area down the side, some adjustment may be needed. It may be preferable to have better continuity around the body and not have the back centered on the same pattern as the front. This would result in shoulder seams that are different front and back, but because of the ease in the back they often do not match anyway.

11. If at all possible, before cutting have someone else check the layout for you; after working with a pattern for an extended time it is easy to miss something that may be quite obvious. *Or,* leave the layout for awhile and then come back and take a fresh look at the matching points.

12. Anchor the pattern securely by placing pins at right angles to the pattern edge.

13. Make a final check to see that foldlines are placed on the fold, that grainlines are parallel to the selvage, and that all necessary pieces are present. Check the number of single pattern pieces to be cut.

14. Cut the pieces in the same order you placed them on the fabric. Check the matching points with the next piece to be cut to double-check yourself.

Cutting

Using bent handle shears, if available, cut smoothly with long strokes, cutting with the grain. For very heavy or thick fabrics, cut each layer singly. Be careful that layers do not slip while you are cutting so that the edges are uneven. Hold shears perpendicular to the table so that the fabric edges are cut straight. Cut all notches outward.

Interfacings

Patterns vary greatly in the number and type of interfacing pieces given. The more expensive designer patterns often give complete patterns for interfacings for all parts of the garment, while other patterns may in-

clude only a minimum sized front interfacing or may not include any interfacings. The size and shape of the interfacing pieces will partly be determined by the method of application you have chosen. If you have not already clarified the method you wish to use, refer to Chapter 9 which describes the different methods of application (traditional and contemporary) with advantages and disadvantages of each.

Cut interfacings as follows:

Front. The interfacing must exactly fit the garment so use the front garment piece(s) as a pattern for the interfacing.

Traditional (Nonfusible):

1. Lay the facing pattern on the front pattern piece.

2. Draw a line beginning 7.5 cm (3'') below the lower armhole and extend it in a downward curve toward the facing edge and within 2.5 cm (1'') from it (Figure 6-4). This extension is important because it will

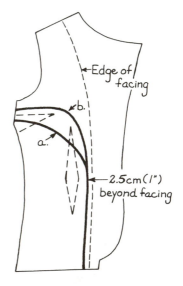

FIGURE 6-4
Interfacing Pattern.

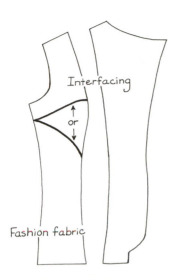

FIGURE 6–5
Interfacing Pattern for Two-Piece Front.

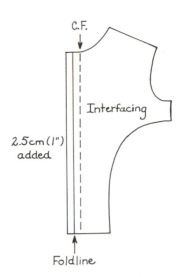

FIGURE 6–6
Interfacing with Extension.

shield and prevent mark-off of the facing edge. A long coat usually has the interfacing the full front length, but for a softer effect, the canvas may stop just below the bottom button.

3.   Allow an underarm dart to be included within any of the curved portion if support is needed through the front area. (See note a in Figure 6–4.) For a softer look, cut the interfacing above the dart area (see note b).

4.   Cut the neckline, shoulder, armhole, and front edge like the pattern and the remainder following the curve line just drawn.

5.   Cut the two-piece front interfacing as illustrated in Figure 6–5.

6.   With a cut-on facing, cut the interfacing to extend 2.5 cm (1'') beyond the foldline (Figure 6–6). This extension will be folded back later to provide a softer appearance and a more desirable edge in the final garment.

Fusible:

1.   Determine the part of the front to be in-

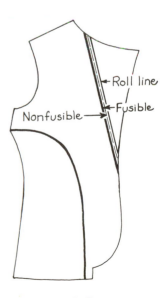

FIGURE 6–7
Interfacing Pattern for a Fused Lapel.

terfaced: the entire front, or the same area as described for traditional interfacing, or the lapel areas with traditional interfacing for the remainder of the front.

2. Cut interfacing following directions for the nonfusible.

3. For a combination, cut the fusible like the lapel, allowing it to extend at least 1.3 cm (1/2'') beyond the roll line and cut the nonfusible 6 mm (1/4'') to garment side of the roll line (Figure 6–7).

Jacket or Coat Back. A lightweight non-fusible interfacing, such as wigan or firm muslin, will give stability to the upper back. *Do not* cut this from hair canvas. If an underlining is used, this additional interfacing may not be required. If an extra layer of fabric seems necessary across the back of the underlined garment cut another layer of underlining in place of the regular interfacing fabric. Remember that this interfacing should be preshrunk before cutting.

1. Begin 7.5 cm (3'') below the armhole

and draw an upward arc to the center back, 23 cm to 25 cm (9'' to 10'') down from the neck edge (Figure 6–8). Cut neck, shoulder and armhole like the pattern and on the same grain as the jacket back. But with a knitted fashion fabric you may wish to cut the back interfacing on the bias to give some stretch. Cut on the straight grain if more stability is desired. Cut the center back on a fold unless the pattern has a curved upper back seam.

2. Cut the two-piece back in two sections and overlap stitching lines and stitch, *or* cut the back in one piece by lapping the pattern pieces at the lower edge of the interfacing and incorporating a dart where the seam spreads at the shoulder (Figure 6–9).

3. For a full or swing back where the garment flares from the shoulder, the upper back interfacing must be cut narrower than the coat back (to fit the wearer). This allows the flare to fall free from the shoulders without causing the garment to slide out on the armhole.

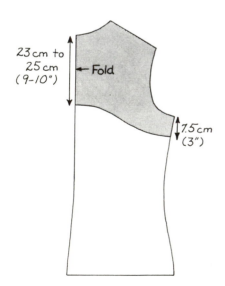

FIGURE 6–8
Back Interfacing Pattern.

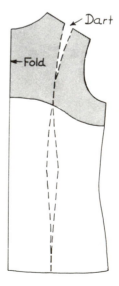

FIGURE 6–9
Two-Piece Back Interfacing Pattern.

4. Use the same interfacing for a back yoke as was used in the fronts; use a lightweight interfacing around the area below the yoke and around the lower armhole (Figure 6–10).

Collar. Use the same kind of interfacing for the collar as was used in the lapels. Use the undercollar pattern with a center back seam on the bias. Keep the *lengthwise* grain the same as for the undercollar. *Note:* When a nonwoven interfacing is used, place the collar so maximum stretch (usually crosswise grain) follows the length of the roll line.

Bias for Hems. A true bias strip is cut for the lower sleeve edge to give crispness to the folded edge. This bias is cut 1.3 cm (1/2'') wider than the sleeve hem, or 2.5 cm (1'') wider if a soft edge is desired, and long enough to fit around the lower sleeve, plus seam allowance. Hair canvas is usually used but a softer interfacing may be used if desired. A softer interfacing (like that used for the back interfacing) is usually used in the jacket hem. Use the same guidelines for cutting this bias interfacing as for the sleeve hems. See Chapter 19 for using fusible interfacing.

Detail Areas. Cut interfacing for pockets and other detail areas like the pattern piece.

Underlinings

If an underlining is to be used, cut all major pattern pieces with exactly the same seam allowances as the fashion fabric. If the traditional method is used, wait to cut the front pieces because only a portion of the front is underlined. Do not underline small areas that will be interfaced, such as pockets, collars, or belts. Unless the fashion fabric is loosely woven or is transparent, generally do not underline the sleeves since underlining may add too much bulk to be comfortable—especially around the elbow.

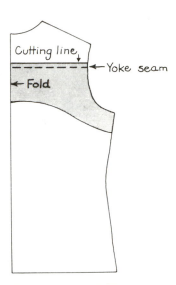

FIGURE 6–10
Interfacing Pattern for Back with Yoke.

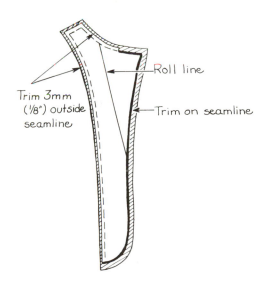

FIGURE 6–11
Fusible Interfacing Applied to the Front Facing.

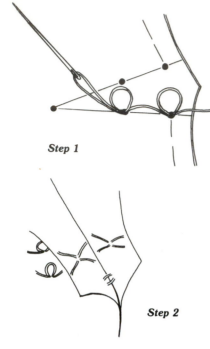

Step 1

Step 2

FIGURE 6–12
Conventional Tailor Tacks.

FIGURE 6–13
Simplified Tailor Tacks.

Note: For lightweight fabrics the upper-collar and lapel facing may be backed with a lightweight fusible fabric to give smoothness and crispness. Cut the collar backing like the upper collar. Cut the lapel like the entire front facing or like the lapel area. Before applying, the full seam allowance should be trimmed away on the front edges and only 3 mm (1/8'') left on the neckline and inside seams (Figure 6–11).

Marking

Markings may be transferred by (1) conventional tailor tacks, (2) simplified tailor tacks, (3) chalk, (4) worn-down piece of soap, (5) tracing wheel and tracing paper, (6) water-erasable marking pen, (7) clip marks, and (8) hand basting.

Conventional tailor tacks are made with a double strand of sewing thread as illustrated in Figure 6–12. Then the layers of fabric are separated, and the thread cut in between. They are time consuming but excellent for delicate and loosely woven fabrics.

Simplified tailor tacks are made with an embroidery needle threaded with colored darning cotton or cotton embroidery floss. Use two strands for lightweight fabrics and more for heavyweight. The needle is pushed straight through the fabric, and a tail at least 2.5 cm (1'') long is left on each side; the layers are then carefully separated so about 1.3 cm (1/2'') of darning cotton is left on either side, and this strand clipped between the layers of fabric (Figure 6–13). Or, pick up one tiny stitch going through both layers. Separate the layers carefully and then cut. Because the strands of darning cotton are soft and loosely twisted, the tack adheres to most fabrics and is easier to remove than the conventional looped tailor tack. Use different colors to denote different pattern markings to simplify joining pieces in construction.

Chalk markings are made by placing a pin through the marking point. Lift the pattern, mark beside the pin, and then turn the fabric over and mark the other side. Because chalk marks rub off easily they are satisfactory for only a short period of time during construction.

Tailor's chalk (a wax chalk) is generally preferred on wool fabrics because it is long lasting. However, never use wax chalk on lining for it leaves a grease mark when the lining is pressed. A worn-down piece of soap with thin edges also makes an excellent marking device.

Tracing wheel and *tracing paper* provide the ideal way to mark *interfacings* and *underlinings* since entire seamlines can be easily marked, and there is no concern that the marks will show on the right side. (But if a light-colored fashion fabric is used, do not mark the underlining with a dark tracing paper.) The general rule is to use the lightest color of carbon possible on the fabric you are marking. This will prevent the possibility of any traced lines being visible through the fashion fabric. Use carbon paper on your fashion fabric and lining with extreme care.

Water-erasable marking pen is excellent to mark notches or other matching points in the seam allowances and to mark the ends of machine-made buttonholes. Marks can usually be easily removed by sponging with a damp cloth. But before using, check your fabric carefully to determine how effectively the pen marks can be removed. Markings are made in the same manner as chalk markings by using a pin to determine the placement.

Hand basting is ideal for marking center front and grainlines on fabrics where grain is not readily visible. It also may be used to transfer markings from the underlining to the fashion fabric, such as pocket placement lines.

Clip marks (no longer than 3 mm or 1/8'') in the seam allowance of *firm* fabrics

are useful for marking ends of center front or center back lines (coat, jacket, skirt, facings, collars, yokes, tops of sleeves, and fold-lines). Experience will help you to determine other areas where they may be useful. Clips are unsatisfactory on loosely woven fabrics. Use the tip of your shears when making the clips to avoid cutting too deeply into the seam allowance.

Marking the Fashion Fabric

Transfer all pattern markings to the fashion fabric unless the garment is to be underlined. In this case markings will be transferred to the underlining except those that must be visible from the outside of the garment.

1. Mark center front and center back with uneven hand basting or machine basting. Generally, hand basting is preferred for marking center front and center back lines because it is less apt to mark the fashion fabric.

2. Hand baste lengthwise and crosswise grain in set-in sleeves.

3. Hand baste crosswise grain in skirt pieces at hip level.

4. Mark seamlines at ends or corners with chalk or tailor's tacks to indicate width of seam. This becomes important because of the width variation of seam allowances.

Marking the Underlining and Interfacing

Seamlines as well as the other markings may be transferred to the underlining and/or interfacing with tracing wheel and carbon paper.

Staystitching

Staystitching keeps curved and bias edges from stretching during the construction process. If the garment is to be underlined or

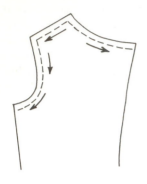

FIGURE 6–14
Staystitching.

fusible interfacing is to be used, proceed to the next chapter before staystitching. If not, follow these guidelines and staystitch through the single layer of fabric.

1. Use regulation length stitch (12–16 st.) in matching *mercerized* thread. Mercerized thread is preferable because it is more stable than a polyester and is easier to remove.

2. Stitch directionally following the diagrams in Figure 6–14. Stitch *on* the neckline seam and 3 mm (1/8'') *from* the seam into the seam allowance in other areas.

3. Do not stitch around corners; cross the stitching lines at angles on the corners.

Note: Practice *continuous stitching* while staystitching (and at any other time possible) by stitching directly off one piece and onto another piece without leaving thread in between the pieces or raising the presser foot. Clip each piece apart after staystitching has been completed. This saves time and thread!

4. Handle your fabric carefully. Recheck fabric pieces with the pattern after staystitching is completed to check for any distortion. If necessary, press to reshape each piece.

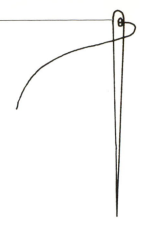

Machine and hand stitching have their own distinctive uses in the construction of any tailored garment. More hand stitching is used in the traditional method than in the contemporary. However, a combination of both hand and machine is a practical solution in many cases. Saving time is a consideration in either method. For example, in some instances hand basting (one of several hand stitches) is a time saver; machine basting can also be effective as a time saver, depending upon the fabric, the seam location, and the skill of the sewer.

Seams form the structural lines of a garment. Their purposes may be functional as well as decorative. If they are primarily functional, they must be flat and as inconspicuous as possible. If they are decorative and intended to add interest to the design of the garment, they may be handled in various ways, depending upon the effect desired.

Regardless of purpose, the way a seam is basted, stitched, and pressed determines the final appearance of the garment. Consequently, accurate stitching as well as correct pressing are of utmost importance.

Stitching

In tailoring, hand sewing may be used for tailor tacking, basting, hemming, sewing on fasteners, finishing zippers in some fabrics, overcasting seams in a ravelly fabric where a machine finish is impractical, finishing piped buttonholes and handworked buttonholes.

For any hand sewing, always cut the thread at an angle, never break or bite it. Cutting at an angle makes threading the needle easier. Thread the cut end through the needle eye, then knot that end. The working length of the thread should be about 46 cm (18'') either single or doubled. For permanent hand stitching, draw the thread over beeswax to reduce snarling.

7

STITCHING AND SEAM CONSTRUCTION

A thimble is a necessary adjunct to efficient hand sewing. It not only protects the third finger of your sewing hand but also makes pushing the needle through the fabric easier.

Basting

Basting is a method used (1) to hold two or more layers of fabric together during fitting, pressing, or permanent stitching, and (2) to mark lines for certain construction areas (termination points of buttonholes, center front and center back of a garment). Basting is often thought of as a hand or machine stitch, but pins, basting tape, and glue stick may be alternatives. The guidelines for basting are as follows:

1. Always work on a flat surface and pin before basting.

2. Select a thread of contrasting color that will show up readily on the fabric being used. *Note:* To avoid discoloration, do not use a dark-colored thread on a white or light-colored fabric.

3. Select a thread and needle size that is compatible with the fabric being used. Heavy thread may mark the cloth if pressing is done before the basting is removed. Heavy-duty cotton thread may be used for heavier fabrics; lightweight threads, such as silk or polyester, are suitable for closely woven fabrics that mark easily. Usually a single strand of basting thread is used; however, a double strand of thread is used for permanent basting in certain areas where additional strength is needed.

4. When hand basting, fasten the ends of the thread with a knot or a backstitch. Work from right to left, unless you are left-handed, then reverse. Allow some ease in the basting line to prevent seam puckering.

5. Clip all bastings at intervals before removing to prevent any pull on the permanent stitching and to avoid damage to the fabric.

6. Use hand basting to "ease-in" an area (i.e., setting in a sleeve) since hand stitches can usually be more easily controlled than those done by machine.

It is well to remember that staystitching in the proper places, the wise use of pins, and skillful machine work can eliminate considerable hand basting. However, another point to remember is that there are places where the quality of work (often achieved by hand basting) may be more important than time-saving efforts.

Because each type of basting performs a certain job, it is well to understand the function of each. The judicious selection of the proper stitch for a particular place will demonstrate the value of basting as a time-saving device.

1. Hand Basting. *Even (short) basting*—These hand stitches are about 6 mm (1/4'') or less in length and are the same length on both sides of the fabric. Even basting is used in areas (1) where close fitting will be done, (2) where easing one side of a seam to another is necessary, and (3) where curved edges occur. Shoulder and underarm seams, darts, tucks, and curved princess lines are areas where this type of basting is frequently used. Because the stitches are quite short, they hold fabric layers well for fitting. With careful pinning, machine basting may replace even basting in some areas of construction.

Uneven (long) basting—A long stitch about 1.3 cm (1/2'') is combined with a short one, about 3 mm (1/8'') long. The long stitch is uppermost on the top surface of the fabric since this basting is used as a guideline for stitching or as a marking line for foldlines, center front and center back lines, and grainlines. At times it may be used for holding seams on which there is no strain in fitting.

Diagonal basting or tailor basting (Figure 7–1)—Diagonal basting stitches appear

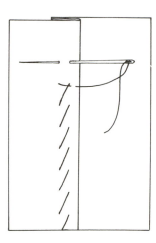

FIGURE 7–1
Diagonal Basting.

long, 1.3 cm to 2.5 cm (1/2'' to 1'') or longer, depending upon the location and are slanted on the topside and are straight and short on the underside. Short diagonal stitches hold faced edges flat and secure while the long diagonal ones are useful for holding underlining and interfacing to the fashion fabric. Also use this basting to hold patterned fabrics for matching. The two layers of fabric will be less likely to slip and become mismatched when diagonally basted than when straight or machine basted. Machine stitch through the center of the short, horizontal stitch.

Slip basting (Figure 7–2)—Slip basting is used where plain seams must be basted from the right side. This situation may occur when matching plaids or stripes or when fitted seams have been altered on the right side. To slip baste, turn under the seam allowance of one side and pin it at right angles to the seamline of the adjoining section. Slip the needle through the fold of the upper section, then into the under layer for another stitch. Seams basted in this manner are easily turned to the wrong side for permanent stitching.

2. Machine Basting. Machine basting may be used in any area where you think that (1) basting is essential, (2) hand basting is too time consuming, or (3) it is as satisfactory as either hand or pin basting. Set your machine about 6 stitches per 2.5 cm (1''). In some fabrics these long stitches may be also used as a marking device. However, in many fabrics used in tailoring this marking is not suitable because of the indentations that may be left in the fabric. Many lining fabrics may be damaged by the needle marks, also. When machine basting, make sure that the seams are adequately pinned to maintain the matching ends of the two fabric layers. It is unnecessary to backstitch at the end of the seam.

3. Alternatives to Hand and Machine Basting. Even though the following are not kinds of stitching, they are a means of holding two layers of fabric together in preparation for either temporary or permanent stitching.

Pin basting—To make pin basting totally effective, pick up a stitch of about 3 mm (1/8'') through all layers of fabric. A small

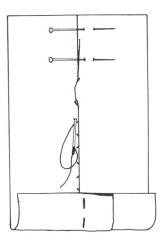

FIGURE 7–2
Slip Basting.

amount of fabric pinned in this manner will hold two layers together more firmly than when a large "pickup" is used. Seams unaffected by fitting and those that fall on the straight grain (or near it) are areas where pin basting may be used effectively. Soft materials that "creep" do not lend themselves to this method of basting, even to the experienced sewer. Careful pinning followed by hand basting is advisable for fabrics of this type.

Basting tape and glue stick—These items may be used in the same locations as pin basting, but they have the advantage of holding the two layers of fabric firmly together to prevent slippage during machine stitching. Thus, they are helpful when matching patterned fabrics and when stitching slippery or bulky fabrics that do not feed evenly under the presser foot. Place the basting tape or a line of glue in the seam allowance *close to,* but *not on,* the stitching line. Remove the tape after stitching the seam. The glue stick is best used on seams that will not be opened since a residue is left on the seam allowance. It works well when attaching underlinings and interfacings to the fashion fabric.

Gathering and Easing

Gathering and easing both require stitches that will control a long edge and allow it to match a shorter edge. Hand or machine stitching may be used.

Gathering Stitches. These stitches, if made by hand, are small running stitches; if by machine, are lengthened according to the weight of the fabric being used. The heavier the fabric the longer the stitch should be. With either hand or machine stitches there must be at least two rows of stitching about 3 mm to 6 mm (1/8'' to 1/4'') apart with the lower line being slightly to the garment side of the seamline. (Use hand basting if the fabric needle marks.) All lines of stitching

must be drawn up with the same degree of tautness, then distribute fullness and stitch *between* the two rows of gathering stitches. Failure to comply with this procedure will result in the formation of pleats instead of gathers.

Ease Stitches. When the long side of a seam is only slightly longer than the short side and no gathers will be formed (e.g., the sleeve cap), place the first row of stitches a thread's width inside the seam allowance and the second row of stitches 3 mm to 6 mm (1/8'' to 1/4'') inside that.

Permanent Hand Stitches

Backstitches. Backstitches are perhaps the strongest of the hand stitches. They are frequently used to (1) begin or finish a line of hand stitching, (2) complete a stitching line into corners where the machine cannot stitch, (3) replace broken machine stitching, (4) topstitch or understitch by hand, and (5) apply zippers by hand. Depending on the purpose of the backstitching, from the right side it may resemble machine stitching or it may appear as a short decorative stitch; from the wrong side the stitches appear overlapped.

1. *Even backstitch* (Figure 7-3) is the strongest of all the backstitches because of its overlapping stitches. From the top, the even backstitch appears like machine stitching, thus it may be used to repair seams.

2. *Half-backstitch* is used to understitch along collar or facing edges to prevent the seam from rolling outward and in other areas where a secure stitch is required.

3. *Pickstitch* is another variation in which backstitches are on the outside with spaces between them. Zippers in certain fabrics may be applied with this stitch.

4. *Combination stitch* is a backstitch combined with several short basting stitches.

This stitch is stronger than a basting stitch and faster to do. It may be used to hold neck and collar seams, to attach overlapping seams of interfacings, and to hold any area where permanent support is needed. A short diagonal basting stitch may supplant the combination if it seems easier and is as effective.

Blanket Stitch. This stitch is traditionally an embroidery stitch (Figure 7–4).

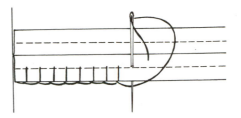

FIGURE 7–4
Blanket Stitch.

Its use in tailoring is minimal, but important at times. It may replace overcasting for seam finishing; it may also be used for covering French and bar tacks.

Buttonhole Stitch. Since this stitch is used primarily for handworked buttonholes, the instructions are given in Chapter 12.

Catchstitch. This stitch may be used for holding raw edges in place (Figure 7–5); it may also be used for a decorative stitch in some areas (e.g., holding ease pleats in linings). The catchstitch is the only hand stitch that is worked from left to right by right-handed persons and the reverse for left-handers.

Fastening Stitch. A fastening stitch may be used to begin or finish a line of stitching. To begin, pick up a small stitch, leaving a tail end of thread about 1 cm (3/8'') long. Lap the tail over, holding it

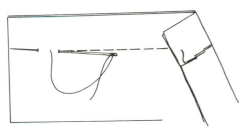

(A) Even Backstitch.

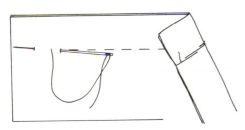

(B) Half Backstitch.

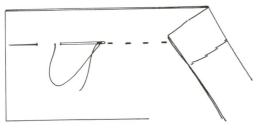

(C) Pickstitch.

FIGURE 7–3

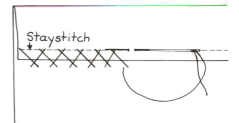

FIGURE 7–5
Catchstitch.

down with your thumb. Take another stitch, crossing over the first at right angles. Use this stitch to end a line of stitching or as an alternative take a couple of tiny backstitches on top of each other.

Hemming Stitches. Refer to Chapter 19 for specific directions for using different types of stitches suitable for tailored jackets, coats, skirts, and pants.

Lining Stitch. Refer to Chapter 20.

Overcast Stitch. Overcasting is the traditional way of hand finishing ravelly seam edges (Figure 7–6). To give additional support along an edge, staystitch about 6 mm (1/4'') from the cut edge, then trim the seam evenly and take each stitch as deep as the staystitched line.

Pad Stitch. The instructions for the pad stitch are given in Chapter 15 since it is used primarily to attach the interfacing to the fashion fabric in the collar and lapel area.

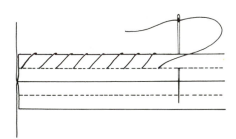

FIGURE 7–6
Overcast Stitch.

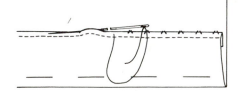

FIGURE 7–7
Slipstitch.

Slipstitch. This stitch is used to hold a folded edge to a flat edge and is essentially a hemming stitch (Figure 7–7). However, it may be useful for attaching patch pockets (if a small stitch is used) and trimmings where an inconspicuous effect is desired. Stitches may be about 6 mm to 1.3 cm (1/4'' to 1/2'') long.

Stabstitch. The stabstitch is used to hold several layers of fabric together (e.g., shoulder pads). Use a double strand of thread, push the needle straight down through all layers, go forward a short distance, about 1 cm (3/8''), and push the needle back up to the top. Depending upon the area to be stabstitched, the stitches may be shortened or lengthened.

Tacks. Tacks have three major functions: (1) to reinforce an area where there is strain, (2) to hold two layers of garment sections together loosely, and (3) to serve as a decoration. Buttonhole twist or topstitching thread is usually preferred for making tacks.

1. *Bar tack* (Figure 7–8) is used to reinforce an area at a point of strain (ends of hand-worked buttonholes, corners of pockets, tops of pleats).

    a. Using buttonhole twist or double strand of strong thread, make a bar tack by taking several stitches, inserting the needle and bringing it out of the same holes.

    b. Finish the bar tack by blanket stitching around the stitches or by taking two or three stitches across the center of the long stitches.

    c. Push needle to wrong side and fasten the thread invisibly.

2. *French tack* (swing tack) is used to loosely hold two parts of a garment together, such as the hem of the lining to the hem of the coat (Figure 7–9). Take several stitches between the two layers of fabrics. Secure the thread, then blanket stitch around the

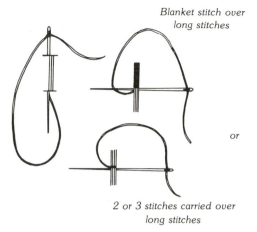

Blanket stitch over
long stitches

or

2 or 3 stitches carried over
long stitches

FIGURE 7–8
Bar Tack.

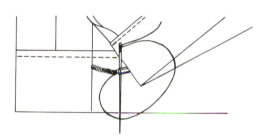

FIGURE 7–9
French Tack.

thread, placing stitches close together. Fasten thread securely. *Note:* A thread chain is a series of loops or slipknots pulled together and is a variation of the French tack in use. It may be made by ''finger crocheting'' a chain or by crocheting with a hook.

3. *Decorative tacks* are used to finish the ends of piped or corded pockets, at stitching ends of pleats or at dart ends, and to add a decorative touch to the garment. The base of the decorative tack touches the end where used.

a. *Arrowhead*

(1) Mark the arrowhead by basting a triangle at the desired position (Figure 7–10, A). Using matching buttonhole twist, start the arrowhead by fastening the thread within the arrowhead. Bring the needle out at the left-hand angle at the base. Then take a stitch across the angle opposite the base, placing the needle in from right to left.

(2) On the baseline push the needle through at a right angle to the base and bring back needle point on the baseline within the first stitch. Repeat the cycle until the stitches on the baseline touch at the center of the base and stitches across the point opposite the base widen out from angle point and cease halfway down the angle sides. Stitches should closely touch each other. Push needle to wrong side and fasten the thread invisibly.

b. *Crow's foot*

(1) Mark the triangle as in the arrowhead. Fasten thread within center of triangle and bring needle and thread through to left angle on the base (B).

(2) Turning triangle from right to left, take a stitch at each angle, pushing needle through from right to left. Each successive stitch widens across the angle as the stitches fill in along the sides. Each stitch should touch closely.

(3) Repeat the operation until stitches meet on each side of the angle; then carry the thread through to the wrong side and fasten securely.

c. *Fabric tack*

(1) Cut a triangle the desired finished size plus a narrow seam allowance with the base on the straight grain of the fabric. Fold each point, then turn seams down along sides of the angle, baste and press (C).

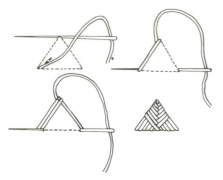

(A) Arrowhead Tack.

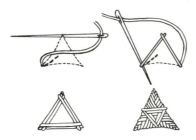

(B) Crow's Foot Tack.

a. Mitered corners—wrong side

b. Seam edges turned back—wrong side

c. Finished triangle —right side

(C) Fabric Tack.

FIGURE 7–10

(2) Place the base of the triangle in position on the garment, baste into place, and closely slipstitch to the garment. Keep stitches under the folded edge.

Topstitching

Topstitching is used to emphasize design lines, to give a finished look to a tailored garment, and to give a firm edge to fabrics that do not take a sharp press. Machine stitching is used more frequently than hand stitching, depending upon the fashion trend. Topstitching is more effective on plain and smooth rather than on patterned and textured fabrics.

Standards for Topstitching:

1. Stitch length is appropriate for fabric and thread. Generally the heavier the thread the longer the stitch should be.

2. Stitches are uniform in length.

3. All stitching is straight and/or a uniform distance from the edge of garment or seamlines.

4. The grain of the fabric is not distorted by the topstitching.

5. Thread ends are invisibly secured.

General guidelines:

1. Use a large machine needle (European size 100 to 110 or U.S. size 16 to 18) with buttonhole twist.

2. Test stitch length and tension on a scrap of fashion fabric, using the same number of layers as is used in your garment. Usually a stitch length of 6 to 8 stitches per 2.5 cm (1''), or the longest stitch on the machine, is satisfactory, depending on your fabric. A shorter stitch may be preferred on lightweight fabrics and is used with a single strand of regular sewing thread.

3. Generally, use regular sewing thread on the bobbin with the twist on the top. If both sides of your garment show at the same time (e.g., tie belts), use buttonhole twist on the bobbin also. When using buttonhole twist only on the the top, tighten the upper tension to create a smooth stitch.

4. When there is a lapel, stitch the collar and the lapel on the facing side. At the top button (or where the lapel turns) stop stitching, cut thread leaving a tail of 7.5 cm to 10 cm (3'' to 4''), and continue stitching from the garment side. Leave another thread tail at a starting point. Stitches should match at stop and start location. *Do not* allow stitches to overlap. With a needle or tiny crochet hook carry tails of thread to the inside of the garment and fasten. In this way the stitching will look continuous.

5. Diagonally baste along edge of areas to be topstitched. To prevent distortion of fabric grain during stitching, stitch multiple rows of stitching in the same direction.

6. All topstitching should be the same distance from the edge or from a seamline. The following may be used as *guides in topstitching:*

    a. A quilting guide if your machine has one.

    b. Width of presser foot if its width is adequate. Machines with a moveable needle facilitate obtaining the desired width.

    c. For edge stitching, a marked throat plate or a strip of opaque tape the required distance from the needle.

    d. Lined topstitching or transparant tape to mark a line if a tape will not damage fabric.

    e. A thread-basted straight line placed *next to, not on,* stitching line.

7. Stitching lapel corners. Note the recommended placement of stitching for a notched lapel (Figure 7-11). Other configurations may be used for special effects.

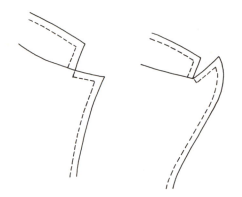

FIGURE 7–11
Topstitching Lapel Corners.

Seam Construction

There are two general classifications of seams. *Exposed* seams are those that join the major parts of a garment and thus have edges that are exposed to friction as the garment is worn. *Enclosed* seams are those in which the edges are not visible, as in collar edges and facings. Each type of seam requires certain procedures to make it satisfactory in appearance and wearability.

Standards for Stitching Seams

1. Stitching usually should extend to seam ends unless otherwise specified.

2. Length of stitch should be compatible with texture of fabric and should be consistent throughout the garment construction. About 12 to 14 stitches per 2.5 cm (1'') is average.

3. Seams should be smooth and unpuckered.

4. Both sides of a seam should be even in width unless different for a reason (e.g., welt seams).

5. Stitching lines should be smooth without any ''wiggly'' lines.

Guidelines for Stitching Seams

1. Stitch with the grain in the same direction as staystitched from wide to narrow (from lower edge of skirt to waist), or in the direction that the cut edge is the smoothest when the finger is run along it.

2. Press seam as stitched, then press open or in its permanent direction.

3. Do not tie off or fasten thread ends of seams which are to be crossed with another line of stitching.

Exposed Seams

The greatest number of seams fall in the exposed seam classification since they include all seams that have turned edges exposed to view (e.g., flat felled and lapped) as well as those that have exposed raw edges (e.g., plain). Because these seams are exposed to friction, ''finishes'' of various kinds are useful in enhancing their wearing qualities. Most exposed seams may require finishing to some degree if the fabric ravels excessively. However, it is usually only in unlined tailored jackets, skirts, and pants that any kind of seam finishing is necessary. If a finish is needed, judgment must be exercised in the selection of the kind to be utilized.

When determining the kind of finish most appropriate to use, consider the (1) type of fabric, (2) kind of garment, and (3) location of the seam. However, keep in mind that a *minimum* finish is all that is necessary. Test your fabric by taking a scrap cut on the same grain as the seams in the garment. Pull gently on the cut edge and note the extent of raveling. If raveling is evident, try pinking the cut edge; then gently pull. This test should help you decide whether any finish, other than pinking, is necessary.

It is not intended that this discussion will cover all possible seam finishes. Only those that are generally applicable to tailored garments will be explained.

Types of finishes:

1. *Plain-trimmed* seams are suitable for fabrics that do not ravel. With heavy fabrics, bevel the seam edges as described on page 119.

2. *Pinked* seams are suitable for fabrics that do not ravel easily, but because of the location in your garment, you may feel that a finish is necessary. Since pinking shears are bulky, extreme care must be taken to prevent ''pinking a hole'' in your garment. Pinking is often used on edges of fusible interfacings where mark-off of a straight edge may be visible on the right side.

3. *Overcast* stitches are illustrated in Figure 7-6. Overcasting and blanket stitching are identical in use in seam finishing. Because hand overcasting is done over a plain-trimmed edge, it is rarely discernible on the right side of the garment after pressing. Machine overcasting may be satisfactory if the seam edge remains flat and smooth. Be sure to test the crosswise grain since at times it produces a heavier edge than on the lengthwise, thus ''ridging'' may be created on the right side after pressing. Use of the multiple zigzag or serpentine stitch rather than the plain zigzag may alleviate this problem.

4. *Hong Kong* seam finish is an excellent *bound edge* finish for unlined jacket and coat seams and hems (Figure 7-12, A). Besides being durable, it is neat and attractive in appearance if properly done. It is more time consuming than most finishes, but the extra time required may be worth the effort. This finish may also be used for lined coats made of ravelly fabric since coat linings are usually hemmed separately from the coat and any excessive raveling may fall below the coat hem. Use the finish only from the bottom of the coat upward, in this case about 30.5 cm (12'').

Because the method for making a Hong

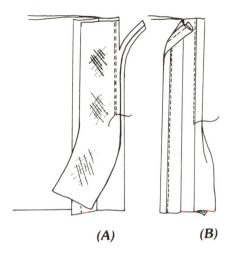

(A)   **(B)**

FIGURE 7–12
Hong Kong Seam Finish.

Kong finish is often misinterpreted, the following directions are included here:

a. For binding, select a lightweight fabric of underlining, lining fabric (cut bias strips 2.5 cm (1'') wide), or prepackaged synthetic bias tape (press edges open). Cotton is usually not satisfactory because it is too bulky for many fabrics.

b. Stitching with the grain, staystitch bias or stretchy seam edges 6 mm (1/4'') from cut edge.

c. Place right sides of seam and tape together and stitch a 6 mm (1/4'') seam on the staystitched line.

d. Make another line of stitching about 3 mm (1/8'') from the first.

e. Trim seam allowance close to the second line of stitching.

f. Fold bias strip over the cut edge and press. From the right side, pin, then stitch in the well of the seam (Figure 7–12, B).

g. The raw edge of the bias is visible on the underside. This makes the Hong

Kong finish different from a regularly finished bound edge. Trim excess bias under seam to about 3 mm (1/8'') from the stitching. *Note:* The narrower the bound edge, the more attractive and less bulky the finish will be. Keep the finished edge as near 3 mm (1/8'') in width as possible. A finish of 6 mm (1/4'') is a bit too wide and appears bulky. As a variation of this finish, lace may be folded and used as a binding.

Types of Exposed Seams

The following exposed seams may be used in tailored garments.

Plain Seams. These are the most frequently used seams in all construction, including tailoring. The plain seam is the first step in the construction of some other seams. This seam often requires more finishing than other seams because the edges are free and thus easily abraded.

Lapped Seam. A lapped seam may be used in (1) joining curved or angular edges of a garment section, and (2) attaching a gathered section to a straight edge. (See Figure 7–13.)

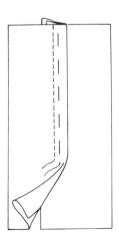

FIGURE 7–13
Lapped Seam.

Joining curved or angular edges:

1. On the section to be overlapped, staystitch *inside* the seamline.

2. Turn under the seam allowance slightly beyond the staystitching and press. Or, make a template by cutting a strip of tagboard the shape of the curved section. Place on seamline and press the seam allowance back over the template.

3. Place the turned edge over the seamline of the adjoining section. Pin at right angles to the seam. Baste and top stitch. *Note:* In tailored garments instead of stitching on the folded edge, you may stitch back from the edge about 6 mm (1/4'') to give a tucked effect.

Attaching a gathered section to a straight edge as in a yoke:

1. Match seamlines of the two sections, being sure that bottom line of gathering stitches lies slightly below the stitching line (folded edge) of the yoke.

2. Adjust gathers, baste, and top stitch. Remove visible row of gathering stitches.

3. Allow seam allowance to turn against yoke. *Do not* try to press open.

4. Flatten gathered section by notching some of the gathers to reduce bulk, then press, making seam allowance as flat as possible. *Note:* If there is a pleat that attaches to the yoke section, after stitching, reduce bulk by trimming the pleat section out of the seam allowance as much as possible. Flatten by pressing.

Welt Seam. The welt seam is popular in both coat and jacket designs (Figure 7–14). Topstitching is used to emphasize a design line, hold a seam flat, and add interest to the fabric. First, make a sample seam to determine the desired length of stitch as well as the proper distance from the turned edge. The distance from the folded edge is determined by the fabric weight,

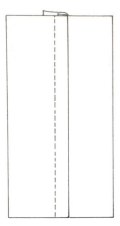

FIGURE 7–14
Welt Seam.

varying from 1.3 cm to 6 mm (1/2'' to 1/4''), with the wider being for a heavier fabric.

1. Make a plain seam with the two right sides of the fabric together.

2. Determine the direction the seam should turn and trim the enclosed layer of the seam to 6 mm (1/4''). Usually the seam allowances are turned as follows: armhole—away from the sleeve; yoke—toward the neck; shoulder—toward the back; and underarm—toward the center (either front or back, depending upon the design features in your garment).

3. Press the seam as stitched to flatten the stitching, then press open. Turn the seams in the desired direction and press again, allowing the top side to roll slightly toward the edge. *Note:* If seam edge is to have a finish, apply the finish before topstitching.

4. From top side, diagonally baste along the turned edge to hold seam in place while you are topstitching. *Note:* Without basting, the top layer of fabric may tend to "creep" as the stitching proceeds. This pushes the grain and mars the effect of the stitching.

5. See suggestions for topstitching.

Double Topstitched Seam. This seam is somewhat related to the welt in that it is decorative as well as functional (Figure 7–15). It may be used on center back seams, princess lines, and in other areas that the welt seam is applicable.

1. Stitch a plain seam and press open. If necessary, finish seam edges.

2. Topstitch along each side of the seamline, keeping an equal distance from the seamline and stitching both lines of stitching in the same direction.

Slot Seam. This is another decorative topstitched seam that provides a more pronounced effect, but is similar to the double topstitched seam (Figure 7–16).

1. Machine baste on the seamline and clip the bobbin thread at intervals of every 5 cm (2'').

2. Press seam open.

3. Cut an underlay of the fashion fabric at least 3.8 cm (1 1/2'') wide. Center it under the seam and hand baste in place. *Note:* If seam edges are to be finished, finish edges of the underlay. Edges of seam may be

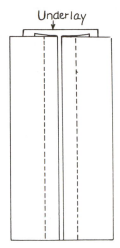

FIGURE 7–16
Slot Seam.

trimmed narrower than underlay if necessary after topstitching.

4. Topstitch an equal distance from the center of each side.

5. Remove basting threads and press.

Flat-Felled Seam. This seam is used perhaps less frequently in tailoring than the other seams (Figure 7–17). Its primary use

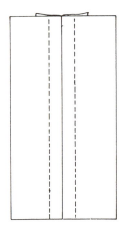

FIGURE 7–15
Double Stitched Seam.

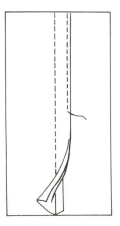

FIGURE 7–17
Flat-Felled Seam.

may be found in handling tailored garments made of reversible, double-woven wool fabrics or on casual unlined jackets. On one side of the garment, the flat-felled seam is visible with its two rows of machine stitching and a folded edge, while on the other side, it resembles a welt seam. Since the flat-felled seam is formed on the right side of the garment, it is necessary to keep all seams even in width with accurate straight stitching.

1. Determine the direction in which the seam is to turn. The straighter and less full side should be on the top since it will be easier to turn. Generally the seams are turned as follows: armhole—jacket over the sleeve; yoke—yoke over the garment; shoulder—back section over the front; underarm—the front over the back.

2. On the uppermost part of the seam, staystitch with the grain about 1 cm (3/8'') from the seamline.

3. Place the *wrong sides* of the garment together and stitch a plain seam.

4. With a steam iron press the seam first as stitched, then open. From the wrong side press in the predetermined direction, pushing the iron *against* the stitching.

5. Trim the underseam allowance to 6 mm (1/4'') and the upper allowance to within 3 mm (1/8'') of the staystitching. *Note:* The width of the finished seam is determined by the weight of the fabric; heavy fabrics require wider seams. Make a sample to determine the best width for your particular fabric.

6. Fold under the upper edge so that the staystitching is not visible. Pin carefully, placing pins at right angles to the seam. Hand baste to hold edges in position. (In some fabrics, pin basting may be used satisfactorily. Press the edge before pinning.)

7. Stitch close to the turned edge from the right side of the garment.

Enclosed Seams

Enclosed seams have edges that are concealed between two layers of fabric. This includes such areas as collars and front facings. The concept of bulk reduction is especially important in handling enclosed seams in fabrics used in tailoring.

Steps in Reducing Bulk in Enclosed Seams. Flattening edges is one of the essential procedures in bulk reduction. Trimming and grading are necessary first steps. Your fabric and the location of the seam will determine which additional steps will need to be considered.

1. *Trimming.*

a. After stitching a plain seam, hold shears parallel to fabric and trim the entire seam allowance to 1 cm (3/8'') for lightweight fabrics or to no less than 1.3 cm (1/2'') for heavy fabrics.

b. To reduce bulk where one seam crosses another line of stitching, trim seam allowance diagonally before stitching the second seam. Note (a) in Figure 7–18. In bulky areas, such as a neckline seam, bulk may be further reduced by trimming away the remaining triangle in the seam allowance after the seam is stitched (b). Do not cut stitching.

2. *Grading.*

a. After seam is trimmed, cut off 3 mm (1/8'') from the facing part of the seam; the longer side of the allowance

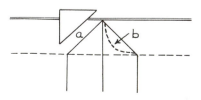

FIGURE 7–18
Reducing Bulk in Seam Allowance.

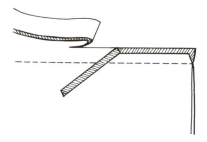

FIGURE 7–19
Grading Seam Allowance.

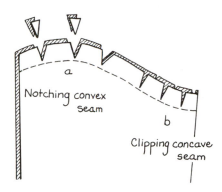

FIGURE 7–20
Handling Curves.

must lie next to the uppermost or visible side (Figure 7–19).

b. To determine if amount of grading is sufficient, turn the seam back, allowing the upper section to roll slightly over the seamline. Note the location of the seam edges on the inside. It may be necessary to trim slightly more than the 3 mm (1/8'') from the facing seam allowance if the enclosed edges fall at the same place and do not appear ''layered'' or graded.

3. *Beveling.* Hold the blades of the shears parallel with the fabric as you trim the seam edges to eliminate prominent edges that may appear on the right side after pressing.

4. *Notching.* Since the outer edge of a convex seam (outward curve) is longer than the distance of the curve at the seamline, the excess fabric must be removed to reduce the bulk and allow the seam to lie flat when it is turned inward. (See (a) in Figure 7–20.)

a. With tips of shears cut small wedges (notches) from the seam allowance. Start by cutting small wedges, then increase width and depth as needed. Sharp curves require more notching than shallow ones.

b. Test by folding back the enclosed seam and feeling the edge. If it feels flat it has been notched sufficiently, if it

feels ''bumpy'' more notching is necessary. The notched edges must lie next to each other to form a continuous, flat seam.

5. *Clipping.* Clips are slashes cut into the seam allowance of a concave curve (inward curve) to allow the seam edges to spread when turned.

a. After trimming and grading the seam, clip *almost* to the stitched line. Clip each seam allowance alternately to prevent indentations from appearing along the enclosed edge.

b. On sharp curves clip frequently; on shallow curves clip less often. (See (b) in Figure 7–20.) However, do not clip any more than is necessary.

6. *''Killing'' the Edges.* This is a process by which bulk is reduced by pressing to flatten seam edges. Refer to Chapter 8 for the procedure.

Understitching. Understitching is a line of stitching holding the seam allowance to the facing, thus preventing the facing from rolling to the outer edge. As a result the enclosed edges are kept sharp and flat. It may be used on facings (fitted and bias), on

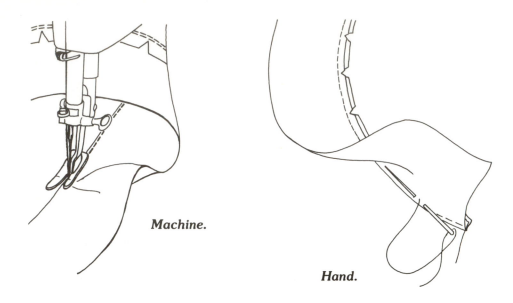

Machine.

Hand.

FIGURE 7–21
Understitching.

any lining that serves as a facing, and on collars or cuffs (Figure 7–21).

While correct pressing is of paramount importance in holding facings in position, understitching is also helpful for stubborn fabrics that will not be topstitched.

1. *Procedure:*

    a. Trim, grade, clip, or notch seam. Press seam open and then turn seam toward the facing.

    b. From the right side, hand or machine stitch through the facing and seam allowances. Stitch close to seamline. Use the half-backstitch when hand stitching (Figure 7–3), which is particularly advantageous if the underside will show at any time.

2. *Limitations of understitching.*

    a. Corners and extreme convex curves cannot be understitched easily.

b. Lapels cannot be understitched easily. Be discriminating in its use in this area.

c. Avoid understitching in areas where both sides of the faced edges will be visible.

Handling Outside Corners. To turn and give a smooth point to a corner of less than 90 degrees, the stitching cannot come to a sharp point. Two or three small stitches across the point and proper trimming will facilitate turning and give the appearance of a sharp point.

1. Directionally stitch the seam to within 2.5 cm (1'') of the corner (Figure 7–22). Change the stitch length from regulation to 20–22 stitches per 2.5 cm (1'') and stitch to within 1 or 2 stitches of the corner. For medium weight

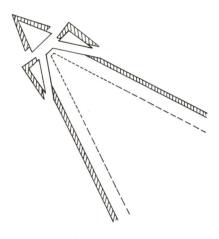

FIGURE 7–22
Handling Outside Corners.

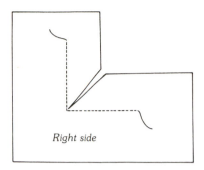

Right side

FIGURE 7–23
Inside Corners.

fabric, take two stitches across the corner, continue with the shortened stitch for 2.5 cm (1''), then continue remainder of seam with regulation stitch. _Note:_ Take three stitches across corner with heavy or bulky fabric.

2. Trim off the point close to the stitching. Then trim at an angle on either side. The more pointed the corner the further back the seam allowances should be tapered. There should be no overlapping of seam edges in the corner when turned.

3. Press the seam open over a point presser, and then turn and press again allowing the upper section to roll slightly to the underside.

Reinforcing Seams

Handling Inside Corners. Design lines in garments often necessitate joining an inside corner to an outside corner or to a straight edge. Because of the strain placed upon this kind of corner, a reinforcement of some kind is necessary. The insertion of a gusset under the

arm illustrates an area where there is an inside corner. The following are methods of reinforcing the inside corner:

1. _Staystitching_ may be used as a reinforcement in some areas, such as on the facing side of a shawl collar where there is little strain.

    a. With a short stitch, 20 to 22 stitches per 2.5 cm (1''), stitch just inside seamline for 2.5 cm (1'') on either side of corner.

    b. Clip _exactly_ to corner, not into stitching (Figure 7–23).

    c. Spread the clipped section in order to fit the piece that attaches to it.

2. _Fabric reinforcement._ In an area where there is considerable strain, a reinforcing piece of thin, lightweight, but firm, fabric is desirable.

    a. Hand baste the stitching line of the corner as a guide for further stitching.

    b. Cut a piece of reinforcing fabric approximately 3.8 cm (1 1/2'') square.

    c. On right side of garment, pin piece in place over the corner to be reinforced. (Fig. 7–24).

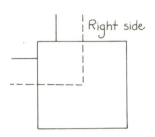

FIGURE 7–24
Placement of Reinforcement on Corner.

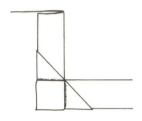

FIGURE 7–26
Reinforcement Pressed and Trimmed.

d.   Machine stitch an acute angle using 20 to 22 stitches per 2.5 cm (1'') as shown in Figure 7–25. Do not stitch angle too sharply but let it round slightly. Allow *one or two stitches across corner.*

e.   Cut carefully to point of angle, turn reinforcement to wrong side, press seam back into position, placing excess fabric into symmetrical folds. Trim reinforcement to seam width. (Figure 7–26).

f.   Spread the reinforced section in order to fit the piece that attaches to it.

3.   *Seam tape reinforcement.*

a.   Follow the same procedure as for the fabric reinforcement (Figure 7–27).

b.   Lap tape edge on itself at the exact corner.

c.   Stitch and cut to point of angle on garment fabric only. *Note:* For gussets use either the fabric or the seam tape reinforcement since both are more durable than the staystitched method.

4.   *Fusible reinforcement.* A circle of woven fusible interfacing may be applied to the corner prior to staystitching. The fusible should be lightweight so that it does not make the area too stiff to be turned easily and there is no mark-off.

Attach *the inside corner to the outside corner* as follows:

1.   Mark the corner and stitching line on the outside corner.

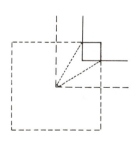

FIGURE 7–25
Corner Stitching

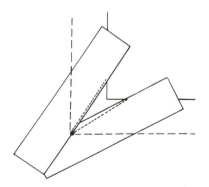

FIGURE 7–27
Seam Tape Reinforcement.

2. Match the points of the two corners and secure with a hand-fastening stitch (Figure 7–28).

3. Match the adjacent seamlines and baste.

4. Stitch with the inside corner uppermost. Shorten stitch to 20 to 22 stitches per 2.5 cm (1'') for 2.5 cm (1'') on either side of the corner. When you reach the corner, keep the needle in the fabric exactly at the corner, raise the presser foot, check accuracy, then proceed with stitching. Refer to discussion of gussets in Chapter 18.

5. Press seam allowance open unless otherwise directed.

Easing In a Seam

To fit over body curves, some seams require slight easing (e.g., in shoulder seams where no dart is present or in princess seamlines).

1. Pin baste, starting by matching notches and the ends of the seam.

2. To distribute ease evenly between markings, hold with the longer side uppermost over the finger or hand. By placing the two layers over a curve the longer outer layer will fit smoothly over the shorter, under layer.

Darts

The function of darts is to give shape to a fabric, thus allowing the fabric to fit smoothly over the body curves. They may be straight darts or curved. Accurate marking and stitching are required for either kind. The following are some general guides for stitching darts:

1. Stitch from the _wide end to the point_ with the last three or four stitches being on the fold. This ensures a smooth point that will curve smoothly over the body. The same rule applies to double-ended darts; overlap

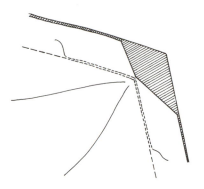

FIGURE 7–28
Attaching Inside Corner
to Outside Corner.

stitching for three or four stitches at the wide (starting point) part of the dart.

2. Never backstitch at the point of the dart. This creates a heavy point that negates the desired smooth point.

3. Tie a quick knot at the dart point and cut the thread leaving a tail of 1.3 cm (1/2'') long (Figure 7–29). This will eliminate the possibility of the thread ends working loose with wear.

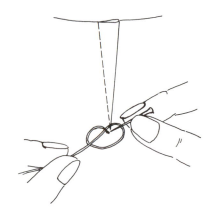

FIGURE 7–29
Quick Knot.

Refer to Chapter 8 for correct pressing of darts.

Dart Tucks. Dart tucks serve somewhat the same purpose as darts except that they may have fullness released at one end or at both ends.

1. For one open end (shoulder tuck) stitch from the top down to the required length and then across to the fold. For two open ends (waistline tuck) begin at the fold, stitch across the width of the tuck, stitch down tuck length, and then across to the fold. By stitching across the tuck in this manner, the ends become stabilized.

2. Examine all tucks for correct stitching, then tie and cut off thread tails leaving about 1.3 cm (1/2''). *Or,* backstitching can be used for tucks since no tapering is involved. Cut off threads at the end of the backstitching.

Follow directions in Chapter 8 for pressing.

Pressing is one of the most important aspects of tailoring. Effective pressing requires the knowledge of a few fundamental facts as well as the patience to work with fabrics. It is time consuming; in fact, you generally will spend as much time at the pressing board as you will at the sewing machine. Pressing is an essential procedure in every phase of fabric preparation and construction.

Pressing Equipment

Since frequent pressing during the construction of a suit or coat is fundamental to the professional appearance of the finished product, a few basic pieces of equipment are necessary. Not all of these pieces are essential. Select those that seem to be the most helpful in meeting your needs. With a little ingenuity substitutions can easily be made.

Combination Steam and Dry Iron. An extra feature in some irons is the "spurt of steam" which provides heavier steam useful when handling hard to press fabrics and for setting creases and pleats. Distilled water should usually be used in most steam irons. Small bottles containing water-distilling crystals are available commercially and are helpful to ensure a ready supply. The sole plate of any iron must be absolutely clean at all times and free from any burned substance. Sizing used in some new fabrics, starch, fusing agents, or synthetics pressed with high heat may stick to the iron. The starchy substances may be removed from a cool sole plate by rubbing with soda or salt. With the prevalence of the use of plastic bags in sewing areas, extreme care must be taken to prevent a hot iron from touching such a surface. To remove this type of material, use an iron warm enough to soften the plastic then scrape off the softened material with any nonscratchable object.

8

PRESSING EQUIPMENT AND TECHNIQUES

125

Additional treatment may be required to completely clean the sole plate. Heating an iron to a high temperature is one method for removing any foreign material. Wipe the sole plate with several layers of paper towel, but use extreme care to prevent personal injury. Fine steel wool is another aid for removing burned substances. Commercial preparations for cleansing the sole plate are also available.

Well-Padded Ironing Board and/or Pressing Board. While an ironing board is a standard piece of equipment in most homes, it may not be as available in a student's living quarters. Thus, a pressing board would be fairly inexpensive and certainly convenient in this situation. To make one, secure a piece of 2 cm or 2.5 cm (3/4'' or 1'') plywood about 35.5 cm (14'') by 76 cm (30'') or larger if one prefers. A board approximately 76 cm (30'') wide by 91.5 cm (36'') long with right angled corners will provide adequate width and length to aid in straightening off-grain fabric. Pad the top surface and cover with a firm, unsized 100% cotton fabric such as drill, muslin, or an old sheet. A *striped* fabric such as pillow ticking, or a checked fabric with checks about 2.5 cm (1'') square is also good for a covering since it provides lines to follow when straightness of grain is being determined. It is important that the fabric is washed well enough to remove any sizing (starch) that may stick to the iron. It is also important to keep a clean cover on the board. When fusing fabrics cover the board with an extra piece of unsized cotton fabric to prevent any fusing material from adhering to the regular cover. When needed, a press board can be easily placed on top of a desk or other stable piece of furniture. To prevent soiling when not in use cover the board with a plastic cover such as those used by dry cleaners. *Note:* If your ironing board has a metallic cover, place a cotton cover over it to prevent shine that sometimes occurs when pressing certain

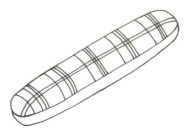

FIGURE 8–1
Sleeve Roll.

fabrics. The metallic cover often causes an accumulation of heat during a prolonged period of pressing (i.e., application of fusible materials).

Sleeve or Seam Roll. A firm cylindrical pad is useful for pressing seams in narrow spaces such as sleeve and pant leg seams. Because of its shape it allows seams to be opened without pressing seam edges into the fabric (Figure 8–1). The roll should be covered with a wool fabric which helps to hold steam and to prevent shine when wool is being pressed. A substitute can easily be made by rolling a magazine tightly and fastening with scotch tape. Cover with muslin or an old sheet and then wrap with a piece of wool fabric.

Pressing Ham (Tailor's Ham). A rounded, firmly packed cushion with a wool covering is useful for pressing curved areas (Figure 8–2).

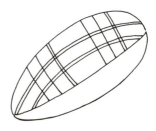

FIGURE 8–2
Pressing Ham.

Point Presser. This piece of equipment is usually made of hardwood and is used uncovered. It is convenient for pressing seams open in areas difficult to reach such as points in collars and lapels. A combination of a point presser and a pounding block is available (Figure 8-3).

FIGURE 8-4
Clapper.

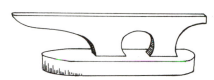

FIGURE 8-3
Point Presser.

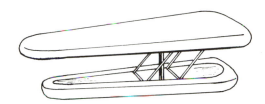

FIGURE 8-5
Sleeve Board.

Clapper Pounding Block. This piece is made of hardwood with slightly rounded edges. It is used to beat steam into the fabric, to flatten bulky edges, and to pro-

used on your regular ironing board or on any firm surface.

Sleeve Board. This board is padded like an ironing or a press board. Because of its size it is convenient for short seams and small areas (Figure 8-5).

Tailor's Board. Made of hardwood with a small flat surface and with shaped edges for pressing straight as well as curved seams (Figure 8-6). If you have a point presser, a tailor's board is unnecessary.

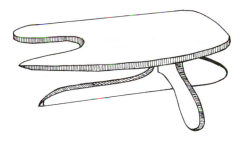

FIGURE 8-6
Tailor's Board.

Seam Stick. Made of a rounded piece of hardwood, resembling a rolling pin with a slice cut off one side. A covering of wool felt is glued to the surface. The curve of the stick is similar to a sleeve roll but because of its hardness and its flatness on one side, pressure from an iron can be applied to seams being opened on it (Figure 8-7).

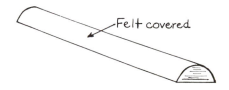

Felt covered

FIGURE 8-7
Seam Stick.

Press Cloths. These are necessary in tailoring to protect your fabric from direct heat. A variety of cloths may be used. A useful one is made of a plain weave piece of wool of medium weight and about 46 cm by 61 cm (18'' by 24''). Any scrap of medium weight wool will be just as satisfactory if the dimensions are sufficient to accommodate seams and other areas, such as collar edges, pockets, and so forth. A fitted wool covering made like the shape of your iron serves the purpose of a press cloth when doing right side pressing. Cotton drill in medium and heavy weights is also useful. Because of its weight it holds moisture well. Be sure to wash it thoroughly before use to remove any sizing.

A lighter weight cloth, such as diaper cloth or any other 100% cotton, such as batiste, is useful for areas where less steam is required.

FIGURE 8–8
Velvet Board.

Velvet Board or Needle Board. Small steel wires are embedded in a heavy canvaslike fabric. It is useful for pressing pile fabrics, such as velveteen, because it allows the pile of the fabric to sink into the wires, thus preventing the fabric from being crushed when steam is lightly applied (Figure 8–8). In lieu of a velvet board careful use of a heavy *Turkish towel* with your steam iron is quite satisfactory.

Pressing Techniques

It is important to understand the difference between ironing and pressing. *Ironing* applies pressure to remove wrinkles from garments or other items that have been washed or creased. The iron is used with a sliding motion *across* the fabric, thus causing the fabric to flatten and be smooth. In contrast, *pressing* is the smoothing or flattening of a fabric by using an up and down motion (lifting the iron after each application to a surface and setting it down again in a new area). The amount of pressure on the iron will vary from a light touch to heavy pressure, depending upon the fabric and the area to be pressed. Light pressure would be satisfactory on a soft fabric while heavier pressure would be necessary to flatten enclosed seams in a heavy fabric. Moisture along with heat and pressure (each in varying degrees) is an essential element in pressing and shaping. Wool fibers respond well to all three of these elements. Thus, a wool fabric is very desirable for tailored garments.

Correct pressing during construction can be a time saver by reducing the amount of basting required. The following are some general guidelines for pressing:

1. Test your fabric to determine the amount of heat, moisture, or pressure it can take as well as the type of press cloth that is most satisfactory. Too much heat and pressure may produce a loss of resilience as well as an overpressed effect. Too much moisture may cause shrinkage as well as a change in surface appearance. It is better to press too little than too much. Once a seam or any part of a garment has been overpressed (pressed too much) it is difficult to return it to its original shape or texture.

Test your fabric in all ways in which it will be handled during construction (e.g., seams, darts, tucks, pleats). Test enclosed seams (lapel and collar edges) by stitching, grading, and handling just as the finished product will be. Always test on a large enough scrap of fabric so that a part can be left unpressed. Seeing the original and the pressed areas together will easily show up differences, if any.

2. To prevent stretching, press by raising and lowering the iron over the fabric surface without sliding the iron.

3. Always press with the grain (usually lengthwise); that is, from the wide to the narrow part of your garment. Be sure the grain is straight (at right angles) before pressing.

4. Before pressing a seam open, press in the position in which it was stitched to settle the stitching into the fabric. This step permits the seam to be pressed open more easily.

5. Always press a seam or dart before crossing it with another line of stitching.

6. Leave some moisture when pressing a wool fabric. Pressing until it is dry will cause wool to lose its resilience and to become stiff. Handle the fabric carefully until it is dry to prevent wrinkling and any fabric distortion.

7. For final pressing of a garment part (i.e., collar), allow it to dry in the position in which it was pressed before further handling.

8. Press lightly over bastings, then remove bastings and repress, if necessary.

9. A garment is usually pressed on the wrong side, but if it is to be pressed on the right side be sure to use a press cloth even though a steam iron is used.

10. To help prevent shine on the right side of your fashion fabric, use a wool press cloth next to the wool. A steam iron can be placed directly on a wool press cloth.

11. Use a clapper (pounding block) to force

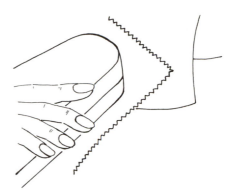

FIGURE 8–9
Using Clapper to Flatten Edge.

steam through enclosed seam edges by placing the clapper sharply and firmly over the press cloth. Hold in place until the steam has dispersed (Figure 8–9).

12. To flatten a cut edge of a seam allowance (especially heavy fabrics), "kill" it by placing the seam edge on a hard surface (edge of point presser), then dip your fingers in water and wet the seam allowance. Place a hot iron directly on the seam edge and press hard. Use a clapper to further flatten the edge. Repeat the process as often as necessary until the desired flatness has been reached. *Caution:* Be sure seam is correctly stitched before killing the edges as the edges become *permanently* flattened.

13. Plan your construction so that difficult areas can be pressed on as small a piece of garment as possible before attaching it to another piece.

14. For wrong-side pressing of a wool seam, press on a firm board with little padding or on a seam stick. This helps to prevent seam edges from ridging or becoming indented on your garment (Figure 8–10). For right-side pressing of seams again use a seam stick or a soft, well-padded board to allow the seam edges to sink into the padding.

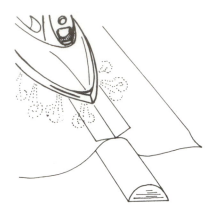

FIGURE 8–10
Using Iron on Steam Stick.

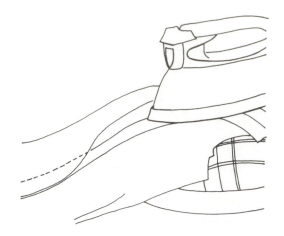

FIGURE 8–11
Pressing Curved Seam.

Construction Pressing

Seams

Press most seams flat in the position in which they were stitched and then press open, even though they will be enclosed later. Exceptions to this rule are seams in gathered areas, seams at back of pleats, lapped seams, armhole seams, and crotch seams. Always press a seam before crossing it with another line of stitching.

Straight Seams. Press a seam open by placing it over a sleeve roll or seam stick and use the tip of the iron to open the seam. Press with the grain and in a straight line. Then place the entire iron on the opened seam. (Refer to Figure 8–10.) The shape of the sleeve roll or seam stick places the weight of the iron exactly on the seamline and prevents edges from leaving an imprint on the right side. A paper towel or piece of heavy paper can be placed under a seam edge to prevent ridging if other equipment is not available. If an imprint does occur, lift the seam edge and press under it.

Curved Seams. To maintain an outward curve (as in a princess-style garment), lay the curved seam over a pressing ham and press the seam open. The side of the seam allowance curving outward will usually be tight against the garment, but it must lie flat. Either stretch the seam allowance by pulling on it as you apply the steam iron to it (Figure 8–11), or, if it does not stretch enough, then clip the allowance only enough to permit it to lie correctly. The inward side of the seam allowance will have some fullness. To reduce this fullness place a piece of paper (curved like the seam) under the seam allowance and shrink in as much fullness as needed. If there is still too much fullness, notching some of the allowance may be required. Do not notch too deeply; the cut edges of the notches should meet to prevent small depressions from appearing on the outside of the garment seam. Both outer edges of the seam allowances must lie perfectly flat when the seam is pressed open.

Seams with an inward curve, such as a fitted side seam, require clipping to within 6 mm (1/4'') of the stitching line. Of, if the

fabric is stretchable, follow the same procedure as just described.

Seams Turned One Direction. Press
the seam open first. Then, from the underside, turn and press the seam in the direction it is intended to go. Seams with gathers
or fullness on one side are not pressed open
but are turned toward the plain side.

Darts

Trim wide darts to 1.3 cm (1/2'') but do not
cut to the end. Press the dart flat, being
careful not to press beyond the point. Then
place the dart over a pressing ham, turn and
press it in the direction it is to go. _Note:_ In
heavy fabrics, slash wide darts along the
fold, from wide to narrow, to the point
where the dart becomes about 1 cm (3/8'')
wide. Press the point open like a box pleat
(Figure 8–12). Insert a knitting needle or a
flat bodkin into the unslashed point.
Dampen the tip of your finger, run it along
the point, and with the tip of the iron press
the dart open.

Bust and elbow darts (horizontal darts)
may be turned upward even though commercial patterns turn them downward. A
dart in either of these locations becomes less
conspicuous if turned up since the eye does
not look directly into the stitched line.

Turn lengthwise darts (vertical darts—
neck, shoulder, waist) toward the center
front and the center back. _Note: To aid in
stitching across a dart in heavy fabrics, slash
through the dart fold as far as the depth of the seam._
On the top layer, clip from the fold to stitching line (Figure 8–13). _Do not clip_ through
both layers of the dart. Press top of the dart
open.

Use a piece of heavy paper or a folded
paper towel under the edge of the dart to
prevent imprints on the right side. Lift the
dart and press under it if an imprint is apparent. For darts that taper at both ends,

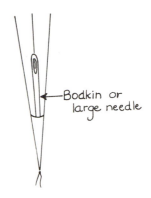

FIGURE 8–12
Box Pleat at End of Opened Dart.

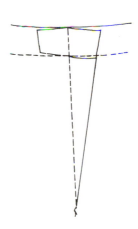

FIGURE 8–13
Slashing Dart at Top of Seam.

clip toward the stitching line at widest part
to allow dart to remain flat (Figure 8–14).
For a fabric that will stretch, try stretching
and pressing the dart at the widest part to
eliminate a clip. Press dart-tucks only as far
as the stitching line to allow the fullness to
fall softly.

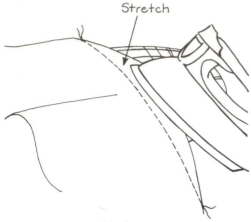

Stretch

FIGURE 8–14
Pressing Dart with Inward Curve.

Pleats

The entire length of the pleat should be hand basted 6 mm (1/4'') from the folded edge. Lay a strip of paper (never newsprint) under the edge and press lightly from bottom to top of the pleat. Leave about 15 cm (6'') unpressed at the lower edge to allow the garment hem to be turned up and finished before the pressing of the pleat is completed. Remove basting and press again, using more pressure. Remember, never open a seam that falls at the back part of the pleat (except at hem). Press only in the position in which it was stitched.

Gathers

1. Press fabric before gathering lines are stitched.

2. Press seam allowance flat in the position it was stitched.

3. Turn the seam allowance away from gathers and press again. Do not allow the iron to extend over the gathered area.

4. If necessary, use tip of iron to press *into* the gathered line, never away from it.

Ease Fullness (Shoulder Seams and Princess Lines)

Press the seam open on a sleeve roll or seam stick. Finish pressing by shaping over a tailor's ham to retain the curved shape. Avoid shrinking the eased side of the seamline.

Buttonholes (Piped or Corded)

Place the buttonhole wrong side up on a wool covered ham. Then use heavy paper or a folded paper towel *under* the edges of the buttonhole and steam press. If necessary, use additional steam and a clapper to flatten the buttonhole. If any imprints remain, run the tip of the iron under the edges.

Additional information on pressing specific areas will be given at appropriate points in the discussion of the construction process.

Pressing Before Lining Application

Before a lining is applied, your garment must be pressed as well as possible. If you have pressed carefully during construction, and if you have handled your garment carefully following pressing (allowed garment to dry before further handling and kept it on a padded hanger when you were not working on it), it is seldom necessary to do much additional pressing. However, a garment that has become somewhat wrinkled may need some additional pressing. You may sometimes feel that a professional presser can handle your garment at this stage better than you can. Generally speaking, this is not to be recommended unless you have a fabric that is especially hard to press. Then, be sure that your presser understands *exactly* what you want in appearance.

Some areas that need a touchup are easily seen. Others may not be as visible. Place your garment on a hanger or on a dress form, if you have one, and stand a distance from it. Areas that may not be flattened enough or where some unwanted shrinkage has taken place will show up better if viewed from a distance. Do wrong-side pressing with a steam iron, but be sure a wool press cloth is between the garment and the press board in areas where greater pressure must be used. Avoid pressing over seam edges. Shaped areas (bustline curves) must be pressed over a tailor's ham from the right side using a wool press cloth next to the garment.

Press gently, being careful not to over-press. Allow the garment to hang several hours or overnight before applying lining.

Final Pressing

The main purpose of final pressing is to remove any wrinkles that appear after the lining has been applied. The lining may require some gentle pressing along edges and hems. Use a dry iron and low temperature for this pressing since linings may be subject to spotting or distortion from too much heat and moisture.

Steam pressing by a professional is *not* recommended at this point. Steam will crush the lining and destroy its smooth appearance. The nice "untouched" effect of the lining will be destroyed soon enough when you have your coat or suit professionally dry cleaned and pressed.

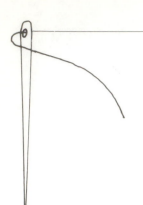

Inner construction that shapes a garment is the hallmark of a finely tailored suit or coat. Underlinings and interfacings are used to stabilize, support, and shape the garment. Interfacings may be shaped by various methods: traditional hand pad stitching, machine pad stitching, or fusing. Carefully study the advantages and disadvantages of each of the following methods before deciding which to use in your garment. Consider the fabric and style of your garment, the time available for construction, your preferences and skills, and the quality of finished product desired.

Refer to Chapter 2 for factors that determine the desirability of underlining. The decision to underline or not to underline should have been made before deciding on a method of shaping and of stabilizing edges since some methods of application apply only to underlined garments.

Stabilizing and Shaping Collars and Lapels

Traditional Method— Hand Pad Stitching

For centuries the custom tailor has applied haircloth interfacings by hand, using pad stitching to ease the interfacing onto the undercollar and to impart shape to the collar and lapels. This causes the interfacing and fashion fabric to behave as one fabric. See Chapter 15 for complete instructions.

Advantages:

1.   The interfacing and fashion fabric are permanently held together by the pad stitching.

2.   The desired degree of roll can be incorporated by easing the interfacing as the pad stitching is done. This is especially advantageous when a gentle roll is desired.

9
COMPARISON
OF METHODS
FOR APPLYING
SUPPORTIVE
MATERIALS

_3._ The firmness of the collar and lapels can be varied by the density of the pad stitches.

_4._ No stitches show on the underside of the lapel or collar if the stitch is correctly done.

Disadvantages:

_1._ Personal skills vary and if you are not adept at handwork, the collar or lapel may not roll correctly or may not be smooth. Thus, your results may be less than professional.

_2._ Handwork is time consuming and includes many hand stitches.

Contemporary Methods—Machine Pad Stitching and Fusing

Modern technology has eliminated most of the hand-sewn inner construction in ready-to-wear, even in expensive tailored garments. The home sewer, too, has other alternatives.

There are two contemporary methods for applying interfacings and shaping the collar and lapels: (1) machine pad stitching of a nonfusible interfacing and (2) application of a fusible interfacing. These methods replace the traditional handwork and are faster to accomplish than the traditional method. These methods can be used with or without underlining.

Either machine pad stitching or fusing work especially well for man-tailored jacket collars[1] that roll sharply and lie flat and for the two-piece collar[2] with a separate stand often found in trench coats.

Fusing and machine pad stitching (especially fusing) are most effective on light to medium weight fabrics. Heavy, thick fabrics are more difficult to handle with these techniques than with the traditional techniques.

Machine Pad Stitching of Nonfusible Interfacings. The nonfusible interfacing is applied in the same manner as in the traditional method. However, machine pad stitching replaces the hand pad stitching. If the garment is to be underlined, stitch the interfacing to the underlining first and then trim the underlining from the areas to be pad stitched. The interfacing is then ready to be applied to the fashion fabric. (See Chapter 10 for complete instructions.)

Advantages:

_1._ Machine pad stitching is faster than hand pad stitching.

_2._ Machine pad stitching, especially if done with the multiple zigzag or serpentine stitch, may produce an undercollar or lapel that is flatter than the hand pad stitched one.

_3._ The firmness of collar and lapels can be varied by the length and density of the stitches.

_4._ The stitching is permanent.

_5._ No hand stitching is involved.

Disadvantages:

_1._ Machine pad stitching shows on the underside of the lapel and collar.

_2._ While some roll may be incorporated by stitching the under layer (fashion fabric) to the interfacing, less control is possible than with the hand method.

Application of Fusible Interfacings. The introduction of fusibles into the home-sewing market gives the home seamstress the opportunity to utilize some of the ready-to-wear techniques. The fusible interfacing

---

[1]For illustration of man-tailored collar, see Figure 16–3 in Chapter 16.

[2]For illustration of two-piece collar, see Figure 16–15 in Chapter 16.

gives stability to the fused area and shape is incorporated by the use of steam. The interfacing may be (1) fused directly to the fashion fabric, (2) fused to an underlining and then fused to the fashion fabric only in the collar and lapel area, or (3) fused only in the collar and lapel, and a nonfusible interfacing used for the remainder of the front. (See Chapter 10 for the advantages and disadvantages of each.)

Advantages:

1. Fusing is faster than hand or machine pad stitching.

2. Fusing produces a very flat, smooth collar or lapel.

3. Fusing stabilizes stretchy, soft, or loosely constructed fabric.

4. No hand stitching is involved.

5. No stitches are visible on the underside.

6. Firmness can be varied by double fusing areas that require more body.

Disadvantages:

1. Roll can only be incorporated by steaming and not by easing, as is done with pad stitching. Therefore, there is some loss of control in the amount of roll that is incorporated. This is especially important to consider in using rigid fabrics that do not ease or compress readily, thus making it difficult to create a roll in a collar or lapel.

2. Unless properly fused, fusible interfacing may loosen with wear and cleaning. It adheres less easily to natural fibers than to synthetics.

3. Some fabrics will show mark-off, or the appearance may be changed when fusible interfacings are applied. Always test a sample and compare that with the original fabric.

Application of Interfacing to Underlining

For the traditional method the underlining is applied early in the construction process and *before* the interfacing is attached to the front. The front underlining extends only 2.5 cm (1'') under the interfacing and is attached by hand to the interfacing *after* the interfacing has been applied.

For the contemporary method, either the fusible or nonfusible interfacing may be applied to the underlining *before* it is attached to the garment front. The following are advantages and disadvantages of this method:

Advantages:

1. The underlining cushions the edge of the interfacing so there is no mark-off.

2. Only the underlining is stitched in the seams, thus reducing bulk along the edges.

3. Garment fronts will look and feel like other areas that are underlined. This is especially important for see-through fabrics. However, only fronts may be underlined if fabric and style do not require underlining throughout the garment.

4. With fusible interfacing, the lapel area may be fused to the fashion fabric without fusing any other areas.

Disadvantages:

1. More steps are necessary to complete the process than when an underlining is not used.

2. The additional layer of fabric may result in some additional bulk or in a different hand.

Stabilizing Edges

Traditionally, cotton or linen tape has been used to (1) strengthen edges that receive constant strain such as the front edge of a garment, or (2) prevent stretching in bias areas such as the roll line of the lapel. Tape may also stiffen and delineate edges where a hard flat line is desired. If the edge has no give when stretched, tape may be unnecessary. Fusible interfacings often give adequate rigidity without the addition of tape, especially in short jackets where there is less stress on the front edge. Also, if the edge is to be topstitched, this will further stabilize the edge. If tape is needed, it may be applied by either (1) the traditional hand method, (2) the machine method, or (3) a combination hand and machine method.

Traditional Hand Method

The tape is applied after the interfacing has been applied to the front and the lapel has been shaped. The tape is then stitched in place by hand. (See Chapter 15 for complete instructions.)

Advantages:

1. Accuracy in placement is easy to achieve because all shaping has been completed.

2. Exact degree of tautness is easy to determine.

Disadvantages:

1. Tape must first be hand basted and then closely stitched on each side by hand.

2. Stitching by hand can be time-consuming.

Contemporary Machine and Combination Methods

The tape is machine stitched to the interfacing before the interfacing is applied to the fashion fabric in one of the following ways:

If the interfacing is lightweight or if an underlining is used, the tape may be stitched along both edges and the interfacing or underlining is then caught in the seam.

If a fusible interfacing is used and the edge will be topstitched, the entire seam allowance of the interfacing can be trimmed away.

For heavier interfacing that should not be sewed into the seam, a combination method may be used in which the tape is machine stitched along the inside edge, the entire seam allowance trimmed away, and the outside edge of the tape attached to the garment by hand. (See Chapter 10 for complete instructions.)

Advantages:

1. Either of the above methods involves less handwork than the traditional method and will be somewhat faster.

2. Tape is securely attached.

Disadvantages:

1. Tape is applied before the interfacing is applied to the fashion fabric, thus there is more likelihood of error in achieving straight edges and accurate seam allowances.

2. It is more difficult to accurately judge the tautness of the supportive tape when it has been applied only to the interfacing material.

Sequence for Applying Supportive Materials

The sequence for applying supportive materials (interfacing, underlining, and tape) for making buttonholes and set-in pockets and for the first fitting varies with the methods used. Decide which method you will use and choose the appropriate sequence from the following list. Should you decide to use a combination of traditional and contemporary techniques, you may need to make adjustments in the sequence. For example, if you use a fusible interfacing but decide to apply tape by the traditional hand method, the tape would be applied as the final step instead of the first step. Carefully think through the sequence you will follow before proceeding.

After each of the procedures you will find the number of the Chapter in which that particular method is described. Steps with an asterisk (*) have a critique in the Appendices.

Traditional Method:

1. Apply underlining—if used (Chapter 10).

2. Staystitch (Chapter 6).

*3. First fitting (Chapter 11).

*4. Buttonholes (Chapter 12) and pockets (Chapter 13).

5. Apply the interfacing material (Chapter 14).

6. Pad stitch lapel (Chapter 15).

*7. Apply tape to front edge and roll line (Chapter 15).

Contemporary Method with Underlining (fusible or nonfusible interfacing):

1. Apply interfacing to underlining—fuse or stitch (Chapter 10).

2. Apply edge tape to interfacing and underlining (Chapter 10).

3. Apply underlining to front—staystitch (Chapter 10).

*4. First fitting (Chapter 11).

*5. Buttonholes (Chapter 12) and pockets (Chapter 13).

6. Fuse (Chapter 10) or pad stitch lapel (Chapter 15).

*7. Tape roll line (Chapter 15).

Contemporary Method without Underlining (fusible or nonfusible interfacing):

1. Apply tape to interfacing (Chapter 10).

2. Apply interfacing to front—fuse or staystitch (Chapter 10).

*3. First fitting (Chapter 11).

*4. Buttonholes and pockets (Chapters 12 and 13).

5. Pad stitch lapel—if nonfusible (Chapter 15).

*6. Tape roll line (Chapter 15).

Whether you use one of these sequences or a combination, it is important that you make your own procedural outline to follow during the construction of your garment. The steps that are similar for all methods of construction are listed in the ''Procedural Outline for Construction of Jacket or Coat'' (Appendices). Complete the outline by filling in the procedures you have chosen for your garment.

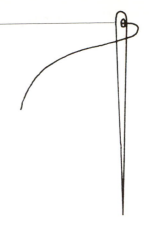

The interfacing should be preshrunk if necessary, adjusted for any changes made in the garment, and cut as directed in Chapter 6 for each method. Mark seamlines, darts, pockets, buttonholes, and the roll line with tracing wheel and carbon. If your pattern has a lapel and does not have a roll line and you have not made a test garment, establish a roll line by following the instructions in Chapter 14. The roll line must be determined before you can shape the lapel. *When the front has been interfaced and taped, use Critique #5 to check your work.*

Application of Tape to Interfacing

The following contemporary methods of taping all involve the application of the tape to the interfacing and/or underlining before these are attached to the fashion fabric. Each method of applying the interfacing will specify the appropriate time and method for applying the tape. The choice of method (or the decision to omit tape) is determined by (1) the type and weight of interfacing, (2) whether an underlining is used, and (3) the style and fabric of the garment. The bridle stay will be attached later (Chapter 15) since it attaches the fashion fabric to the interfacing and underlining. *Note:* Be sure the tape has been preshrunk and then stretched and pressed to eliminate any possible stretch.

Standards:

1. Edge of tape along seamline is straight or smoothly curved.

2. Tape lies flat and smooth, curves are notched or clipped and corners are mitered.

3. Taped edge does not stretch when pulled.

10 CONTEMPORARY METHODS FOR APPLYING INTERFACING, TAPE, AND UNDERLINING

Method I: Machine Method

The advantage of this method is that the tape is completely attached by machine. The disadvantage is that the nonfusible interfacing will be sewed in with the seam to hold it in place. This increases bulk, thus only lightweight nonfusible interfacings can be used. The seam allowance on the fusible interfacing may be trimmed away, especially if the edge will be topstitched.

Procedure:

1. Pin lapel and front edge of interfacing (if a fusible, place nonfusing side up) to the paper pattern or duplicate of the pattern to prevent interfacing from stretching.

2. Pin tape to the interfacing with the edge on seamline, tape lying on the garment side of the seam. Hold tape taut below the roll line, ease for 2.5 cm (1'') at the roll line, and ease slightly around the lapel (Figure 10–1).

For additional reinforcement end tape 1 cm (3/8'') past the point where the lapel and gorgeline meet (Figure 10–2). If jacket has a curve at the lower edge, ease tape along the curve so that the outer edge lies smooth (inner edge will ripple). (See Figure 10–3.)

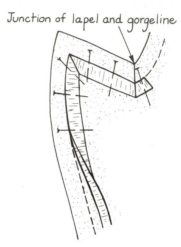

FIGURE 10–2
Reinforcement at Junction of Lapel and Gorgeline.

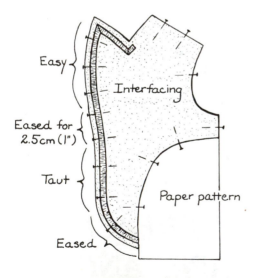

FIGURE 10–1
Tape Pinned to Interfacing Which Is Pinned to Paper Pattern.

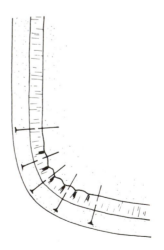

FIGURE 10–3
Taping a Curve.

3. Machine stitch with a straight or small zigzag stitch along the *outside* edge of the tape. Stitch through tissue paper if duplicate pattern is used to maintain the shape; otherwise, remove the pattern before stitching.

4. Notch tape around lower curve so it will lie flat (edges of notches just meet). (See Figure 10–4.) Miter tape at point of lapel and trim away excess tape, but do not clip through outer edge of tape at any time. Stitch inside edge of tape (Figure 10–5). Zigzag across the cut edges of the miter to hold them flat if you wish. *Note:* If the garment has no lapel, follow the same procedure but bring tape 1 cm (3/8'') past the center front line at the neckline (Figure 10–6).

Method II: Combination of Machine and Hand Method

For nonfusible interfacings, this method reduces the bulk more effectively than Method I since the tape is secured along the seamline and no interfacing is stitched into the seam. With fusible interfacing the non-topstitched edge will be more secure.

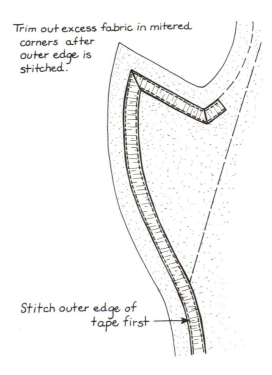

Trim out excess fabric in mitered corners after outer edge is stitched.

Stitch outer edge of tape first →

FIGURE 10–5
Mitering and Stitching Tape.

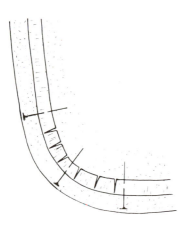

FIGURE 10–4
Tape Notched on Inner Curve.

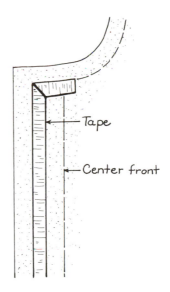

—Tape

←Center front

FIGURE 10–6
Taping the Garment Without a Lapel.

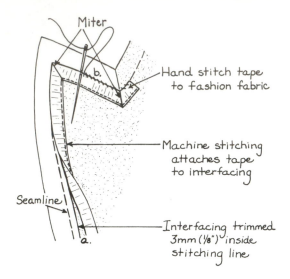

FIGURE 10–7
Machine and Hand Method of Taping.

**Procedure (Steps 1 and 2
are the same as in Method I):**

1. Pin lapel and front edge of interfacing, nonfusible or marked side up, to paper pattern or duplicate of pattern to prevent interfacing from stretching.

2. Pin tape to the interfacing with the edge on seamline, tape lying on the garment side of seam. Hold tape taut below the roll line, ease for 2.5 cm (1'') at the roll line, and ease slightly around the lapel (Figure 10–1). For additional reinforcement end the tape 1 cm (3/8'') past point where lapel and gorgeline meet (Figure 10–2). If jacket has a curve at the lower edge, ease tape along the curve so that the outer edge lies smooth (inner edge will ripple).

3. Notch tape around lower curve to allow the tape to lie flat (edges of notches just meet). Miter tape at point of lapel, trim away excess tape but do not clip through outer edge of tape at any time. Machine

stitch *inside* edge of tape. (Outside edge is *not* stitched) (Figure 10–7).

4. Trim interfacing 3 mm (1/8'') inside seamline so tape extends slightly beyond edge of interfacing.

5. *After the lapel has been pad stitched or fused,* hand stitch the edge of the tape to the fashion fabric as is done in the traditional method.

Method III: Machine Method with Underlining (or Lightweight Seam Allowance)

The advantage of this method is that the interfacing is attached to the seam without any hand stitching. This method is faster than Method II and utilizes the underlining to secure the tape and interfacing at the seamline.

Procedure:

1. Follow Steps 1 to 4 of Method II but *do not* catch the underlining in the stitching.

2. Lay taped interfacing over a piece of lightweight fabric that is wide enough to extend beyond the taped edges. (If front is underlined, the underlining forms the extension.) Pin in place and stitch close to the *outside* edge of the tape (Figure 10–8).

Alternative: Use the garment front pattern to cut a shaped strip of lightweight fabric as shown in Figure 10–9. This method may also be used to catch the interfacing into other seams such as shoulder, neckline, or side seams.

3. Trim fabric to form a 1.5 cm (5/8'') seam allowance on the front edge and the lapel. Trim away excess fabric under the tape about 3 mm (1/8'') from the stitching line so fabric meets the interfacing edge (Figure 10–10).

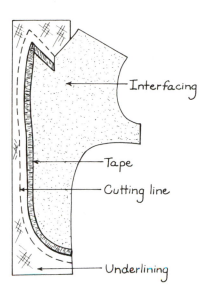

FIGURE 10-8
Lightweight Extension Beyond
Taped Edge.

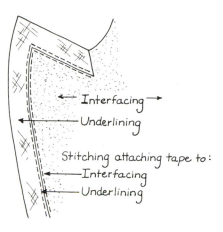

FIGURE 10-10
Underside of Taped Lapel.

4. If front is underlined, trim the lapel underlining 6 mm (1/4'') beyond the roll line, thus exposing the interfacing that will be attached to the fashion fabric (Figure 10-11).

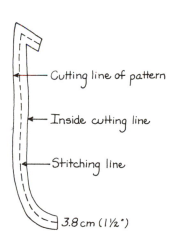

FIGURE 10-9
Cutting a Shaped Fabric Underlay.

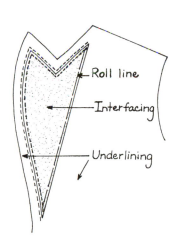

FIGURE 10-11
Underside of Taped Lapel
with Underlining
Trimmed from Lapel Area.

Interfacing Applied to Underlining

For the contemporary method, either the fusible or nonfusible interfacing may be applied to the underlining before it is attached to the garment front, or the fusible interfacing may be applied directly to the garment front. The following are advantages and disadvantages of applying the interfacing to the underlining:

Advantages:

1. The underlining cushions the edge of the interfacing so there is no mark-off.

2. Only the underlining is stitched in the seams, thus reducing bulk along the edges.

3. Garment fronts will look and feel like other areas that are underlined, especially important for see-through fabrics. However, only fronts may be underlined if fabric and style do not require underlining throughout the garment.

4. With fusible interfacing, the lapel area may be fused to fashion fabric without fusing any other areas.

Disadvantages:

1. More steps are necessary to complete the process.

2. An additional layer of fabric may result in additional bulk or in a different hand.

Application of Nonfusible Interfacing to the Underlining

The interfacing, cut in the traditional manner, is applied to the underlining as follows:

1. On the interfacing, trim away the seam allowances on the seamline at side seam, shoulder, neckline, and hemline. If tape is to be applied, trim 3 mm (1/8'') *inside* the stitching line at the front edge *below* the lapel. The seam allowance remains around the lapel. Remove any darts or welt pocket rectangles that may be present in the interfacing by cutting on the stitching line. Trim rectangles for fabric buttonholes 3 mm (1/8'') larger than the buttonhole (Figure 10-12).

2. Position interfacing on the underlining (Figure 10-12), match and pin seamlines at shoulder, neckline, and front. If any discrepancies occur due to inaccurate cutting, allow the armhole or shoulder to shift but keep the grain straight.

3. Use a multiple zigzag (serpentine), a zigzag, or a straight stitch. Stitch close to all edges of the interfacing except around the lapel (Figure 10-13).

4. Apply tape following Method III. Instructions for applying the prepared underlining to the garment front are given at the end of this chapter.

Optional: When hair cloth interfacing is used with wool, take advantage of the ability of the two fabrics to cling together.

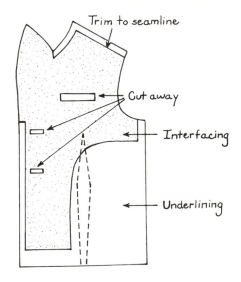

FIGURE 10–12
Trimmed Nonfusible Interfacing Placed on Underlining.

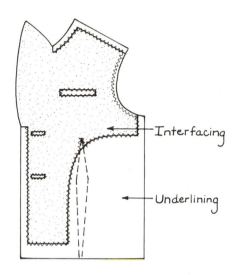

FIGURE 10–13
Interfacing Stitched to Underlining.

lines match. Place the front on a flat area that is large enough to support the entire area to be fused. (Towels on a table or floor are satisfactory if the pressing surface is too small. Protect the surface from heat and moisture.) Steam baste (lightly fuse) the interfacing to the underlining by lightly pressing with an up and down motion, resting the

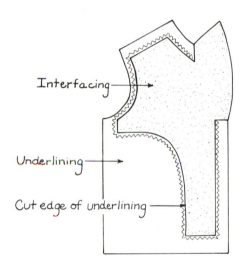

FIGURE 10–14
Optional: Underlining Trimmed Away to Expose Interfacing (Viewed from Wrong Side).

Do this by trimming the underlining away from the interfacing leaving the underlining attached along the edges (Figure 10–14).

Application of Fusible Interfacing to Underlining

The interfacing is cut as in the traditional manner and is applied to the underlining as follows:

1. Trim the interfacing on all seamlines and hemlines except the armhole. If front and lapel are to be taped, also trim 3 mm (1/8'') inside the stitching line on the front edge and the lapel. If using a firm interfacing, trim darts and/or welt pocket rectangle along stitching line. If fabric buttonholes are to be made, trim a rectangle 3 mm (1/8'') larger than the buttonhole rectangle (Figure 10–15).

2. Place the fusible side of the interfacing on underlining front so that the stitching

steam iron only a second in each spot. *Do not* steam baste or fuse the lapel area. Check to see that the interfacing is correctly placed and that both sides are smooth, then permanently fuse following the manufacturer's instructions. Allow the fused piece to cool before moving or handling.

3. Apply tape following Method III.
   Option: Stitch the interfacing to the underlining with zigzag or straight stitch

along the seamlines where the interfacing will not be caught or where an enclosed edge will not be topstitched. This will prevent any possibility of the fusible releasing along the seams.

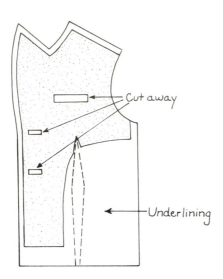

FIGURE 10–15
Trimmed Fusible Interfacing Placed on Underlining.

4. Trim away underlining 6 mm (1/4'') beyond the roll line, thus exposing the fusible interfacing which will later be fused directly to the fashion fabric (Figure 10–11). Instructions for fusing the lapel are given at the end of this chapter with other directions for applying the underlining to the garment.

Note: If the roll line has not been established, fuse only the outer shoulder and lower front. Do not trim at the roll line. Baste the body of the garment together. Lap the neckline edge of the undercollar over the neckline seam of the garment. Pin or baste. (Refer to instructions for establishing the roll line in Chapter 14.) After marking the roll line, remove the collar.

Application of Fusible Interfacing Directly to Fashion Fabric

The instructions for applying fusible interfacings are shown for a garment with a shaped lapel, but both Methods I and II are equally as applicable to the garment without a lapel that has a seamed or a cut-on facing.

Method I: Fusing the Entire Front (often used in men's jackets)

There are several advantages of using this method. Since the entire front is fused, there is no problem with mark-off, and lightweight, stretchy, or unstable fabrics can be stabilized. Also, a more lightweight fusible interfacing can be used than would be used for lapels alone, and buttonholes and pocket areas are stabilized. But there is one disadvantage. Unless the interfacing is chosen carefully and is compatible with the fashion fabric, a too rigid look may result and/or the garment front may feel too heavy.

Procedure:

1. Cut fusible interfacing from garment front(s) pattern. Use a tracing wheel, and tracing carbon to mark seamlines, roll line, darts, and all markings on right side of fabric.

2. Apply tape to the interfacing following Method I, II, or III.

3. Trim the neckline, armhole, and shoulder seams so that only 3 mm (1/8'') extends beyond the stitching line. Trim the bottom edge or hem foldline and the side seam on the stitching line. Unless the interfacing is very lightweight, trim away darts and welt-type pocket rectangles on the stitching line. Trim rectangles for fabric buttonholes 3 mm (1/8'') larger than the buttonhole (Figure 10–16).

Note: With a princess-type seam over the bustline, trim the interfacing *on* the stitching line. Interface the entire side front section or only at the top (or not at all) as explained in Method II.

4. Place the interfacing on the garment front so that the stitching lines match (Figure 10–16). Then, place the front on an area that is large enough to support the entire area to be fused. (Towels on a table or floor will work if the pressing surface is too small. Protect surface from heat and moisture.) Steam baste (lightly fuse) front by lightly pressing with an up and down motion, resting the steam iron only a second in each spot. *Do not* steam baste or fuse the lapel area. Check to see that the interfacing is correctly placed and that both sides are smooth, then permanently fuse front following the manufacturer's instructions. Allow the interfaced piece to cool before moving or handling.

5. The lapel may be fused flat or some roll may be incorporated as follows. After fusing the front, roll the lapel over your hand as it will be worn and pin along its edge. Place over a pressing ham and lightly steam press. The lapel cannot be permanently fused over a curved surface because it is difficult to make adequate contact between a flat iron and a curve. By rolling the lapel and lightly fusing the layers together, the interfacing will be slightly fuller than the fashion fabric. When it is laid flat for fusing, the interfacing will be temporarily shrunk but will expand when reshaped and when steam is applied. Thus, a better roll will result than if it were fused flat. However, be certain the interfacing will shrink in and lie flat before fusing. Rigid fabric may not ease and should not be rolled before fusing.

Lay lapel on a flat surface and fuse according to the manufacturer's instructions.

Note: If more body is desired in the lapel, cut a stay the shape of the lapel, minus seams and about 6 mm (1/4'') narrower than the roll line. Fuse it to the lapel before applying the interfacing. If extra body is needed only in the point of a lapel, such as a sharply pointed one, stay only that area (Figure 10–17). An *alternate method* of giving body to the lapel is to fuse a lightweight in-

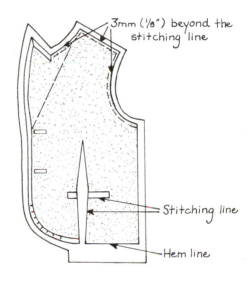

FIGURE 10–16
Taped and Trimmed Interfacing Placed on Fashion Fabric.

terfacing to the lapel facing. This technique has the added advantage of providing a smooth lapel, especially important for lightweight fabrics that may tend to ripple. Fuse the entire facing or only the lapel area. This procedure was noted on page 142.

6. Stitch darts or seams *after* fusing is completed. Fold dart so that stitching lines exactly match. Press the foldline and stitch along the trimmed edge of the interfacing.

Method II: Fusing Traditionally Shaped Interfacing

Advantages: The front is softer than Method I because the interfacing only partially covers the front. Also, for a garment with a princess-type seam, the front section may be completely interfaced and the side section only interfaced across the shoulder and perhaps around the armhole.

Disadvantage: Some fabrics may show mark-off along the edge of the interfacing

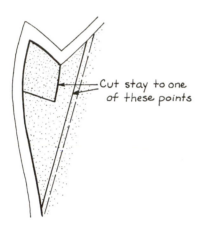

FIGURE 10–17
Optional Lapel Reinforcement.

and/or the fused area may hang differently than the nonfused area.

Procedure:

1. Cut fusible interfacing following the directions for the traditional method as discussed on page 146. If there is a princess-type seam or a vertical dart at the waistline, extend the interfacing to this point ending at the seamline. If garment has front shoulder

gathers, pleats, or ease, cut the interfacing 1.3 cm (1/2'') wider than the complete length of the facing rather than extending the interfacing across the shoulder. Pink or sawtooth the inside edge of the interfacing if it does not end at a dart or seam to prevent mark-off.

2. Follow Method I for marking, trimming, taping, and fusing.

Application of a Combination of Fusible and Nonfusible Interfacings

For this method fusible interfacing is used in the lapel, and a nonfusible is applied to the front following the traditional method.

Advantages: No mark-off occurs from the edge of the interfacing, and no adverse effects will result from fusing the interfacing to the back of the fashion fabric. Also, better control may be achieved in lapel and fronts since different interfacings may be used (i.e., the fronts may be soft and the lapels may have more body).

Disadvantage: The method is more time consuming than fusing a single interfacing to the whole interfaced area.

Method I: Use of Two Different Kinds of Interfacing

1. Cut the *nonfusible* interfacing following the traditional method in Chapter 6, except cut away the lapel 6 mm (1/4'') to the garment side of the roll line. Cut a piece of *fusible* interfacing the shape of the lapel minus seams (allow to extend 3 mm [1/8''] into the neckline seam) and about 1.3 cm (1/2'') beyond the roll line (Figure 10–18).

2. Prepare and apply the nonfusible interfacing following the traditional method

(Chapter 14). Place the fusible lapel interfacing over the edge of the garment interfacing, overlapping edges 6 mm (1/4''). Pin lapped edges. Fuse lapel following instructions under Step 5, page 147. Or, fuse the lapel section first and then apply the interfacing to the garment front. The edge of the nonfusible interfacing will be secured when the stay tape is applied to the roll line.

Method II: Use of a Fusible Web

The nonfusible interfacing cut to include the lapel may be fused to the lapel by inserting a piece of fusible web the shape of the lapel (as shown in Figure 10-18) between the inter-

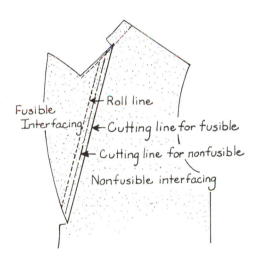

FIGURE 10-18
Fusible Lapel Interfacing and Nonfusible Front Interfacing.

facing and the fashion fabric. Follow the manufacturer's instructions for fusing. Generally, the fusible web makes the area stiffer than a fusible interfacing, so be sure to test the combination for compatibility with the unfused area.

Application of Underlining to Garment

The function and selection of the underlining was discussed in Chapter 2, and the underlining was cut like the major pieces of the fashion fabric, as directed in Chapter 6. If following a contemporary method, the interfacing and tape have been applied to the underlining. If following the traditional method, the underlining will be attached to the garment prior to the interfacing. When applying the underlining to the wrong side of the fashion fabric, remember that the fabric will need to conform to the body curves when it is constructed. Because the inner circumference of a circle is always smaller than the outer circumference, the greater the degree of curve the fabric will take, the smaller the inner layer (underlining) will need to be. For example, the curve of the sleeve is much greater than the curve of the body of the garment, and therefore the circumference of the underlining of the sleeve will need to be reduced more than the circumference of the coat body.

Nonfusible Underlining

Follow these steps to apply nonfusible underlining (with or without interfacing) to the fashion fabric.

1. Lay the fashion fabric wrong side up on a flat surface.

2. Position the underlining, with markings up, on the fashion fabric with cut edges matching. Smooth the two pieces with your hands beginning at the center of the piece

and moving outward. Slight irregularities in cutting may result in minor variations in the edges of the two pieces.

3. Place a row of pins on the lengthwise grain through the center of the piece. If the piece will lie relatively flat on the body, allow the underlining to be *slightly* more taut than the fashion fabric, then pin the edges of the pieces together. If the piece will curve, as a back section of a jacket or coat, follow this method for evenly reducing the circumference of the underlining.

 a. Fold a magazine and lay the fold on top of the center line of pins. Fold the underlining over the magazine. Then fold the fashion fabric over the magazine on top of the underlining. You will note that the edge of the underlining will extend past the edge of the garment fabric—the heavier the fabric, the more the underlining will extend beyond the edge of the garment fabric.

 b. Pin the edges together every 7.5 cm to 10 cm (3'' to 4''), allowing the edges to remain uneven until the edges are controlled by basting.

 c. Folding once will be adequate for pieces that will curve gently. For pieces that will go over sharp body curves, such as sleeves and pant legs, reverse the magazine so the fold is facing the opposite direction and repeat the process with the opposite edges of the fabric.

4. Using stitches about 7.5 cm (3'') long tailor baste the two fabrics together along the center line of pins. Use a fine thread for delicate fabrics. Place curved pieces, right side up, over a curved surface, such as a pressing ham or your thigh, to distribute ease and baste from the right side. Repeat vertical lines of tailor basting at 7.5-cm to 10-cm (3'' to 4'') intervals across the piece.

Note: Permanent tailor basting is desirable to keep unstable fabrics from stretching between widely spaced seamlines. With the garment wrong side up, use fine matching thread and stitch through both layers of fabric catching only a few fibers from a yarn in the fashion fabric. The length of the stitches and the closeness of the rows of basting will be determined by the amount of stabilization needed. Stitches may range from 2.5 cm to 7.5 cm (1'' to 3'') in length. Keep stitches slightly loose so they will not be visible from the right side. The garment lining will protect the long basting threads.

5. Use an uneven basting stitch along the seamlines, except around the lapel, to hold the layers together until seams are permanently stitched. Baste all layers together along the roll line. For a garment without lapels (buttons to the top), baste the entire front edge.

Note: Alternatives to hand basting are the use of a glue stick or machine basting. If the glue stick works well on your fabric, it is excellent to hold the seamlines in place. For machine basting pin carefully and do not allow the layers of fabric to slip as they are stitched.

6. Directionally staystitch stress areas as discussed in Chapter 6. If nonfusible interfacing is to be applied in the traditional manner and hand or machine pad stitched, the underlining will be cut away from under the interfacing, and the edges lapped and basted together as directed in Chapter 14. Therefore, staystitch only the fashion fabric at neckline, shoulder, and armhole.

If lapel is to be fused, follow procedure in Step 5, page 147.

7. To keep the layers of fabric together when stitching darts, machine baste or hand baste through the center of the darts, then fold and stitch. Slash darts and press open, or slash the underlining and press the dart to one side. To reduce bulk in heavy fabrics, stitch the darts in the fashion fabric and the underlining separately prior to applying the underlining. Then slash the darts and press open or press the two darts in opposite directions so that they lie side by side and not on top of each other. Do not slash small darts in stress areas.

Fusible Underlining

Although conventional underlinings are usually preferred, occasionally a fusible underlining is advantageous to stabilize very soft or loosely woven fabrics. Apply the fusible underlining following the instructions for applying fusible interfacing.

11

FITTING THE GARMENT

The amount of fitting that will be required at this point depends to a large extent on the amount of previous fitting that was done in the pattern and/or test garment and the style of the garment. If the garment is to be underlined, the underlining should be applied using either the traditional or the contemporary method before fitting. If a very heavy interlining or lining (i.e., quilted or backed) is to be used, baste this together to try on under the outer garment. If a test garment was made or the garment has little fit, (except across the shoulders), it should be safe to complete the fabric buttonholes and slashed pockets (welt type) before fitting the garment. However, it is well to remember that there may be some change in the way the fashion fabric fits as compared to the test garment, especially if your fabric is not firm and stable or is heavy. If there is *any* question whatsoever about buttonhole or pocket placement, check the fit first. If supportive materials are to be applied by the contemporary methods described in Chapter 10, apply them before checking the fit. If the garment requires reinforced corners, these should usually be made before the fitting, unless they occur in a fitting seam and the fit was not checked in a test garment. In general, follow the same fitting procedure as discussed in Chapter 4.

The discussion in this chapter centers on general suggestions related to the preparation of your garment for fitting and the procedure following that process.

Garment Preparation

The following are some general suggestions to consider when basting your garment together for fitting:

1. Before basting, remember that all fitting seams (shoulder, side, back of skirts, inseam and outseam of pants) were cut with a

2.5-cm (1'') seam allowance, design seams with 2 cm (3/4''), and all other seams with 1.5 cm (5/8'') as shown on your pattern.

2. Use either hand or machine basting for attaching the garment pieces. Hand basting with short, even stitches is preferable with heavy and delicate fabrics and for intricate seams that require greater accuracy than can be obtained by machine basting. Machine basting, even though quicker to do, is more difficult to remove and may leave marks on some fabrics. Also, the layers of heavy fabrics may tend to shift, and inaccurate stitching lines may result.

3. For ease of permanent stitching later, leave the seam allowances free where one seam crosses another. This permits easy stitching and pressing without having to clip previously basted seamlines, an additional advantage of hand basting.

4. Do not press a basted seam open. If machine basting has created a puckered seam, lightly press the seam flat as basted. Since the stitching lines may be altered during fitting, a creased line will be difficult to handle.

Jacket or Coat:

1. Pin and baste all darts or tucks in front, back, and sleeves.

2. Pin and baste the seams in the following order:

   a. Yokes to garment section.

   b. Princess seams, if in the design.

   c. Lengthwise back seams.

   d. Underarm seams.

   e. Shoulder seams. (The back shoulder seam is usually eased onto the front shoulder.)

   f. Lengthwise sleeve seams.

Note: Remember that set-in sleeves are not basted into the garment for the first fitting. In the raglan or dolman design, the sleeves must be basted into position before fitting the garment since they form a part of the neckline. Complete instructions for preparing and setting in the sleeves are given in Chapter 18.

3. Pin up all hem allowances to check proportion.

Skirt or Pants:

1. For skirt, pin and baste darts and seams.

2. For pants, pin and baste darts and/or pleats, pocket underlay (if pocket forms a part of the waistline), outseam, inseam, and crotch.

3. Pin fitting band in place.

4. Pin up hem allowances.

Conducting the Fitting

Refer to the fitting guidelines listed in Chapter 4 and *use the second copy of Critique #2*. Refer to the adjustments shown in Chapter 3 to correct any fitting problems.

Procedure Following Fittings

Remove your garment carefully so that the pins used in fitting will not be lost. Mark any adjustments that were made during fitting by using an appropriate method for your fabric.

Jackets and Coats:

1. If traditional stabilizing and shaping methods will be used, separate fronts and backs at the shoulder and the side seams by cutting through the basting lines so that the bastings will stay in the fabric to mark seamlines. If fronts have been stabilized and shaped by contemporary methods, separate

only the side seams for ease in working with the garment.

2. Stitch and press darts and design line seams. (Refer to Chapter 8 for pressing details.)

3. Continue with the next step in the construction sequence you have chosen in Chapter 9.

Skirts and Pants:

1. Hand baste the waistline seam location below the *lower* edge of the fitting band if the position is different from the normal seamline.

2. Stitch and press darts and seams in skirts. For pants, stitch and press the outseam, inseam, and the crotch seams in this order.

3. From Chapter 22 select alternative methods for further construction of your garment. Or, follow the procedures given in your pattern guide sheet.

Follow your procedural outline for your next step.

Buttonholes are an important feature of a tailored garment. Because they are generally located on the center front of a coat or suit, they become an obvious design element of your garment. Consequently, extreme care must be taken to see that a buttonhole is correctly positioned and is as perfectly constructed as you are capable of doing. Poorly constructed buttonholes of any type can mar the appearance of an otherwise well-tailored garment.

Remember, first of all, that in women's garments the right-hand side usually carries the buttonholes and overlaps onto the left which holds the buttons. On men's garments the left side carries the buttonholes. However, designers have been known to overlap women's in the same manner as men's as a means of carrying out the unisex idea.

Types and Selection of Buttonholes

There are three types of buttonholes and your choice depends upon (1) the design of the garment, (2) the fashion fabric used, (3) your ability to sew, and (4) the time available. The types of buttonholes are as follows:

Fabric buttonholes are those employing the use of the garment fabric, or other fabrics related to it, in forming the buttonhole lips. They are traditionally known as *bound* but, in truth, they are really *piped* or *corded*. Recall the difference in the appearance of a bound edge versus a piped or corded edge, and you can understand the reason for the authors' preference for the use of the term *fabric* as a general descriptive term.

Fabric buttonholes are those most frequently used on women's tailored suits and coats to give a professional appearance.

12

BUTTONHOLES AND OTHER CLOSURES

However, they may not be as appropriate on women's sportswear and are usually not used in men's tailored garments. Worked buttonholes, either hand or machine, are more suitable for garments of this type. Fabric buttonholes are difficult to construct in heavy, thick fabrics, and they are more time consuming to make than machine buttonholes.

Worked buttonholes are those which may be hand stitched using buttonhole twist or machine stitched using regular sewing thread. Hand-worked ones are generally used in high quality menswear and in women's blazers and jackets designed for a man-tailored effect. Skill and time are necessary to make them satisfactorily for tailored garments. Machine-made buttonholes are suitable for many children's coats and jackets as well as for adult sportswear. A combination of both may be used by first making the machine buttonhole and then covering the machine stitches with the hand buttonhole stitch. This method can also improve the appearance of machine-made buttonholes in commercially produced garments.

Inseam buttonholes are those which are small openings in a seam. These are easily constructed if the design has a band in which the seam forms the center front of the garment or there is some other design feature which makes an inseam buttonhole possible.

General Guides for Making Fabric Buttonholes

1. The length of the buttonhole must be either on the lengthwise or crosswise grain. Exception: Novelty effects may be achieved by placing buttonholes on an angle to center front (Figure 12–1).

2. Spaces between buttonholes or between a series of buttonholes must be even. Some changes from the pattern may be necessary because (1) the pattern may have been altered in length, thus requiring respacing of

FIGURE 12–1
Angled Buttonholes.

buttonholes; or (2) during fitting, a change in location may have been found to be desirable (i.e., difference in waist length).

3. All buttonholes must be the same length and correct for button size. To determine the length, measure the width plus the depth of the button, plus 1.5 mm to 3 mm (1/16'' to 1/8''). Fabric-covered buttons require a larger buttonhole than the button actually measures to allow ease in buttoning and to reduce strain on the buttonhole as well as the button.

To determine length for a ball- or dome-shaped button, cut a strip of paper 6 mm (1/4'') wide and wrap it around the button. One-half of the total length of the strip indicates the required length of the buttonhole. *Note:* To test for correct length, place a piece of interfacing under a scrap of your fashion fabric and cut a slit the necessary length through both layers. The button should slip through easily. This may not be an accurate test but it does give some indication of the required size.

4. The buttonhole width should be as narrow as your fabric will allow to maintain a professional look. Keep within range of a total width of 6 mm (1/4''). Lightweight fabrics may require slightly narrower buttonholes while heavy fabrics may require slightly wider ones.

5. The area under a buttonhole must have a firm but lightweight interfacing abut 5 cm (2'') wide by 2.5 cm (1'') longer than the buttonhole. A fusible interfacing may be used if satisfactory for your fabric and if it is lightweight. Never make a fabric buttonhole through a hair canvas interfacing because this adds bulk and is difficult to press.

6. Always make a test buttonhole on a scrap of your fashion fabric before making it in your garment. Try at least two methods of making buttonholes, if undecided about the method to use, to determine (1) how your fabric responds and (2) how your ability suits the method.

7. Complete the same step on all buttonholes during construction before proceeding to the next step. Thus, comparisons and corrections may be made at the appropriate time. Try to complete all buttonholes in one period of work.

8. To ensure accuracy in stitching, draw parallel stitching lines on magic transparent tape (tape on which pencil lines can be· drawn) and place over the area to be stitched.

9. For permanent stitching, use short stitches (20-22 per 2.5 cm [1'']). When stitching a rectangle, start and stop stitching in the middle of one long side, overlapping 2 or 3 stitches. Never start at a corner because this weakens an area that must remain stable.

10. When stitching two parallel lines, do not backstitch at the ends but leave threads at least 7.5 cm (3'') long. This will allow the length of the stitched lines to be easily adjusted by removing a stitch or by carrying a thread through a needle and adding a stitch or two. Tie thread ends when accuracy is assured. Do not trim threads until the ends of the buttonhole have been stitched.

11. When cutting a buttonhole that has two parallel lines of stitching, cut between the lines extending no deeper than 6 mm

FIGURE 12–2
Cutting the Buttonhole.

FIGURE 12–3
Improper Cutting.

(1/4'') from the ends. Cut diagonally to the center of the last stitch at each corner, being careful not to cut the stitching (Figure 12-2). Cut a rectangularly stitched buttonhole in the same manner, except cut exactly *to the corner* stitch. *Never* cut diagonally *from center* out to corners because the anchoring space between the stitching and the cutting lines becomes too narrow and may readily pull out (Figure 12-3). Compare cutting lines with Figure 12-2.

When cutting any buttonhole, use only the tip of sharp pointed shears or scissors. Cut into the fabric, using tiny snips to avoid cutting too deeply.

Standards for Fabric (Piped and Corded) Buttonholes

1. The lips should meet and be even in width and no wider than 6 mm (1/4'') for most fabrics.

2. The corners must be square without a ravelly or a puckered appearance.

3. The opening must be long enough to allow the button to slip through easily without any strain.

4. The buttonholes must be exactly "on grain" of the garment unless they are on an angle for a decorative reason.

5. The facing finish on the back must be as long as the finished buttonhole. The buttonhole can be no longer than the finish on the facing. Hand stitch lightly around the opening of the facing.

6. The lips must be on the same grain unless they are cut on the bias. Bias strips on a fabric with a prominent twill weave must all be cut on the same angle. The lips should be firm (corded if fabric is stretchy). When buttonhole sample is made, use *Critique #3* to check your sample. Also use it to check buttonholes in your jacket or coat.

7. The buttonhole must lie flat. Reduce the bulk around the buttonhole as much as possible by grading and pressing.

Construction of Fabric Buttonholes (Piped and Corded)

The lips of fabric buttonholes are often cut on the bias, especially for corded buttonholes; however, fabric on the lengthwise grain is also frequently used—with the grain going the length of the lip. Crosswise grain is rarely used unless you are attempting to match a stripe, plaid, or check. Patterned fabrics cut on the bias offer a pleasing contrast to the garment, thus, eliminating matching. As long as you are making a fabric buttonhole, why not plan for one which will show in your garment and not try to conceal it?

Fabric buttonholes are constructed *prior* to the application of the traditional front interfacing, but if a fusible interfacing is being used, the buttonholes are generally made after the fusible has been applied.

There is a variety of methods for making fabric buttonholes. Our discussion will focus on (1) the five-line patch, (2) the butterfly with a faced opening, and (3) the corded strip, along with some suggested variations. We will also discuss the advantages and limitations of each method.

Pre-preparation—Making the Buttonhole Ladder

1. The center front line has previously been *hand basted* on the exact grain on both left and right fronts, and the location of the buttonholes has been marked.

2. Pin a piece of lightweight fabric 5 cm (2'') wide and 2.5 cm (1'') longer than the buttonhole under each buttonhole area, centering the interfacing over the location mark for the buttonhole. This step may be omitted for the butterfly method and when a lightweight fusible interfacing is used. *Note:* Instead of separate pieces of interfacing, one continuous strip extending 2.5 cm (1'') over each end of the total length of the buttonhole area may be substituted. After each buttonhole has been turned and pressed, cut the strip between each buttonhole and trim off excess fabric.

3. Baste a second line 3 mm (1/8'') from center front toward the cut or open edge of the garment on the side that will carry the buttonholes (right for women, left for men). See Figure 12–4 (note line a).

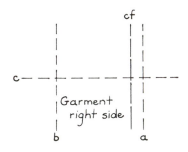

FIGURE 12–4
Buttonhole Ladder.

4. Determine length of buttonhole as previously discussed and baste a second line (b) parallel to line a.

5. Baste the location of the buttonhole (c) at right angles (on exact grain) to a and b. Extend basting at least 1.3 cm (1/2'') beyond the vertical lines a and b. Baste as many crosswise lines as needed for the required number of buttonholes.

Five-Line Patch Method

This method is suitable for medium to light weight fabrics, not for heavy ones. It is also unsuitable for fabrics that needle mark.

1. Cut a bias or straight strip (piping material) for each buttonhole, making each strip 5 cm (2'') wide and at least 2.5 cm (1'') longer than the buttonhole length. Remember that if your fabric has a *prominent* twill weave, be sure that all bias strips are cut in the same direction. To determine the most pleasing effect, fold your fabric with the bias running one direction and then the reverse direction. Sometimes a fold (bias) not quite on true bias is pleasing, especially with a prominent twill weave.

2. Fold the strips in half lengthwise and lightly press a crease line.

3. On the right side of the garment, place the creased line of the piping material exactly on top of line c, right sides together (Figure 12-5). Pin in place along outer edges of the patch.

4. With a sharp pencil draw five parallel lines on a piece of magic transparent tape. The distance between the lines determines the width of the lips and can vary from 1.5 mm (1/16'') to 3 mm (1/8'') depending upon the fabric weight. The heavier fabrics require the wider width. If 1.3 cm (1/2'') tape is used, the edges of the tape will form lines 1 and 5 for a buttonhole with 3-mm (1/8'') lips (Figure 12-6). An alternative is

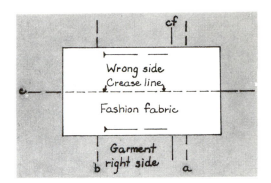

FIGURE 12-5
Patch for Five-Line Buttonhole.

to draw the lines on the interfacing instead of the tape. One disadvantage of this method is that the interfacing may not be sufficiently firm to accept well-defined pencil lines. Another way is to cut a piece of 3-mm (1/8'') graph paper 2.5 cm (1'') longer than the buttonhole and 2.5 cm (1'') wide. Number the lines as indicated in Figure 12-6. The center line (line 3) will lie exactly on the buttonhole location line.

5. Then on the wrong side of the garment, place the tape (or graph paper) with line 3 on top of the basted buttonhole marking.

6. From wrong side, baste stitch on line 3 (the center line) to hold the buttonhole patch in place. Check grain of patch and garment.

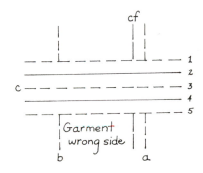

FIGURE 12-6
Markings on Transparent Tape.

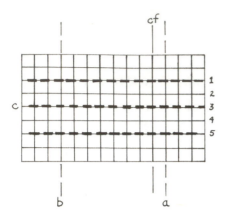

FIGURE 12-7
Markings on Graph Paper.

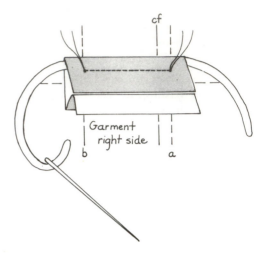

FIGURE 12-9
Cording the Lips.

Then baste the length of the patch exactly along lines 1 and 5 (Figure 12-7).

7. On the right side press the edges of the patch on lines 1 and 5 toward the center, pushing the iron against the basting. Cut edges should stand up and not overlap. Pin in place.

8. With matching thread and a short stitch (20-22) and with the wrong side up, stitch on lines 2 and 4, using the graph paper or marked lines as guides. Start and stop ex-

actly on vertical basting lines that mark the ends of the buttonhole (Figure 12-8). Leave threads about 7.5 cm (3''); pull the ends through to the right side. Check stitching for accuracy and for even lips. Make any necessary corrections before proceeding. Then tie threads in a firm knot but do not cut.

9. Remove all crosswise bastings (lines 1, 3, and 5). A cord or soft yarn, often needed to give stability to bias lips, may be drawn through pipings (tucks) if desired. Thread a tapestry needle and draw the cord through each tuck, leaving about 6 mm (1/4'') at each end (Figure 12-9).

10. Place your fingers underneath to hold the lips and seam allowances away from the cutting area. Then from the wrong side, cut between the lines of stitching no closer than 6 mm (1/4'') from the ends. Cut diagonally to the center of the last stitch at each corner, being careful not to cut the stitching. Corners must be cut *to,* but *not through,* the end stitch or the buttonhole will not turn with square corners.

11. Pull the buttonhole piece through the slash to the wrong side. Gently pull ends and

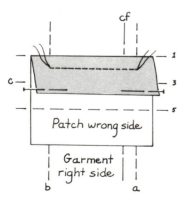

FIGURE 12-8
Stitching the Lips.

sides in place. Diagonally baste lips together, catching firmly at each end.

12. With the garment right side up place the buttonhole piece next to the feed dog, fold the garment back, grasp the ends of the knotted threads and hold taut to aid in making square corners. Then stitch across the triangles, catching the knots. This end stitching should start away from the edge of the buttonhole piece, coming to the exact corner of the triangle and curving slightly around to the opposite corner and beyond. Stitch back and forth over the triangle several times to flatten the ends and to make them secure (Figure 12–10).

13. Trim the buttonhole pieces to 1 cm (3/8'') on ends and sides.

14. With the wrong side up place garment on a press pad. To prevent edges from showing on the right side, place a piece of brown paper or a paper towel under the seam allowance and press carefully. Use a slightly damp cloth over the buttonhole.

15. The back of the buttonhole is finished later after the facing has been applied.

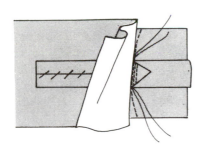

FIGURE 12–10
Stitching Buttonhole Ends.

Butterfly Method (Faced Opening)

This method in which the butterfly forms the buttonhole lips is suitable for most fabrics used in tailoring. It is especially ad-vantageous for heavy fabrics because all three layers of the seam allowances around the buttonhole can be graded at different lengths to reduce bulk. Other methods are less easily graded. The butterfly method requires a piece of firmly woven, lightweight fabric that *matches* the fashion fabric as closely as possible. Extreme care must be taken that the facing does not show around the finished buttonhole, thus the reason for a matching fabric. Some lightweight crepe lining fabrics are satisfactory for use in this area.

Preparing the Butterfly:

1. Cut two pieces of garment fabric 3.8 cm (1 1/2'') wide by 2.5 cm (1'') longer than the finished length of the buttonhole, either on grain or on true bias.

2. With right sides of the strips together *machine* baste lengthwise down the center of the strips. Leave a 5-cm (2'') tail of thread on each end to allow for easy removal of the basting (Figure 12–11).

3. Open the butterfly you have just made and carefully press (Figure 12–12).

Making the Faced Opening:

This procedure for making a faced opening is also used for finishing the facing back of the buttonholes.

1. Cut a rectangle on the straight lengthwise grain of a lightweight, closely woven

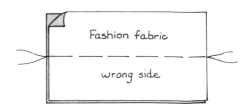

FIGURE 12–11
Making the Butterfly.

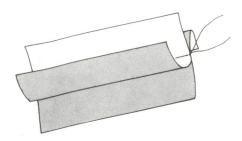

FIGURE 12–12
Pressing the Butterfly.

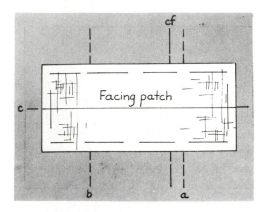

FIGURE 12–13
Positioning the Facing.

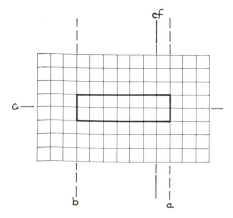

FIGURE 12–14
Rectangle Marked on Graph Paper.

fabric (e.g., crepe, organza, batiste). This should be about 5 cm (2'') wide and 3.8 cm (1 1/2'') longer than the length of the finished buttonhole.

2. Fold the strip lengthwise and finger press a crease line the entire length. On the *right* side of the garment, center this rectangle over the position for the finished buttonhole. Pin or hand baste in place (Figure 12–13).

3. With a sharp pencil draw three parallel lines on a piece of magic transparent tape. Or, lines may be drawn directly on the facing rectangle. The distance between the lines determines the finished width of the buttonhole lips and is influenced by the weight of the fabric. For a coat or suit the lines should be about 3 mm (1/8'') apart. On the wrong side of the garment, place the tape with the center line of the tape on the buttonhole location line. Using the buttonhole ladder as a guide, draw the ends to complete the rectangle. Or, using graph paper, draw a rectangle the exact size of the buttonhole. Position it on the buttonhole location line on the underside and pin in place (Figure 12–14).

4. With matching thread and a short stitch (20–22) and with wrong side of the garment up, stitch on the rectangle starting in the center of one long side, pivot at corners and accurately stitch around rectangle, overlapping stitches at starting point (Figure 12–15). Remove paper or tape. *Check for accuracy* and make any necessary corrections before the next step.

5. Cut between the lines of the stitching, stopping 6 mm (1/4'') from the ends. Clip diagonally *to* each corner, being careful not to cut the stitching. The corner will not be square unless slashed *exactly to* each corner (Figure 12–15).

6. Pull the facing through the slash to the wrong side. Place the opening over a ham or a padded surface and gently pull ends and

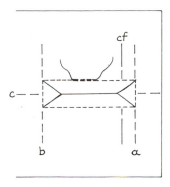

FIGURE 12–15
Stitching and Cutting Rectangle.

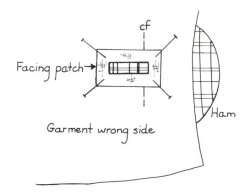

FIGURE 12–16
Pressing Faced Opening.

sides into place. Pin facing at corners and press (Figure 12–16). Make sure that the facing is not visible on the right side. The faced opening is now the finished width of the buttonhole.

Applying the Butterfly:

1. From the right side, position the butterfly behind the faced opening aligning the seam of the butterfly exactly in the center of the opening. Hold the butterfly in place for stitching by one of these methods:

    a. Apply glue stick or basting tape to the faced side of the opening and press the butterfly firmly in place.

    b. Place strips of fusible web on the faced side of the opening (Figure 12–17). Hold iron above and steam until the web becomes sticky and adheres to the facing. Center the butterfly over the opening and fuse, using a press cloth to protect the iron.

    c. From the right side, slip baste long sides of rectangle, catching into butterfly strip (Figure 12–18).

2. When the lips are perfectly centered within the opening, fold back the fashion fabric along the long side to expose the wrong side of the facing and stitch (20–22) exactly on top of previous stitching across width of facing. Be careful not to catch the

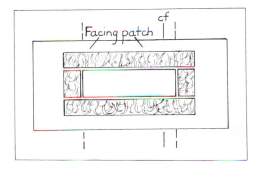

FIGURE 12–17
Fusible Web for Holding Butterfly.

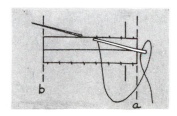

FIGURE 12–18
Slip Basting the Lips.

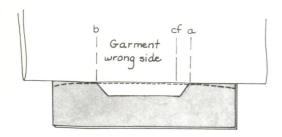

FIGURE 12–19
Stitching Lips.

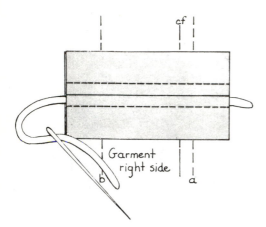

FIGURE 12–20
Cording Lips.

fold of garment at end of buttonhole (Figure 12–19). *Check for accuracy.* Be sure that the facing does not show at the edge of the buttonhole and that the lips are even. Make any necessary corrections before continuing.

3. To make corded or padded lips, use a soft cord or yarn threaded through a tapestry needle. Pull needle through each lip leaving cord barely extending beyond buttonhole length (Figure 12–20).

4. With the garment right side up, place the buttonhole piece next to the feed dog, fold the garment back, and stitch across the

end of the facing. Stitch back and forth over the triangle several times to flatten ends as shown earlier in Figure 12–10.

5. Trim and grade the butterfly to 1 cm (3/8'') on ends and sides.

6. With the wrong side up, place garment on a press pad. To prevent edges from showing on right side, place a piece of brown paper or a paper towel under the seam allowance of the buttonhole. Press carefully with a slightly dampened cloth.

7. Remove the machine basting which holds the lips together. The back of the buttonhole will be finished later after the facing has been applied. Follow directions later in this chapter. *Note:* The butterfly method may be adapted easily to buttonholes of different shapes (e.g., triangular, round, oblong, diamond).

Corded Strip Method

While cording can be inserted at the proper time into the lips of any of the previously described fabric buttonholes, this method differs in the time the cord is added and in the fact that cord is always used. When using this method the size of the cord is critical. The cord size selected must produce the correct size buttonhole lip when the fabric is folded around it. A soft cord may be twisted to give it more body or two cords may be twisted together to increase its size.

Making the Buttonhole Lips:

1. Cut as many pieces of the garment fabric as there are buttonholes to be made. They should be cut either on the true bias or straight grain and at least 2.5 cm (1'') longer than the planned buttonhole opening and 5 cm (2'') in width. Baste a line across the center length of the strips. *Note:* Two pieces of fabric may be used instead of one, particularly in a fabric with stripes where certain colors are desired in the buttonhole lips.

2. Cut twice as many pieces of soft yarn or cord as there are buttonholes.

3. Place the yarn or cord within a fold of the strip (right side out) and hand baste it in place using small stitches with matching mercerized thread (Figure 12–21). *Or,* using a zipper foot, machine baste the cord in place. This basting is not removed. Baste a second cord in place, keeping the two cords about 6 mm (1/4'') apart (Figure 12–22). The distance between the two bastings should measure approximately 6 mm (1/4''). Test the width by holding the fabric taut, crosswise of the cords. Push the cords with the thumbnail to the center; the two cords should touch. If the cords are too far apart, the lips will gap; if too close together, the lips will overlap and crowd the opening.

Applying the Lips to the Garment:

1. Position the lips on the ladder on the right side of the garment with the cut edges up, so that the exact center between the two basted lines is on the cross marking of the ladder. Hand baste carefully over the previous basting. Mark the ends of the buttonhole by placing (1) a strip of tape so that the edge of the tape defines the exact ends of the buttonhole, or (2) mark across the ends with hand basting.

2. Machine stitch (20–22) the exact length of the buttonhole, using a narrow zipper foot and then stitch as close as possible to the cord. Leave long thread ends to allow for any necessary correction (Figure 12–23).

3. Check each buttonhole from the interfacing side for accuracy of stitching. Does the stitching start and stop exactly on the ladder positions? Is the distance between the two lines of stitching correct in width and are they parallel? Now pull the thread ends to right side and tie, leaving long ends.

4. From the wrong side hold apart the two standing edges of the lips. Cut between the lines of stitching no closer than 6 mm (1/4'')

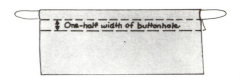

FIGURE 12–21
Basting Cord in Lips.

FIGURE 12–22
Cord Basted for Lips.

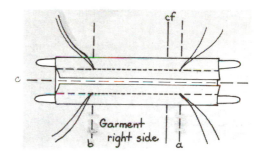

FIGURE 12–23
Stitching Corded Lips.

from the ends. Cut diagonally to the center of the last stitch at each corner, being careful not to cut the stitching. (Refer to Figure 12–2.)

5. Carefully pull the lip piece through to the underside. Tailor baste the lips together from the top side. To prevent the lips being pushed apart as the triangle ends are being stitched, whip the two lips together at each end of the buttonhole. Clip basting at ends of the lip piece and carefully cut away the cord ends to reduce bulk.

6. With the garment right side up, place the buttonhole piece next to the feed dog, fold the garment back, grasp the ends of the knotted threads and hold taut to square the corners, and stitch across the triangles, catching the knots. This end stitching should start at the edge of the buttonhole piece, come across the exact corner of the triangle, curve slightly around to the other corner, and continue off the edge. Stitch back and forth over the triangle several times to flatten the ends. (Refer to Figure 12–10.)

7. Trim ends of the lip fabric to within 1 cm (3/8'') of the machine stitching and grade. Trim off corners at an angle to prevent a corner from becoming folded under.

8. With the wrong side up, place garment on a press pad. To prevent edges from showing on right side, place a piece of brown paper or a paper towel under the seam allowance of the buttonhole. Press carefully.

9. The back of the buttonhole will be finished later after the facing has been applied.

Finishing the Facing for Fabric Buttonholes

Finishing the buttonhole facing cannot be done at this point because the front facing and the collar have not been applied. So, disregard the following steps until it is the proper time for this procedure.

When a garment has a front closing as in coats and jackets, the finished back of the buttonhole is exposed to frequent view. Thus, it is important that the facing side of your garment look as well handled as the front. Two methods are described, but Method A is highly recommended because it is neat and durable and may be used to finish the back of fabric buttonholes regardless of the construction method used. If this opening is finished inconspicuously, the buttonholes on the facing side will appear the

same as on the outside of the garment. However, great accuracy is necessary with this method to make the two rectangles lie exactly on each other.

Method A—Faced Rectangular Opening:

1. After the facing has been carefully pressed in place and the lapel has been rolled and pinned into position, carefully check the position of the facing against the back of the buttonholes, grain on grain. Pin around each buttonhole to hold the facing in place for marking.

2. Mark the facing by pushing pins through each corner of the lips from the outside of the garment (Figure 12–24). Hand baste the rectangle formed by the pins (Figure 12–25). *Or,* place a pin between the lips at each end of the buttonhole and hand baste a straight line following the opening. Then baste lines across each end (Figure 12–26).

3. Follow Steps 1 through 6 in "Making the Faced Opening" for the butterfly method.

4. Trim the patch to 1.3 cm (1/2'') on all sides.

5. Pin facing to the garment, making sure that the faced opening falls exactly on the stitching lines of the piped buttonhole. Then pin around each buttonhole to hold the faced opening securely in place.

6. Closely slipstitch the facing around each buttonhole (Figure 12–27).

7. Remove all bastings. Press buttonhole carefully by placing the right side on a padded surface and using a wool press cloth under the iron.

Method B—Oval Opening:

This method produces an oval finish around the buttonhole. While it generally is not as neat as Method A, it is satisfactory in casual-type jackets but is unsuited for fabrics that ravel.

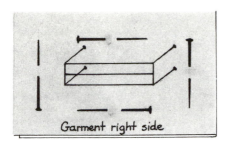

FIGURE 12–24
Marking Facing from Garment Side.

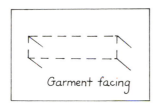

FIGURE 12–25
Marking Rectangle on Facing.

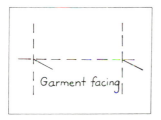

FIGURE 12–26
Alternate Method of Marking Rectangle.

1. From the right side insert pins at each end of the buttonhole at the place where the lips meet.

2. From the facing side, slash the facing *on the exact grain* from pin to pin, cutting about one or two threads more at each end than the pins indicate.

3. Starting along one side, turn under the slashed edge and carefully hand stitch in place, using a *short* invisible stitch (Figure 12-27). Use your needle to assist in rolling the facing under as you approach the ends. Reinforce the ends by making two stitches on top of each other.

4. Press, using a wool cloth between the facing and the iron.

Construction of Worked Buttonholes

Worked buttonholes are among the last details to be constructed on your garment. All construction and final pressing have been completed. Worked buttonholes are almost always used in men's garments and are also suitable for women's jackets. The keyhole shape is desirable because the enlarged end (the end nearest the garment edge) allows space for the button shank to

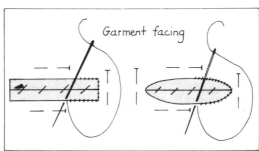

(A) Rectangular Finish.   **(B) Oval Finish.**

FIGURE 12–27

set, thus preventing the buttonhole from spreading around the button.

Since worked buttonholes are made through all thicknesses of your garment, carefully check the grain of both the garment front and the facing; they must be the same. *Recheck buttonhole location.*

General Guides for Making Worked Buttonholes:

1. Always make a test buttonhole.

2. Baste or pin around each buttonhole area through all layers of fabric.

3. Buttonhole must be on grain.

4. Complete one buttonhole at a time.

Handworked Buttonholes

Practice and skill are required to make attractive, professional looking buttonholes. Unless you are very proficient, it is recommended that you either (1) have your buttonholes made by a professional tailor, or (2) make a machine buttonhole and finish by covering with hand buttonhole stitches.

Standards for Handworked Buttonholes:

1. Use buttonhole twist or topstitching thread since these are heavier than the thread for normal stitching; they provide greater stability to the buttonhole. A double strand of regular thread is *not* satisfactory because it is too difficult to form an even stitch with the two strands.

2. Wax the thread either by pulling the thread over a piece of beeswax or over a piece of soap to prevent knotting and curling of thread. After waxing, pull the thread through your fingers to remove excess wax.

3. Stitches must be close together, evenly spaced and even in depth.

4. Finished edge (purled) is even and smooth.

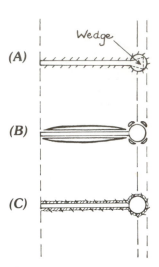

FIGURE 12–28
Methods for Worked Buttonhole Preparation.

Procedure for Handworked Buttonhole:

1. Cut a keyhole by using sharp scissors, Cut a small wedge at the end of the buttonhole nearest the front garment edge, then round out the wedge. See Figure 12–28, (A). *Or,* from the top side use a stiletto to punch a round hole. Lightly trim around the hole from the underside to help keep the hole open. Cut exactly on grain from the hole to the required length of buttonhole. Tailors use a special buttonhole shear that cuts the keyhole and the buttonhole length in one operation.

2. With a fine thread, overcast around the cut edges to hold them together and to prevent raveling. Untwist some of your regular sewing thread (silk is excellent) to acquire a *fine* thread.

3. Pad the buttonhole in either of two ways:

    a. With buttonhole twist take a small stitch at the back end of the buttonhole, then at the beginning of the keyhole at the opposite end. Continue around the keyhole with short stitches, then repeat for the second side (B). *Or,*

b. Take a length of buttonhole twist, double in the center of the length and twist together. Lay the twisted thread around the buttonhole and with fine matching thread lightly overcast the twist to the opening (C).

4. Fasten the thread invisibly (no knot) and bring the needle out at the cut edge at the straight end of the buttonhole (end away from the garment edge). To make the buttonhole stitch, work from right to left. Make the buttonhole stitch as follows (Figure 12–29):

a. Place the needle down through the opening, up through the fabric 3 mm (1/8'') or less from the cut edge, and around the padding. (Needle should point toward you.) Bring the thread from the needle eye under the point of the needle, going from right to left. (*Warning:* Be sure that the needle catches through all layers of fabric.)

b. Pull the thread away from the buttonhole edge. This leaves a ''purl'' at the cut edge of the opening. *Note:* The purl gives a sturdy, finished effect which is not produced by using any other stitch (e.g., blanket stitch). Try making a blanket stitch and note the difference in the finished edge.

c. Keeping stitches the same depth and close together, repeat this operation to the keyhole. Spread stitches fanwise around this end. Then continue stitches to end of second side. *Note:* If stitches are too close together, the purled edge will be bumpy; if too far apart, there will be too much space between the purls and a less durable edge will result.

5. Make a bar across the straight end by taking three or four stitches across the full

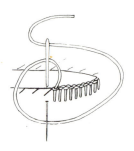

FIGURE 12–29
Buttonhole Stitch.

width of the buttonhole. Each stitch should lie on top of the previous one. Finish this end using one of these three methods:

a. Make two or three stitches (one on top of the other) directly in the center of the long stitches. Place needle through all layers of fabric and then through the opening so these short stitches encompass the long ones. See (A), Figure 12–30. This method is easy to do and provides a neat effect.

b. Buttonhole stitch around these long stitches (B).

(A)

(B)

(C)

FIGURE 12–30
*Methods for Finishing Bar
at End of Buttonhole.*

c. Wrap the thread closely around the stitches, thus covering the entire width (C).

6. Pull thread to wrong side and fasten invisibly in the stitches around the buttonhole.

Machine-Worked Buttonholes

These are appropriate on sportswear (both men's and women's) and on children's jackets and coats. Any zigzag machine will make buttonholes, but an attachment is needed on a straight-stitch machine. Such an attachment makes *keyhole* buttonholes and may be used on a zigzag machine if the attachment will fit. Follow your machine manual for specific instructions.

In contrast with handworked buttonholes, which are slit first and then stitched, the machine-worked ones are stitched first and then slit.

Standards for Machine-Worked Buttonholes:

1. Stitches should be close together and deep enough to hold all layers of fabric.

2. A small space must be left between the two rows of stitches to prevent cutting the stitches when the buttonhole is slit open.

3. Opening should not appear ravelly after it is cut. Trim away any loose threads.

Suggested Guides for Making and Cutting Buttonholes:

1. When using a buttonhole attachment, stitch a second row over the first row of stitching for added stability. For a zigzag machine, shorten the stitch length so that stitches lie close together.

2. Place straight pins at each end of the buttonhole before cutting. This reduces the chance of cutting too far.

3. If using small, sharp scissors for cutting, start in the center of the buttonhole

and cut to the ends. If using a seam ripper, cut from the ends toward the center.

4. If interfacing shows after cutting the buttonhole, use handworked buttonhole stitches to cover the edges or color with a matching indelible pen.

Combination Machine-Worked and Handworked Keyhole Buttonholes

The easiest way to obtain a professional looking keyhole buttonhole is to begin with a machine-made buttonhole (buttonhole attachment with keyhole template) and finish it by hand. The following suggestions may be helpful.

1. Set attachment for widest stitch width and set machine length so that stitches are about 1 mm (a scant 1/16'') apart.

2. Choose the keyhole template that is the nearest size needed. If the length is too long for your button, adjust this by making a sample buttonhole beginning and ending at the straight end of the keyhole template. Leave buttonhole under the machine, hand rotate the knob to move the attachment so that the needle is at the point of the desired buttonhole length (at straight end). Remove the sample and place the garment under the attachment with the needle at the end of the buttonhole marking furthest from garment edge. Stitch around the buttonhole ending opposite the starting point. Hand rotate the knob until the attachment is at the starting point of the first stitching. Remove the finished buttonhole. The attachment is in position to begin your next buttonhole.

3. Cut buttonhole and trim out keyhole as close to stitches as possible.

4. Follow instructions for handworked keyhole buttonhole beginning with Step 4. Use machine stitches as a guide for depth of the hand stitches.

Construction of Inseam Buttonholes

Openings may be left in either a vertical or horizontal seam to serve as buttonholes. If fabric buttonholes are used in the garment, but one buttonhole falls on a seamline, an inseam buttonhole may be used at that point.

Standards for Inseam Buttonholes:

1. Both sides of the opening should be firm.

2. The seamline should appear straight and continuous.

3. Openings should be the correct size for the buttons.

4. The back of the buttonhole should be neatly finished.

Procedure for Inseam Buttonholes:

1. On the seams that will be stitched together, mark the location for the ends of each buttonhole. Baste the entire seam.

2. Cut strips of organza or a lightweight fabric on the lengthwise grain 2.5 cm (1'') wider by 2.5 cm (1'') longer than the buttonhole, or use seam tape or a strip of lightweight fusible interfacing. There should be two pieces for each buttonhole. These are to become a stay.

3. On the wrong side, place the stay over the buttonhole markings on each side of the seam with one edge slightly over the seamline. Pin with right sides together, match the buttonhole markings, and baste the entire garment seam. See (a), Figure 12–31.

4. Stitch the seam, stopping at the buttonhole marking. Backstitch about three stitches at each end of the buttonhole (b). Press the seam open (c) and remove the basting. *Note:* Occasionally more firmness and support is desired in an inseam buttonhole than the stay supplies. To add support after stitching the seam, turn and press the seam open, then insert a cord along each edge. With a hand backstitch, inconspicuously stitch each cord in position. The shorter and finer the backstitch (each stitch about 3 mm or 1/8'') the less conspicuous it will be.

5. If there is a seam in the facing, make identical openings in the facing seam, eliminating the stay. After pressing the facing back over the buttonhole, carefully

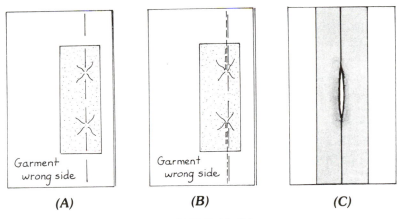

(A)   (B)   (C)

FIGURE 12–31
Inseam Buttonholes.

slipstitch the facing in place. *Or,* if there is no seam in the facing, carefully position the facing over the inseam opening. Follow either Method A or B for finishing the buttonhole backs.

Fabric Loops

Button loops may be substituted for buttonholes, providing the loops are in accord with the design of the garment. Buttonholes are not workable in some fabrics, such as a fabric with heavy crosswise slub yarns. Hence, loops may serve as an appropriate answer for a closing.

Loops may be made of (1) tubing made from your fashion fabric, (2) braided ravelings from your fabric, especially where there are heavy crosswise yarns, and (3) commercially made cord or braid. Your choice will depend upon your fabric and the design of your garment.

Making the Tubing

The well-made loop or tubing is round like a cord. If it is flat, it indicates that the tubing is not well filled. This may be altered by having more seam allowance inside the tubing, by using a larger cord when making the tubing, or by stitching closer to the cord.

It is always advisable to make a sample to determine the desired size of tubing before making longer cords for the loops. To make *corded tubing* from your fashion fabric, cut a true bias strip 2.5 cm to 5 cm (1'' to 2'') wide and the length desired. It is easier to make one long strip and then cut into the desired length for each loop. Obtain a cable cord (which becomes a filler inside the tubing) that is more than twice the length of the bias strip. The bias strip will become longer as it is stretched in stitching, hence the need for a longer cord. If there will be little strain on the loop or some stretch is desired, omit

the cord and let the seam allowance serve as the filler.

Fold the bias over the cord (Figure 12–32), wrong side out, with cut edges matching and half of the length of the cord inside the bias strip. Using a zipper foot, sew across the end as shown in Figure 12–33, then turn and make a funnel as you stitch downward. The funnel provides more room for starting the turn of the tube. Hold the edges of the bias together while stitching. Stitch close to the cord, but be careful that you do not catch into it. Stretch the bias as you stitch, pulling from both ends. If you do not stretch the bias at this time, the threads of the stitching will break when the tube is stretched in turning (Figure 12–34).

FIGURE 12–32
Placing Cord in Bias Strip.

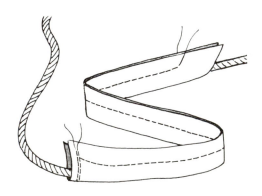

FIGURE 12–33
Funnel End for Easy Turning.

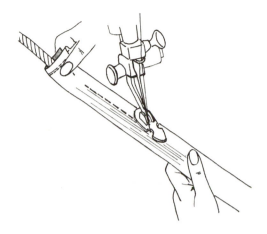

FIGURE 12–34
Stretching Bias While Stitching.

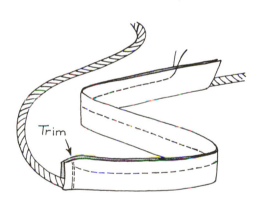

Trim

FIGURE 12–35
Trimmed Seam.

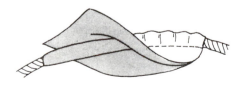

FIGURE 12–36
Pulling Bias over Cord.

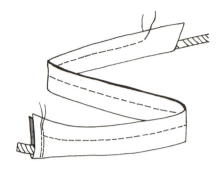

FIGURE 12–37
Uncorded Tubing.

Trim extra seam away where cord was attached at top (Figure 12–35). This will reduce bulk at the starting point, thus making it easier to get the fabric started in turning. Gradually push the fabric up over the place where the cord is attached (Figure 12–36), thus pulling the fabric right side out and encasing the opposite end of the cord inside the bias strip. Continue pushing the fabric gradually over the cord, not allowing it to become bunched in one place or you will find it almost impossible to turn. After all is turned, cut off the cord at starting point. *Note:* For uncorded tubing, follow this method except omit the tail extending outward from the end of the tubing. The cord must remain inside the tubing to make it possible to turn the tubing after stitching. Stitch several times across the end of the cord to hold it firmly in place. Leave the seam allowances wide enough to fill the tube to give the rounded effect (Figure 12–37).

Applying the Loops

Loops may be applied in different ways, depending upon the effect desired. They can be applied singly (cut) or as a continuous row, contingent upon the fabric weight and the spacing desired. For tailored suits and coats, the single loop is more popular.

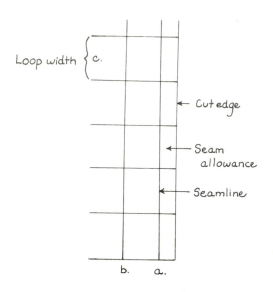

FIGURE 12–38
Paper Guide for Loops.

However, continuous looping may be effectively used, especially in suits where buttons may be smaller than those used for coats.

Making a Pattern for Loop Placement:

1. On a strip of lightweight paper draw a line the width of the seam allowance from the edge. Note (a) in Figure 12–38.

2. Draw another line (b) parallel to (a) the distance that the loops are to extend (about half the button diameter, plus the cord thickness).

3. Draw crosswise lines indicating the width of the loop and the distance between the loops. For the width, make each loop the button diameter plus twice the thickness of the cord.

Applying the Single Loop:

1. Cut each loop the required length for the button plus two seam allowances.

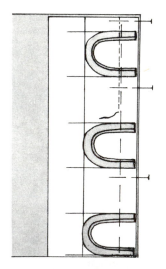

Single loops.

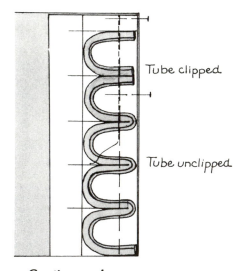

Continuous loops.

FIGURE 12–39
Making Loops.

FIGURE 12–40
Single Loops.

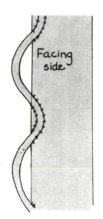
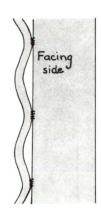

FIGURE 12–41
Continuous Loops Attached by Hand.

2.   Pin paper pattern on the right side of garment and with the seamed side uppermost, pin or use basting tape to hold each loop in position, extending away from the seam edge (Figure 12–39.) Remove pins. The seam of the tubing should lie on the inward curve of the loop.

3.   Baste stitch through paper, loop ends, and garment close to the seamline but within the seam allowance.

4.   Remove the paper.

5.   To reduce bulk, trim cord (if used) away from cut ends of loops.

6.   Flatten ends of loops by applying steam and pressure (clapper).

7.   Apply the facing (stitch, turn, and press) and then fold facing back, allowing the loops to extend out beyond the seam edge. Press again (Figure 12–40).

Applying the Continuous Loop

Continuous loops attached by hand may be attached to the edge of the closing or attached under the edge (Figure 12–41). The ends will be flatter than if stitched into a seam. To attach a continuous loop *in a seam,*

follow the instructions for single loops except allow a loop of tubing to extend 1.3 cm (1/2'') into the seam allowance between buttonhole loops (Figure 12–42). After stitching, trim away the inside loops to reduce bulk and press.

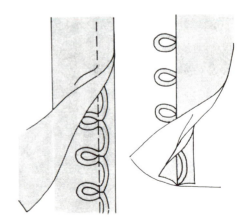

FIGURE 12–42
Continuous Loops Stitched into Seam.

Frogs

Frogs may be used as decorative closings on some tailored jackets and coats with the Chinese knot being the button most frequently used with them.

1. Make tubing as for the loops.

2. Twist the loops into the desired design to produce a neat looking frog. Keep the seam of the tubing turned under as you work (Figure 12–43).

3. After you have formed the design, firmly hand stitch the areas where crossing of the tubing has occurred.

4. Slipstitch tubing to the garment, leaving the button loop free.

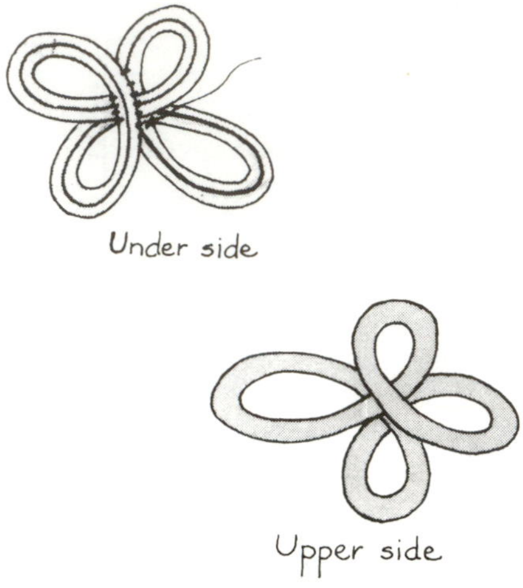

Under side

Upper side

FIGURE 12–43
Frogs.

Pockets can be classified in three major categories. (1) *Applied* pockets are separate pieces that are attached to the right side of a garment. (2) *Slashed* pockets are inset through a slash in the garment with only the opening visible. They include the double welt or corded (like a large fabric buttonhole), stand or single welt, and flap. (3) *Inseam* pockets are set into a seam or a design line. Fashion influences the choice of pocket style, but all three types are usually used.

Visually, applied pockets appear larger in scale and are more dominant than slashed or inseam pockets because the total pocket is visible. Slashed or inseam pockets may be dominant if they have flaps or decorative welts. Inseam pockets may be very inconspicuous if they are contained in a seam or design line. All may be equally functional.

Pocket placement is usually determined by the designer of a commercial pattern; however, if the pattern is altered or the type of pocket is changed, some adjustment may be necessary in the pocket placement. If the pocket is to be functional, it should be placed so the hand can be comfortably inserted in it. A short jacket may, of necessity, have pockets placed high and thus they are usually considered decorative rather than functional.

The style of pocket shown in the pattern can be changed quite easily. To do this, here are some general suggestions:

1. Experiment by cutting from paper or muslin the visible part of the pocket (patch, flap, or welt) and pinning it in place on the test garment for the first fitting. Be sure that the hem of the jacket or coat is turned up so the relationship of the pocket piece to the total area can be seen.

2. Place top of slashed pocket on same line as the applied pocket it is to replace.

3. The lower end of an angled slashed pocket should be dropped about 3.8 cm (1½'') from the original horizontal position.

13

POCKETS

4. Unless a pocket is placed on the diagonal, place top of pocket level with garment hem, and thus also level with the floor.

5. The exposed parts of the pocket usually match the grain of the garment unless cut on the bias for a decorative effect. The bias is often used with patterned fabrics so matching is not necessary, but remember this will also make the pocket more noticeable than if it is matched to the background.

Applied Pockets and Flaps

The construction of applied pockets and pocket flaps are similar, thus they will be discussed together. Patch pockets are the most common type of applied pocket. They may be used alone or with a flap. The saddle bag and the gusset or bellows pockets are variations of the patch and allow for more to be carried in the pocket without distorting the garment. They also present a different visual appearance.

Standards for Applied Pockets and Flaps:

1. Paired pockets or flaps should be identical in size and shape.

2. Corners should be smoothly curved or have perfectly formed angles.

3. Edges must be straight.

4. Pocket or flap is cut on grain.

5. All possible bulk is reduced in seams.

6. Topstitching, if used, is even and suitable for fabric.

7. Layers of pocket or flap lie smoothly together.

8. Pocket and garment lie smoothly over body curve when worn.

9. Paired pockets or flaps are placed the same distance from the front edge and the same height at the front of the pocket.

Note: An asymmetrical figure may cause a jacket to vary on each side. In this case, the variation in the pocket placement should occur at the back edge of the pocket, not the front.

10. In patterned fabrics, pocket or flap should match the garment at the front edge. If the pocket or flap crosses a seam or dart, total matching is impossible.

Patch Pockets (and Flaps)

Patch pockets may vary greatly in size, shape, and placement. Because the total pocket is visible, the placement and relationship to the total space is especially important to the appearance of the garment, and the scale is important as it is related to the wearer. Determine whether the pocket is primarily for appearance or whether it will be used often. Choose the method of application accordingly. The pocket which is attached with machine stitching will be more durable than one applied by hand.

Applying Interfacing. Patch pockets and flaps in tailored garments usually require interfacing to hold their shape and to ensure sharp edges. Interfacing may be a nonfusible type or a fusible if the fashion fabric is not changed in appearance by fusing. Fusible interfacing usually gives a smooth, sharp appearance and is easy to apply. Consider using a lighter weight fusible for pockets and flaps than would be used for collar and lapels. Follow this procedure for either type of interfacing:

1. Cut the interfacing on the same grain and the size and shape of the finished pocket or flap less 1.5 mm (1/16'') on sides and lower edge. You may wish to make a tagboard template the exact size of the finished pocket. This may be used as a pattern to cut the interfacing as well as to shape the hand-lined pocket.

Note: If pocket has a hem at the top and additional firmness is desired at this foldline, allow the interfacing to extend 1.3 cm to 2.5 cm (1/2'' to 1'') beyond the fold.

2. Position the interfacing on the wrong side of the pocket or flap. Be sure fusing agent is down when using fusible interfacing. (See Figure 13–1.)

3. Apply the fusible interfacing according to the manufacturer's instructions, or follow the directions with each method of lining application for nonfusible interfacings.

Applying Lining (Facings to Flaps).
A patch pocket may be unlined in some garments, but a tailored garment will be much nicer and more serviceable with lined pockets. The lining finishes the inside of the pocket by covering raw seams and the interfacing. Before lining the pocket, read ahead and decide how the pocket will be applied.

If the pocket pattern has no lining, follow one of these methods to cut one:

1. For a pocket pattern with a hem, fold the hem into place on the paper pattern. The lining should extend a seam allowance above the stitching line on the hem (line b, Figure 13–2) to allow lining to be sewed to the hem. Cut lining to line a, Figure 13–2.

2. For a pocket pattern without a hem, a hem may be added and the lining cut as above, _or_ the lining may be cut exactly like the pocket with a seam at the top of the pocket (usually less desirable).

A flap is always faced using either self-fabric or lining fabric, depending on the weight of the fashion fabric. Use self-fabric only if the fashion fabric is lightweight. The facing is cut exactly like the flap.

Facings are usually applied to flaps by machine, but the hand method may be advantageous for heavy fabrics. Linings may be applied to pockets either by machine or by hand.

FIGURE 13–1
Applying Interfacing.

Machine Method:

1. If fusible interfacing is _not_ being used, position the nonfusible interfacing on pocket or flap. (See Figure 13–1.) Place over a curve to help shape, then pin and catchstitch around all edges.

2. For pocket with a hem, stitch lining to hem leaving a 5-cm (2'') opening in the center of the seam. Press seam toward the lining.

3. Trim 3 mm (1/8'') off the sides and lower edge of pocket lining or flap facing. This will cause the seam around the outside to roll slightly under so the lining will not show after turning.

4. With right sides together, match side and bottom cut edges. Pin at close intervals. The fashion fabric must ease slightly and will appear to bubble in the center.

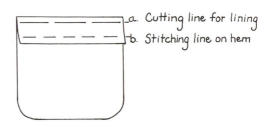

FIGURE 13–2
Cutting the Pocket Lining.

FIGURE 13–3
Machine Method of Lining Pocket.

FIGURE 13–4
Stitching Angle of Less Than
90 Degrees.

FIGURE 13–5
Pocket Shaped over Template.

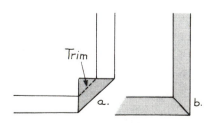

FIGURE 13–6
Mitering the Corner.

5. Stitch on the seamline around the cut edges. Use a shorter stitch on curves and corners. For a pocket without a hem, leave an opening at lower edge for turning (Figure 13–3). For a flap, leave the top edge open.

Note: When stitching a seam with less than a 90 degree angle, shorten the stitch length as the point is approached and take one or two stitches across the point. This will make the point easier to turn, and it will be sharper and less bulky (Figure 13–4).

6. Press lining seam allowances toward the pocket to facilitate turning. Trim and grade seams. The seams on the flaps may be graded to 3 mm and 6 mm (1/8'' and 1/4'') and seams on pockets slightly wider, especially with heavy fabrics. Notch any curves and angle the corners so seam allowances will lie flat when turned (Refer to Figure 13–3). Turn gently through the opening and carefully push out corners. Roll the seam so it is not visible from the right side and press. Slipstitch the opening on the pockets.

Hand Method:

1. If pocket or flap is curved, machine baste 6 mm (¼'') from the cut edge.

2. Place a tagboard template, cut to the size of the finished pocket or flap, on the wrong side of the pocket or flap and match template edge to seamlines.

3. Draw up basting stitches on curved pocket, thus permitting the pocket to assume the exact shape of the template (Figure 13–5). Miter corners of a square pocket by pressing the corner toward center (Figure 13–6, note a), and then fold the seam allowance over the template (b). Steam press in shape. Trim the seam to 1.3 cm (1/2'').

4. Remove the template and insert non-fusible interfacing in its place (unless a fusible was applied earlier). Place pocket over a pressing ham with fashion fabric on top of interfacing. Pin the two layers together.

Remove from ham and catchstitch the seam edge to the interfacing, _or_ if pocket is to be topstitched, baste the interfacing in place. Lay pocket over ham and press carefully.

5. After all pockets of this size have been pressed over the template, trim 3 mm (1/8'') off sides and bottom of template. For curved pocket, ease stitch 1.3 cm (1/2'') from cut edge around curves on pocket lining. Press the lining over the template in the same manner as the pocket. Trim the seam close to the ease stitching leaving about a 1 cm (3/8'') seam allowance.

6. With right sides together, match top edges of lining and pocket and stitch. Press seam toward lining.

7. Fold lining to cover pocket and pin in place (Figure 13–7). For a pocket that will be applied by the standard hand or machine method, slipstitch the lining to the pocket or to give additional durability to the pocket, yet a custom look, the lining may be machine stitched to the garment and the pocket applied by hand over the lining. If this method is desired, _do not_ slipstitch lining to pocket, but follow instructions under "Reinforced Application of Hand-Stitched Pocket."

Standard Pocket Application. Pockets may be applied by hand or by machine.

For lightweight fabrics the pocket may be attached to the garment as the pocket is topstitched. With heavier fabrics this causes the pocket to be distorted and the edges to flip up unless topstitched very close to the edge. For best results, topstitch the pocket before it is attached. Follow this procedure to apply pocket:

1. Place the garment over a surface that simulates the curve of the area the pocket covers (such as the front hip), then pin the pocket in place. Pin edges carefully so the curve is retained.

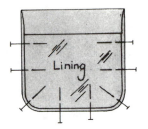

FIGURE 13–7
Lining Pinned to Pocket.

2. Place a small piece of interfacing on the wrong side of garment fabric under the top corners to reinforce areas of strain.

3. Machine topstitch, or from the wrong side hand stitch by working a small backstitch through garment into the pocket. If the pocket has been topstitched, prior to application catch into the topstitching; if not, place stitches about 3 mm (1/8'') in from the edge of the pocket. Be sure that these stitches do not show on the right side and that they are not too tight. Reinforce top corners with extra stitches. If topstitching is a distance from the pocket edge and edges do not lie flat, a second row of hand stitches may be needed about 3 mm (1/8'') from the pocket edge.

Reinforced Application of Hand-Stitched Pocket. Position pocket (prepared by the hand-lined method) as previously instructed.

1. Place pins parallel to edge and about 2.5 cm (1'') from it.

2. Roll back the edge of the pocket and closely pin the lining to garment, placing pins at right angles to the edge. The seam allowance will be visible (Figure 13–8).

3. Remove the pins holding the pocket and flip the pocket up to expose the lining.

4. Machine stitch about 3 mm (1/8'') from

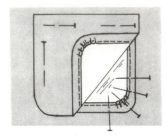

FIGURE 13–8
Pocket Lining Pinned to Garment.

the edge of lining, ending at top edge of pocket. Stitch a small triangle at the beginning and the end to reinforce the top corners (Figure 13–9).

5.   Flip pocket back over the lining, place over a curved surface and pin pocket in place being sure it is correctly positioned over the lining. Roll the garment fabric back to expose the edge of the lining. Hand stitch the pocket to the edge of the lining *or* backstitch the pocket to the garment as in the standard pocket application.

Inside Stitched Patch Pocket. This pocket gives the same appearance as the hand-applied pocket without topstitching, but because it is machine stitched it will be more durable. This method is satisfactory with light to medium weight fabrics. The bottom corners of the pocket *must* be curved, not square, and the pocket must be medium or larger in size. Inside-stitched pockets require more practice and skill than the hand-stitched pocket. Proceed as follows:

1.   Cut pocket lining the same size as the finished pocket plus seam allowances on all four sides. Trim 3 mm (1/8'') off sides and bottom edges.

2.   For ease in handling, interface the pocket with a fusible that is lightweight and flexible.

3.   Press the seam allowance to the inside along the top of pocket. Press the top seam allowance of the lining 6 mm (1/4'') *below* the stitching line.

FIGURE 13–10
Lining Stitched to Pocket.

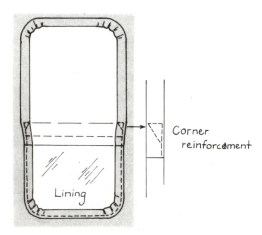

FIGURE 13–9
Lining Stitched to Garment.

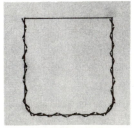

FIGURE 13–11
Pocket Zigzag Stitched to Garment.

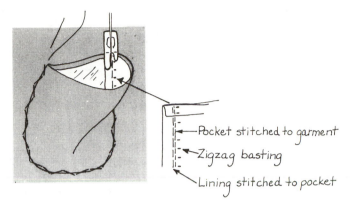

FIGURE 13–12
Stitching Inside the Pocket.

4. With *right* sides together, match cut edges of sides and bottom. The top fold of lining will be 6 mm (1/4") below the top edge of the pocket (Figure 13–10). Fashion fabric will ease slightly and bubble in center.

5. Stitch 1.3 cm (1/2") from the sides and bottom. Leave top edges free.

6. Notch curves. Trim seams to 1.3 cm (1/2"). See Figure 13–10.

7. Turn pocket right side out. Press rolling the stitching line of pocket slightly under.

8. Place garment over the appropriate curve to match body curve. Position pocket and pin in place. Using a narrow, long zigzag stitch and contrasting thread, stitch over the edge of the pocket catching alternately into the pocket and the garment (Figure 13–11). For fabrics that may mark, slip baste the pocket in place.

9. On the inside of pocket between fashion fabric and lining, machine stitch as close as possible on the pocket side of the stitching that attaches the lining to the pocket (Figure 13–12). Keep fabric smooth immediately in front of the presser foot. Secure ends by backstitching at the top edges of pocket.

10. Remove bastings. Fold top edge of pocket seam to form a miter (Figure 13–13). Slipstitch lining to pocket 6 mm (1/4") from the top edge.

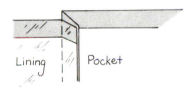

FIGURE 13–13
Miter Pocket Seam Allowance.

Patch Pocket with Flap

A patch pocket may have (1) a flap that is an extension of the pocket and turns back over the pocket (see flap Figure 13–14), thus the opening of the pocket is above the flap, or (2) a separate flap that is applied above pocket to cover the pocket opening (Figure 13–15).

Patch Pocket with Self-Flap:

1. Add depth of flap plus seam allowance to the top of the pocket pattern, and cut one

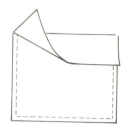

FIGURE 13–14
Pocket with Self-Flap.

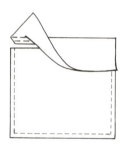

FIGURE 13–15
Pocket with Separate Flap.

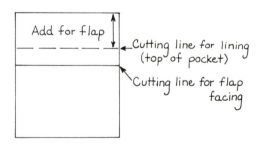

FIGURE 13–16
Cutting the Pocket with Flap.

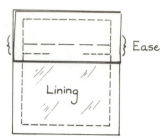

FIGURE 13–17
*Stitching the Lining and Flap
to the Pocket.*

FIGURE 13–18
Topstitching the Separate Flap.

2. Interface large pocket section with fusible or nonfusible interfacing following previous instructions.

3. Stitch lower edge of flap to lining. (For machine method leave an opening to turn the pocket). Use either the hand or machine method for lining the applied pockets and flaps. Remember that the top side of flap will need additional ease to fold down, so ease the upper flap at foldline at the top of the pocket (Figure 13–17). Ease (bubble) remainder of upper flap so the seam will roll under.

4. Attach pocket to garment following any of the methods previously discussed. Fold flap in place. Light pressing may be necessary, but allow it to maintain a soft turn.

Patch Pocket with Separate Flap:

1. Prepare and apply pocket. Interface and line the flap according to previous instructions, except begin and end stitching on

of fashion fabric. Cut the upper flap facing, also of fashion fabric, the width of the pocket and the depth of the flap plus three seam allowances (one for the top and two for the bottom to allow for seaming to lining). Cut lining the width and depth of pocket (Figure 13–16).

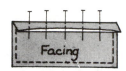

FIGURE 13-19
Seam Allowance Folded Under
to Allow Ease.

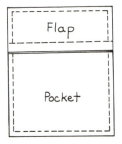

FIGURE 13-20
Flap Stitched to Garment.

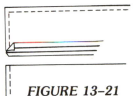

FIGURE 13-21
Finishing the Flap Seam Allowance.

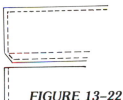

FIGURE 13-22
Seam Allowance Stitched in Place.

the seamline. (Retain 1.5-cm [5/8''] seam allowance on the open edge.) Topstitch (if desired) as shown in Figure 13-18.

2. To allow flaps to lie flat when folded, press seam allowance toward the facing being careful that all layers of flap are smooth (Figure 13-19). Pin cut edges together and baste. The top layer will appear bubbled when flap is placed flat.

3. Place flap above pocket with right sides together and with cut edges meeting. Stitch on flap seamline and secure ends (Figure 13-20) by back stitching.

4. Fold back uppermost seam allowance of flap. Trim lower seam allowance close to stitching. Turn upper seam allowance under 6 mm (1/4'') and fold ends diagonally (Figure 13-21).

5. Hand or machine stitch along edges of folded seam allowance (Figure 13-22). Press flap down. If necessary, place a few slip-stitches at the upper corners of the flap to hold it down.

Saddlebag Pocket

The finished saddlebag pocket is similar in size to the patch pocket, but is used primarily on sportswear. This pocket is stitched to the garment at the top edge only, permitting the bag to hang away from the garment. The pocket is cut in three pieces.

1. For each pocket, cut two pieces of fashion fabric the length of the pocket and

the flap, and the width of the pocket with seam allowances all around. The flap may be shaped to suit your taste and is usually from 5 cm to 7.5 cm (2'' to 3'') in depth. Consider the relationship of the flap to the pocket in planning the size and shape.

2. Cut one of the pieces along the foldline (Figure 13-23). These two pieces form the facing for the flap and the front of the pocket. For heavy fabrics, the flap facing may be cut of lining fabric.

3. Interface flap and pocket as needed according to the firmness of the fabric. A fusible interfacing would be appropriate for these areas. Cut top of pocket interfacing 1.5 cm (5/8'') below the foldline.

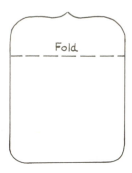

FIGURE 13–23
Cut One Pocket Piece on Foldline.

4. Turn seam allowance on top edge of front pocket section to wrong side. Hand catchstitch or machine stitch. Match pocket front to pocket back, right sides together. Slightly ease front to back. Pin, baste, and stitch (Figure 13–24).

5. Match flap facing to top of the pocket, easing the pocket edge to the facing. Pin, baste, and stitch (Figure 13–24). If lining fabric is used for facing, trim 3 mm (1/8'') from lining to allow lining to be concealed when turned. Trim away corners to stitching, grade the seams by trimming the flap facing narrower than the pocket flap and the pocket back narrower than the pocket front. Notch all curves.

6. Turn pocket and flap right side out, slightly rolling seam to the wrong side. Press flat. Catchstitch the lower raw edge of the flap facing to the pocket. Topstitch (if desired) around pocket edge, stitching 6 mm to 1 cm (1/4'' to 3/8'') from the edge before the pocket is applied to the garment. Stitching must be from right side on both pocket and flap to maintain the same appearance (Figure 13–25).

7. Baste the pocket into position on the garment and machine stitch just under the flap along the catchstitching at lower flap edge (a).

8. Press flap down over pocket opening and topstitch across pocket top the same distance from top of flap as the previous stitching was from the edge (Figure 13–26).

Gusset or Bellows Pocket

The gusset or bellows pocket derives its name from the pleat along the sides and bottom that allows it to expand. It lies flat when not in use and is found primarily in sportswear. Usually there is a flap attached to the garment that keeps the top of the pocket flat.

Use Figure 13–27 as a guide to make your own pattern. If the fashion fabric is firm, no interfacing is needed, but if more support is desired, use a fusible interfacing. Construct the pocket as follows:

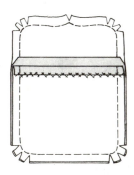

FIGURE 13–24
Stitching the Front and Back Pocket Pieces.

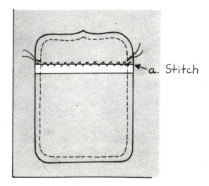

FIGURE 13–25
Topstitched Pocket Stitched to Garment.

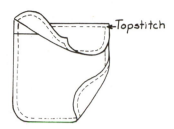

FIGURE 13–26
Completed Saddlebag Pocket.

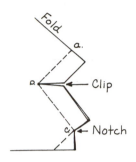

FIGURE 13–28
Stitching the Corner.

1. Press seam allowance under at top edge. Seam tape may be used to finish the seam edge on heavy or ravelly fabrics. Machine or hand stitch in place.

2. Fold pocket right sides together so that points b-b and c-c match (Figure 13–27). Stitch from cut edge to c, pivot and stitch to b, pivot and stitch to a, then backstitch (Figure 13–28). Fold the second corner and stitch in same manner.

3. Clip seam allowance to point b, notch at c (Figure 13–28). Trim seam and press open.

4. Turn point a to right side. Press foldlines so pleat is formed under pocket. Seam allowances will extend beyond pocket. Turn pocket wrong side up. Press seam allowances under so folded edge is even with

pocket edge. Miter top edge of seam. Inside fold may be stitched close to edge (Figure 13–29).

5. Place pocket in position on garment. Pin lower edge of expansion pleat to garment. Place a piece of interfacing behind upper corners for reinforcement. Stitch close to the edge of sides and bottom.

6. If a flap is used, construct flap following the previous instructions. Place the flap with its foldline slightly above the pocket edge. Turn flap up and stitch on top of previous stitching. Catchstitch or machine zigzag over lower raw edge of seam allowance that extends inside the pocket (Figure 13–30), or finish as for pocket with separate flap (Figure 13–19 through 13–22).

Note: The folds of the gusset may be topstitched to hold them in place. The flap is usually made with a buttonhole so it can be buttoned onto the pocket to hold the pocket closed (Figure 13–30).

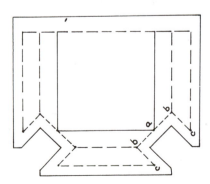

FIGURE 13–27
Bellows Pocket Pattern.

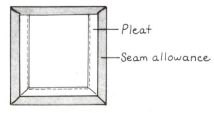

FIGURE 13–29
Inside of Completed Pocket.

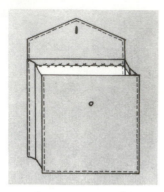

FIGURE 13–30
Pocket and Flap Applied to Garment.

Slashed Pockets

High quality tailored garments often have slashed pockets. When these are precision made they add greatly to the tailored appearance of a garment, but if they are poorly made, they can shout "homemade." Make a sample pocket on a scrap of your fashion fabric before you make one in your garment.

Slashed pockets are similar to fabric buttonholes except they are on a larger scale. A *double-welt* pocket has two welts, like the buttonhole lips. Each welt is commonly 6 mm (1/4'') wide but it may be wider or narrower and corded. It usually is straight, but the corded welt pocket may be curved (Figure 13–31). Single-welt pockets are of two types. (1) An *inside single welt* (similar in construction to the double welt) has a seam at the top of the welt and the ends are stitched into the ends of the opening like a buttonhole. (2) The *outside single welt* completely covers the opening and is stitched at the ends by hand. A very wide outside single welt is called a *stand* if it is turned upward (often it is shaped) or a *flap* if it is turned downward. The latter is the simplest type of flap pocket. The flap pocket may also be constructed like the inside single welt with

the flap inserted above the welt. Or, the flap may be inserted between the welts of the double-welt pocket so one welt is visible above the flap.

Standards for Slashed Pockets:

1. Corners must be square without a ravelly or a puckered appearance.

2. Pockets must be exactly "on grain" of the garment unless, for a decorative reason, they are on an angle.

3. Welts should be firm and have adequate body for garment.

4. The pocket must lie flat with surrounding bulk reduced as much as possible.

5. Paired pockets should be identical in size and shape.

6. Welt or flap is cut on grain or on true bias if a special effect is desired.

7. Pocket and garment lie smoothly over body curve when worn.

8. Paired pockets are placed the same distance from the front edge.

9. In patterned fabrics, pocket should match the garment at the front edge. If the pocket crosses a seam or dart, total matching is impossible.

General Information for All Slashed Pockets

Since all slashed pockets are similar in construction to fabric buttonholes, reference will be made to buttonholes to prevent extensive repetition. The following information is applicable to all slashed pockets.

1. A lightweight interfacing should be used to reinforce the opening of all slashed pockets. A nonwoven or woven interfacing may be used, but it must be stable on the crosswise grain. If the fabric does not show mark-off, a fusible interfacing prevents fraying and stabilizes the opening. Since it will be sewed in a seam that must be pressed

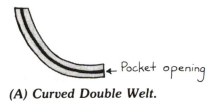

(A) Curved Double Welt.

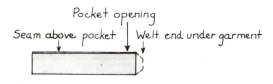

(B) Inside Single Welt.

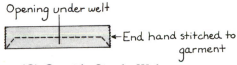

(C) Outside Single Welt.

(D) Stand Pocket.

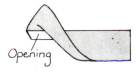

(E) Simple Flap.

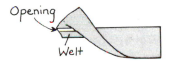

(F) Single Welt with Flap.

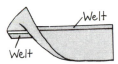

(G) Double Welt with Flap.

FIGURE 13–31
Types of Slashed Pockets.

back, it should be lightweight. Hair canvas is not recommended because it is too resilient to be pressed flat.

2. Cut the interfacing about 2.5 cm (1'') wider and longer than the pocket rectangle formed by the pocket stitching lines. Mark the rectangle on the interfacing. Then match it to the rectangle marked on the wrong side of the fashion fabric, and fuse or baste in place.

3.   The *pocket bag* or pouch is usually of lining fabric in women's garments and of a durable cotton pocketing or twill in menswear. A strip of the fashion fabric is sewed across the visible part of the pocket bag or the entire side of the bag may be made of the fashion fabric (for the double- or single-welt pocket without flap). When a pocket opening is parallel to the lower edge of the garment, the fashion fabric section is sewed to the upper edge, the lining section to the lower edge. In a perpendicular pocket, the fashion fabric section is sewed to the back edge, the lining to the front edge of the opening. The bag is usually cut as a rectangle on straight grain whether the pocket is straight or angled. However, for the angled pocket, the end of the bag that attaches to the welts will be cut on an angle.

Note: After the pocket is completed and before stitching the pocket bag, check to see that the bag will fit above the hem of the garment and not interfere with buttons and buttonholes. The pocket bag may be shortened by stitching across the bottom or angled at the sides or given rounded corners. Lint is more easily removed from pockets with rounded corners than square corners.

4.   The welt, stand, or flap may be cut on the same grain as the garment. The ends of flap pockets will usually be on straight lengthwise grain whether the flap is placed straight or on an angle. The welt without a flap may be square at the ends even though it is placed on an angle. Thus, the welt ends would not match the garment grain. For interfacing, a fusible applied to the upper layer is recommended. On women's hipline pockets the welt or flap is usually about 15 cm (6'') long and men's are about 17.5 cm (7'') long. The following instructions are given for the 15-cm (6'') pocket; add 2.5 cm (1'') to measurements for the 17.5-cm (7'') pocket. The breast pocket is usually 9 cm to 11.5 cm (3 1/2'' to 4 1/2'') long.

Welt (Outside Single), Stand, or Flap Pockets

In these pockets a separate piece is completely constructed and then attached to either the top or the bottom of the pocket opening. The flap is attached to the top while the welt or stand is attached to the bottom. The welt or stand is attached to the outside of the garment at its ends. The flap is attached only at the top. The outside welt is commonly used for men's and women's breast pockets. The stand pocket is simply an enlarged outside welt that is often shaped differently from a rectangle.

Constructing the Welt, Stand, or Flap:

1.   Construct *flaps* according to instructions at the beginning of this chapter. The finished flap should be exactly the same length as the pocket opening or about 3 mm (1/8'') longer if the flap goes over a curved area. After the flap has been turned and pressed, press the seam allowance toward the facing being careful that all layers of flap are smooth. (Refer to Figure 13–19.) Baste along seamline, then trim seam to 6 mm (1/4''). This will allow the flap to lie flat.

2.   Construct a pocket *stand* like the flap except it may require a slightly firmer interfacing. The stand does *not* need to be rolled before the raw edges are basted together since the seam allowance does not need to turn back against the stand.

3.   The *welt* is usually no more than 3.2 cm (1 1/4'') wide for a breast pocket, but may be wider for hipline pockets. Welts are usually placed on the same grain as the garment but may be placed on the crosswise or bias for special effects. The welt is constructed as follows:

   a.   Cut the welt the length of the pocket opening plus two seam allowances and twice the desired width plus two seam allowances. The welt is usually folded, creating a self-facing, but for heavy fabrics or for wide welts, it may be constructed with a seam on three sides, and the lining fabric used for the facing. For a lined welt, follow the instructions at the beginning of this chapter for pocket flaps.

b. Cut interfacing the size of the finished welt. Fuse, or catchstitch non-fusible interfacing, to wrong side of welt (Figure 13–32).

c. Fold welt in half lengthwise with right sides together. Ease the interfaced side slightly at side seamlines so it is slightly longer than the facing side. This will allow the seams to roll under at the ends. Stitch from the fold to the seamline, and backstitch at the seamline (Figure 13–33).

d. Grade seams at ends of welt. Press seam open, turn and press again. Baste long cut edges together along seamline. Trim seam to 6 mm (1/4'').

4. If _welt, stand,_ or _flap_ is to be topstitched, complete topstitching. Trim diagonally across the corners of the seam allowance (Figure 13–34).

Constructing the Pocket:

1. Interface the pocket opening by fusing or basting a rectangle of interfacing about 7.5 cm (3'') deep and slightly longer than the pocket behind the pocket rectangle. Mark exact size of rectangle on the interfacing. If the ends of the pocket rectangle are square, angle them slightly so the ends of the opening will not show at the end of the finished flap or welt. The lower edge for flap, or upper edge for welt or stand, should be about 5 mm (3/16'') shorter at each end (Figure 13–35).

2. With right sides together, baste welt or stand to garment matching seamline to lower edge of pocket rectangle. Baste flap to upper edge (Figure 13–36). If fabric is patterned (plaids, stripes, checks), check to see that the pattern matches.

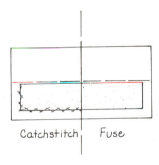

Catchstitch | Fuse

FIGURE 13–32
Interfaced Welt.

FIGURE 13–33
Upper Side of Welt Eased to Facing.

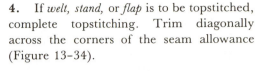

FIGURE 13–34
Completed Welt.

Flap attaches here
5mm (3/16")
Flap pocket

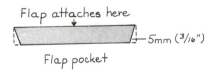

Welt or stand attaches here
5mm (3/16")
Welt or stand pocket

FIGURE 13–35
Angled Ends of Rectangle.

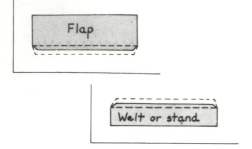

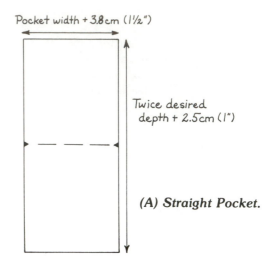

Pocket width + 3.8 cm (1½")

Twice desired depth + 2.5cm (1")

(A) Straight Pocket.

FIGURE 13–36
Position on Garment.

3. To form a pocket bag from lining fabric, cut a rectangle two times the depth of the desired pocket plus 2.5 cm (1'') and the width of the pocket plus 3.8 cm (1 1/2''). See Figure 13–37, A. For the angled pocket reduce the depth of the back edge of the pocket to coincide with the angle of the pocket (Figure 13–37, B). Fold rectangle in half lengthwise and mark the foldline with clips on each end.

4. With the *right* sides together, place the center of the rectangle (marked with clips) on the top edge of the pocket rectangle. The welt or flap now lies between the garment and lining. Pin the lining in place. From the *wrong* side of garment, stitch across the top and bottom of rectangle, ending exactly at the end of the welt or flap and the marked rectangle. Check to see that both ends of stitched line are even. Pull threads to wrong side and tie, leaving long thread ends (Figure 13–38).

5. Carefully cut through all layers of fabric, as you would for a buttonhole (Figure 13–39). End the center cut 1 cm (3/8'') from each end of rectangle. Direct the point of scissors to the middle of the end stitch and cut. Clip exactly to the corner, or the corner will not turn squarely.

6. Turn pocket to *wrong* side of garment. Carefully press the seam allowances away from opening. Turn flap or welt in its permanent position and press.

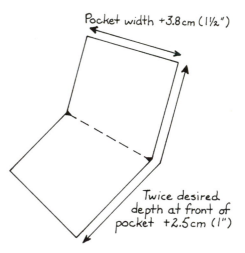

Pocket width + 3.8 cm (1½")

Twice desired depth at front of pocket + 2.5cm (1")

(B) Angled Pocket.

FIGURE 13–37
Pocket Bag.

7. Fold the upper pocket section down over the opening, in line along the sides with the lower section, and pin (Figure 13–40). If lower pocket edges are not even, trim. Check size and shape of pocket bag as previously discussed.

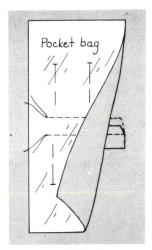

FIGURE 13–38
Stitching Top and Bottom
of Pocket Rectangle.

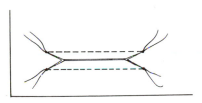

FIGURE 13–39
Cutting the Pocket.

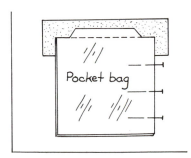

FIGURE 13–40
Bag Pinned in Position.

end of pockets catching knots, then proceed to stitch around the bag (Figure 13–41).

9. Turn *welt* or *stand* upward, and if it will be worn over a curved area such as the bustline, place over a similar curve. Pin ends of welt or stand and slipstitch in place (Figure 13–42). Be sure the opening is com-

8. With right side up, flip garment back to expose the pocket. Fold the end of the welt or flap so it will not be caught when the end of the pocket is stitched. Hold long thread ends taut and stitch across the triangle at

FIGURE 13–41
Stitching the End of the Pocket
and the Bag.

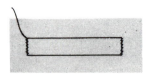

FIGURE 13–42
Slipstitch Ends of Welt or Stand.

pletely covered at the ends. The *flap* has been pressed down and usually needs no further stitching. If necessary, it may be tacked at the top corners.

Double-Welt Pockets (With or Without Flap)

Any method for making fabric buttonholes may be used to make a double-welt pocket, but two methods, adaptations of the butterfly and the five-line buttonholes, will be given. Either method may have a flap inserted. The butterfly method may also be used for an inside single-welt pocket. Both of these methods produce a pocket with inside or set-in welts (i.e., the ends of the welts are stitched under the garment fabric, and there is a seam that lies at the top of the single welt). Some consider the double-welt pocket with a flap to be the epitome of tailoring and quite difficult, but the following methods simplify the procedure.

The choice of method will be determined by the fabric and personal preference. The five-line method is not suitable for fabrics that show basting marks. The butterfly method is more suitable than the five-line method for heavy fabrics, primarily because the seam allowances can be graded at wider intervals and will lie flatter. The butterfly method also will be the easier if matching must be done.

For both methods the welts should be interfaced unless (1) the fabric is very firm, (2) a flap will be used, or (3) the welts will be corded. The lining serves as the interfacing in the five-line method. For the butterfly method use lightweight fusible or nonfusible interfacing similar to that used to face the pocket opening.

Flaps should be constructed according to directions given earlier, but if matching is necessary or your stitching is sometimes not perfectly accurate, cut and construct the flaps after the double welt is completed. In this way there is better assurance of an exact

fit and match since the flap must *exactly* fit the opening.

Five-Line Double-Welt Pocket (With or Without Flap). The five-line method is satisfactory for women's garments if the fabric is lightweight. It is also excellent for the inside pockets on men's jackets and men's back pants pockets.

1. Cut a piece of lightweight interfacing (preferably a nonfusible nonwoven that will not ravel and will be easy to mark) 7.5 cm (3'') wide and 20 cm (8'') long. Pencil a line lengthwise through the center, then draw two lines 6 mm (1/4'') apart on either side (Figure 13–43). These guidelines will make each welt 6 mm (1/4'') in width. The spacing of the lines determines the width of the welts, thus they can be varied according to the design. Pockets with flaps may have slightly narrower welts, those without flaps slightly wider welts. Heavy fabrics necessitate slightly wider welts than lightweight fabrics.

2. Place interfacing on pattern (or garment) and mark ends of pocket opening. Lines 2 and 4 will match the pocket rectangle. Mark ends between these lines to form a box. Use interfacing as a pattern to cut the welt from a piece of fashion fabric. The end of the pocket denotes the lengthwise straight of grain in many instances, but check the pocket marking on the garment to be sure the grain is correct. The welts will usually match the grain of the garment. (See

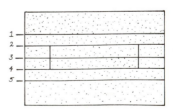

FIGURE 13–43
Guidelines Drawn on Interfacing.

Figure 13–31.) However, they may be placed on the bias for a straight pocket or on the straight grain for an angled pocket.

3. Cut the lining for pocket bag 20 cm (8'') wide and 38 cm to 46 cm (15'' to 18'') long. *For an angled pocket,* fold the rectangle in half (it will be about square), and trim the cut edges opposite the fold on the same angle as the pocket placement line. *Note:* Illustrations are given for the straight pocket, but the relationship of the pocket opening to the cut edge will be the same for the angled pocket.

4. Place welt piece right side up on right side of lining at one end. Stitch raw edges together and zigzag over raw edge of fashion fabric (Figure 13–44).

Note: For a double-welt pocket *without a flap,* cut a 7.5 cm by 20 cm (3'' by 8'') strip of fashion fabric on the same grain as the garment and apply it to the other end of the pocket lining in the same manner. For a patterned fabric, wait to cut and stitch this piece to the lining until the pocket welts are completed so it may be matched. If *cotton pocketing* is used for the pocket bag (as in a man's garment) and there is a flap, cut a piece of lining fabric and apply it to the pocket bag. Turn the edge of the lining under and stitch rather than zigzag over the raw edge; otherwise the edge will ravel.

5. Place interfacing on wrong side of gar-

ment matching the pocket rectangle. Be sure the ends of the rectangle are on straight of grain unless otherwise designed. Pin. With small stitches begin in the center of line 2 (Figure 13–45) and stitch to the end mark, pivot, stitch end to line 4, pivot, and continue to stitch around rectangle overlapping stitches at the starting point.

6. On right side of garment, center the welt piece that is attached to the pocket bag over the stitched rectangle with the bag extending downward. Pin along edges. If matching is necessary, match at the upper front corner of rectangle.

7. To construct the pocket, follow the instructions for the five-line buttonhole, pages 159–160, Steps 6 through 11.

8. *If a flap is not used,* diagonally baste welts together so they lie in place. (For patterned fabric, refer to note above. *If a flap is used,* make the flap to exactly fit the opening, or it may be 2 mm (scant 1/16'') longer to curve over the lower welt. From *right* side, insert flap into opening, matching seamline of flap to stitching line of welt. Pin seam allowance of flap to welt only (Figure 13–46). Or, for exact matching hand baste from the *right* side in the seamline above the welt (Figure 13–47).

9. From the *wrong* side, turn upper welt seam allowance down and stitch on top of previous stitching to secure flap to welt (Figure 13–48, A). On wrong side, fold

FIGURE 13–44
Welt Piece Stitched to Pocket Bag.

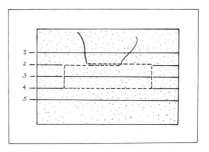

FIGURE 13–45
Stitching the Rectangle.

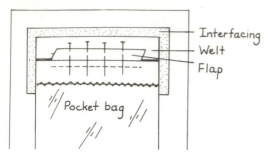

FIGURE 13–46
Seam Allowance of Flap Pinned to Welt.

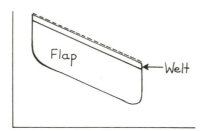

FIGURE 13–47
Flap Hand Basted to Welt.

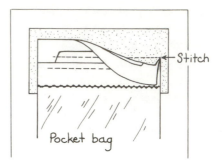

(A) Stitching Flap to Welt.

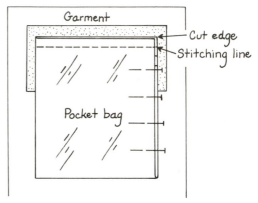

(B) Pocket Bag Folded for Stitching.

FIGURE 13–48

pocket up so cut edge matches cut edge of welt. Pin seam allowances. Fold garment back to expose upper welt stitching and stitch on top of previous stitching to secure pocket lining. (Stitch as shown in Figure 13–48, B).

10.   Turn back the garment at the ends of pocket to expose each triangle. Gently pull threads which were knotted to make the corners of the pocket square. Stitch across knots and triangle and continue stitching pocket bag (Figure 13–49). Additional rows of stitching may be made across triangles to reinforce and flatten the ends of the pocket.

Butterfly Double- or Single-Welt Pocket (With or Without Flap). This method results in an inside single-welt pocket in which there is a seam at the open edge of the single-welt and the ends are stitched to the inside like a buttonhole.

Cut lining for pocket bag 20 cm (8'') wide and about 38 cm (15'') long. *For an*

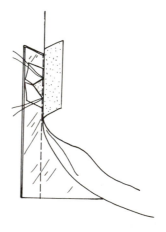

FIGURE 13–49
Stitching Pocket Ends and Bag.

angled pocket, refer to cutting instructions in Step 3 of the "Five-Line Double-Welt Pocket," page 194. Trace pocket rectangle from the pattern on the wrong side of one end of this piece. Center the rectangle 2.5 cm (1'') below the top edge (Figure 13–50). The rectangle is usually 1.3 cm (1/2'') wide which makes each welt 6 mm (1/4'') in width. As stated earlier, the width of the welts is determined by the rectangle width.

Note: If heavy pocketing fabric is used (as in menswear), place a 7.5-cm (3'') strip of lining or lightweight fabric, _right_ sides together, on one end of the pocket piece and stitch. Press seam toward lining. Draw the pocket rectangle from the pattern, on the wrong side of this fabric.

For a _pocket without a flap,_ apply a 7.5-cm by 20-cm (2'' by 8'') piece of fashion fabric right side up to the right side of the lining at the opposite end from the rectangle. Stitch raw edges together and zigzag over the raw edge of the fashion fabric (Figure 13–50). If fabric is patterned, this piece should be cut on the same grain as the garment, but wait to cut and apply it until the pocket has been completed so it may be easily matched.

Constructing the Welts:

1. Cut welts as follows:

    a. _Double welt._ Cut two welts each 5 cm by 20 cm (2'' by 8''). These usually match the grain of the pocket opening. However, they may be placed on the bias for a straight pocket or on the straight grain for an angled pocket. If pocket is slanted and welts are to be matched in a patterned fabric, make a pattern by tracing the pocket rectangle on a 5-cm by 20-cm (2'' by 8'') piece of paper. The end of the rectangle should be placed on the same grain as the end of the rectangle on the garment. For patterned fabric, use the center of the front end of the rectangle and the center of the welt as matching points.

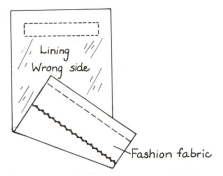

FIGURE 13–50
Pocket Rectangle Marked on Bag.

    b. _Single welt._ Cut one welt 7.5 cm by 20 cm (3'' by 8'') following the above instructions. If welt is slanted, match pattern at the top of the front end of the rectangle and the center of the welt strip.

2. Stabilize welts by fusing a lightweight interfacing to the wrong side or by including a piece of lightweight nonfusible interfacing. _Or,_ for slight stability without bulk, a strip of fusible web may be inserted after the butterfly is completed.

3. Prepare the welts as follows:

    a. _Double welts._ Place welts right sides together and machine baste lengthwise through the center forming a "butterfly." Open the butterfly so the wrong sides of each welt are together. Press flat (Figure 13–51).

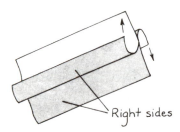

FIGURE 13–51
Butterfly for Double Welts.

b.   *Single welt.* Fold welt in half lengthwise, *wrong* sides together, and press. Cut edges may be basted together.

Making the Faced Opening:

1.   If fabric is very lightweight or loosely woven, apply a 7.5-cm by 20-cm (3'' by 8'') rectangle of interfacing to wrong side of fashion fabric behind pocket. Firm fabrics will be adequately stabilized by the lining fabric which faces the rectangular opening.

2.   Pin right side of pocket lining to right side of garment matching rectangles. Using small stitches, begin at the center of one long side, pivot at corners and accurately stitch around rectangle. Overlap stitches where they meet. (Refer to Figure 13–45.)

For a single-welt pocket with a flap, the ends of the welt may be angled in slightly so welt will not show at ends of flap. Redraw rectangle before stitching, so lower edge is about 5 mm (3–16'') shorter at each end (Figure 13–52).

Completing Faced Opening and Applying Welts:

1.   Follow instruction for butterfly buttonhole, page 162 (Step 5) through page 164 (Step 4).

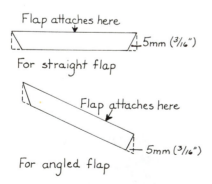

FIGURE 13–52
Faced Opening for Single-Welt Pocket with Flap.

FIGURE 13–53
Lower Edge of Butterfly Attached to Bag.

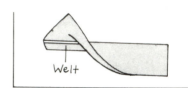

FIGURE 13–54
Single Welt with Flap.

2.   Turn pocket away from garment. Grade seam below lower welt so outside layer is longest. Zigzag over cut edge to secure seam allowance to pocket bag. Be careful not to catch garment (Figure 13–53).

Completing the Pocket:

1.   *If a flap is not used,* diagonally baste the double welts together so they lie in place. Follow the last two paragraphs in the discussion of the five-line double-welt method, pages 195 and 196 to complete the pocket.

2.   *If flap is used,* with either a single or a double welt, follow the steps described on page 195 to construct and insert the flap and complete the pocket. *Note:* For the flap with a single welt, the welt is hidden under the flap and is not visible unless the flap is raised (Figure 13–54).

Curved   Corded   Pocket.   Corded pockets may be made parallel or perpendicular to the floor, on a diagonal, or on a curve. A straight corded pocket may be made by the butterfly or five-line patch pocket methods by reducing the width of the welts and inserting cord. A curved corded pocket can be made only by the following method.

Usually the fabric for the cording is cut on the true bias, but if the fabric has a stripe and the stripe is used for a trim, the fabric may be cut on the straight grain. Cut in the same direction diagonally across the fabric so that the grain will all run one way.

Constructing the Corded Pocket:

1. For each pocket cut two bias strips the pocket length plus 2.5 cm (1'') for seams and 2.5 cm (1'') wide.

2. Fold the bias closely around a cord that is slightly smaller than the desired finished cording. With matching thread and fine hand stitches, or by machine using the zipper foot, stitch as close as possible to the cord.

3. Cut off surplus seam allowance until seam edge from basting is equal in width to corded edge from basting (Figure 13–55).

4. Fuse or baste interfacing in place behind the pocket opening. Mark the pocket position with a single line of basting (Figure 13–56).

5. Place the two corded strips along marked pocket position with cut edges touching. Pin and baste into position (Figure 13–57). Baste across the pocket ends, having bastings at right angles to pocket opening. Ease the cord slightly on the upper edge (a) and hold cord slightly close (stretch) on the lower pocket edge (b). This will allow the two corded edges to match

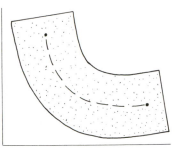

FIGURE 13–56
Basted Pocket Position.

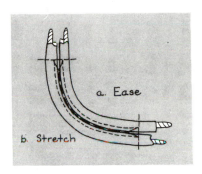

FIGURE 13–57
Cording Positioned on Right Side
of Garment.

smoothly when pocket is cut and cords meet along the opening.

6. With narrow zipper foot and small stitches, stitch closely against the cord, forming two parallel rows of stitching. Leave long thread ends. Tie and *do not* trim. After both inner and outer edges of pocket are stitched, survey each from the wrong side to check the accuracy of width between the stitchings.

7. Cut through the center to within 6 mm (1/4'') of end of stitching. Holding seam allowance of cording out of the way, diagonally cut to the middle of each end stitch (Figure 13–58). Turn the seams through the opening to the wrong side. Clip lower seam allowance to allow the pocket to lie flat. Notch the upper allowance, if necessary, to reduce bulk.

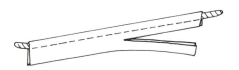

FIGURE 13–55
Trimmed Cording.

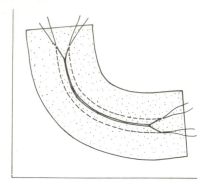

FIGURE 13–58
Cutting the Pocket.

8. From the right side, tailor baste the two corded edges together along the pocket length and press carefully. *Note:* The cord on the lower side may be pulled slightly to conform to the curved opening. The bias covering the cord on the upper side may be stretched slightly.

9. With the garment right side up, place the corded pocket next to the feed dog, fold the garment back, grasp the ends of knotted thread and hold taut to square corners, and stitch across the triangles at the ends of the pocket, catching the knots. This end stitching should start at the cut edge of the corded strip, come across the exact corner of the triangle, curve slightly around to the other corner, and continue off the edge. Trim away excess cord inside the bias at pocket ends to relieve bulk. Stitch back and forth over the triangle several times to flatten the ends (Figure 13–59).

Constructing and Attaching the Pocket Bag:

1. Make the pocket bag in the desired shape with the opening edge on the same grain as the pocket opening. Cut the upper pocket bag of lining and have the top edge end at the line of the pocket opening. From fashion fabric cut the lower bag piece so it extends twice the width of the cording above the pocket opening (Figure 13–60).

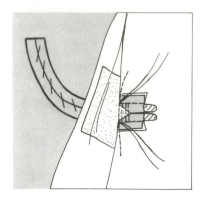

FIGURE 13–59
Stitching the Pocket Ends.

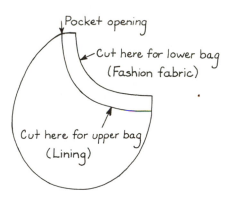

FIGURE 13–60
Cutting the Pocket Bag.

2. Staystitch along pocket opening of lining bag the width of the cording from the edge. Clip to staystitching. Place right side of bag piece against lower seam allowance of pocket with staystitching on top of previous stitching. Baste reverse curves together (Figure 13–61). With lining piece down, fold the garment back to expose the stitching line and stitch on top of previous stitching to secure lining.

3. Pin right side of fashion fabric bag against the upper seam allowance of the

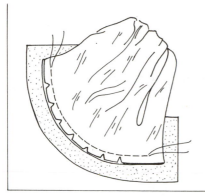

FIGURE 13–61
Bag Lining Basted to Lower Seam
Allowance of Pocket.

FIGURE 13–62
Stitching the Pocket Bag.

pocket. With the pocket piece down, fold the garment back to expose the stitching line. Stitch on top of previous stitching to secure the bag (Figure 13–62).

4. Baste the edges of the two bag sections together and stitch from end to end, catching through triangles at ends of pockets (Figure 13–62).

5. Decorative tacks, bar tacks, or fabric triangles may be used at each pocket end for a finishing touch and to reinforce the pocket ends against strain (Figure 13–63).

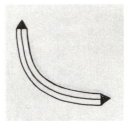

FIGURE 13–63
Decorative Tacks at Ends
of Corded Pocket.

Inseam Pockets

The inseam pocket is made in a construction seam of the garment. It may be invisible, and thus is the least obvious type of pocket, or it may have a welt or topstitching added for decoration. Inseam pockets are often used in women's garments when an inconspicuous pocket is desired, but seldom are they used in menswear.

Standards for Inseam Pockets:

1. The line of the seam should appear to be continuous.

2. Topstitching, if used, should appear to be continuous.

3. The edge of the pocket should be firm and not stretch.

4. The opening should be placed in a functional position.

5. The welt used with an inseam pocket should be:

    a. Firm and smooth with inconspicuous seams along the edges.

    b. Identically shaped to a paired welt.

    c. An appropriate size and shape, and placed to enhance the garment design.

Inseam pockets may be constructed in two ways (Figure 13–64). (1) The pocket bag may be attached at the regular seamline

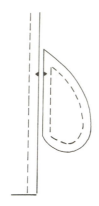

(A) Bag Attached at Seamline.

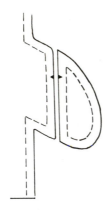

(B) Bag Attached to Extension.

FIGURE 13–64

(A); or (2) the pocket bag may be attached to an extension on the garment piece, (B). The use of the extension is preferable for heavy fabrics and has the advantage of not having a seam on the under layer at the opening to the pocket.

The *inseam pocket* without a welt may be constructed in either way, but if the separate inseam pocket is used, the lower bag piece must be cut from fashion fabric or have a piece of fashion fabric applied along the opening.

The *inseam pocket with a welt* must have a seam along the upper pocket opening. An extension may be used on the back (or lower) seam if desired.

Reinforcing the Opening:

When a welt is not used, the front or outside seamline (foldline) should be reinforced with tape to keep it from stretching.

1. Cut a piece of tailor's tape, straight seam tape, or a strip of lining selvage 5 cm (2'') longer than the pocket opening.

2. Place the tape on the wrong side of the fabric, centered in the pocket opening, with an edge against the seamline or foldline and tape in the seam allowance or pocket extension (Figure 13–65).

3. Stitch 3 mm (1/8'') from the edge of the tape closest to the seamline.

Cutting the Pocket Bag:

1. In tailored garments the pocket bag is usually made of the lining fabric. If a sturdier pocket is desired, the lining fabric may be backed or underlined with a firmly woven cotton. These two fabrics may be quilted together, or simply basted together and constructed as one fabric.

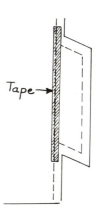

FIGURE 13–65
Taping the Opening.

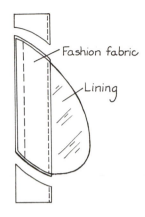

FIGURE 13–66
Fashion Fabric Strip Applied
to Pocket Bag.

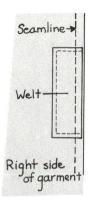

FIGURE 13–67
Attaching the Welt.

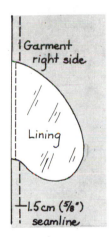

FIGURE 13–68
Upper Bag Attached with 1-cm
(3/8") Seam.

2. Cut four (two for each pocket) shaped pocket bag pieces of lining fabric for the inseam pocket with a welt.

3. For an inseam pocket without a welt in which the under pocket bag attaches at the regular seamline of garment, cut the lower bag of fashion fabric if it is lightweight. If fashion fabric is heavy, cut a facing strip of fashion fabric 5 cm (2") wide by the length of the pocket opening plus 7.5 cm (3") for each pocket. Turn under 6 mm (1/4") on one long edge and press, or to reduce bulk, zigzag over the raw edge when applying to lining. Pin facing right side up on right side of pocket piece (lining) with cut edges even. Stitch close to the folded edge of facing strip. Baste raw edges together. Trim strip even with top and bottom of pocket (Figure 13–66).

Constructing the Inseam Pocket:

1. _If a welt is to be used,_ prepare a narrow, straight welt according to instruction on page 197, or prepare a larger, shaped welt according to instructions for pocket flap at the beginning of this chapter. Topstitch the welt, if desired. Place welt between pocket opening markings, right side of welt against right side of garment, cut edges even, and baste (Figure 13-67).

2. With right sides together, match pocket opening markings and stitch the upper bag piece to the reinforced front seamline or to the extension. For the inseam pocket without a welt, stitch a 1-cm (3/8") seam so the lining attaches 6 mm (1/4") from the seamline (Figure 13-68). (If welt is present, it lies between the garment and pocket bag, and stitching must be exactly on the seamline.)

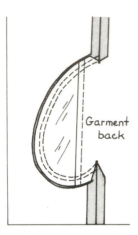

FIGURE 13–69
Extension Clipped to Allow Seam to Open.

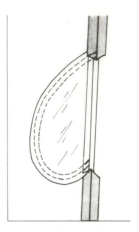

FIGURE 13–70
Stitching the Pocket Bag.

Grade the seam and press toward the pocket bag.

3. With right sides together, stitch lower bag piece to the back seam. Press the seam open if the seamline is continuous, or press the extension toward pocket bag.

4. Place garment pieces right sides together with pocket markings matched and pocket bags extended. Pin and stitch the seam above and below pocket opening. Reinforce by backstitching at each end of the opening. Press the garment seam open; press the pocket toward the front. The back seam allowance will need to be clipped to allow the seam to lie flat (Figure 13–69).

5. Pin pocket sections together. Double stitch to reinforce the pocket bag (Figure 13–69 or 13–70).

6. *Topstitching.* If the entire seam, including pocket opening, is to be topstitched, (1) topstitch seam above and below pocket opening. Leave long thread ends, pull to back and tie. (2) Topstitch pocket opening matching stitching exactly to stitching above and below opening (place opening over free

arm on machine, if available). Leave long thread ends so they can be threaded into a needle if an additional stitch is needed to join stitches. Pull threads to wrong side and tie. Stitching should appear to be continuous.

7. *Welt.* Slipstitch the ends of the welt securely in place. Position stitches slightly under the edge so they do not show. Or, on lightweight fabrics the ends may be machine stitched if the welt has been topstitched.

Pocket Inset in a Design Line

A pocket placed in a horizontal or slanted design line of a garment is made in the same manner as the previously described inseam pocket. Brief instructions follow for the pocket in a slanted front seam.

1. Cut lower pocket bag as part of side section, if possible (Figure 13–71). If not, a bag of fashion fabric may be attached by stitching a 1-cm (3/8'') seam so that the seam edge does not show when the pocket is finished (Figure 13–72). Press seam open.

2. Cut upper pocket bag of lining fabric (Figure 13–73). Or, it may be cut as an ex-

FIGURE 13–71
Lower Bag Cut with Garment.

FIGURE 13–73
Upper Pocket Bag.

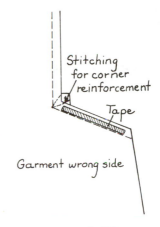

FIGURE 13–74
Tape Placed Along Seamline.

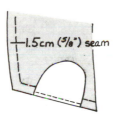

FIGURE 13–72
Lower Bag Attached with 1-cm
(3/8") Seam.

tension of the front. The top of the separate pocket bag matches the angle and grain of the pocket opening.

3.   Place a stay tape on the wrong side of the garment, one edge touching the seamline (or foldline if the pocket is cut with front) with the tape within the seam allowance. Stitch along both edges of tape (Figure 13–74).

4.   Reinforce the corner at the turn of the seam. The fabric patch reinforcement (des-

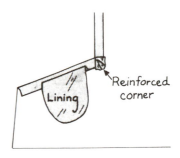

FIGURE 13–75
Upper Bag Attached to Garment with
1-cm (3/8") Seam.

cribed in Chapter 7) is recommended for strength.

5.   Baste the lining pocket bag section into position with right sides together. Stitch a 1-cm (3/8'') seam instead of a 1.5-cm (5/8'') seam. This prevents the bag's showing at the folded pocket edge when finished.

6.   Turn the seam edge along seamline and press (Figure 13–75).

7.   Complete the pocket by following the instructions for the inseam pocket beginning with Step 4. A flap may be added as shown in Figure 13–76.

FIGURE 13–76
Design Line with Flap.

An ideal interfacing for traditionally tailored garments is hair canvas which contains animal hair. It is considered ideal because the hair (often goat hair) will cling to the wool fashion fabric and thus, it becomes as one fabric in the way it feels. Hymo is a general name given to interfacings of this type. The technique used for interfacings containing animal hair is also applicable to interfacings without hair content. Another interfacing, wigan, as used in this chapter indicates a lightweight, firm, cotton fabric and is similar to muslin of the same weight. Wigan serves as an interfacing across the back shoulders and is interchangeable with muslin in its use.

At this point in construction (1) your garment has been underlined (if necessary); (2) staystitching has been completed; (3) seams (except shoulder and underarm) and darts have been stitched and pressed; and (4) the garment has been adjusted for any changes made during fitting. (Identical changes must be made on the interfacings.)

In addition the interfacings have been shrunk and pressed on grain, cut to suit your garment needs, marked along seamlines with tracing wheel and carbon. *Note:* If the fashion fabric is white or pastel in color, be careful about using carbon for marking. In this case use the very lightest colored carbon that will show on the hymo. In case of doubt, tailor tacks may be used more safely.

Application of Front Interfacing (Hymo)

Before the interfacing can be applied, it must be shaped to conform to the shape of the garment. The garment and interfacing are then placed together so they conform to the body curves.

14
TRADITIONAL METHOD FOR APPLYING SUPPORTIVE MATERIALS

Stitching Darts and Seams

There are several methods for handling darts in the front section of a garment where hymo interfacing is used. Because hymo may be a relatively heavy interfacing, depending upon the selection for your fashion fabric, darts must be stitched in a different manner to reduce bulk. Any of the three methods shown are applicable to any dart or seam in heavy to medium interfacings. While Method I may take longer to construct, it will produce a flatter surface than the other methods.

Method I:

1. Cut out any marked darts (Figure 14–1).

2. Cut a strip of wigan or muslin on the lengthwise grain 2.5 cm (1'') wide and 2.5 cm (1'') longer than the dart. Crease or draw a line down the center length of the strip to use as a guide for the next step.

3. Butt the two cut edges of the dart together at the center of the wigan strip. Place pins at right angles to the cut edges through both layers of fabric.

FIGURE 14–1
Cutting Marked Darts.

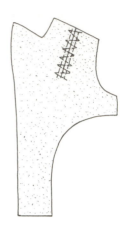

FIGURE 14–2
Butted Cut Edges Stitched
with Underlay.

4. Secure the cut edges of the dart to the strip by stitching with (1) multiple zigzag through the center, then straight stitch or zigzag along each side. Or, (2) straight stitch about 3 mm (1/8'') from each cut edge, stitching downward on both lines. Then stitch back and forth over the cut edges to secure them. The latter method is for straight-stitch machines. (See Figure 14–2.)

5. Press over a curved surface.

Method II:

1. Cut down the center of the marked dart. Overlap stitching lines and pin.

2. Place a small piece of wigan abut 2.5 cm (1'') square at lower end (point) of dart.

3. Stitch downward on the stitching line of the dart. At the point where lines cannot overlap, zigzag over that area through the wigan to give sufficient support and press (Figure 14–3).

Method III:

This is used primarily for curved design seamlines.

1. Overlap stitching lines, carefully matching notches over curved areas where

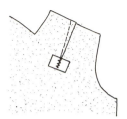

FIGURE 14–3
Stitching Lines Overlapped with
Patch Reinforcement.

curves are of two different arcs. Pin and hand baste.

2. Test before stitching by laying the interfacing inside the wool garment. *They must fit each other exactly.*

3. From the shoulder stitch downward on the stitching line. Stitch another row 3 mm (1/8'') from the first row.

4. Trim interfacing to within 3 mm (1/8'') of stitched lines on both right and wrong sides and press (Figure 14–4).

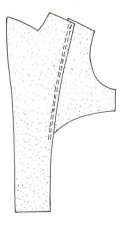

FIGURE 14–4
Overlapped Stitching Lines
on Curved Seam.

Positioning Interfacing

If the front was to be underlined, the underlining was cut like the area *not* covered by the interfacing plus 2.5 cm (1'') extra on the edge next to the interfacing. Refer to Chapter 5, Figure 5–17. There is no difference in the way the front interfacing is applied to the underlined or to the non-underlined garment. However, with the underlined garment first lay the underlining in place, pin and tailor baste it into position before applying the interfacing. After the interfacing is positioned, the two cut edges of the interfacing and the underlining will overlap. Permanently tailor baste these two overlapping edges together. Now, apply the interfacing as follows:

1. Place the garment front on the table with the right side down.

2. Lay the interfacing into position, matching vertical seams and darts. Pin in place. If there are no seams or darts, pin vertically through the interfacing.

3. Now, reverse position of the garment, thus allowing the right side to be uppermost. Place the curved bust area over a ham, or lacking that, lay the front over your bent knee. The piece should *not* remain on a flat surface at this time because the fashion fabric must assume an outer curved position. Thus, it will be eased slightly over the hymo, making the hymo extend slightly beyond the cut edges of the fashion fabric.

4. Pin the interfacing into place from the *right* side of the front section.

Establishing the Roll Line

The roll line is formed when the lapel, an extension of the front, turns back against the body. The turn is determined by the location of the top button and the position of the collar as it joins the lapel. Since the collar aids in controlling the roll line placement, it will be necessary to have the undercollar sec-

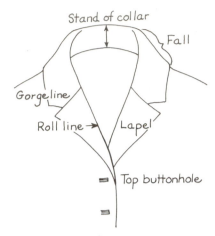

FIGURE 14–5
Establishing Lapel and Collar Roll Lines.

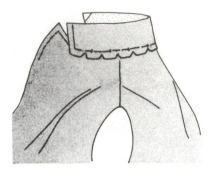

FIGURE 14–6
*Undercollar Pinned to Neckline
Before Marking Roll Line.*

tion ready to be pinned around the neckline. As you can see in Figure 14–5, the lapel roll line makes a continuous line around the collar. Thus the roll line of the lapel and the roll line of the collar can be established at the same time. Follow this procedure:

1. Baste front and back shoulder seams together.

2. Stitch the center back seam in the undercollar and press it open.

3. Stitch the collar interfacing, overlapping the seamlines at the center back. Trim the surplus seam allowance, leaving about 6 mm (1/4'') on each side. Lay the interfacing next to the undercollar and baste the neck edges together.

4. Clip the neckline seam of the undercollar, if necessary, to allow it to lie flat as it is placed around the neck of the garment.

5. Holding the garment uppermost, pin the undercollar to the neck of the garment, overlapping seamlines, and pin on the stitching line and parallel to it (Figure 14–6).

6. Place the garment on your figure or on a dress form and pin fronts together through

the buttoned area. With a marking pen or pencil (or with pins), lightly mark the collar and lapel roll line on the right-hand (overlapping) side from the top button to the center back of the collar (Figure 14–7).

7. At this time check to see that the seamline of the outer collar edge *covers* the back neckline seam. If it lacks a little, plan to reduce the width of the seam allowance on the outer collar edge.

8. Remove the garment, true the drawn lines and transfer the marking to the left side.

9. Separate collar, front and back.

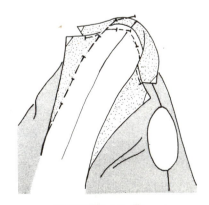

FIGURE 14–7
Marking Roll Line.

FIGURE 14–8
Marking in Preparation for Pad Stitching.

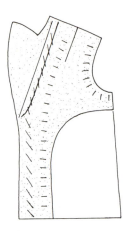

FIGURE 14–9
Basting Hymo to Garment.

Basting Interfacing

Garment with Lapel:

1. Draw a "second line" 2.5 cm (1") back from the roll line and parallel to it. About 3.8 cm (1 1/2") above the buttonhole, curve or slant this seamline to meet the roll line at the buttonhole location. This will allow the pad stitching to clear the top buttonhole (Figure 14–8).

2. From the hymo side, beginning 3.8 cm (1 1/2") below the shoulder seam, tailor baste along the second line with stitches about 2 cm (3/4") long. With each stitch pick up only a 3-cm (1/8") bite, making sure that you catch into the garment along with the hymo. Continue basting as far as the top buttonhole.

3. Lengthen basting stitches to 3.8 cm (1 1/2") and continue down the front about 2.5 cm (1") back of front edge seamline (Figure 14–9).

Note: Basting too close to the front edge will require some extra basting later since the hymo will be trimmed slightly more than

the seam allowance before the taping is done.

4. With the garment *right side out,* continue tailor basting with the 3.8-cm (1 1/2") stitch length. Over the bust area, baste over a curved surface to maintain the bust shape. Continue basting rows about 6.5 cm (2 1/2") apart until hymo is completely held in place (Figure 14–10). Notice that the tailor

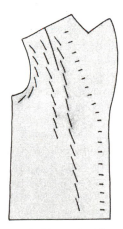

FIGURE 14–10
As Front Appears from Right Side After Basting.

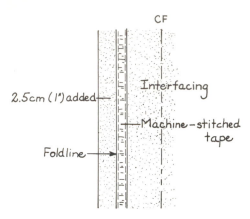

FIGURE 14–11
Taping Front of Extended Interfacing.

basting stitches appear like short straight stitches from the hymo side. If hymo is used to support the entire front, basting rows will continue the full length. Also note that the lapel area is free of any basting.

5. Baste around the armhole.

Garment Without Lapel:

If there is a seam along the front edge, baste the interfacing in place as explained in Steps 3, 4, 5. If the front facing is cut on the garment and you have followed instructions by cutting the hymo 2.5 cm (1'') beyond the front foldline of the garment (refer to Chapter 6, Figure 6–10), then your next step is to apply the tape before applying the hymo. Follow this procedure:

1. Press back the added 2.5 cm (1'') on the foldline.

2. Open the fold and place the shrunk and pressed tape on the hymo next to the foldline. Pin into position, making sure that the tape is not pulled too tightly. At the same time it must be taut enough to prevent the garment front from sagging and stretching. Baste, if necessary.

3. Machine stitch along both edges of the tape, stitching from neck to hem on both edges (Figure 14–11).

Application of Back Interfacing (Wigan or Muslin)

To apply the back interfacing, proceed as follows:

1. Fold and stitch shoulder or neck darts. *Do not slash open;* where strain is placed on the back, slashing would cause weakening of the dart, and these darts are usually small.

2. Press the dart toward the armhole, allowing the wigan dart to lie *next to* the garment dart, not on top of it.

3. With right side of the fabric next to a table, lay in the wigan, matching neckline and center back. From center back push wigan out slightly beyond edges of the fashion fabric. Pin in place.

4. With right side of garment out, try on the garment or place on a dress form to determine whether there is smoothness across the back—or whether the interfacing

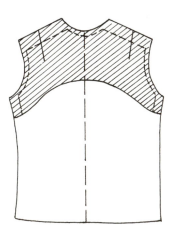

FIGURE 14–12
Applying Back Interfacing.

has been eased out too much, thus causing the interfacing to be tighter than the garment. The fashion fabric must fit smoothly with no wrinkling in either layer of fabric. Adjust, if necessary.

5.   Tailor baste 3.8 cm (1 1/2'') below the shoulder seam and near the seamline of the armholes (Figure 14–12).

Your next step is contingent upon the garment design. *With lapels* padstitch the lapels and tape the fronts (Chapter 15). *Without lapels,* construct the collar (Chapter 16).

15

PAD STITCHING AND TAPING

Traditionally, pad stitching and taping have been hand techniques. The contemporary method in which (1) fusing replaces hand pad stitching, and (2) the tape is applied by machine was discussed in Chapter 10, because these steps were necessarily completed earlier in the construction process. At this point in construction, however, hand or machine pad stitching and taping are done after the completion of the pockets and the buttonholes. Use *Critique #5* when the pad stitching and taping have been completed.

Pad Stitching

The advantages and disadvantages of hand and machine pad stitching were discussed in Chapter 9. If you are undecided as to which method to use, review that chapter. The function of *any* type of pad stitching is to give body, shape, and stability to the lapel or collar.

Standards for Pad Stitching:

The following standards may be applied when either the hand or machine method of pad stitching is used.

1.　Pad-stitched area has desired degree of roll and firmness.

2.　The interfacing lies smoothly over the fashion fabric.

3.　The interfacing and fashion fabric are held together at uniform intervals.

4.　Corners on the lapel or the collar roll under slightly and are somewhat firmer than the major portion of the lapel or collar.

Hand Pad Stitching

The pad stitch is used to fasten the interfacing into the garment and at the same time shape and roll the lapels and the undercollar. A well-handled hand pad-stitched area will permanently keep its shape. While hand pad stitching is barely visible on the fashion fabric side, it is used on lapels that are generally worn turned back. If a garment has a lapel that is sometimes worn closed and sometimes open, invisible hand pad stitching lightly done with few stitches will give body without incorporating a roll. This is very difficult in fabrics with a smooth, hard finish, however, because pad stitches, even though tiny, will tend to show a pricked effect on the garment side.

Types of Hand Pad Stitches. The pad stitching is essentially the same as diagonal or tailor basting, except that the stitch is smaller and remains permanently in the garment. The pad stitches may be arranged in either of two ways: (1) in a chevron pattern in which the stitches are placed in a straight line and (2) in a series of pyramids in which the apexes of the triangles are perpendicular to the roll line (Figure 15-1).

The chevron is more quickly stitched than the pyramids for some sewers. How-

ever, others prefer the pyramid. Both give good coverage, if properly done, but the pyramids tend to produce a smoother and firmer effect because of the proximity of the stitches to each other.

Guidelines for Hand Pad Stitching:

1. Use a matching, single thread no longer than 46 cm (18'') of silk or fine polyester and a small, fine needle (#10 recommended).

2. _Do not_ knot the thread end but use the fastening stitch to anchor the end (Chapter 7).

3. Use a thimble to protect your finger and to expedite your sewing.

4. Hold the garment so that the direction of the roll is parallel to the index finger of the left hand (right hand for left-handers).

5. Take a tiny stitch through the interfacing, catching a yarn (or fibers of a yarn) of the fashion fabric.

6. Make stitches shorter and rows closer together in areas where more firmness is desired (i.e., on sharp roll lines and the points of collars and lapels). The closer together the stitches, the firmer the area will be. For soft tailoring, stitches may be spaced farther apart.

7. The size of pad stitches are defined as:

    a. Small—stitches spaced 6 mm (1/4'') apart.

    b. Medium—stitches spaced 1 cm (3/8'') apart.

    c. Large—stitches spaced 1.3 cm (1/2'') apart.

8. _Do not pad stitch within the seam allowances._ Stop a minimum of 3 mm (1/8'') inside the seamline because the seam allowances will be trimmed before taping.

9. Practice pad stitching on a scrap of your fashion fabric and interfacing that are on the same grain as the area to be pad stitched in

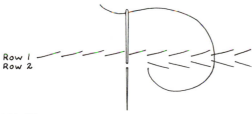

(A) Chevron.

(B) Pyramid.

FIGURE 15-1
Types of Hand Pad·Stitches.

FIGURE 15–2
Determining Interfacing Ease over Lapel.

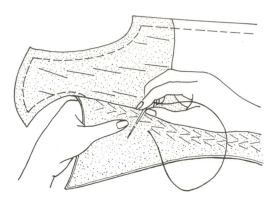

FIGURE 15–3
Holding Lapel for Pad Stitching.

your garment. This will help you to learn the stitch as well as to determine the amount of ease to incorporate.

Procedure for Hand Pad Stitching the Lapel. Before starting to pad stitch, test for the amount of ease that will be necessary to allow the lapel to roll as desired. Do this by rolling the lapel over your hand or over a magazine, allowing the interfacing to ease over the fashion fabric. Then pin at frequent intervals along the edges. Note that the garment fabric extends a bit beyond the interfacing edge (Figure 15–2). This should give an indication of the amount of easing that will be required to give the desired roll. If during the pad-stitching process this difference between the two edges *increases* considerably, then you are easing too much across the lapel surface. If *no difference* appears, you are not easing enough and no roll is being incorporated. Remove pins before beginning to pad stitch.

1. Hold the garment correctly by placing the interfacing side of the garment on the table with the front edges of the garment away from the table edge. Now, bring the

lapel forward over your hand with the thumb uppermost (Figure 15–3).

2. Start pad stitching on the "second" line and 3.8 cm (1 1/2″) below the shoulder seamline. (This space will permit the front interfacing to be placed over the shoulder seam after it is stitched and pressed.) Using either the chevron or pyramid type of stitches, fill in the area between the second line and the roll line, allowing the lapel to lie easy over your finger. The filled in area will permit the lapel to begin to turn before the roll line is reached. Make rows of stitching alternately from right to left, then left to right without changing the position of the lapel in your hand. Do not allow excessive ease in this area.

3. Determine the sharpness of the roll desired. A "man-tailored" garment has a lapel that lies quite flat with a sharp turn at the roll line. For a sharp, firm roll, make small pad stitches in the turn area and medium stitches in the flat part of the lapel. Other lapels may roll gradually so all of the lapel can be pad stitched with the same size stitches. Remember, the closer the stitches, the firmer the lapel will be.

4. At the roll line start to ease more by holding the garment fabric slightly taut over

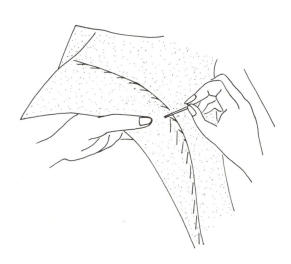

FIGURE 15-4
Position of Thumb to Push Ease.

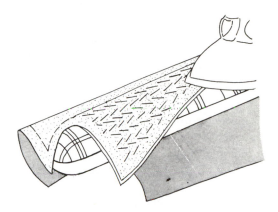

FIGURE 15-5
Pressing Pad-Stitched Lapel.

your finger and with your thumb push on the interfacing to incorporate more roll (Figure 15-4). Push at right angles to the roll line to prevent distortion of the grain of both layers of fabric. Check your stitching frequently to see that you are maintaining a smooth roll across the surface. Complete the lapel. The corner or point should tend to roll under slightly so use small stitches in this area.

5. Place the pad-stitched lapel over a curved surface (sleeve roll, ham, or press pad) and press to set the stitches into the fabric and to smooth the lapel (Figure 15-5).

Machine Pad Stitching

Only lapels that will *always* be worn turned back may be machine pad stitched because of the visibility of the stitching. Machine pad stitching may be done with (1) a straight stitch, (2) a plain zigzag stitch, or (3) a multiple zigzag or serpentine stitch.

1. Straight stitching works well if the rows are placed fairly close together (6 mm to 1

cm or 1/4'' to 3/8''), but bubbling is likely to occur between rows if they are placed too far apart. This will result in a bumpy surface. Also, straight stitching is apt to push the fabric ahead of the machine and distort the grain more than the other methods.

2. The plain zigzag gives good coverage, but the stitches tend to show on the fabric side.

3. The multiple zigzag gives the most coverage for each row of stitches because its short stitches progress on the diagonal. Thus it is less likely to push the fabric ahead. For these reasons it is often the preferred method.

Guidelines for Machine Pad Stitching:

1. With scraps of your fashion fabric and interfacing cut on the same grain as the collar or lapel, experiment with the type of stitch, the stitch length, and the distance between the rows of stitches before pad stitching your garment.

2. To reduce bulk, trim the seam allowance of the interfacing. To determine the amount to trim, roll the collar or the lapel and pin. Measure from the edge of the fashion fabric and mark the seam allowance on the interfacing. Trim on this line.

3. Use a standard stitch length for straight stitching or zigzag. For multiple zigzag, set your machine for a short stitch length and the maximum width. Again, the smaller the stitches and the closer the rows, the firmer the pad-stitched area will be.

4. Stitch with the straight of grain for areas that are to remain relatively flat.

5. To incorporate a roll, hold the fashion fabric taut (slightly stretched) at a right angle to the roll line. Stitch parallel to the roll line.

Preparation of Lapel for Machine Pad Stitching. If the garment front is underlined using the contemporary method in which the nonfusible interfacing has been sewed to the underlining, the underlining has been trimmed away from under the lapel. All layers are basted together along the roll line with the lapel left free (Chapter 10).

Machine Pad Stitching the Lapel:

The stitches should not extend closer than 3.8 cm (1 1/2'') below the shoulder seam so the interfacing may be placed over the shoulder seam after it is stitched and pressed.

1. Beginning at least 5 cm (2'') above the lower end of the roll line (more for a narrow lapel), stitch one line of multiple zigzag stitches (or two lines of straight or small zigzag stitches) about 1.3 cm (1/2'') to the garment side of the roll line. This row of stitching serves as a permanent basting before pad stitching the lapel.

2. Roll the lapel, interfacing side out, over your hand or over a folded magazine, allowing the interfacing to be eased over the fashion fabric. Thus, the cut edge of the interfacing will be shorter than the fashion fabric. (Refer to Figure 15–2.) Pin the cut edges. For a sharply creased lapel, flatten the fold of the magazine and repin the lapel along the outside of the roll.

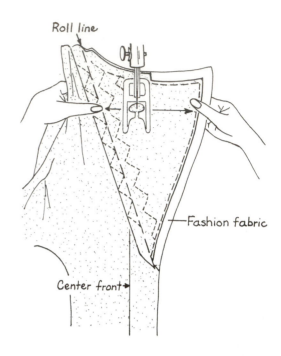

FIGURE 15–6
Fabric Being Stretched During Stitching.

3. Hand or machine baste 2 cm (3/4'') from the outer edge of the fashion fabric and remove the pins. Check the roll of the lapel. Are layers smooth when the lapel is rolled?

4. Trim the interfacing close to the basting to reduce bulk in the seam.

5. Determine the distance between the stitching lines by the amount of body desired and the type of stitch. For medium firmness, center the rows of multiple zigzag stitches about 1.3 cm (1/2'') apart. Straight stitches will need to be closer together.

6. Start to sew by holding the fashion fabric on each side of the machine needle (at right angles to the roll line) and slightly stretch across the area where the stitching will be placed (Figure 15–6). Beginning close to the roll line, make rows of stitching parallel to that line. Extend the stitching through the seam allowances where the interfacing has been trimmed away. The fashion fabric should conform to the eased interfacing to produce a smooth, rolled lapel.

7. Place the pad-stitched lapel over a curved surface (sleeve roll or press pad) and press to set the stitches into the fabric and smooth the lapel while retaining the desired shape. (Refer to Figure 15-5.)

Hand Application of Edge Tape

The function and methods of stabilizing the garment front and lapel edges with tape were discussed in Chapter 9. The machine method necessitates the application of tape to the interfacing _before_ the interfacing is applied to the garment. With the traditional hand method taping must be done _after_ the interfacing has been applied and the pad stitching has been completed.

Standards for Hand Taping:

1. The edge of the tape is firm and resists stretching.

2. The tape lies flat and smooth and is attached along both edges.

3. Hand stitches are not visible on the right side.

Preparing the Front for Taping. At this point the interfacing has been applied to the garment front and pad stitching, if used, has been completed and pressed.

1. If the lapel has been hand pad stitched, measure and mark with pencil about 2 cm (3/4'') from the cut edge of the fashion fabric, starting at the end of the gorgeline (the point where the collar attaches to the lapel as shown in Chapter 14, Figure 14-5) and extending to the lower edge of the front.

2. Trim on the marked line. If a jacket is curved at the lower front, trim around the curve.

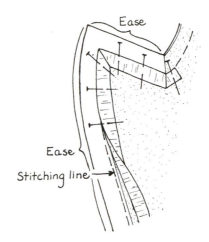

FIGURE 15–7
Taping Lapel.

3. Shrink the tape and then press. Pull on the tape as you press, since it is necessary to remove all of the stretch before applying it to the garment. Keep the tape on a straight line since the edge of the tape will form the stitching line when attaching the facing.

Procedure for Taping:

1. Lay the garment flat on the table with the interfacing up.

2. Pin the tape in place, starting 1 cm (3/8'') beyond the end of the gorgeline (toward the shoulder) and placing it so that the tape edge covers the edge of the interfacing by a bit less than 3 mm (1/8''). Slightly ease the tape over the point or curve of the lapel and down to 1.3 cm (1/2'') above the lower end of the roll line. Place pins at right angles to the tape edge (Figure 15–7).

3. Ease tape more for 2.5 cm (1'') across the roll line. (Roll lapel over your finger.) From that point to the bottom of the garment, hold the tape taut. If there is a curve at the lower edge, slightly ease the tape around the curve, keeping the outer edge of the tape (on the seamline) smooth. The inner edge will ripple (Figure 15–8). Stop the

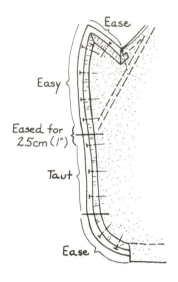

FIGURE 15–8
Pinning Tape.

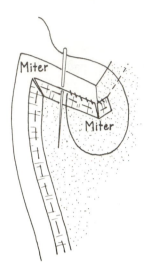

FIGURE 15–9
Mitered Corners.

tape at the hemline for a right-angled front corner.

Note: For a garment without a lapel, place the starting end of the tape 1 cm (3/8'') toward the shoulder from the center front and then continue on down the front.

4. Baste the tape in place. Pull along the edge of the garment. Is it firm or does it have some give? Make any necessary adjustment (loosen or tighten).

5. Have your assistant stand behind you and hold the garment front on your figure at the shoulder and underarm. Does the lapel roll correctly and does the front edge hang perfectly straight? If the front curves inward, the tape is too tight. If the front curves outward, the tape is too loose. If the lapel does not roll at the roll line, the tape may not be eased enough across the end of the roll line. Also note how closely the roll line lies to the body. Does the garment need to be eased in to conform to the body?

Note: Without an assistant, you can check the front fairly well on yourself. It

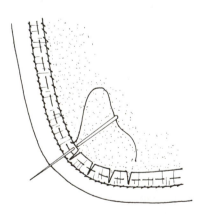

FIGURE 15–10
Stitching Inside Edges of Tape.

may not be as accurate but at least you can obtain an idea as to the way the garment hangs.

6. Follow exactly the same procedure for pinning and basting the tape for the second side. Be sure that both sides are identical: lapel shape, length of front, curve at lower edge.

Note: A template cut like the finished lapel and/or lower curve is helpful to achieve identical angles and curves.

7. With stitches about 6 mm (1/4'') long, hand stitch the *outer* edge of the tape to the fashion fabric, picking up a few fibers of the fashion fabric.

8. Miter the tape at point of the lapel by trimming the excess tape but do not clip through the outer edge of the tape at any time (Figure 15–9). Notch the tape around the lower curve to allow it to lie flat (edges of notches should meet). Hand stitch the *inside* edge of the tape catching only the interfacing, *not* the fashion fabric (Figure 15–10).

Taping the Roll Line

Tape is applied along the roll line to (1) stabilize this bias area to prevent stretching and/or (2) to hold the roll line close to the body for a smooth fit. This taping is called the *bridle stay*. A long roll line, as found in a one- or two-button jacket, may be eased as much as 1.3 cm (1/2'') while a short roll line may require only stabilization or slight ease. A low, full bust may require more ease along the bridle stay to permit a good fit. For a convertible neckline, the tape *only* stabilizes. If desired, the roll line may be taped *before* the taping is done along the lapel and front edge.

Standards for Taped Roll Line:

1. The roll line is firm and resists stretching.

2. Tape lies flat and smooth.

3. Stitching that attaches tape is not visible when the lapel is rolled.

4. Lapel rolls smoothly and is not distorted by tape.

Methods of Applying Bridle Stay. Tape may be applied either by hand or by machine. The initial steps are the same for both methods; only the method of stitching varies.

1. *Hand stitched.* Both edges of the tape are attached by hand, a time-consuming process. The stitching is invisible on the right side and it permits better control of the ease than the machine-stitched method.

2. *Machine stitched.* The tape can be quickly attached with either a single line of a multiple zigzag stitch or two rows of straight stitching, one on each edge of the stay. A disadvantage may be that the stitching shows under the lapel on the right side.

Procedure:

1. Pin one end of the tape where the roll line crosses the neckline, placing one edge of the tape 1/4'' to the garment side of the marked roll line and toward the armhole side.

2. Carry the tape to the front facing seamline and mark this point on the tape. Cut the tape allowing about 2.5-cm (1'') extra. Place the same amount on the opposite lapel. Pin both tapes in place and try on to check the amount of ease or stabilization needed. If the lapel needs to hug the body more closely, ease in one end of the tape. Pin in place and recheck the fit.

3. To distribute ease on the garment, if easing is necessary, place a pin at the top of the tape and another at the front seamline. Hold the tape taut and pin at close intervals (Figure 15–11).

4. Baste the stay in position.

5. Hand stitch in place along each edge, catching into the interfacing only. Or, machine stitch, as previously described, ending the stitching about 5 cm (2'') above the lower end of the stay to prevent the stitching from showing when the lapel is rolled.

6. Keep both sides of the garment identical. *Use Critique #5 to check the fronts.*

Taping Other Areas

A collarless garment may be taped around the entire neckline for greater stability after the shoulder seams have been stitched. Clip the tape as necessary to allow it to lie flat around the curve. *Do not* clip through the edge of the tape lying next to the neck seamline.

Other seams that are somewhat bias or stretchy and will receive strain when the garment is worn may be reinforced also with tape. For instructions see Chapter 17 (Shoulder seams), Chapter 18 (armholes), Chapter 13 (pockets).

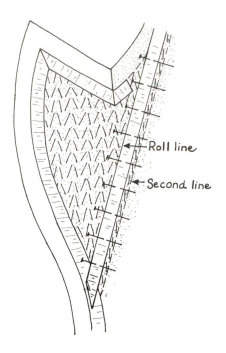

FIGURE 15–11
Taping Roll Line.

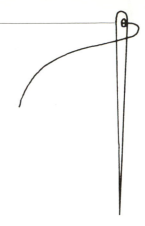

The collar forms a frame around the face. Thus it is important that it is carefully handled during its construction. In fact, a poorly constructed collar can shout that the garment has been ''homemade'' more quickly than any other feature. In view of this, the heavier and more highly textured fabrics commonly used in tailoring require even more careful attention in collar making (as well as in all other aspects of construction) than do the lighter weight materials.

Collars are stabilized and shaped by attaching the interfacing to the undercollar. As discussed in Chapter 14 this may be accomplished (1) by hand or by machine pad stitching, or (2) by fusing. By now you have probably chosen the method that best suits your fabric, the collar design, your personal skills and preferences, and your available time.

The procedure in constructing and applying the collar presented here is probably different from the method used in your pattern guide. Most pattern guide sheets instruct you (1) to stitch the undercollar to the garment, (2) to attach the uppercollar to the two front facings, and then (3) to join the outer edges of the uppercollar and undercollar and the lapels in one operation. But the collar and lapels can be more easily and effectively shaped by completing and shaping the collar and the lapels separately and then joining them at the neckline seam. With this method you can be certain that enough ease has been allowed in the uppercollar and in the lapel facings to allow the ends of the collar and the lapels to lie smoothly and the outer seams to roll toward the underside. The neckline seam can also be adjusted, if necessary, so that the upper and under neckline seams will lie directly on top of each other. Then with the neckline seams of both collar and facing sections pressed open, more flatness and smoothness around the neckline will result.

16

CONSTRUCTION OF COLLARS

Criteria for Evaluating Tailored Collars. To help you judge desirable qualities in a well-made collar, regardless of the stabilization method used, look for these features:

1. Smooth fit around the neck indicating sufficient clipping of the neck seam.

2. Equal lengths in both collar ends and both lapel notches (Figure 16–1). Collar end and lapel notch may not be the same length.

3. Well-pressed flattened edges with seam rolling toward the undercollar, making the seam invisible from the upper side.

4. When on a figure the outer edge of the collar covers the neck seamline of the garment.

5. A smooth uppercollar without excessive ease or ''rippling'' across the surface.

6. Slightly ''curled under'' collar ends and/or lapel points indicating adequate ease over the surface.

Types of Collars

Collars may be classified as those (1) with lapels and (2) those without lapels. As discussed in Chapter 15 the lapel requires pad stitching and thus more work is involved in its construction. The effort in-

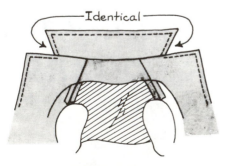

FIGURE 16–1
Checking Collar and Lapel Notch.

FIGURE 16–2
Softly Rolled Collar.

volved in making those without lapels is dependent upon the size and shape of the collar. With all collars a back neck facing is usually recommended because it provides greater wearability to the garment and permits a flatter finish around the neckline.

The shape of the collar and the manner is which the collar frames the face is controlled to some degree by the lapel. Without a lapel a collar may have various shapes.

Collars with Lapels

The typical tailored collar has two sections (upper and under) and lapels with separate front facings. Women's garments often have softly rolled collars and lapels (Figure 16–2) while men's and man-tailored women's garments often have lapels that lie quite flat against the garment and collars that roll sharply and hug the back of the neck (Figure 16–3).

The collar may be found in a variety of different shapes when the collar and lapel roll permanently as a unit. The shape of the collar pattern may be quite straight or somewhat convex on the neckline edge, with the roll line extending only part of the length of the collar (typical of the softly rolled collar as shown in Figure 16–4). Or the neckline may angle sharply at the end of the roll line where the gorgeline begins typical of the

FIGURE 16–3
Man-Tailored Collar.

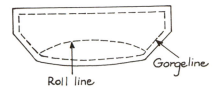

FIGURE 16–5
Pattern Shape of Man-Tailored Collar.

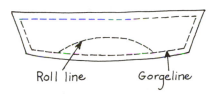

FIGURE 16–4
Pattern Shape of Softly Rolled Collar.

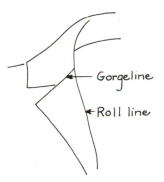

FIGURE 16–6
Location of Gorgeline.

man-tailored collar as shown in Figure 16–5. As you can see the gorgeline is the part of the neckline seam that joins the collar to the lapel (Figure 16–6).

The shawl collar is similar to the collar with lapels except that the uppercollar is cut as one with the lapel facing, thus making a center back seam necessary (Figure 16–7). The outer edge may be smooth or it may be notched or have a special design. Some fabrics with a prominent twill weave may be unsuitable for this collar design since the effect at the center back will appear mismatched.

Collars Without Lapels

The Flat Collar. The shape of the collar determines whether the collar will roll around the neck or lie flat. The closer the

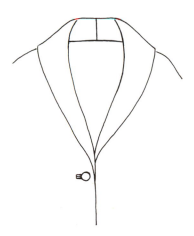

FIGURE 16–7
Shawl Collar.

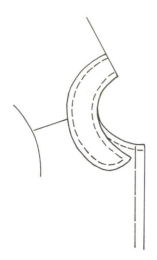

FIGURE 16-8
Neckline Curve of Flat Collar.

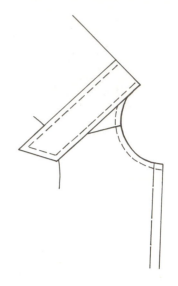

FIGURE 16-10
Neckline Curve of Rolled Collar.

neck edge of the collar follows the same curve as the neckline of the garment, the flatter the collar will lie (Figure 16-8). The flat or slightly rolled collar will not roll back to form lapels when it is worn open, but is designed to be worn closed at the neck (Figure 16-9).

The Rolled Collar. The straighter the neckline of the collar, the more the collar will stand up around the neck (Figure 16-10). The collar stands up from the neck edge (i.e., the *stand*) and falls down to rest on the garment (i.e., the *fall*). The line where the collar begins to fall is the roll line (Figure

16-11). This collar fits closely to the neck when the top button is buttoned as noted in Figure 16-11 or may form a *V* if worn unbuttoned. Thus it is often called the convertible collar and is one kind of a rolled collar (Figure 16-12).

The Standing Collar. The standing collar has a band that extends above the neckline, but has no fall. It may be a straight piece of fabric or curved so it is slightly smaller in circumference at the upper edge

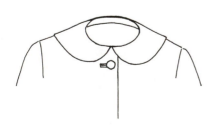

FIGURE 16-9
Flat Collar.

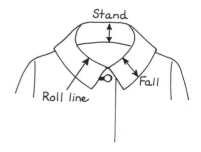

FIGURE 16-11
Rolled Collar.

FIGURE 16–12
Convertible Collar.

FIGURE 16–14
Two-Piece Collar.

FIGURE 16–13
Standing Collar.

to conform to the shape of the neck (Figure 16-13). A two-piece collar which has a separate stand and fall, such as collars used on shirts and some trench coats, is a variation of the stand collar (Figure 16-14).

Stabilizing and Shaping the Collar

The advantages and disadvantages of traditional (hand pad stitching) and contemporary (machine pad stitching, or fusing) methods of shaping and stabilizing the lapel and collar were discussed in Chapter 9. A combination of these methods may also be used. Consider the following:

1. Machine pad the stand and hand pad the fall. Since the stand is padded flat, smaller time-consuming hand stitches can be replaced by the machine stitching.

2. Use a piece of fusible web between the interfacing and fashion fabric to fuse the stand and hand pad the fall for the reasons just mentioned.

3. Fuse the total interfacing and machine pad the stand to give it more body and to shrink the stand slightly.

Although the same method is usually used to shape and stabilize the collar as was used in the lapels, this is not a requirement. However, they must look the same when the garment is completed. In case of doubt it might be well to do some testing of your fabric using possible interfacing choices to determine the best method for the desired effect.

Preparing the Collar

This step is essentially the same for all types of collars with the exception of the shawl collar. (The procedure for constructing the shawl collar is discussed in Chapter 17 since its top collar and facing are in one piece and must be applied to the garment at the same time.) The two-piece collar is handled exactly like the one-piece collar except that the stand and fall are separate pieces. Pad stitch or fuse each piece separately and then stitch the stand to the fall before pressing the shaped undercollar.

1. Stitch center back seam in undercollar. Trim to 6 mm to 1 cm (1/4'' to 3/8'') allowing the greater amount for bulky fabrics. Flatten the seam edge by pounding or "killing" it. (Refer to Chapter 8.)

2.   Overlap the center back stitching lines of the interfacing which has been cut like the undercollar and stitch two parallel lines 3 mm (1/8") apart (Figure 16–15, A). Use a zigzag stitch in place of two rows of straight stitching, if desired as in (B). Trim excess fabric close to the stitching. Alternates: (1) cut off seam allowances, butt ends together over a strip of wigan or muslin, and stitch as the darts were handled as in (C); or (2) apply a fusible to cover and hold the butted edges together.

3.   Place the interfacing to the wrong side of the garment undercollar with center backs matching. Hand or machine baste *neck* edges together *on* the seamline. Trim off corners of the interfacing about 6 mm (1/4") back of the seamline (Figure 16–16).

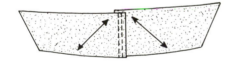

(A) Straight-Stitched Lapped Seam.

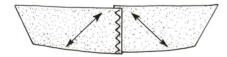

(B) Zigzagged Lapped Seam.

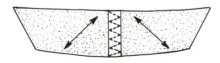

(C) Butted Seam.

FIGURE 16–15
Methods of Stitching Interfacing.

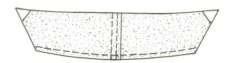

FIGURE 16–16
Interfacing Applied.

Note: If either (1) or (2) alternate method is used and if you have a lightweight fashion fabric, place the interfacing with the wigan or the fusible strip uppermost. This provides a shield for the sharp cut edges of the hymo which may "stick through" the uppercollar.

4.   If you made a test garment and the collar roll line and/or the lapel roll line was established, then with a pencil lightly transfer those lines to your interfacing (Figure 16–17). You are now ready to pad stitch the collar. If you did not make a test garment, follow the procedure discussed in Chapter 14, pages 209 and 210, for establishing the roll line of the collar.

Hand Pad Stitching the Collar

Remember that the undercollar and the interfacing are basted together on the neck seam *only*. (Refer to Figure 16–16 and review Chapter 15). Pad stitch the stand first by holding the interfacing side uppermost with the neck edge *toward* you. Starting at the neckline seam, pad stitch in an arc following the curve of the roll line. Stitch to the roll line, holding the collar as shown in

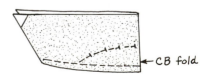

FIGURE 16–17
Roll Line Transferred.

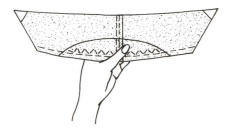

FIGURE 16–18
Pad Stitching the Stand.

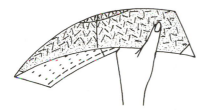

FIGURE 16–19
Fall Pad Stitched.

Figure 16–18). The stand area must remain flat. Reverse the collar in your hand so that the _outer_ edge is _toward_ you. Continue to pad stitch, again following the curve of the roll line and allowing the collar to roll slightly over your finger as you stitch (Figure 16–19).

Remember: (1) The shorter the stitch, the firmer the padded area becomes. Not only the stand but also the collar points are usually more effective if short stitches of about 6 mm (1/4'') in length are used. (2) _Do not pad stitch within the seam allowance_ because this area will be cut away later. (3) To determine the seam allowance measure from the fashion fabric side—not the interfacing. (4) Smoothness must be maintained over the entire pad-stitched area. If ridges start to form, stop, remove stitches, press if undesirable wrinkles are present and stitch again. ''Ridging'' may occur if too much interfacing is eased over the undercollar.

Machine Pad Stitching the Collar

The interfacing has been basted to the collar along the neck edge. Trim 1.3 cm (1/2'') off the interfacing at the neckline edge so only 3 mm (1/8'') extends _beyond_ the basted seamline. Thus the machine stitching may continue through the seam allowance without causing difficulty in grading the seam allowance later.

Note: Depending upon the shape of the collar, the gorgeline is part of the neckline seam, but the angle of the seam may change. Note in Figure 16–20 the marking (x) where the lapel meets the collar. This is the end of the gorgeline.

Now, analyze the shape of the collar before beginning to stitch. A man-tailored collar that has a fall only slightly deeper than the stand and has a sharp turn at the roll line will fit better if the stand is eased in and shrunk slightly along the length of the stand. A collar that rolls more gradually will not need the roll line to be shrunk and the roll line should not be as definite.

Stitching the Stand—The Man-Tailored Collar:

1. Machine stitch the stand using a short stitch (about 14 stitches per 2.5 cm or 1'') along the roll line while stretching the collar (Figure 16–21). To stretch, grasp the neckline seam with one hand and the outer collar edge with the other. Move hands and continue to stretch as the machine moves the length of the roll line.

2. Continue to stretch the undercollar in the same manner as you make additional

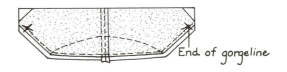

End of gorgeline

FIGURE 16–20
Gorgeline.

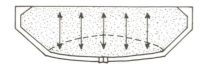

FIGURE 16–21
Stretching the Undercollar When Machine Stitching.

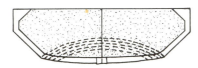

(A) Stitching for a Firm Stand.

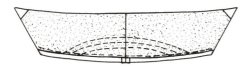

(B) Stitching for Less Firm Stand.

FIGURE 16–22

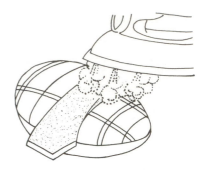

FIGURE 16–23
Steaming the Roll Line.

rows of stitches parallel to the roll line. Make rows 3 mm to 6 mm (1/8'' to 1/4'') apart depending on the amount of firmness desired. The closer the rows, the firmer the collar will be (Figure 16–22,A).

The Softly Rolled Collar:

1. Machine stitch the stand in the same manner as for the man-tailored collar but do not stretch as you stitch.

2. Place the rows of stitching farther apart than for the man-tailored collar to provide a less rigid stand (Figure 16–22, B).

Preparing and Stitching the Fall:

1. Before stitching either type of collar, fold the collar along the roll line and lightly steam without pressing a sharp crease

(Figure 16–23). The man-tailored collar can be creased more sharply than the softly rolled one. While rolled, pin the outer edges of the undercollar and the interfacing together. This allows the interfacing to be slightly eased to the undercollar.

2. Hand or machine baste 2 cm (3/4'') along the *outer* edge of the undercollar. The interfacing should be slightly shorter than the undercollar.

3. ·Trim the interfacing on the seamline 3 mm (1/8'') outside the basting to reduce bulk in the seamline when the uppercollar and undercollar are stitched together.

4. Stitch the fall from the fashion fabric side of the collar to allow the feed dog to ease slight fullness into the interfacing. Stitch the fall with the grain of the fabric to prevent distortion of the collar shape. Use either a straight stitch or a multiple zigzag (Figure 16–24). Determine the distance between the stitching lines by the amount of body desired in the collar. Better overall coverage is achieved by using the multiple zigzag, thus fewer rows will be needed. If using straight stitching, place rows about 6 mm to 1.3 cm (1/4'' to 1/2') apart.

Note: If you encounter any difficulty in easing the interfacing smoothly, grasp the outer edge of the collar in one hand and the neck edge with the other and stretch slightly with the grain as you stitch.

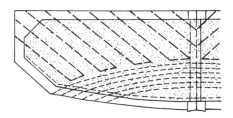

(A) Pad Stitching with Straight Stitch.

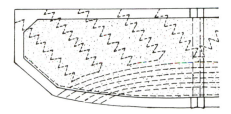

(B) Pad Stitching with Multiple Zigzag.

FIGURE 16–24

Making the Fused Collar

The fusible interfacing you choose and the method of application determines the firmness of the collar. A woven interfacing that contains hair will be the firmest and will give a crisp effect. Medium weight fusibles, woven or nonwoven, give moderate firmness and lightweight ones give slight firmness for a very supple collar. Generally, heavier fabrics require firmer treatment than lightweight fabrics.

1. Cut the fusible interfacing from the undercollar pattern placing the center back seam on the bias if using a woven fusible interfacing, or on the lengthwise grain if using a nonwoven fusible that has lengthwise stability and crosswise stretch. Using tracing paper, mark the seamlines and the roll line. Trim the interfacing so that only 3 mm (1/8'') extends into the *center back* and *neckline*

(including gorgeline) seams. Carefully trim the outer edges *on* the seamline. If the collar will not be topstitched, you may wish to leave 3 mm (1/8'') beyond the outer seamline. This will be included into the seam and will add more bulk.

2. Lay the two sections of the undercollar wrong side up on the pressing board and carefully position the interfacing on them with wrong sides together. Match the seamlines. Be sure that the placement is accurate and steam baste lightly. Permanently fuse according to the manufacturer's instructions. Allow the fabric to cool before proceeding further.

3. Stitch the center back seam and press open. Trim to 6 mm to 1 cm (1/4'' to 3/8''), allowing the greater amount for bulky fabrics. Flatten the seam edges as much as possible.

Optional: For a firmer stand in the collar, place a second piece of fusible interfacing in this area. Cut the fusible on the same grain and the same shape as the collar stand. Carefully place in position and fuse over the center back seam (Figure 16–25). Usually fusing *over* a seam is not permissible.

Note: The seam allowances in the stand may be fused *prior* to applying the second layer of interfacing. Place a strip of fusible web under each seam allowance and fuse. This is advisable for heavy, springy fabrics.

4. Stitch along the roll line edge of the stand interfacing using a short stitch and stretching slightly. To stretch, grasp the neckline seam with one hand and the outer

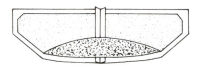

FIGURE 16–25
Second Layer Fused to Stand.

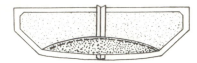

FIGURE 16–26
Interfacing Stitched Close to Roll Line.

edge with the other as was done with the machine pad stitching. Move your hands and continue to stretch as the machine moves the length of the roll line. This stitching helps to shape the collar and keeps the edge of the fusible from loosening along the roll line (Figure 16–26).

Pressing After Pad Stitching or Fusing

Regardless of the method used for stabilizing the collar (hand or machine pad stitching or fusing), the pressing procedure at this point will be the same for all methods. Proceed as follows:

1.   Roll a Turkish towel firmly from end to end. Shape into a curve.

2.   Lay the pad-stitched or fused collar over the curved towel. Press using a damp cloth and a dry iron. The damp cloth will provide concentrated steam which will aid in shaping the collar (Figure 16–27).

Warning: Before pressing over a roll, remove water from the iron to avoid injury from spilled hot water.

FIGURE 16–27
Steaming the Undercollar.

FIGURE 16–28
Undercollar Shaped on Ham.

3.   If the undercollar is too wide for the rolled towel, first press over the stand area and the roll line. Then shift the collar in order to complete pressing. The completed undercollar section must be perfectly smooth and free of any wrinkles.

4.   Allow the undercollar to dry thoroughly by placing it around a ham or on a dress form (if available) or around your own neck. Pin in the same position in which it will be worn on the garment (Figure 16–28).

5.   *Before proceeding, check your undercollar using Critique #6 in the Appendices.*

Completing the Collar

Changes may have occurred in fitting which may have altered the length of the neckline. For example, small neckline darts may have been added or the shoulder seam may have been let out or taken up. This changes the neckline measurement, and consequently, the collar will need adjustment.

Check for Correct Collar Length

The logical time to check the collar length for accuracy is prior to the application of the top collar. Follow this procedure:

1. Pin shoulder seams, matching stitching lines. (Instructions for stitching are at the beginning of Chapter 17.) Pin the pad-stitched or fused collar section along the inside neck edge of the garment just as you did in determining the roll line of the collar. For a collar that hugs the neck, the garment neckline should be eased slightly 6 mm to 1.3 cm (1/4'' to 1/2'') to the collar. Where there is a lapel, reverse and ease the collar slightly for 2.5 cm (1'') at the point where the collar roll (b) meets the lapel roll line (a), as shown in Figure 16–29.

2. Mark the right-hand side of the collar where it touches the lapel notch (c) or where it meets the center front, depending on the design. *Note:* Recheck to see that the collar adequately covers the neckline seam of the garment.

3. Remove the collar and mark the length on the *left-hand* side from the marking on the right-hand side. Lightly pencil a line across each newly marked collar end.

Pressing the Uppercollar

Lay the uppercollar (right side up) over the undercollar and lightly mark with pins the roll line onto the uppercollar. Using a lightly dampened cloth or a steam iron, shrink in

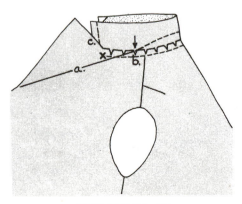

FIGURE 16–29
Checking Correct Collar Length.

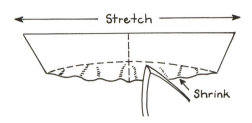

FIGURE 16–30
Shaping Uppercollar.

the stand area of the uppercollar. Soft fabric will shrink easily, but firmer fabric such as gabardine will be more difficult to shrink. Shrinking this area becomes essential since that section of the uppercollar becomes the inner part of a curve as it fits around the neck. Thus, it should be smaller than the undercollar to which it will be attached.

Lightly stretch the area from the roll line to the outer edge of the collar. (Figure 16–30). Now determine that the uppercollar is wide enough to slightly extend over the outer seam after it has been stitched, turned and pressed. To do this lay the uppercollar over the undercollar, matching marked seamlines. *Remember:* The neck seam allowance of the uppercollar was cut about 1.3 cm (1/2'') wider than the pattern, so be sure that you are matching seamlines, *not* cut edges.

The uppercollar should extend 3 mm to 6 mm (1/8'' to 1/4'') beyond the outer edge of the undercollar. The amount of extension is dependent upon the weight of the fashion fabric; a heavy fabric will require more length to cover the seam than will a lightweight one.

If there is not enough uppercollar to cover the undercollar adequately, allow the neck seam of the uppercollar to slip upward. In case there is not enough allowance at that position, reduce the seam width of the outer edge of the uppercollar by 3 mm (1/8'') or more, depending on the fabric available and the amount required.

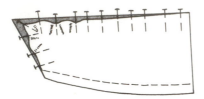

FIGURE 16-31
Uppercollar Pinned to Undercollar.

Applying the Uppercollar

Place uppercollar to undercollar with right sides together and with center backs matching. Start pinning at center back, placing pins at right angles to the seam. Allow the collar to assume the position it will have when worn. Across the collar ends, slightly "bubble" or ease the fabric (Figure 16-31).

Hand baste along the seamline of outer edge and ends and turn the collar right side out to obtain a clue as to the accuracy of the amount of ease. If the amount of the uppercollar is adequate, turn the collar wrong side out.

To ensure accuracy when stitching, measure from the fabric edge and pencil mark a stitching line on the interfacing side. (On the fused or machine-padded collar the edge of the interfacing serves as the guideline for stitching.) Trim the interfacing along the marked seamline. Stitch on this line, starting at center back. For a pointed collar, pivot and take one or two tiny stitches across the point of the collar. The heavier the fabric the more stitches across the point will be required to allow the point to turn smoothly.

Trim seams to 1 cm to 1.3 cm (3/8" to 1/2") depending on the fabric. Grade the undercollar seam allowance to at least 6 mm (1/4"). *Remember* to bevel the edges as you trim.

Caution: When grading a seam in a heavy fabric keep the wider part of the seam at least 1.3 cm (1/2") wide. This allows for an edge which can be pressed flat. A narrow seam allowance produces what appears to be a ridge rather than a flattened edge when the collar is turned.

Pressing and Shaping the Completed Collar

To press, use a point presser, first laying a wool press cloth over its surface. Press the seam open (Figure 16-32). Or, if you do not have a point presser, lay the collar flat on a press board, fold the upper seam allowance back, and press the seam open (Figure 16-33).

Turn right side out and with the underside uppermost, roll the seam slightly with your fingers so that the uppercollar edge

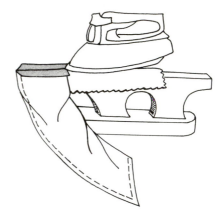

FIGURE 16-32
Pressing with Point Presser.

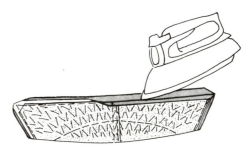

FIGURE 16-33
Pressing without Point Presser.

becomes visible. Lay a *damp* press cloth over the part of seam held in place with your fingers. Press for about 2.5 cm (1'') before shifting the fingers to the adjacent section of seam. Press only the seamed edges at this point.

When all stitched edges have been pressed to your satisfaction, again lay the collar over the rolled Turkish towel. Using a damp cloth and a *dry* iron press the top surface. Refer to Figure 16–27 for position on the towel. A smooth appearance must be maintained over the roll line, and the edges must be sharp (in most fabrics). Allow the collar to dry as was done with the undercollar.

If the collar will not be topstitched and the collar will always be worn turned down, the outside seam of the collar may be understitched to help keep the seam rolling to the underside. You cannot machine stitch to the points, but you can with hand backstitching (usually preferred for the professional look). Pull or fasten the threads to the inside of the collar and secure the ends.

Carefully tailor baste all collar layers together *along the roll line*. Again, make sure that the seamline remains *under* the collar edge and that smoothness is maintained on the uppercollar.

Hold the collar in a curved position and with pins transfer the stitching line of the undercollar to the uppercollar. *Be accurate.* These seam allowances may not be the same width. Hand baste this line of pin markings. These two stitching lines *must* lie on top of each other. Trim off any excess neck seam allowance from the uppercollar. *Before proceeding any further, use Critique #7 in the Appendices to check your collar.*

17

APPLICATION OF FACINGS AND COLLAR

Since facings are an integral part of a collar or any neckline finish, they must be handled with as much care as the collar. The same principles—easing, stitching, grading, and pressing—apply to the application of any facing.

At this point, lapels have been shaped by pad stitching or fusing and steaming, and front edges and roll line have been taped and pressed.

Attaching Facing to Garment

Because one edge of the previously applied tape was placed next to the stitching line, the tape edge now forms the stitching line when attaching the facing. With right sides together, match the front facing to the garment. Ease the facing for about 1.3 cm (1/2'') on either side of the lower end of the roll line and pin in place. This ease allows for the reverse in the direction of the facing as it turns from the outside of the lapel to the inside of the front. Lay the layers of the lapel together smoothly and pin to within 7.5 cm (3'') of the lapel point. Ease and pin the facing to the lapel around the point of the lapel to the collar notch (Figure 17–1). This "bubbles" the facing across the lapel point and allows the seam edges to roll under when turned. From the top button (end of roll line) to bottom of garment hold the facing *slightly taut* and pin in place.

If the garment has a rounded lower front edge, check to see that the facing will lie smoothly to the lower edge, then slightly ease the garment to the facing through this area. (See Figure 17–1.) Then baste the front edges along the seamline, turn the facing to the right side, and check to see that the lapel point has been bubbled adequately to allow the seam to roll under. Also check to see that the total facing length is correct as it lies smoothly from neckline to the hem

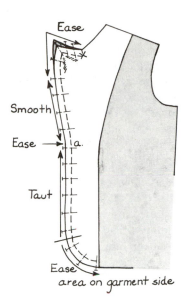

FIGURE 17–1
Application of Front Facing.

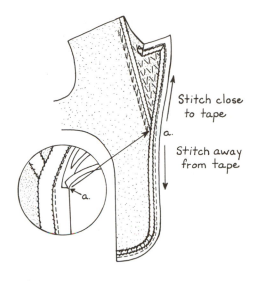

FIGURE 17–2
Stitching and Grading Front Edge.

and that the seam on the lower curve (if there is one) rolls under slightly.

From the interfacing side, stitch through the two garment thicknesses next to (not on) the tape edge from collar notch (end of gorgeline) to lower end of roll line (a). Stitch 1 mm to 2 mm (1/16'') (more for heavier fabrics) from the tape below the roll line (a) so that the seam can roll slightly to the inside (Figure 17–2).

Grade and trim the seam allowance following the same procedure as was used for the collar. However, change the wider part of the seam allowance from *garment to facing* at the turn of the lapel (a). Press the seam open, fold the facing back, turn the lapel right side out and press, handling the pressing as was done on the collar seams. Press the lapel over a curved press pad to maintain the roll created by pad stitching.

Lay the garment flat on the table and beginning at the lower end of roll line smooth the facing to the garment, keeping crosswise grain straight. Pin in place. Mark

First, press.

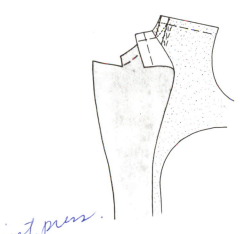

FIGURE 17–3
Marking Neckline Seam of Facing to Match Garment.

neck and shoulder seams on the facing with hand basting. The result is illustrated in Figure 17–3. Trim away any excess seam allowance on the facing, which may occur as a result of easing the garment to the bridle stay.

Shoulder Seams

Check yourself at this point to see that (1) the interfacing in the back of the garment has been basted into position; (2) the front facing has been applied to the garment; (3) the neckline of the back facing has been staystitched; and (4) a hand basting marking the exact stitching line has been placed around the neckline of the garment, the garment facing, and the upper and under neckline seams of the collar.

Note: Generally speaking, for many women's garments a back facing of the fashion fabric is desirable. (Men's jackets do not use a back facing.) Without a back facing the lining will be required to cover the raw edge across the back of the neck. This is often the first place to show wear in the lining. If your pattern does not include a facing, use the back pattern piece as a guide. Place the pattern on a fold if there is a center back seam in the pattern. Cut the facing like the neckline and at least 6.5 cm (2 1/2'') wide. This width is determined by the width of the front facing at the shoulder; they should be equal. Staystitch next to the neckline seam.

Before proceeding further consider whether a reinforcing tape is needed along the shoulder seam to prevent stretching. Knits and shoulder seams that are quite bias or stretchy deserve special consideration in this respect. If taping is needed, cut a strip of seam tape (or lining selvage) the length of the front shoulder seam. (Front shoulder seam is usually shorter than back.) Pin shoulder seams together easing the back to the front. Attach the reinforcing tape to the back side of the shoulder seam, positioning the edge 3 mm (1/8'') into the seam allowance. Stitch directionally with the tape side up to be certain that the tape is being caught. Or, stitch the seam, press open, then lay the tape on the stitching line and

hand stitch the tape to the seam allowances. *Continue as follows:*

1.   Permanently stitch the shoulder seams *without* incorporating the interfacings. *Note:* If a contemporary technique has been followed in which fusible interfacings have been used and/or the interfacing has been attached to an underlining, the underlining or edge of the interfacing will be caught with the seam. Omit Steps 3 and 4.

2.   Leave a 2.5-cm (1'') seam allowance on most fabrics. The additional seam allowance in light and medium weight fabrics provides some padding across the shoulder. However, trim heavy fabrics to 2 cm (3/4'') and bevel the edges. Press the seam open and kill the edges to reduce bulk if necessary.

3.   Lay the back interfacing over the opened shoulder seam and the heavier front interfacing over the back. With the right side out, place garment over a curved surface to duplicate your shoulder shape. Adjust the interfacings to fit smoothly over the shoulder. Pin along seamlines through all layers of fabric.

4.   Using a double strand of thread, permanently tailor baste the interfacings in place at the shoulder, using stitches about 1.3 cm (1/2'') in length. Catch into the seam allowances of the garment to hold the interfacings securely.

5.   Pin the back neck facing to the garment back, overlapping shoulder seams. Allow the neckline to assume the curve that it will have when worn and test to see that the facings will fit the inner curve of the garment neckline. Note that the seam allowance of the facing in Figure 17–4 is now wider than the garment shoulder seam. Adjust the facing seam to match the shoulder seam.

6.   Mark the new lines and stitch the facing seams at the shoulder. Trim to at least 1.3 cm (1/2'') and press open. Flatten the seam edges as much as possible.

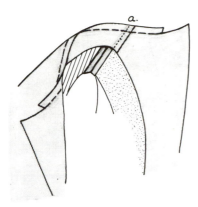

FIGURE 17–4
Check Length of Back Facing.

FIGURE 17–5
Uneven Collar Points.

Joining Collar to Garment

The principle of joining a collar to a tailored garment is essentially the same for all types of attached collars. But there is a difference in the way the collar sets and rolls. The collar with a lapel rolls *across* the neckline seam whereas a collar that closes to the neckline rolls *over* the neckline seam at the front. Thus, when the garment is closed the left-hand side of the collar must roll over the additional thickness of the overlap. Consequently, the left-hand side appears shorter even though it is the same length as the right-hand side. (See Figure 17–5.) The heavier the fabric the more apparent this difference becomes. If you will usually wear the garment buttoned to the neckline and wish to have the collar ends appear the same, you may make *one* of the following adjustments when you attach the collar to the garment: (1) decrease the seam allowance on the left collar front, or (2) increase the seam allowance on the right.

Before joining the collar to the garment, check to see that your collar has been (1) pressed well, (2) tailor basted along the roll line to prevent shifting of the uppercollar, and (3) marked and basted at stitching lines of both upper- and undercollar. Now proceed as follows:

1. At center back pin the undercollar and the garment neckline stitching lines together, making sure that they match. Then pin the collar ends at the correct position on the front where the lapel and collar meet. Hold with garment side uppermost as you pin. Follow the same procedure for pinning the facings and uppercollar together. Carefully hand baste along the neckline seamline of the garment and the collar, using stitches about 4 mm (3/16'') in length to hold the collar securely in position during stitching (Figure 17–6). *Precaution: Do not baste over the*

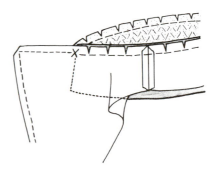

FIGURE 17–6
Neckline Seams of Collar
and Facing Basted.

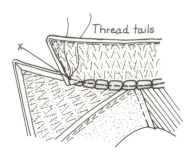

FIGURE 17–7
Stitch Neckline Seam only to x.

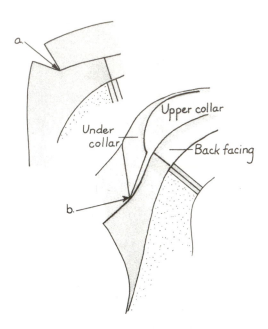

FIGURE 17–8
Effect of Correct Stitching at Neckline.

enclosed seam in collar ends but leave as free-standing seam to allow for better turning and pressing in this area after permanent stitching is completed (Figure 17–7). Check to see that (1) the collar ends are of equal length, (2) the lapel points are the same length, and (3) the opened neckline seams lie on top of each other when the collar is rolled in its correct position.

2. Starting at center back, stitch to the matching point in front first on the garment side and then on the facing side. Repeat for the second side. Again, be certain that you *do not stitch over* the free-standing seam at the collar end. Refer to Figure 17–7. Leave a 10-cm (4'') "tail" of thread to permit hand closing of a small hole that may appear at the collar ends. If the collar has been correctly stitched, the notch at the lapel will form a sharp V. (See a, Figure 17–8.) The stitching lines should appear to be continuous from the lapel through the collar. (See b, Figure 17–8.)

3. Trim uppercollar and neckline facing seam allowances to 1.3 cm (1/2'') and undercollar and garment allowances to 1 cm (3/8''). Clip as much as necessary to allow the seam to lie flat. If the collar rolls correctly but the neck seamlines do not lie directly on top of each other, allow them to

remain uneven. The appearance of the collar is more important than forcing the neckline seams to be in perfect alignment. However, grade the seams so that the edges do not lie directly on top of each other.

4. Trim the front garment interfacings as close to the stitched lines as possible; do not trim the back interfacing any closer than 6 mm (1/4'') because of strain which it may undergo as the garment is worn. *Press* both neckline seams open (Figure 17–9). If necessary, clip the seams more deeply to allow them to lie flat when pressed. *Do not notch.* Diagonally trim the free-standing ends of the seam to reduce bulk. Again, check to see that uppercollar sets smoothly and, if possible, the neckline seams match as they lie on top of each other.

5. With uppercollar, undercollar, and facings in correct position and with neckline

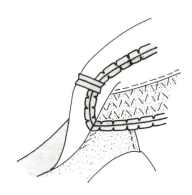

FIGURE 17-9
Neckline Seams Pressed Open.

seams open, pin through both neckline seam allowances exactly on the seamlines. Fold the facings back over the collar so that the raw edges are exposed. Pick up the two lower seam allowances which extend downward, and with a double strand of matching thread permanently baste the two seams together with stitches about 1.3 cm (1/2'') long (Figure 17-10). Do not pull the bastings tightly or the neckline seam may appear dimpled. This basting will hold the neckline seam firmly so that the uppercollar

will not shift as the garment is worn. If there is no back facing, allow the uppercollar seam allowance to lie on top of the opened back neck seam. Using a combination stitch (Chapter 7), securely stitch the uppercollar seam to the neckline seam.

Check your completed collar and lapel using Critique #8 in the Appendices.

The Shawl Collar

The shawl collar differs from the regular tailored collar in that its uppercollar and lapels are combined into one pattern piece. This eliminates the visible seam (gorgeline) characteristic of the tailored collar but it also means that there must be a center back seam in both the undercollar and the uppercollar. While the outer edge of the collar is usually a smooth unbroken line, its appearance may be altered by placing a notch or some other variation along the edge.

The shawl collar may be cut with the front of the garment and the undercollar in one piece as in Figure 17-11 or it may have the undercollar cut as a separate piece as in Figure 17-12. In either case the uppercollar

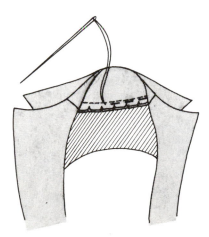

FIGURE 17-10
Permanently Baste Neckline Seams.

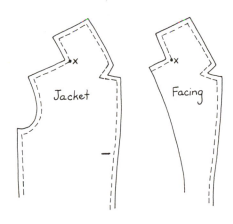

FIGURE 17-11
One-Piece Shawl Collar (Reinforce at x).

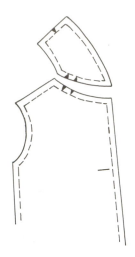

FIGURE 17–12
Two-Piece Shawl Collar.

(facing and lapel) will be applied in the same manner. Generally, the latter method is easier to construct because the first method requires a corner reinforcement.

Both fusible and nonfusible interfacings are applicable to shawl collars and are discussed in this chapter.

The garment with the shawl collar is fitted in the same manner as the suit or jacket with a set-on collar. Check the way in which the back of the garment sits around the neck. If it does not fit closely, neckline darts may be incorporated so that the collar can fit more closely around the neck. If darts are added, the back collar will need to be shortened to fit the smaller neckline.

Nonfusible Interfacing Application

Two different methods are presented for applying nonfusible interfacings. In Method I, the front and back of the garment are permanently stitched at the shoulder and the neck *before* the interfacings are applied. This requires the handling of the combined front and back of garment when pad stitching is done. In Method II, the fronts are joined at

the center back of the collar *only* before pad stitching. The shoulder seams are not joined at this point. This method is probably easier to use for full-length coats, whereas Method I might be more appropriate for jackets and short coats. However, either method may be satisfactory.

For either method the beginning steps are as follows:

1. Prepare interfacings (front and back) by stitching and pressing darts and/or seams. If edge tape is applied by machine as discussed in Chapter 10, begin taping 2.5 cm (1'') above the top button and continue downward to the turn of the hem.

2. For the collar cut with the front, reinforce the corners on the garment where shoulder and neckline seams meet. (See Chapter 7). Clip diagonally to corner. Note corners in Figure 17–11.

3. Stitch the center back seam of the undercollar (regardless of style) and press open. For medium to heavy fabrics the center back seam of the collar may be tapered outward from the neckline to the edge to allow the collar to set over the neckline seam more easily. The uppercollar may be let out slightly more than the undercollar.

4. Position garment *back* interfacing, pin and baste in place as described in Chapter 15. The basting around neck, shoulders, and armholes should be about 3.8 cm (1 1/2'') from cut edges to allow garment seams to be stitched and pressed open. This leaves the interfacing free to be lapped over the garment seams later.

Method I (Shoulder seams stitched):

1. Pin, baste, and stitch shoulder and neckline seams. Clip the neckline seam allowance as necessary and press open.

2. Lap the *back* interfacing *over* the neckline and shoulder seams. Pin in place.

3. Check the fit of the interfacing across the back by placing garment right side out over a curved surface. The interfacing must lie smoothly inside the garment. Repin if necessary.

4.   Place the *front* interfacing into position in the garment, match and pin center back, neckline, and shoulder seams. To aid in the placement of the interfacing it will be helpful to either place the garment with right side out on yourself or place on a dress form (if one is available). This allows the interfacing to assume the same position it will have when the garment is worn. Pin together on the center front full length of garment.

5.   Clip the interfacing to the corner where the garment was reinforced at the shoulder. This will allow the front interfacing to lap over the opened shoulder seam and the back interfacing at neck and shoulder. It is unnecessary to reinforce the interfacing at the corner. Note x in Figure 17–3.

6.   Continue to fit the interfacing in place and pin, allowing the center back of the collar interfacing to overlap the seam on the undercollar. Trim off excess seam allowance at center back, leaving about a 1-cm (3/8'') overlap. Permanently baste or stitch the interfacing seam at center back collar, avoiding catching into the undercollar of garment. The interfacing must be free to shift as the collar is pad stitched.

7.   Clip the interfacing along the neckline seam to allow it to lie flat.

8.   Using a double strand of thread, permanently tailor baste the interfacings in place at neckline with stitches about 1.3 cm (1/2'') in length. Catch into the seam allowances of the garment.

9.   Draw a diagonal line from the shoulder x to the seamline opposite the top buttonhole marking. This line serves as a placement line for the bridle stay. (See Figure 17–13.) Tailor baste along the diagonal line, continue to baste the entire front to the garment side of the seamline as described in Chapter 14.

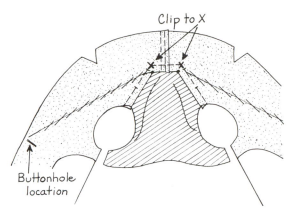

FIGURE 17–13
Placement Line for Bridle Stay.

Method II (Shoulder seams open):

1.   Place *front* interfacing into position on garment, match and overlap the center back seam allowance over the garment undercollar seam. (See Figure 17–13.)

2.   Trim off the excess interfacing seam allowance at the center back, leaving about a 10-mm (3/8'') overlap. Permanently tailor baste this seam catching through the interfacing *only*. The interfacing must be free to shift its position as the collar rolls.

3.   Baste the interfacing to the undercollar on the collar neckline seam from shoulder to shoulder. Mark and baste the front as described in Step 9 of Method I.

4.   If the roll line of the collar was not previously established in the test garment, clip the back neckline seam allowance as deep as the staystitching and clip the interfacing at the corners as far as the reinforced corners in the garment were clipped. *Temporarily* join the garment front to the garment back by overlapping shoulder and neckline seams and pinning in place.

Shaping the Shawl Collar

Place the garment again on a figure, match center fronts, and pin together starting at

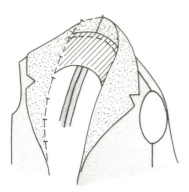

FIGURE 17–14
Marking the Roll Line with Pins.

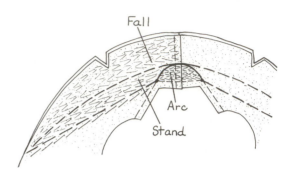

FIGURE 17–15
Pad Stitching the Arc, Stand, and Fall.

the location for the top button. The roll formed along the collar from around the neck to the top button indicates the front roll line as well as the back collar stand. Before proceeding check to see that the back neckline seam will be well covered by the collar when the facing is applied. Lightly pencil the roll line from center back to the top button on the front on the right-hand side only, or place a row of pins parallel to and *on* the roll line (Figure 17–14). Remove the garment and mark the left side like the right. (For Method II remove the garment back.)

Pad Stitching:

The shawl collar may be hand or machine pad stitched following the instructions for the lapel and collar previously explained. Proceed as follows:

1. Mark an arc on the interfacing from shoulder seam to shoulder seam, curving the arc about 1.3 cm (1/2'') below the collar stand at center back (Figure 17–15).

2. Hand or machine pad stitch this arc in exactly the same manner as in a separate collar.

3. Fill in the remainder of the stand between the roll line and the diagonal line that

extends from the shoulder to the top button, keeping this area flat.

4. Pad stitch the fall utilizing one of these procedures:

a. Starting at center back, fill in one side and then fill in the other (generally preferred), *or*

b. Pad stitch from the top buttonhole around the collar to the opposite side; continue from side to side.

5. Press over a rolled towel as shown with the tailored collar.

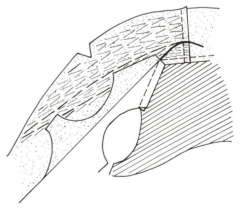

FIGURE 17–16
Exclude Interfacing from Shoulder Seam.

Completion of Method II:

1. Pin and stitch the garment fronts and back at the neckline and shoulder. Include the interfacing into the neckline seam but not into the shoulder seam (Figure 17–16).

2. Press seams open. Clip where necessary to allow the neckline seam to lie flat and open. Trim the excess fabric at the corners where the neckline and shoulder seams meet.

3. Lap the back interfacing over the neckline and shoulder seams. Then lap and pin the front interfacing in place over the shoulder seam. Check for smoothness, then permanently tailor baste the overlapping seams lightly catching into the seam allowance of the fashion fabric.

Fusible Interfacing Application

Apply the fusible interfacing to the garment front and to the undercollar (if there is a separate one) prior to stitching any seams. Extend the interfacing 3 mm (1/8'') into the armhole, shoulder, neckline, and center back seam allowances, but trim the front edge on the stitching line (Figure 17–17).

Note: Prior to fusing, tape may be applied by machine to the front edge from 2.5 cm (1'') above the top buttonhole to turn of hem. (See Chapter 15.)

Stitch and press open the collar center back seam. Reinforce the corners on the garment where the shoulder and neckline seams meet by stitching with short stitches on the seamline for about 2.5 cm (1'') on either side of corner. If the roll line of the collar was not previously established in the test garment, clip the back neckline to the edge of the fusible interfacing and clip to the corners. Join garment front to garment back by lapping and pinning shoulder seams and neckline seams. Place the garment on a figure and follow the instructions on pages 243 and 244 to establish and mark the front roll line and the back collar stand.

If more body is desired in the stand than supplied by the fusible, fuse a second layer of interfacing in the stand area. To do this mark an arc on the interfacing from shoulder seam to shoulder seam, curving the arc about 1.3 cm (1/2'') below the collar stand at center back. Cut a piece of fusible interfacing in the shape of the stand, minus the neckline seam, and fuse on top of the first layer of interfacing and center back seam, which has been trimmed to about 6 mm (1/4''). Stitch close to upper edge of stand (Figure 17–18).

Stitch any darts or seams in nonfusible

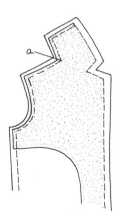

FIGURE 17–17
Fusible Interfacing Application.

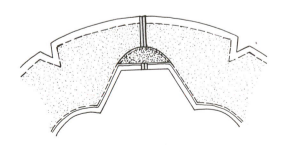

FIGURE 17–18
Reinforcing Stand.

back interfacing and position interfacing on garment back, pinning at shoulder and neck edges. The back interfacing will be stitched into the neckline and shoulder seams to balance the fusible front interfacing that also will be stitched in the seam.

Pin, stitch, and press open the shoulder and neckline seams. Trim away excess fabric at the corner so the cut edges meet. Clip where necessary to allow the neckline seams to lie flat.

Taping Garment with Shawl Collar

Place tape for the bridle stay from point where the shoulder and neckline meet to the top button. (Refer to Figure 17–19.) Follow same procedure as for the lapel on page 220. Carry the front edge tape 2.5 cm (1'') above top button, following the same procedure for trimming, basting, hand stitching, and pressing discussed in Chapter 15. *Note:* Do not tape the outer edge of the collar as it may create a tight outer edge, thus pushing the collar upward around the neck.

Completing the Shawl Collar with Back Neck Facing

If the garment has a back neck facing, check the length of the facing as was done with the

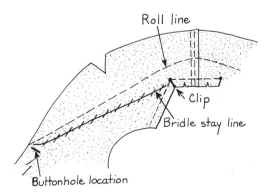

FIGURE 17–19
Roll Line and Bridle Stay Line Marked.

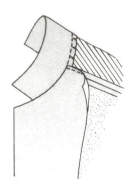

FIGURE 17–20
Collar Without Back Neck Facing.

tailored collar. Reinforce the corner (see Figure 17–11) and attach the back facing to the front facing at neckline and shoulder. Stitch the center back seam of the top facing and press the seam open. Use the same procedure for applying the facing as was followed for the tailored collar. *Note:* It is important that these facings are well pressed—with edges as flat or as rounded as fashion decrees.

Check your completed collar using Critique #8 in the Appendices.

Completing the Collar Without a Back Neck Facing

The garment without a back neck facing of the fashion fabric requires the lining to be extended to the neck edge to hold the uppercollar in position:

1. Pin the uppercollar in place across the back of the neck following the procedure outlined earlier. Remember that this seam has been clipped and pressed open.

2. Use a combination stitch and stitch through the uppercollar to the opened garment neckline seam (Figure 17–20).

3. Fasten the shoulder facing seam in the same manner after the shoulder shapes have been applied.

Problem Areas in Collars

Even though you may feel that you have followed directions exactly in making the collar, it still may be possible to have a result which does not meet all the criteria for judging a good collar. Check yourself with these questions:

1. Does the collar fit smoothly around the neck?

2. Are both lapel notches as well as collar ends equal in length?

3. Are seams flattened and rolled to the underside of collar?

4. Does the outer edge of the collar cover the neckline seam of the garment?

5. Is the uppercollar smooth across the surface?

6. Do the collar ends and lapel points curl under slightly?

One of the common faults which may be corrected at this point is related to #6 above. The collar may tend to turn upward across the back as well as curling upward at the ends. This may be because an error was made in determining the correct neck seamline on the uppercollar. Thus, when the opened neckline seams were permanently basted together, the uppercollar lacked sufficient ease to allow the collar edge to roll under as it should. To correct this:

1. Lift the neck facing and clip the permanent basting which holds the uppercollar to the neckline seam.

2. Hold the collar as it will set when worn and ease the uppercollar toward the outer edge. This will result in the two seamlines no longer lying exactly on top of each other.

3. Pin the uppercollar in place along the crack of the seam, and then: (1) replace the permanent basting if the seam allowance permits this or (2) from the top side use tiny backstitches about 1.3 cm (1/2'') apart and *on* the neck seamline of uppercollar, stitch through that area *into* the layer below. Do not pull the thread too tightly as this may cause dimples to appear along the neckline seam. Other errors may be helped by pressing or by utilizing your own ingenuity.

Completing the Facings

Since the shoulder shapes will be partially covered by the facing and they cannot be applied until after the sleeves are mounted, a recommended procedure is to defer anchoring the facings to the interfacing until the sleeves are applied (Chapter 18) and the garment is hemmed. To do this follow through Step 6, then proceed with hemming as described in Chapter 19.

1. Place an ease line along the edge of the facing opposite the roll line. This will allow for easing-in and shrinking any extra ease that may appear in the front shoulder area (Figure 17-21).

2. Lay the garment flat on the table with the facing side uppermost.

3. Fold the lapel on its roll line, carefully smooth the facing over it and then pin along the folded edge through all layers of fabric. This will hold the facing in place over the lapel until the facing is stitched (Figure 17-22).

4. Smooth all of the facings in place, being sure that grainlines of the facing and the garment coincide.

5. Press the facings and shrink out any ease that may appear along the edges. Carefully pin facings in place along the cut edges.

6. Finish buttonhole facings as described in Chapter 12. Press after completing this process.

Note: For a garment to be lined by the

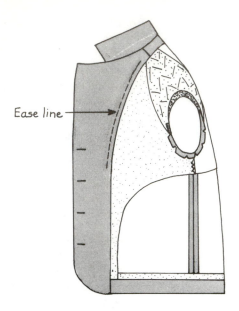

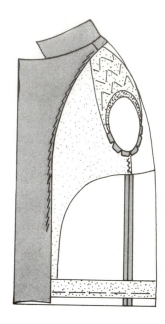

FIGURE 17–21
Easing in Facing
(Hemming Has Been Completed).

FIGURE 17–23
Tailor Basting to Anchor Facing
(Hem Ready for Completion).

Ease line

FIGURE 17–22
Lapel Pinned to Hold Ease.

machine method, omit Step 7 because all facing edges must remain free. For the *unlined* garment, finish the facing edges after the fitting has been checked. The Hong Kong finish is an appropriate and neat finish for the facing. Loosely and invisibly catchstitch the facings to darts, seams, and shoulder pads. *Do not* attach facings to the fashion fabric.

7.   Starting about 20.5 cm (8'') above the hemline for a coat and less for a jacket, use a double strand of matching thread and tailor baste around all facings, catching into the interfacing *only*. Keep stitches about 2 cm (3/4'') long and within the seam allowance of the facing (Figure 17–23). Tailor basting will usually hold the interfacings more securely than will catch stitching.

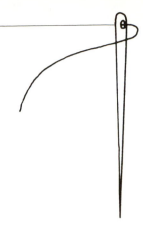

Sleeves are an important feature of a tailored coat or jacket. A properly hung sleeve, one which falls perfectly balanced, is another hallmark of fine tailoring.

The types of sleeves used in tailored garments fall into three basic categories: (1) set-in, (2) raglan, and (3) kimono. Our discussion will focus on the set-in (mounted) sleeve because it is the type traditionally used in tailoring and is more difficult to apply than either the raglan or the kimono sleeve.

At this point:

1. If the body of the garment has not been stitched, stitch and press all seams and darts. For the unlined garment, all visible seams should be appropriately finished.

2. Critiques for buttonholes, pockets, lapels, taping, collar, and facings have all been checked at the proper intervals.

3. Collar has been completed and attached, or carefully basted to the garment neckline and to the neck and the front facings.

Note: It is unnecesary to have the collar permanently attached at this stage. After the sleeves are hand basted in position, then the collar and sleeves can be checked at the same time.

Occasionally the addition of sleeves to a garment may alter the set of the collar around the neckline; hence, any necessary change will be easier with basted seams than with permanently stitched ones.

4. Shoulder pads (if used) of the correct size are ready for insertion into the coat or jacket.

5. The interfacing across the back has been carefully checked to see that it is smooth and that it is not tighter than the garment.

18

SLEEVES

Set-In (Mounted) Sleeves

Sleeve Designations:

The following numbers correspond to those in Figure 18–1.

1. *Lengthwise grain marking.* A hand-basted line (uneven) on grain from the top of the sleeve to the hem used in determining correct hang of the sleeve. To determine the grain to follow, fold the sleeve lengthwise, matching the underarm location points. *Do not follow* the lengthwise grain marking on the pattern because it is usually not centered in the sleeve.

2. *Crosswise grain marking.* Also a hand-basted line at right angles to the lengthwise marking and from the lowest part (base) of the cap curve. Also aids in determining hang.

3. *Cap.* The top part of the sleeve above the crosswise grain, or base marking, as noted in (A), line 2.

4. *Sleeve cap depth.* Distance from the top of the sleeve to the base line (line 1 to 4, A).

5. *Underarm location point.* Lowest point of the cap curve (B and C, dotted line 5).

6. *One-piece sleeve* with an underarm seam (A).

7. *Two-piece sleeve* with seams at the front and back. Underarm location point about middle way in the underarm sleeve section (B).

8. *Simulated two-piece sleeve.* The front seam of the two-piece sleeve is eliminated, thus leaving a seam along the elbow side. Underarm location point is at lowest part of sleeve curve (C, dotted line 5).

Standards for a Set-In Sleeve:

1. The sleeve should appear balanced (an equal amount of ease at the front and back of arm) with the lengthwise grain falling straight from the shoulder to the elbow and the crosswise grain parallel to the floor.

2. Ease around the cap is evenly and smoothly distributed with the major fullness being in the front and back where the cap is on a bias. The sleeve cap is smooth with no "dimples" or indented areas.

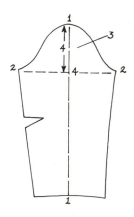 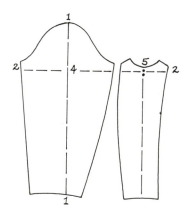 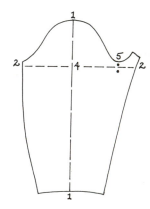

(A) One Piece.   *(B) Two Piece.*   *(C) Simulated Two Piece.*

FIGURE 18–1
Sleeve Designations.

3. There are no diagonal (drag) lines in the cap area.

4. The position of the sleeve on the body is appropriate for the current style and for the shape of the figure.

5. There is ease for comfort and movement across the cap and around the elbow.

6. Elbow ease or darts are centered over the elbow.

7. The curve of the armhole must be smooth.

8. Length is appropriate to the current fashion and to your figure.

Preparing the Armhole

Some loosely woven fabrics may require more support around the armhole than the interfacing provides. Or, if the armhole stands away from the body under the arm, it may need to be drawn in slightly before the sleeve is attached. The following choices for stabilization are optional:

Method I. Using a regulation stitch length, staystitch on the seamline through all layers of the garment (interfacing plus fashion fabric).

Method II. Pin and baste a 6-mm (1/4") twill tape over the armhole seam, slightly easing the garment to the tape in the underarm area if the garment tends to stand away from the body. The tape will be included in the permanent stitching of the sleeves. This method is not recommended for coats because it allows less give in the armhole area.

Method III. Around the armhole seamline use a pull-up stitch (a chain stitch). See Figure 18-2. To make this stitch:

1. Use a waxed double strand of your sewing thread and from the interfacing side, place stitches just outside of the seamline (toward cut edge).

FIGURE 18-2
Chain Stitch to Support Armhole.

2. Take all stitches through both layers of fabric. Slightly draw in the stitches through the underarm area if you feel the garment should fit your body more snugly. *Caution:* Be careful about drawing in too much since the stitching is primarily for stabilization.

Preparing the Sleeves

Preliminary checking. Before continuing, recheck the shape of the sleeve cap to determine the curve of the cap shape and to be sure that both sleeves are not made for the same armhole. Remember to always mark the wrong side of the fabric with chalk if the right side is not readily distinguishable. To check the shape:

1. For a one-piece sleeve, fold the sleeve lengthwise through the center with the stitching lines matching. The back curve of the cap should be wider than the front curve (Figure 18-3).

2. For a two-piece sleeve, overlap the seamlines about 7.5 cm (3") down toward the elbow and pin. Fold the sleeve lengthwise through the center and place a pin at the underarm location point. Check the cap curve as above.

If the sleeve is not curved correctly, it is advisable to superimpose a well-fitting sleeve cap onto the sleeve and baste a line on what would be the new cutting line.

Preparing the Sleeve Cap. There are two methods for preparing the sleeve cap.

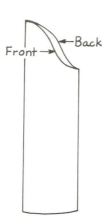

FIGURE 18–3
Checking Shape of Sleeve Cap.

Method I uses a hand-basted ease line and Method II uses the more common double machine ease stitching. Method I is a slower process but its results are often more satisfactory because a hand-stitched ease line is more easily adjusted than machine stitching. For either method proceed as follows:

1. Hand baste (uneven basting) lengthwise and crosswise grainlines (Figure 18–4,

A). Remember that machine basting is not recommended for marking lines in wool fabrics.

2. Baste and stitch darts and/or seam(s) if you are sure of the location of ease over the elbow and are sure of the ease allowance in the sleeve. Otherwise, *baste only* until final checking is done.

3. Ease stitch the cap.

    a. *Method I.* Using a *double* strand of thread, place a small hand run ease line on the stitching line around the entire cap, beginning and ending at the top of the sleeve. Leave thread ends of about 7.5 cm (3''). See Figure 18–4, B. Tie knots in the ends. If the lengthwise seams are basted, leave the seams standing free and not basted flat to the cap. This will allow the seam to be permanently stitched later without removing the sleeve from the armhole after the fitting has been done.

    b. *Method II.* Machine baste two rows of stitching from notch to notch across the top of the cap with one row placed on the seamline and the second row 6 mm (1/4'') from the cut edge. The two rows of stitching will tend to flatten the seam, thus making it easier to handle.

4. Shrink in some fullness in the sleeve cap seam allowance since the cap is usually 3.8 cm to 5 cm (1 1/2'' to 2'') larger than the armhole. To shrink:

    a. Measure armhole distance over shoulder from notch to notch.

    b. Draw up the ease line between notches on the cap to conform to a little less than the measurement of the armhole.

    Note: Pull on both machine basting threads simultaneously to form a curve in the cap, then pull the outer thread more than the inside so that the ease lines are the same length. (Since the

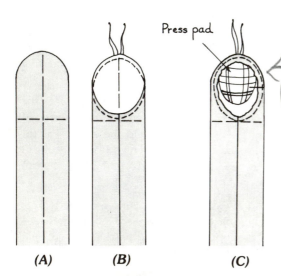

(A)　　　**(B)**　　　　　**(C)**

FIGURE 18–4
Preparing Sleeve Cap.

outer thread is on the wider side of the curve, it will be longer.)

c. Adjust the sleeve cap over a small pressing pad or over a small Turkish towel rolled into a firm curve if a pad is unavailable. Distribute the ease (Figure 18-4, C).

d. With a steam iron (or if more moisture is needed, use a damp press cloth) shrink in ease on the seam allowance *only*. Firm fabrics, such as garbardine, will not shrink readily and may require additional handling later to master the ease, or use this alternate method.

Alternate Method for Rigid Fabrics (fabrics that do not ease):

1. Cut a 30-cm by 3.8-cm (12'' by 1 1/2'') bias strip of muslin or similar fabric for each sleeve.

2. Beginning at one notch on the sleeve cap, place the bias strip on the wrong side of the sleeve cap with cut edges even.

3. Next to the stitching line (toward cut edge of seam allowance) machine baste the two layers of fabric together, stretching the bias as you stitch. As the bias is stretched, the sleeve cap is automatically eased.

4. Check the measurement of sleeve and armhole between the notches. If the sleeve is smaller than the armhole, the bias was stretched too much; if the sleeve is larger, bias was not stretched enough. A larger sleeve can be eased into the armhole, but if the sleeve is smaller, remove the basting and restitch, stretching the bias less.

5. Trim off excess bias that extends beyond notches. Sleeve is now ready to be set into the armhole.
Note: This bias strip usually replaces the sleeve head that may be used to give a "lift" across the top of the sleeve. If additional lift is needed, an extra sleeve head may be added after the sleeve has been stitched in

place. Instructions for making and applying sleeve heads follow later in this chapter.

Fitting the Sleeve into the Armhole

The sleeve may be applied by two methods: Method I requires either (a) a dress form on which to fit your garment or (b) an assistant who can adjust the sleeves while the garment is on you. Method II requires neither an assistant nor a dress from but will produce good results. It is more of a trial and error approach to fitting, however.

General Suggestions:

1. Fit both sleeves along at the same time alternating from one to the other to prevent pulling the garment off center.

2. The notches and dots in the sleeve cap do not necessarily have to match those in the armhole, nor do the underarm seams of the sleeve and garment have to match. Consider these location points as guides only.

Procedure for Method I:

1. Place the shoulder pads (if used) in position, extending them almost as far as the seam allowance and pin in place from the outside.

2. On a dress form or on you, if you have an assistant, pin the garment together, matching center front lines.

3. Place one sleeve into position; match the shoulder marking and fold the seam allowance exactly on the ease line. The ease line provides stability and makes turning under the seam allowance easier.

4. Adjust the sleeve so that the lengthwise grain marking is perpendicular to the floor. This marking usually falls slightly in front of the shoulder seam. Then pin at the top of the sleeve, using a small pin stitch parallel to, and on, the folded edge (Figure 18-5, A).

5. Adjust the crosswise line so that it is

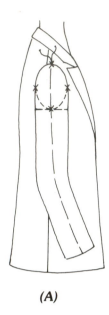 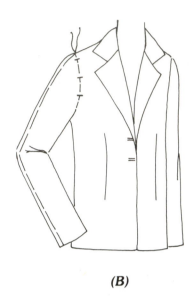

(A)   **(B)**

FIGURE 18–5
Adjusting Sleeve on Figure.

parallel to the floor and pin on the folded edge at widths of chest and back.

6. Place the forefinger and the thumb in the garment at the underarm, bring the two edges of the sleeve and garment together. Pin in place.

7. Repeat for the second sleeve and check the general appearance of both sleeves.

8. Hold onto the end of the hand run ease thread, pull up the thread slightly, if necessary, and continue to pin the sleeve into position, using one or two pins between the chest pin and the top and between the back pin and the top (Figure 18–5, B).

9. Repeat for the second sleeve.

10. From the outside, slip baste the sleeve into the armhole.

Procedure for Method II:

1. Following the directions in your pattern guide, match and pin notches, dots at top of shoulder, and underarm markings.

2. With the sleeve side up allow the seam to roll over your fingers and pin baste with pins at right angles to the seam. Work from notches on each side to the top (Figure 18–6).

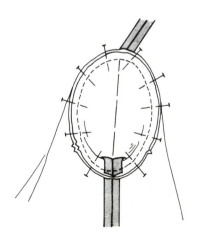

FIGURE 18–6
Pinning Sleeve into Armhole.

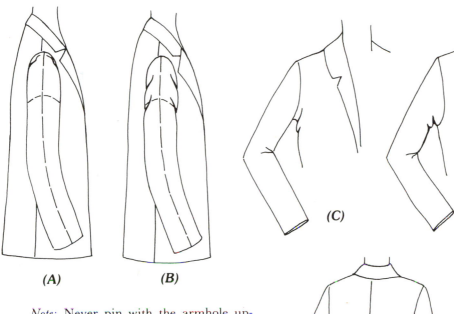

(A)   **(B)**

Note: Never pin with the armhole uppermost for this will allow ease to form on the armhole side of the seam. *The ease must always be in the cap.*

3. Hand baste along the seamline leaving lengthwise seam allowances free from the bastings if the underarm sleeve seams are not permanently stitched. Machine basting is not advised at this point since it may cause too much shifting of the seam.

4. Try on and check the fit with the shoulder shapes in place.

Checking the Fit

Regardless of the method used to insert the sleeve, check to determine whether the sleeve meets the standards outlined at the beginning of this chapter. Also *use Critique #9 in the Appendices to check for correctness and possible adjustments.*

Apparent discrepancies in the hang of the sleeve require certain adjustments:

1. Diagonal wrinkles from the highest point of the cap, indicating that the cap is too short (Figure 18–7, A).

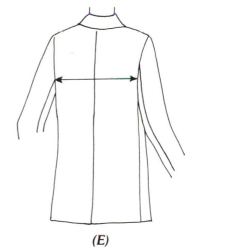

(C)   **(D)**

(E)

FIGURE 18–7
Check Points for Sleeves.

To adjust: Unpin the cap at the shoulder top and let out the seam of the sleeve cap (if seam will allow it) and repin. If wrinkles do not disappear, raise the underarm seam of the sleeve on the armhole of the garment from the underarm up toward the width of the chest and of the back. Repin, raising the entire lower section of the sleeve. This automatically increases the depth of the sleeve cap.

2. Diagonal wrinkles along the upper front and the back of the cap, indicting improper distribution of ease (Figure 18–7, B).

To adjust: Using the ease threads, lift the cap, pushing more ease along the front and back until the crosswise line is parallel with the floor.

3. Underarm wrinkles in garment, indicating that the garment sets too high at the underarm (Figure 18–7, C).

To adjust: Clip the lower section of the armhole so that any wrinkling is released as the arm drops naturally. The new stitching line on the garment should be about 1.3 cm (1/2'') below the clips. Allow the stitching line on the lower portion of the sleeve to fall on the new stitching line of the garment.

4. Underarm wrinkles in sleeve, indicating that the sleeve is too high at this point (Figure 18–7, D).

To adjust: Clip the lower portion of the sleeve, then raise the sleeve on the armhole of the garment, thus reshaping the contour of the sleeve cap.

5. Lengthwise seams in a two-piece sleeve appear at different levels on the back of the garment (Figure 18–7, E).

To adjust: Realign the ease in the sleeve cap. It may require some shifting in both sleeves.

Stitching the Sleeves

After determining that the sleeves are hanging properly and there is adequate ease across the back and through the upper arm and elbow areas, you are ready to stitch them permanently. If the lengthwise seams of the sleeve were not permanently stitched before setting in the sleeve, now stitch and press, trying to avoid disturbing the armhole basting.

Note: Because the seams were left free standing at the time the sleeves were basted in place, it is now possible to stitch and press

the sleeve seams without removing them from the garment.

If you slip basted the sleeves in place and the slip basting appears uneven, turn the sleeve to the wrong side and rebaste using an even basting stitch. The basted line serves as a guide in stitching, so it must be even.

Stitch around the armhole from the sleeve side, stitching next to the basted line. Remove the basting. If a second row of stitching is desired to give stability, stitch *exactly* on the previous line of stitching.

Handling the Armhole Seam

From the wrong side of the sleeve, and with the tip of the iron, press the seam allowance (as it was stitched) about 1.3 cm (1/2'') into the sleeve (Figure 18–8). Notch out any excess folds across the cap and then trim the seam to 1.3 cm (1/2''). Allow the upper portion of the seam to extend into the sleeve to help fill out the cap. However, for a dropped shoulder or a flat effect across the top of the cap the seam may be pressed open.

The *lower* portion of the armhole (between notches) may be handled in either of two ways. In *Method I* the seam is clipped

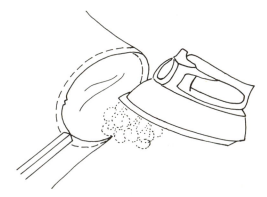

FIGURE 18–8
Pressing Armhole Seam.

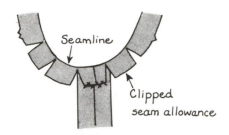

FIGURE 18–9
*Pressing Lower Armhole Section
Back on Itself.*

and pressed open, and in *Method II* the seam is double stitched, trimmed to 6 mm (1/4''), and left standing. Men's garments and close fitting women's garments are usually made by Method II because it is less bulky. Unlined garments should follow Method II so that the seam can be bound. Method I leaves a slightly larger armhole and thus is advantageous for coats that will be worn over bulky garments. It also allows the lining to fit more smoothly over the underarm seam allowance.

Method I:

1. Double stitch the lower armhole seam between notches, stitching exactly on top of the first line of stitching. From notch to notch clip the seam about every 1.5 cm to 2 cm (5/8'' to 3/4'').

2. Press this portion of the seam open and then fold the seam back on itself and press to sharpen the underarm seamline (Figure 18–9).

Note: To hold thick or springy fabrics more securely, catchstitch the armhole seam allowances at the intersection of the underarm and sleeve seam.

Method II:

1. Stitch 3 mm (1/8'') toward the cut edge from the stitching line between the notches in the lower armhole.

2. Trim the seam to 6 mm (1/4'') between notches. Overcast the seam if the fabric ravels excessively. The seam will remain standing under the arm and the lining will fit over it. If the sleeves are unlined, bind the entire seam. For a neat apperance, make the binding as narrow as possible. If the garment will be partially lined, do not bind the armhole seam until the lining has been inserted.

Applying the Shoulder Pads

With your garment on, adjust the pads to fit your shoulders, with the pad extending about 1.3 cm (1/2'') beyond the shoulder or armhole seam. Pin the pads in place from the outside (Figure 18–10). Remove garment and check the pad alignment. Straighten if lopsided, and then recheck fit.

Note: A pad with a curved armhole edge will follow the armhole seam, extending beyond the seam at the shoulder and tapering to the seam at the lower ends. A pad with a straight armhole edge often will not reach the armhole seam at the lower ends. In this case, attach the edges of the pad to the interfacing. The armhole edge of the pad may be trimmed, if necessary, for narrow shoulders or to ensure a better fit.

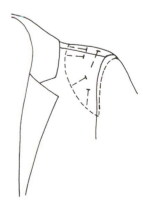

FIGURE 18–10
Pinning Shoulder Pads.

With a double strand of matching thread and from the *outside,* stabstitch through the armhole seam going through both pad and garment. Take a tiny backstitch with each stitch in the well of the seam but *do not pull tightly* since it will cause a dimpling in the seamline. If you desire, use the same kind of stitch across the shoulder seam. From the inside, again with a double strand of thread, diagonally baste along the outer edges of the pad, catching through the pad and the interfacing in both front and back. If the interfacing is fused, *very loosely* catchstitch the edges of the pad to the interfacing.

Note: For an *unlined garment* in which the shoulder pads will be visible, cover the pads with lightweight self-fabric or with matching lining fabric. Fold fabric on a true bias over the armhole edge of the pad. Cut the double thickness 1.5 cm (5/8'') larger than the pad. With right sides together stitch a 1-cm (3/8'') seam, leaving an opening large enough to insert the pad. Turn the seam, press, insert the pad, and then stitch through all layers of lining to make the seam lie flat.

Making and Applying Sleeve Heads

Sleeve heads are used to smooth the armhole seam across the top and to give additional shaping and support. They are especially useful in giving a lift to the seam where there is extra cap fullness or where there is a hollow in the upper cap area. If the cap is smooth, sleeve heads may be unnecessary. They are not used in unlined jackets unless the sleeves are lined.

To make and apply sleeve heads:

1. Cut a bias strip about 7.5 cm by 25 cm (3'' by 10'') for women, about 30 cm (12'') long for men, of lamb's wool or soft flannel.

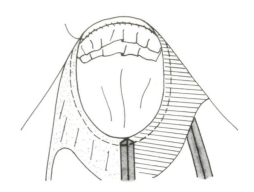

FIGURE 18–11
Applying Sleeve Head.

2. Make about a 2.5-cm (1'') fold along the length of the strip.

3. Center the strip over the top of the sleeve with the fold lying on the seamline between the seam allowance and the sleeve. The wider portion of the strip should lie next to the sleeve (Figure 18–11).

4. Permanently hand baste the strip in place, using a double strand of thread.

Note: If more padding is desired in the sleeve cap, make a 3.1-cm (1 1/4'') fold along the length of the strip, place folded edge even with edge of *seam allowance* and permanently baste along the seamline. Thus, four layers of fabric are placed between the seam allowance and the sleeve with the fold and the two cut edges of each different lengths.

5. Put your garment on and examine the sleeves. Slash the wide layer of the sleeve head or trim, if necessary; it should lie smoothly inside the sleeve. *Note:* To smooth a hollow in the upper cap (for a person with small upper arm), do not trim the sleeve head, but slash to allow the slashes to overlap. For a heavy upper arm, a narrower sleeve head is usually needed to fill out the shoulder above the upper arm.

Raglan Sleeves

Since raglan sleeves form a part of the neckline, they must be applied before any fitting is done. They may have a dart for fitting along the shoulder line or a seam extending from the neck the full length of the sleeve. The seam generally provides an easier means of fitting across the shoulder than does the dart. To apply:

1. Stitch and press open the underarm seam of the sleeve.

2. Match the armhole notches of the sleeve and garment, pin and hand baste in place.

3. Fit the garment, noting the smoothness of the fit across the shoulder line as well as the body ease. Some adjustment can be made at this time on a dart, shoulder, and /or armhole seam to accommodate a square or sloping shoulder.

4. Stitch and press the seams open. If topstitching is to be done on a shoulder seam (welt seam in Chapter 7) turn the seam toward the front and press again. If the armhole seams are to be topstitched, press them downward and topstitch from the neck to the armhole notches or the length of the straight portion of the seam.

Note: A shoulder dart is usually curved over the top of the shoulder and should taper gradually toward the end. The length may be extended to achieve a tapered, smooth point. Slash a shoulder dart open to the place where the dart is 1 cm (3/8'') wide. Follow the usual procedure for pressing opened darts.

5. The lower armhole seam may be slashed and opened or trimmed and left standing as described for the set-in sleeve, Method I or II.

Kimono Sleeves

Kimono sleeves are usually more popular in suits than in coats, primarily because of the design which may create too much bulk under the arm in heavy fabrics. Kimono sleeves may be designed in four different ways. They all require some type of reinforcement in their construction.

Designs

A normal underarm curve creates more folding under the arm, thus making it less applicable to coats of heavy fabric. It will require some kind of reinforcement since the curve will be clipped to allow the seam to be flat and not "bunch up" under the arm. Either one of two methods may be used to reinforce the seam:

Method I. This is the easiest and least conspicuous method (Figure 18–12).

1. Before the underarm seam is stitched, center and pin a length of tape 10 cm to 12.5

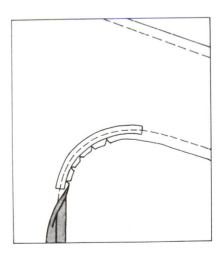

FIGURE 18–12
Kimono Sleeve Reinforcement.

cm (4'' to 5'') over the curved underarm area.

2. Stitch through tape when the seam is stitched, shortening the stitch slightly along tape length.

3. Clip (not notch) seam allowance along curve. Press seam open.

Method II. This is the most secure method, but stitching will be visible on the right side (Figure 18–13).

1. Stitch underarm seam, clip, and press open.

2. Center, pin, and baste a length of tape 10 cm to 12.5 cm (4'' to 5'') over the opened seam.

3. From the right side stitch through all layers of fabric, close to the seamline on each side. Fasten thread ends. Or use a half backstitch to make stitching less visible on the outside of the garment.

4. Remove basting and press.

An angular underarm curve permits a close fit to the body (Figure 18–14), but requires a gusset to allow for up and down arm move-

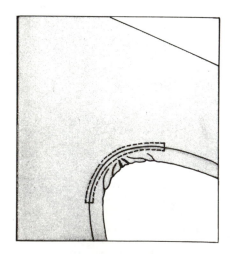

FIGURE 18–13
Kimono Sleeve Reinforced.

FIGURE 18–14
Angular Underarm Curve
Requiring a Gusset.

ment. Directions for constructing a gusset follow.

Kimono sleeve combined with a yoke gives a close underarm fit without the construction of a gusset. The shoulder seam extends from the neck over the shoulder to the hem of the sleeve, while the underarm section is cut like a normal set-in sleeve (Figure 18–15, A). A reinforced corner is required at the point where the armhole meets the yoke (Figure 18–15, B).

The *kimono* may be combined with a raglan. This gives the appearance of a raglan in the back and a kimono in the front. Or, it may be combined with a set-in sleeve so that the front has an armhole seam and the back is a kimono style.

Gusset Information

A gusset is either a triangular- or diamond-shaped piece of fabric set into a slash, extending from an underarm curve of the sleeve toward the neck. It provides room for arm movement in a garment. While gussets may appear to be difficult to construct, they are not hard *if* you follow instructions.

Gusset Patterns. The *diamond-shaped* gusset (Figure 18–16, A) may be one-piece (some-

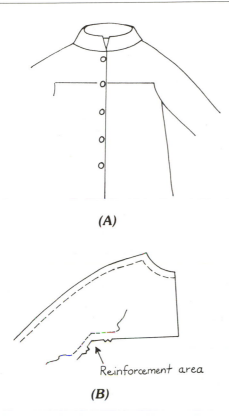

(A)

(B)

Reinforcement area

FIGURE 18–15
Kimono Combined with a Yoke.

triangular-shaped gusset is that it can be *inserted before* the underarm seam is stitched.

The *combination* gusset (E and F) forms part of (1) the underarm section of a sleeve, or (2) a side section of the garment. This is a popular style in coats as well as in jackets. The combination piece may be cut as one piece (E) or as two pieces (F).

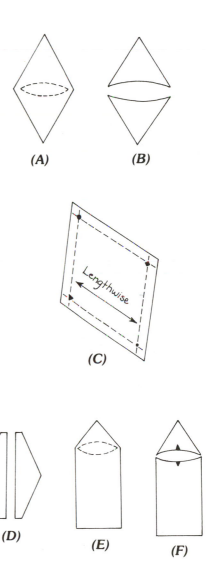

(A)   **(B)**

Lengthwise

(C)

(D)   **(E)**   **(F)**

FIGURE 18–16
Gusset Shapes.

times darted) or cut in two pieces with a curved crosswise seam (B). Either a dart or a curved seam through the middle of the piece is useful in reducing bulk. The regular diamond-shaped gusset has four corners each with a different shaped marking (□ △ ○ ○) as in (C). The gusset piece is applied *after* both the sleeve and garment underarm seams have been stitched.

The *triangular-shaped* gusset (two-piece) (D) may be converted from a diamond-shaped pattern by first determining (by checking the pattern markings) which halves of the gusset correspond to the front and back of the garment. Then cut in half lengthwise and add seam allowances along each newly cut edge. The advantage of the

General Suggestions for Inserting Gussets:

While your pattern includes instructions for inserting gussets, the following suggestions may supplement your pattern guide sheet and will apply to all gussets, regardless of the shape desired.

1. Tailor tack each corner, using a different color darning cotton on both gusset and garment. For example, use yellow for the □ symbol, blue for △, and so forth. By matching colors to your garment, you can be sure of inserting the gusset piece correctly.

2. Carefully mark the seamlines on both the gusset and the garment where the gusset is to be inserted. To make well-defined lines, hand baste or use a sharp marking pencil.

3. Always reinforce the point of the slashed opening. The fusible and the fabric patch are recommended reinforcements for loosely woven fabrics. Refer to Chapter 7 for an appropriate method.

4. Match the gusset stitching lines and the slashed opening exactly. The slashed seamlines will vary in width while the gusset seamlines will be even.

5. Carefully pin and then hand baste the gusset in place before machine stitching.

6. Leave a pin in place at the end of the slash and using a regulation stitch, stitch from the garment side toward the end of the slash. When 2.5 cm (1'') from the point, shorten the stitch to 20–22 and stitch to the point (remove pin as you approach point), pivot, take one or two stitches across the point, pivot again, and continue to the end of the gusset side.

7. Press the seam open or turn toward the garment side, depending upon your fabric and the effect desired. A pressed-open seam will be less conspicuous.

8. To firmly hold a turned gusset seam,

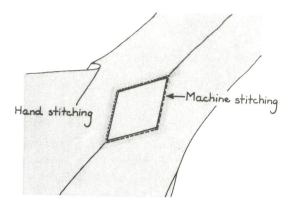

FIGURE 18–17
Gusset Topstitched.

from the right side of the garment use an inconspicuous hand backstitch along the turned edge. Keep these stitches at least 3 mm (1/8'') apart, depending upon the weight and structure of the fabric (Figure 18–17). Machine stitching may be used on casual garments.

Cuffs

Cuffs vary in popularity in tailored coats and suits almost as much as they vary in design. Because of this variation, the discussion in this text will deal only with general suggestions that may not be found in your pattern guide sheet.

Turnback Cuffs

When making cuffs we are generally concerned with (1) the prevention of wrinkling in the sleeve as the cuff is turned back, and (2) the reduction of bulk around the lower edge of the sleeve. Both of these concerns are necessarily interrelated. Keep this in mind as you are handling any hem or facing in terms of grading seams, pressing techniques, increasing an outer edge, or reducing an inner area.

Unless a fabric requires support through the lower sleeve area, eliminate interfacing in a hem or cuff to reduce bulk. Or, use a more lightweight interfacing than in the other garment parts. A lightweight fusible may be the best interfacing to use.

Prevention of Wrinkling in Sleeve with a Turnback Cuff. Wrinkling may occur in sleeves with turnback cuffs that are an extension of the sleeve or with cuffs that have been applied with a facing. To prevent wrinkling in a one-piece sleeve, taper the lower part of the sleeve.

The amount of necessary tapering will depend upon the weight of your fabric. The heavier the fabric, the more room will be needed on the outer edge of the cuff as it is turned. To determine the amount to taper, place pins on the seamline and parallel to it. Fold the cuff back and see if any puckering is discernible. This method gives only a ''guess'' as to the amount of tapering required.

When stitching the sleeve seam, taper the seam inward as you approach the turn of the cuff. Then taper outward through the cuff area. This allows the outer edge of the cuff to be wider than the sleeve at that point, thus helping to prevent wrinkling in the lower sleeve area (Figure 18–18).

A slash effect may be used to allow the outer edge of the cuff to expand (Figure 18–19). In a one-piece sleeve this is placed approximately one-half the distance between the middle top of the sleeve and the underarm seam. In a two-piece sleeve in which an extension has been allowed for a turnback cuff, an opening may be left in the lower part of the elbow seam. In this case the facing of the cuff also forms the hem which is turned back into the sleeve. The opening, as it is faced, allows the same cuff expansion as in the one-piece sleeve.

Reduction of Bulk Around the Sleeve Edge with a Turnback Cuff. If some preliminary planning was done before an at-

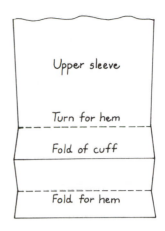

FIGURE 18–18
Shaping Sleeve to Reduce Wrinkling in Cuff.

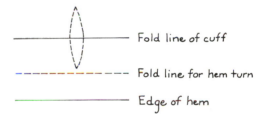

FIGURE 18–19
Stitching for a Slashed Effect in Cuff.

tached cuff was cut, as suggested in Chapter 5, bulk can be reduced and a smooth cuff will result. Two methods are suggested:

Method I. For a straight cuff, where the facing of the cuff was extended to form the hem of the sleeve, follow this procedure:

1. Stitch the under section of the cuff to the lower edge of the sleeve. Press the seam open.

2. Apply the top cuff (facings), remembering the methods for easing the outer layer of the cuff and for tapering the turn of the hem. Allow the facing to extend over the

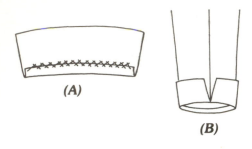

(A)

(B)

FIGURE 18–20
Detachable Cuff.

pressed open seam before turning the hem. This procedure extends the sleeve length by the width of the seam that attaches the cuff to the sleeve.

Method II. While this procedure may not be considered a way of reducing bulk, it allows for the circumference of the cuff to be larger than the sleeve and thus ensures that the cuff will lie smoothly. It is especially advantageous for the shaped cuff which must have a seam along the lower edge. Also, the cuff can be easily removed when no longer in vogue, leaving a finished sleeve edge. With this method, straight or shaped cuffs can be hand stitched to the finished sleeve by following this procedure:

1.   Finish the hem of the sleeve as directed in Chapter 19.

2.   Make the cuff; it should be long enough to go around the outer circle of the sleeve. Trim off the seam allowance of the lower edge of the underside of the cuff. Fold the top (facing side) over the cut edge and catch-stitch to the under part of the cuff (Figure 18–20, A). Press over a sleeve roll.

3.   Fit the cuff around the sleeve, allowing it to extend about 3 mm (1/8'') beyond the turn of the hem. Pin in place and carefully slipstitch the cuff to the fold of the hem (Figure 18–20, B).

Shirt-Style Cuffs

Cuffs of this type are often popular in casual jackets. Follow the directions in your pattern guide sheet for applying the shirt-style cuff. You may already have made adjustments in the cuff before cutting by following the suggestions listed in Chapter 5. However, consider these points in the construction of the cuff.

1.   To permit ease across the top surface of the cuff and to maintain a straight grain on the ends of the cuff (especially on plaids) *reduce* the inner circumference, rather than increasing the outer.

2.   To maintain a curved position, press the cuff, right side out, over a sleeve roll.

3.   To reduce bulk in the seam where the cuff attaches to the sleeve, consider the suggestions previously discussed in terms of pressing, killing edges, and grading seams.

Tailored Plackets. Sleeve plackets are less frequently found in strictly tailored jackets than in the casual type. Knit fabrics are partially responsible for the increased use of simple plackets in many informally styled jackets. Most pattern guide sheets give adequate directions for making plackets of this type. However, tailored plackets, which are considered to be more desirable and decorative than other types, are perhaps less used because they appear to be difficult to make (Figure 18–21). The directions given here are for making a two-piece tailored placket and are easy to understand and to construct if you follow the step-by-step instructions. Patterns for the two-piece placket are found in the Appendices and are for a 2.5 cm (1'') wide placket. At the end of the instructions you will find a pattern layout and directions for matching placket pieces to a sleeve of a plaid or striped fabric.

A tailored placket is applied *before* the underarm seam is stitched so that the sleeve may remain flat for easy construction.

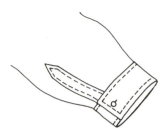

FIGURE 18–21
Shirt-Style Cuff.

Constructing the Placket. The follow-ing directions and illustrations are for a placket for the right sleeve. Reverse the directions for the left. It is advisable to make the two plackets simultaneously.

Precaution: After cutting, mark the wrong side of each piece with chalk. Re-member that the placket should open toward the underarm seam. Thus, the underlap will be placed toward the back on the side of the opening closer to the sleeve seam.

1. Pencil or chalk a straight line on the wrong side of the sleeve the length of the underlap piece and at the correct location. *Do not cut* the slit until after the overlap and

underlap have been stitched in place (Figure 18–22).

2. Fold the narrow upper section of the overlap in half lengthwise, right sides together, and stitch a 6-mm (1/4'') seam across the top. Tie threads, trim corner, and finger press the seam open. Turn right sides out to make a point. The seam should be *ex-actly* in the center of the point (Figure 18–23). *Note:* Shaded areas represent right side of fabric in this and all following il-lustrations.

3. Turn on indicated foldlines of both the underlap and overlap sections and press. The width of the overlap is now 2.5 cm (1'') and the width of the underlap is 2 cm (3/4'') when folded on the center line (Figure 18–24).

4. Edge stitch the overlap to within 1 cm (3/8'') of the ''jog'' level as illustrated. Pull the thread to underside and tie ends (Figure 18–25).

5. Place the right side of the underlap and overlap sections on the wrong side of the sleeve with the underlap closer to the under-arm seam allowance. The raw edges of the underlap and overlap should meet exactly on the placement line of the sleeve. Pin to

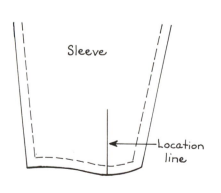

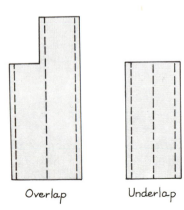

FIGURE 18–22
Placket Location Line and Placket Pieces.

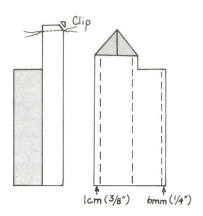

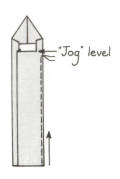

FIGURE 18–25
Stitching Open Edge of Overlap.

FIGURE 18–23
Making Pointed End on Overlap.

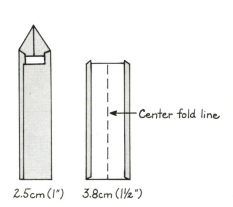

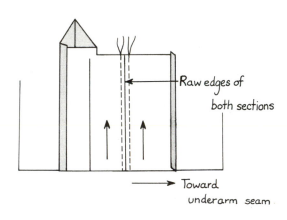

FIGURE 18–26
Stitching Sections to Sleeves.

FIGURE 18–24
Folding and Pressing Overlap
and Underlap.

hold in place and stitch 6 mm (1/4'') from the cut edges, using the crease line as a guide. Stitch from the bottom of the sleeve to the upper edges of both the underlap and overlap. Pull threads to the wrong side and tie (Figure 18–26).

6. Cut the sleeve along the placement line exactly to the top of the placket sections (Figure 18–27).

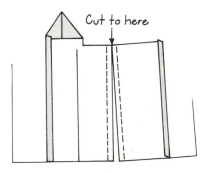

FIGURE 18–27
Cutting Placket.

FIGURE 18–28
Stitching Underlap.

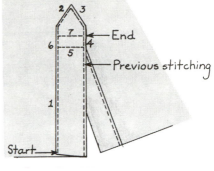

FIGURE 18–30
Final Stitching Left Placket.

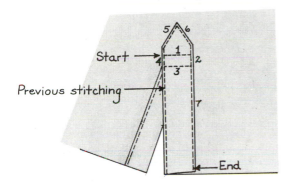

FIGURE 18–29
Final Stitching Right Placket.

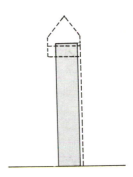

FIGURE 18–31
Stitching Showing on Wrong Side.

7. Turn the underlap to the right side through the slit. Pin the open side in place and stitch close to the edge, stitching from the bottom of the sleeve to the top of the underlap. Backstitch or tie threads (Figure 18–28).

8. Turn the overlap to the right side through the slit. Lap the placket sections as the completed placket will appear, pin, and topstitch in place as indicated in Figures 18–29 and 18–30. Figure 18–31 shows the stitching as it will appear on the wrong side of the sleeve.

Layout and Instructions for Matching Plaids or Stripes:

1. Place the broken center line of the overlap pattern on the same plaid position as the placket cutting line on the sleeve (Figure 18–32). The bottom edge of the placket should be on the same crosswise plaid as the lower sleeve edge. Place the underlap pattern on the same crosswise grain as the lower edge of the overlap. The placket cutting line on the sleeve can be shifted slightly either way in order that it comes on a center unit of the plaid for easier matching.

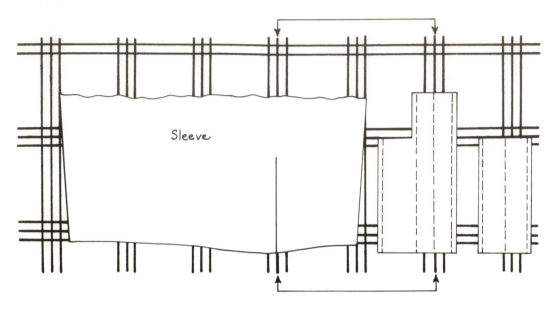

FIGURE 18–32
Pattern Layout on Plaid.

2. To test for accurate matching, cut a slit in a scrap of fabric the same length and on the same plaid unit as the placket location line of the sleeve. After the underlap and overlap sections have been prepared (Steps 2, 3, and 4), pin them first to the sample and turn through the slit to see if they will match accurately.

The overlap of the shirt-style cuff should match the overlap of the placket.

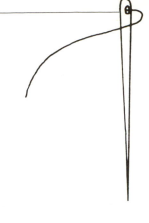

An inconspicuous hem is one of the marks of quality in construction. Almost every step from the measuring of the length of the garment to the final hand stitching and pressing is directed toward this end. As you work with heavy fabrics, such as those found in many tailored garments, the importance of hem handling becomes readily apparent. In fact, hems provide an excellent vehicle to illustrate the part that fabrics play in the dictating of methods to use in construction.

Standards for Hems:

1. Appropriate depth with uniform width.

2. Even in appearance from the floor and/or on the figure.

3. Reduced bulk in seams.

4. Even distribution of ease.

5. Appropriate finish for cut edge.

6. Easy and inconspicuous hand stitches with fine, matching thread.

7. Appropriate pressing for the type of fabric and style of garment.

8. Invisible from the right side.

Hemming Stitches

All hemming stitches should be loose and usually no closer together than 1.3 cm (1/2''). A fine hand-sewing needle (#9 or #10) is essential in making stitches inconspicuous; the thread should be your regular matching sewing thread.

For tailored garments the following hand stitches should be used:

1. The *inside hemming stitch* (also known as blind hemming or blind catchstitch, tailor's hemming stitch, running hemming) is highly recommended not only for hems but for attaching interfacings in hems as well as hems in linings. In addition, it is quick and easy to do. All stitches are made on the in-

19
HEMS

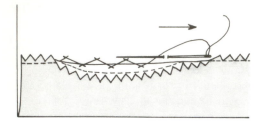

FIGURE 19–1
Inside Hemming Stitch.

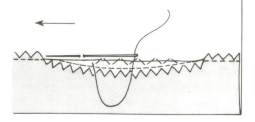

FIGURE 19–2
Inside Running Stitch.

side, between the hem and the garment. The stitches may be made in either of two ways:

a. Anchor the thread at a seam and then with the needle pointing toward the left, take a tiny stitch about 6 mm (1/4'') *toward the right* in the garment. Take a second stitch in the same direction into the ease line of the hem (Figure 19-1).

Continue alternating stitches in this manner, keeping stitches about 1.3 cm (1/2'') apart on each side (garment and hem). You will recognize this stitch as a catchstitch, but *between* two layers of fabric rather than *over* a hem edge. *Or,*

b. Anchor the thread and instead of working left to right, work from right to left with the needle pointing left. Alternate stitches from garment to hem with stitches about 6 mm (1/4'') in length. This stitch is faster to do than the one just described, but it is less durable if the thread ends are not securely anchored (Figure 19-2). A backstitch into the hem every 5 cm to 7.5 cm (2'' to 3'') will make the hem more secure.

2. The *slipstitch* (described in Chapter 7) is useful for hemming coat linings if the edge of the hem has been turned and stitched. It has other uses within the garment such as attaching the lower edge of the facings to the hem.

3. The *catchstitch* (Chapter 7) may be used when attaching an edge to an interfacing. Be careful about using it for a hem not interfaced or underlined unless the fabric is very lightweight. Catching *over* an edge will usually result in a ridge on the right side of the garment, especially in medium or heavy fabrics.

Hem Preparation

Hand baste a marking line along the foldline of the hem. After measuring and marking the desired hem depth, trim off the excess fabric. Turn on the marked line and lightly press, carefully holding the hem in place with your fingers. Avoid using pins which may leave an imprint if pressing is done over them. *Note:* For an underlined garment, trim the underlining about 2.5 cm (1'') longer than the foldline (less for more circular hem). To hold the underlining more securely lightly baste to foldline, if desired.

Grade the seam allowances through the depth of the hem by trimming about 3 mm (1/8'') on each side of the seam for a 1.5-cm (5/8'') seam and 6 mm (1/4'') for a 2.5-cm (1'') seam width (Figure 19-3). Machine stitch an ease line 6 mm (1/4'') from the cut edge. Draw in the ease as much as necessary to allow the cut edge of the hem to lie flat on the garment but be careful about drawing in

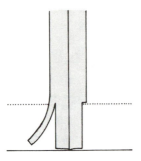

FIGURE 19-3
Grading Seam Through Hem Allowance.

too much. Shrink in fullness, placing a paper towel under the eased-in edge to prevent the cut edge from showing on the outside.

Note: For the *unlined garment,* use the Hong Kong finish (as described in Chapter 7) along the edge of the hem to control the ease and to provide a finish, or finish as the seams are finished. Straight hems in lightweight fabrics may be turned and stitched.

For the *lined garment,* jacket hems do not require a finish because the lining completely encases the garment hem. The coat lining covers the hem but it hangs free along the lower edge. Coat hems do not need a finish unless the fabric is ravelly.

The Interfaced Hem

Interfacing gives the hem body and prevents the cut edge of the hem from showing on the right side. Depending on the desired effect, the hem may have a soft or a sharp hemline turn which is determined by (1) the interfacing, (2) the method of application, and (3) the pressing techniques. For a *sharp hemline,* a heavier interfacing is usually used with the cut edge placed *on the foldline.* For a *soft hemline,* a light to medium weight interfacing is carried *past the fold* of the hem to form a double thickness at the turn. If the garment is underlined, the bias interfacing is not essential since the underlining itself will give support and add softness to the turn of the hem.

If a lightweight interfacing is used, follow the method for the soft hemline. However, the turn can be pressed so that it is quite sharp, if that is the effect desired or it can be soft. The soft hemline that is interfaced with a medium weight interfacing will not show wear along the fold as much as the sharp hemline. This is particularly important for sleeve hems where there is considerable wear.

For either the sharp or the soft effect, the interfacing extends *above* the cut edge of the hem to prevent "ridging" on the outside. For unlined garments the interfacing cannot extend above the hem and should end about 1 cm (3/8'') *below* the cut edge of the hem.

Applying the Nonfusible Interfacing.
Cut a strip of true bias interfacing at least 3.8 cm (1 1/2'') wider than the hem depth for a soft edge or 1.3 cm (1/2'') wider for a sharp edge. The strip should be long enough to extend the full circumference of the hem plus 2.5 cm (1''). *Note:* For jackets and coats exclude the bias interfacing from the front interfaced area. The additional 1.3 cm (1/2'') on each end allows the bias to extend *under* the front unterfacing for extra support. If piecing is necessary to make the interfacing the correct length, overlap the cut edges (preferably those on the lengthwise grain) and stitch. *Do not make a regular seam* that will add bulk to the hem.

For the *soft* hem, fold the bias strip so that it is as wide as the hem plus 1.3 cm (1/2'') and lightly press a crease line the entire length. With the hem opened flat, match the crease line of the bias strip to the foldline of the hem (Figure 19-4, A). Or, for a *sharp* turn, lay the cut edge of the bias to the foldline of the hem. As you lay in the opened strip, pull gently to reduce the circum-

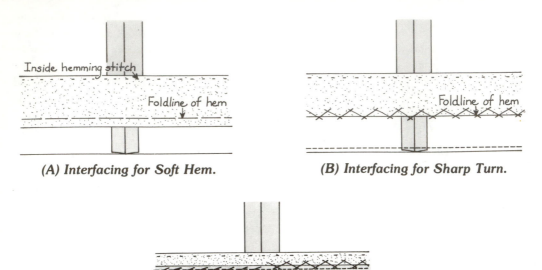

(A) Interfacing for Soft Hem.

(B) Interfacing for Sharp Turn.

**(C) Methods of Holding Hem
to Interfacing.**

FIGURE 19–4
Methods for Interfacing Hems.

ference of the bias as it lies next to the out-side curve of the garment.

Use an uneven hand-basting stitch about 2.5 cm (1'') long. From the bias strip side, carefully and loosely (but permanently) baste through the creased lines of both garment and the bias strip (or catchstitch the raw edge to the foldline as in Figure 19–4, B). Be sure that the stitch does not show through the garment. However, if it does show slightly, it will not be visible to a viewer because of its location on the fold.

Attach the interfacing to the garment along the upper edge with an inside hemming stitch. Then permanently tailor baste or catchstitch the fashion fabric to the interfacing along the ease line or to the underlining, if used (Figure 19–4, C). Lightly press the entire hem.

Applying the Fusible Interfacing. Woven, nonfusible interfacing is generally used for hems but if the fabric accepts a *fusible interfacing,* without mark-off or distortion, it may be applied like that for a soft or sharp edge. Cut a lightweight woven fusible on the bias or cut a nonwoven fusible with cross-wise stretch to fit the hem edge. Apply as for the nonfusible interfacing with the fusible side next to the garment. Fuse according to manufacturer's instructions. *Do not fuse over seams.* Place the fusible interfacing *under* the seam allowance before fusing. *Note:* Do not fuse to a hem unless the hem is perfectly straight. A fused curved hem will not ease.

Jacket Hems

Jacket designs frequently have curved or angled lower fronts. It is necessary that the hemline of the jacket coincide with the seamline of the curve or angle. Thus, at this point a jacket length cannot be lengthened, but it may be shortened by changing the location of the curved lower edge.

Recall from Chapter 4 that the jacket hems should usually be no less than 3.8 cm (1 1/2'') in depth. Some designs may require a wider hem allowance, and occasionally, facings, serving as hems, may be wider than 3.8 cm (1 1/2'').

Measuring the Length

The accompanying skirt should be tried on with the jacket. If the skirt hem is not ready to be permanently stitched, have your assistant pin it up at approximately the proper location since the total effect of jacket length to skirt length must be considered. Turn the jacket hem on the planned hemline and pin at right angles to the hem edge. Pinning in this manner sharpens the edge and makes checking for evenness easier. Put the jacket on and pin matching center front lines. Then analyze the jacket length in relation to the skirt length as well as to your figure. Adjust the length as needed.

Note: Often a more pleasing effect can be achieved by slightly lowering the front edge. However, plaids and checks may give a better appearance if turned *on* a line. In any case, the length must look well balanced on the figure.

Recheck to ascertain that the fronts appear equal in length even though this may mean that the overlapping side is slightly longer than the left underlap. Remove the jacket and lay it full width out on a table and analyze the appearance of the lower edge. Adjust, if necessary, to create a smooth hemline.

Procedure for Hemming. Follow the instructions for the interfaced hem, unless you have decided that the interfacing is not needed (i.e., because it is underlined or the fabric has sufficient body and weight). Before doing the permanent hand stitching, proceed as follows:

1. Attach lead weights (optional) to the seam allowance of the side seams. (Directions for handling weights are given at the end of this chapter.)

2. For a right-angled front corner trim the lower edge of the *facing* 1 cm (3/8'') below the hem foldline and trim the lower edge of the *front* 1.5 cm (5/8'') below the hem fold. Allow the end of the hem to extend under the facing at least 1.3 cm (1/2''). (See Figure 19-5, A.) This trimming allows the seam allowances to be graded when the facing is in place.

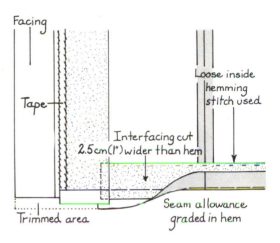

(A) Handling Jacket Hem.

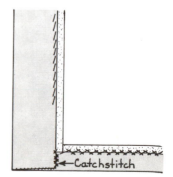

(B) Handling Jacket Facing Edge.

FIGURE 19-5

3. Fold back the front facing and turn up along the lower edge of the hem. Allow the facing to be slightly shorter than the hem and then press.

4. Slipstitch the lower edge of the facing to the jacket. Then with a short catchstitch attach the *raw* edge of the facing to the hem (Figure 19–5, B).

5. Lightly press the completed hem.

Handling Vents

Many tailored jackets have vent openings in the back or in the elbow seam of a sleeve. The vertical edges of the vent should be interfaced, usually in the same manner as the hem. However, you might wish to use a fusible interfacing along the vent edge and not in the hem.

A *mitered corner* (the diagonal joining of two lines at a corner) is a recommended procedure for handling a vent hem in a jacket. It is neat in appearance, eliminates bulk in the vent area, and allows both the hem and the vent edge to be smooth. Because some of the hem is trimmed in mitering, rarely would you use this method for a coat or skirt vent, unless the hem width is fairly narrow or unless there would never be any need for lengthening.

A mitered corner is most satisfactory when the hem and facing are the same width so that the miter is on a 45° angle. If the hem or the vent and at the lower edge of the jacket differ in width, the vent overlap may be handled like the front facing rather than mitering the corner.

To Make a Mitered Corner:

1. Press a crease line along the turn of the hem and the turned edge of the vent.

2. Fold back the corner of the fabric (bias fold) so that the fold touches the intersection of the two converging pressed lines. The grain of the folded back triangle should be the same as the grain underneath. Press in place (Figure 19–6, A).

3. Open the corner and fold the hem area on the bias. The right sides should be together and the raw edges should meet. Machine stitch (or hand backstitch) the two angled creased lines together. (Figure 19–6, B). *Or,* slipstitch the folded edges together after pressing and trimming.

4. Trim off the corner to within 6 mm (1/4'') of the stitching. At the corner, taper the seam allowance to eliminate bulk (Figure 19–6, B and C).

5. Press the seam open over a point presser, turn and press again.

The *vent underlap,* in a lined garment, has its seam allowance pressed to the underside before the hem is turned. The raw edge

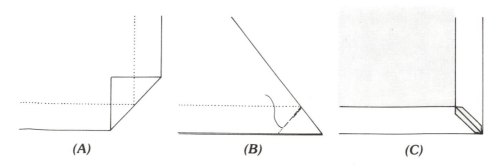

(A) *(B)* *(C)*

FIGURE 19–6
Mitered Corner.

of the vent is covered later by the lining. In the unlined garment, the underlap usually has a facing and is handled like the overlap. Finish the raw edges before slipstitching the vent to the hem.

Coat Hems

Generally a coat hem cannot be turned and pinned, as was the jacket, before the coat is tried on; fabric and body variations may cause the hem to be uneven. However, if you do not have an assistant for measuring, an alternative would be to use the jacket method.

Do not wear full-length pants with the coat when measuring unless you plan to wear them with your garment.

Coat hems may vary in width from 5 cm to 7.5 cm (2'' to 3'') depending upon the fabric as well as the design of the garment. For example, a flared coat will have a curved lower edge. Consequently, less width can be utilized since considerable fullness must be handled along the cut (or longer edge) when the hem is turned. Another consideration is that if a ''lengthening'' trend seems inevitable, the coat hem width may be extended to a bit more than 7.5 cm (3'') providing the fabric is not too heavy and bulky, or, the fabric is one in which the lines of a pressed or of a worn hem edge will not be noticeable. In other words, napped fabrics which are soft and fuzzy tend to wear along the edges, and the worn edge line will be discernible when the coat is lengthened. Likewise, heavily creased hem edges will be difficult to remove from a garment if the hemline is lowered.

Measuring the Hemline

A point to consider here is that the shoes you wear at the time a coat or a skirt hem is being measured can greatly affect the total appearance of the garment. Wear the shoes with the heel height approximating that which will be worn with the coat.

Put the coat on and pin, overlapping the fronts on the center front line. Be sure both fronts are held together at the same lengths.

The hem of a full-length coat should be about 2.5 cm (1'') longer than the longest skirt to be worn with it. Have your assistant use a marking device (see Chapter 1). To measure the hem, your assistant should move around you. This avoids any shifting of the coat that may occur *if you turn.*

Before removing the coat, have your assistant turn up the hem on the marked line and pin at right angles to the hem edge. Scrutinize for proper length and for evenness. Do not be afraid to adjust for different lengths in order to achieve a satisfactory appearance. Sometimes shortening a hem slightly from center back to the side seams will produce a neater effect. Otherwise it may appear as if the garment is longer in the back than in the front, especially if your coat tends to slide back from your shoulder. However, if you were properly fitted, this should not occur.

Preparing the Hem (Without Interfacing):

1. Follow the general instructions for hem preparation.

2. The hem of the facing should be turned up about 6 mm (1/4'') shorter than the hem measurement, tapering toward the front edge. Making the facing slightly shorter will prevent the facing from showing below the lower edge of the coat.

The facing should have the same hem depth as the rest of the coat, since it must allow for any lengthening of the garment later (Figure 19-7). This is a deviation from the treatment on the jacket facing as shown in Figure 19-5, A.

3. Stitch an ease line 6 mm to 1 cm (1/4'' to 3/8'') from the cut edge of the hem. Ease in to fit the garment.

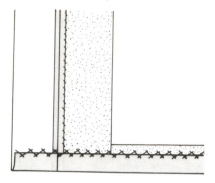

FIGURE 19–7
Handling Coat Hem.

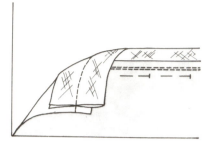

(A) Hem Edge Shield.

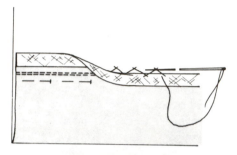

(B) Hemming Shielded Edge.

FIGURE 19–8

4. To help shield the cut edge of the hem from the outside, cut a 5-cm (2'') strip of lightweight fabric which matches the coat in color (batiste, or a similar weight fabric). Fold lengthwise through the middle and lightly press.

Note: If a soft hem roll is desired in a comparatively lightweight coat fabric, follow the instructions for the interfaced hem.

5. Place the cut edges of the strip *under* the edge of the hem. The fold should extend at least 1.3 cm (1/2'') above the cut edge of the hem and the entire hem length with the exception of the facing. It must fit smoothly. Pin in place (Figure 19-8, A).

6. Hold the strip in place by machine stitching on top of the ease line and then press again.

7. Pin the hem in place; place pins parallel to the cut edge and about 1 cm (3/8'') below the ease line.

Stitching and Completing the Hem

With your regular sewing thread and with "easy" stitches, hand hem, using a loose inside hemming stitch. (See Figure 19-8,B.) *Note:* For a wide hem, give additional support by placing a loose hemming stitch *inside* the hem and about 2.5 cm (1'') above the

hem before the final stitching is done (Figure 19-9).

For fabrics that do not hold a crease, fold the facing back. In order to hold it firmly, place pins parallel to the front edge and about 1.3 cm (1/2'') from it. Fold the

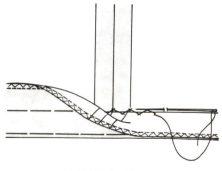

FIGURE 19–9
Double-Stitched Hem.

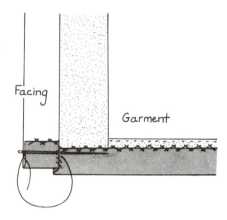

FIGURE 19-10
Holding Facing in Coat Hem.

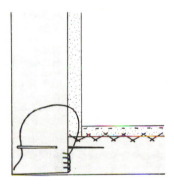

FIGURE 19-11
Finishing the Loose Facing Edge
of Coat Hem.

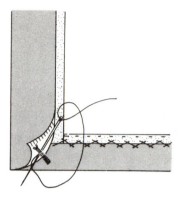

FIGURE 19-12
Tack for Holding Facing to Coat Hem.

either a blanket or an overcasting stitch. This permits the edges to remain flat, rather than "ridgy," the result if both edges were turned inward (Figure 19–11).

To loosely hold the facing to the hem, use a French tack (Chapter 7), placing it about 2.5 cm (1'') from the hem edge and from the facing edge (Figure 19–12).

Sleeve Hems

Establishing the Hemline

Since arm lengths vary and since the same amount of hand should be visible in both sleeves, the hem for each sleeve must be measured separately. While you have the garment on, have your assistant turn and pin the hem of one sleeve (pins at right angles to the edge) so that it looks well on your hand. The usual guide for turning is to cover the wrist bone. However, personal preference and the prevailing fashion may alter this location. _Note:_ A close fitting sleeve has a downward curve on the elbow side to allow the extra length needed as the elbow is bent. Follow this curved line in measuring. A wide sleeve has a straight lower edge.

For the second sleeve, measure from the

facing back over the pins and with a double strand of matching thread, hand whip the two layers of the hem together and then press (Figure 19–10). With a stitched-on facing, grading of the seam and hard pressing will be required to flatten the edge before doing the inside stitching. _Note:_ If topstitching is to be done, this hand stitching is unnecessary.

To prevent any possible raveling and to give a finish, stitch through both layers of the vertical facing and hem edges, using *tip* of the thumb to the sleeve edge and turn the hem to that measurement. Measure from the *tip* of the little finger to the hem to determine that location. Fold up the hem on these marks, pin, and analyze the location on both hands. Adjust for visual balance.

Baste *along* the folded edge (*on it, not* through it) as was done on the jacket hem. Fold the hem on the basted line and with the right side of the sleeve uppermost, place the hem edge over a sleeve roll and lightly press, turning the sleeve roll as you press. Be sure to use a wool press cloth next to the fabric.

Note: All pressing on a sleeve hem must be handled with the sleeve in the same position as it is worn to allow the hem to ease to the inside curve.

Finishing the Sleeve Hem

Sleeve hems should usually be no less than 3.8 cm (1 1/2'') in width. A good general rule is the wider the sleeve, the wider the hem should be to prevent the lining from becoming visible as it extends toward the lower edge of the sleeve. Proceed as follows:

1. Measure and mark the hems for the correct width. Trim and then grade the seam allowance(s) as was done in the previous hems.

2. Cut the interfacing following the instructions for the interfaced hem.

3. Follow instructions for inserting the interfacing with this exception: turn the sleeve wrong side out and *stretch* the bias slightly as you insert it since it must fit the inner curve smoothly.

4. Turn the right side out and check for a smooth fit. There must be no ''rippling'' of the bias. If there is, then turn the sleeve and again slightly stretch the bias strip. Check for smoothness.

5. Since the hem must also fit smoothly *inside* the sleeve, check the way it fits. If there is too much fullness, stitch the seam(s)

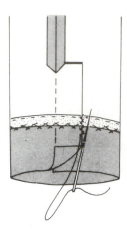

FIGURE 19–13
Finishing Sleeve Vent.

deeper, starting at the cut edge of the hem then tapering to the turn. Grade the seam and press.

6. Overlap the ends of the interfacing about 6 mm to 1.3 cm (1/4'' to 1/2'') and permanently hand baste in place.

7. With a loose stitch, catchstitch the hem edge to the interfacing.

8. Use the inside hemming stitch to hold the interfacing in place along the upper edge.

9. Again lightly press the hem over a sleeve roll.

Sleeves with Vents

The traditional sleeve vent has an overlap which is loose at the hem (held in place by buttons) and an underlap that is tacked to the sleeve hem.

For the *overlap,* follow the instructions for jacket vents. The mitered corner is particularly advantageous for sleeve vents since both the sleeve and vent edges are readily visible.

Note: Occasionally a pattern shows the vent facing cut as an extension of the sleeve hem. This results in a seam along the edge of the vent overlap. This is satisfactory in lightweight fabrics, but too bulky for heavy cloth.

The *underlap* in a *lined* jacket needs no finish. So closely catchstitch the lower 2.5 cm (1'') of the raw edge of the underlap to the sleeve hem to hold it in place and to keep the edge from raveling (Figure 19–13). The lining will cover most of the raw edge. For an *unlined* jacket, face the underlap or finish the raw edges as other seams are finished.

Skirt Hems

Measuring the Hemline

The skirt hem should be measured in the same manner as the coat hem. Choose the length that is within current fashion and most flattering to your figure. Straight skirts are usually a bit longer than full skirts but for a suit, the jacket length is also important. Consider the relationship of jacket length to skirt length. The proportion is usually more pleasing if the bottom of the jacket does not divide the total garment exactly in half. Skirt hems may vary in width from 2.5 cm (1'') or less in circular hems to 7.5 cm to 10 cm (3'' to 4'') for straight skirt hems, depending on the fabric. An A-line or slightly flared skirt will usually look best if it has at least a 5-cm (2'') hem.

Procedure. Skirt hems may have a soft or a sharp edge. For light to medium weight fabrics a lightweight interfacing such as batiste or organza gives added weight and smoothness to the straight or slightly flared hemline. An underlining will serve this purpose in the underlined skirt. If you wish to interface the hem, follow the previous instructions in this chapter.

For the underlined skirt or the noninterfaced hem follow the preliminary preparation for the interfaced hem. If an edge finish is needed, use the least bulky edge finish

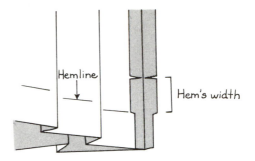

FIGURE 19–14
Seam Clipped at Backfold of Pleat Before Hemming.

that will prevent excessive raveling. Catchstitch the skirt hem to the underlining. Use the inside hemming stitch to hold the non-interfaced hem to the garment.

Pleats in Hems:

For the pleat that has a seam at the backfold edge:

1. Grade the seam in the hem allowance and press the seam open. Clip the seam at the top of the hem, then stitch the hem (Figure 19–14).

2. To hold the seam of the pleat flat, stabstitch through all layers about 3 mm (1/8'') from the seamed edge. Lightweight fabric may be machine stitched (Figure 19–15).

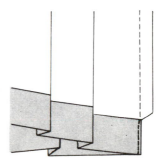

FIGURE 19–15
Flattening Pleat Seam.

FIGURE 19–16
Handling Seam after Hemming.

Alternate Method:

For a pleat in heavy fabrics or for a pleat cut with an angled seam:

1. Turn the hem, press, and hand stitch *before* stitching the lower 15 cm (6'') of the vertical seam.

2. Stitch the vertical seam, matching hemlines exactly.

3. Fold the seam allowance to form an angle and hand stitch the edges together (Figure 19–16).

Vents. Handle the vent in a skirt like the vent in a jacket or coat. *Do not* miter the corner or trim out the hem under the facing if you ever anticipate lengthening the skirt.

Pant Hems

Measuring the Hemline. Mark the pants at the desired length. Ordinarily, pants should not break over the instep and may be about 6 mm (1/4'') longer at the back over the heel.

A wider hem 6.5 cm to 9 cm (2 1/2'' to 3 1/2'') will give more body and weight to the pant leg, thus it will hang better than the pant leg with a narrow hem.

Procedure. Like skirts, pant hems may be interfaced for added weight and smoothness. The interfacing will also cushion the turned edge so that it is less likely to show wear. Follow the instructions for hem preparation; ease stitching will be needed only if the pant leg is flared. For tapered pant legs the seams through the hem should be tapered *out* below the foldline so the circumference of the hem will match the pant leg when the hem is turned up in place.

The tailor's hem (inside stitched) will be the least conspicuous, but the foot can catch in the loose edge. To reinforce the hem, take a fastening stitch into the hem every 2.5 cm to 5 cm (1'' to 2'') *or,* very loosely catchstitch over the edge to hold it close to the pant leg.

Cuff Suggestions:

1. The cuffed pant is constructed like the turnback cuffed sleeve (Chapter 18). Note the section on ''Prevention of Wrinkling in Sleeves,'' which describes tapering the seams.

2. Turn up the cuff before pressing a crease in the top folded edge of the cuff. Allow the inside layer of the fabric to lie smoothly inside the outer layer, then press both the top and bottom turns of the cuff.

3. Since the cuff covers the hemming, it need not be invisible, but can be securely stitched. Secure the cuffs at inseams and outseams with short French tacks.

Weights

Weights are optional in the construction of a jacket but are helpful in ''settling'' and holding a jacket in place on the figure. Two types are frequently used in tailoring— round *lead* weights like those in draperies and *chain* weights. The lead weights are ap-

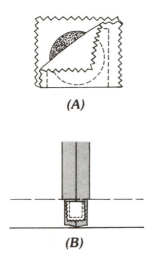

(A)

(B)

FIGURE 19–17
Lead Weight for Jacket Hem.

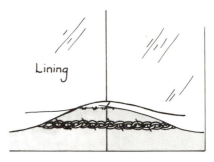

Lining

FIGURE 19–18
Chain Weight.

plied at the time the jacket is hemmed while the chain is attached after the lining has been stitched in place. Round lead weights are preferred to the square ones because in dry cleaning the shape of the corners of the square ones may become distorted.

Lead weights are used in hems at the underarm seams and at other seams where desired. Cut a strip of lining fabric large enough to make a pocket in which to enclose the weight (Figure 19–17, A). Fold the strip around the weight and enclose the weight by basting around it. Leave about 6-mm (1/4'') fabric around the three sides. Permanently hand baste the weight to the hem side of the seam allowance. Be careful about "jam-

ming" the weight to the turn of the hem (Figure 19–17, B).

Chain weights are available at notion counters and are used in the hems of jackets when even weighting is needed to hold the garment in place. They are usually used on jackets that are shorter than hip length, tend to "hike up" when the arms are raised, and will not settle into place when the arms are lowered. They are both functional and decorative.

To make the chain inconspicuous, attach it *under* the ease pleat at the bottom of the lining, thus allowing the lining to fold down over the chain (Figure 19–18). Pin the chain in place, remembering that it must assume an inner curve position. With hand whipping stitches (use a double strand of thread) attach the chain, sewing the ends of the chain to the front facing or as far as it will extend. Since the chain is attached *after* the jacket is completed, it can be easily removed when the garment is dry cleaned.

Lining the garment is the final major step in the construction process, and thus is one of the most exciting steps in tailoring. It means that another type of fabric comes into use—a fabric that can be elegant in color, design, and/or weave. Whatever the nature of the lining, the same careful attention must be given to its application as was given to the garment in earlier stages.

A jacket is used to illustrate the steps in lining construction, but the same procedure is applicable to a coat with the exception of the lining hem.

Standards for Linings Are as Follows:

1. Adequate ease across the back shoulders.

2. Smooth, but easy fit inside garment.

3. Seams pressed open, except seam at back of pleat in center back pressed as stitched, not opened.

4. Underarm seams attached loosely to garment seams.

5. Lower edge of lining equal distance from edge of garment.

6. Lining edges straight or smoothly curved and adequately cover facing edges.

7. Inconspicuous stitching attaches lining to facings.

8. Sleeves, back neck, and shoulder seams securely stitched.

9. Coat hem neatly finished; jacket ease fold adequate for vertical ease.

10. Ease fold in sleeves inconspicuous when arm is raised.

Methods of Application

Three methods of applying the lining are (1) by machine, (2) by hand, and (3) by a combination of the two. The *machine method* is popular for those who are interested in a

20

LINING APPLICATION

quick application since all portions of the lining may be stitched together (including the sleeves) before its insertion. This method is used almost exclusively in ready-to-wear apparel, especially in less expensive garments. Unless handled carefully, its chances of being poorly fitted are greater than with the other two methods.

The *hand method* involves the application by hand of each separate piece of lining to its counterpart in the garment. A minimum amount of machine stitching is involved and is done primarily on lengthwise sleeve seams, darts, and tucks. This method is durable (if the hand stitching is well done) and probably provides the best fit because of the way in which it is applied. However, it is time consuming due to the handwork involved. Also, all seams are essentially lapped seams, and in some rather heavyweight linings, this type of seam may be unsuitable.

The *combination method* utilizes some of both of these methods. All lengthwise seams in the body of the lining as well as in the sleeves are stitched and pressed open. Open shoulder and armhole seams provide an opportunity for adjusting the lining to fit smoothly in these important areas. By matching the side seamlines, adjustments can be made in the front along the facing edges and in the center back pleat. The outer edge of the lining covers the facing edge and is hand stitched in place.

In this text the combination method is synonymous with "traditional," while the machine method is considered "contemporary." The hand method is not included in the following discussion.

Preparing the Garment for Lining

If you have practiced good construction techniques, your garment should require very little additional attention at this time.

However, the following should help you to decide whether you have met the standards for a well-constructed garment up to this point.

Inspection of Garment:

Open your garment wide for close inspection.

1. Are all bastings removed and loose threads clipped?

2. If lining is to be inserted by the traditional method, are facing edges attached with firm permanent tailor basting, about 6 mm to 1 cm (1/4'' to 3/8'') from the cut edge? Are the facings left loose for the contemporary method?

3. Are hemming stitches inconspicuous?

4. Are all seam edges trimmed, beveled, and flattened (especially in heavy fabrics) to reduce a bulky appearance?

Use Critique #11 to check specifics. Refer to previous critiques for any specific areas already checked. Now, place your garment on a dress form or a well-padded hanger. Stand back about 1 m to 1.2 m (3' to 4') and carefully scrutinize the total appearance. A distant view gives a perspective that is not discernible at close range. If you have an assistant, put the garment on and stand in front of a full-length mirror. While you look at the front, your assistant will be able to survey the back. Be critical. Then ask yourself these questions:

1. Are any "puffy" spots apparent? If so, this indicates that shrinkage has taken place unevenly over the fabric surface.

2. Are there any imprints of bastings or pins along facing edges or hems?

3. Do hems appear even and pressed as flat as fashion dictates?

4. Does the collar roll evenly and are edges flattened?

When you are satisfied that all conditions have been met, then you are ready for the lining.

Note: Many times a question has been raised regarding the advisability of having a tailored garment pressed professionally before attaching the lining. If you feel that professional pressing is essential, now is the time to have it done. However, in most instances your careful attention to pressing details during construction, with a few minor press up jobs at this point, is usually all that is necessary unless your fabric is very rigid and resists pressing. As the creator of this garment, you have the greatest interest in it, much more so than the average professional presser. However, if you decide upon professional pressing, it may be wise to point out to the presser the area(s) where special attention should be given.

Preliminary Planning for Lining

Decisions as to whether to underline your lining or to interline your garment should have been made prior to this time. Refer to Chapter 2. If your lining is soft (i.e., China silk) an underlining of a firm, sheer, and supple fabric may be applied to the lining to provide opaqueness as well as durability. If the decision is to underline the lining, you must now combine the two fabrics before stitching the lengthwise seams. Refer to Chapter 10.

If an interlining is to be incorporated, decide on the method to use. Again, refer to Chapter 2. The easier procedure to use is to apply the interlining to the lining, thus allowing the interlining to act as an underlining in its treatment. The procedure is to tailor baste all layers together, stitch the lengthwise seams, and then permanently machine or hand baste along the outer edges about 1.3 cm (1/2'') from the cut edge. This basting will be covered when the lining is

folded over the facing. Trim the interlining about 3 mm (1/8'') from the basted line. From this point, follow the directions for either the traditional or contemporary method for application.

Certain couture touches can individualize a lining and make an ordinary plain lining look elegant. The addition of any of these touches will increase the time involved, but will be worth the effort if you enjoy fine clothing.

Decorative Stitches for Linings

Some of the couture touches must be planned for *before* the lining is applied. The following are suggestions to consider:

Decorative *hand* stitches are applied after the lining has been basted in place. A popular one is a chain stitch made of silk buttonhole twist or of polyester topstitching thread. (Refer to Chapter 7.) The thread may match or may be of a contrasting color. Care should be taken that each stitch is pulled only enough to maintain a chain effect. A stitch about 6 mm (1/4'') is a good length and will be less apt to get caught and pulled out of shape than a longer stitch. The chain stitch, or a variation, may be used to anchor the lining to the facing. Other hand stitches can also be used, depending upon the ingenuity of the sewer.

Machine stitches (decorative) can be used effectively, but they must be applied *before* the lining is attached to the garment. The first step is to establish the exact foldline of the lining. This provides a guideline to follow when the decorative stitching is applied. To do this lay the lining front on the garment front, matching the lining side seam to the garment side seam. Pin the two layers together and fold the front edges over the facing (allow some ease) to determine the foldline on the lining. Lightly crease the line and then apply the decorative stitching toward the garment side of the lining.

Cording is another method that can give

a simple but distinctive couture addition. A fabric-covered cord can easily be prepared by using a small cord and covering it with a bias strip of lightweight fabric, often of a contrasting color. The cord must be small enough to avoid adding excessive bulk to the garment. Lightweight fabrics should use a tiny cord to give a faint line along the lining edge; heavy fabrics can carry a heavier cord no larger than 3 mm (1/8'') in diameter.

To make the cording, hand or machine baste the cord in a folded bias strip of matching or contrasting fabric about 2.5 cm (1'') in width. Purchased rayon bias binding is also usable and, if the right color is available, will involve less work. Then pin the strip along the entire facing edge, allowing the stitching lines to match. Then, with a double strand of thread, permanently hand baste the cording in place. Machine stitch the cording on the facing if the lining is to be applied by machine.

Braids also offer a pleasing effect to a lining. A variety are available on the market but they must be selected with care because they tend to be bulky and hence can be used more often on coat weight fabrics than on jackets. Either a matching color or a contrasting one can be effective. If the braid is carried around the curve of the neck facing, use one narrower than 1.3 cm (1/2'') since it will curve more easily. Braids are applied inconspicuously by hand *after* the lining has been stitched.

Trapunto (also known as Italian quilting) can be used effectively in a lining in the form of a monogram or in other simple designs. It is better suited to curved rather than to abrupt, sharp lines. Any couture technique should be located where it is visible when the garment is opened. Thus, a monogram should be on the right-hand side of the lining on a woman's garment and at a level visible when the front is opened. A monogram could be placed on the inside pocket of a man's jacket. A point to remember is that the lining will be reversed with the raw seam edges matching those of the garment. Think about this before applying a decorative feature such as a monogram.

The design for trapunto is raised with padding while the background is left plain. To handle the trapunto:

1.   Place a soft, porous fabric under the area for the design.

2.   Draw your design on tissue paper and place on the right side of the lining. Pin in place.

3.   Either machine stitch or hand backstitch the outline of the design.

4.   Remove the tissue and with a tapestry needle and a soft yarn, fill in the stitched area from the wrong side.

Note: Do not pad too heavily since it may tend to make the design puckered. *Do not press.* However, if pressing seems necessary place the design face down on a heavy towel to avoid flattening the raised design.

Machine embroidery or *hand embroidery* can also be used in monograms or small designs. It may be applied to a patch pocket of lining fabric and attached as a separate piece to the lining or placed directly on the lining.

Preparing the Lining

Since the lining should fit smoothly into the jacket or coat, make the same changes in it that may have been made in the garment during fitting. Refer back to the adjusted paper pattern or to your test garment to determine where changes (if any) were made. *Note:* Do not use wax chalk for marking on lining fabric since it will leave a grease mark when pressed.

Before stitching the lengthwise lining seams, check in the following manner:

1.   Hand baste the center back ease pleat in place the full length of the lining.

2.   Pin the lengthwise seams with the pins parallel *to* and *on* the seamline.

3.   Lay the opened lining next to the opened garment (wrong sides together) and match the seams. Do they match or is the lining too wide or too narrow? It is still possible to decrease or to increase the seam allowances at this point.

4.   Slip the pinned sleeve lining into the garment sleeve. Open your hand wide and draw your hand through the sleeve length. Is the lining too large? Because the lining assumes the inner circle position within the sleeve, it usually requires wider seam allowances to reduce the circumference.

5.   Staystitch the back neck edge 1.3 cm (1/2'') from the edge.

6.   Then stitch lengthwise seams *only,* including the seam at the center back pleat (unless the pleat was laid on a fold). Stitch darts in the back shoulder, neck, and underarm and any long darts that function as a fitting seam.

7.   Pink the seams only if the fabric ravels excessively. If the fabric is translucent, do not pink the edges since straight edges are less visible in a fabric of this nature.

8.   Press the seams open with a dry iron after first testing to determine the proper temperature for your fabric. *Note:* Do not press the back ease pleat in place at this time in case it may be necessary to take in back fullness or to let out some ease during the lining process.

9.   Pin to a hanger or lay the sections on a flat surface until ready to apply.

Optional Adjuncts to Linings

A *permanent lining shield* is often desirable to absorb additional wear in the underarm section of the garment, particularly in jackets where the fit is close to the body. A jacket lining is frequently of lightweight fabric which may tend to show signs of wear more quickly under the arm than in any other place. The shield is easily removed from the jacket later if and when it shows wear, thus leaving an exposed unworn area.

See pattern in Appendices. To construct:

1.   Place notched edges together and stitch, using a 1-cm (3/8'') seam allowance.

2.   Press the seam open and turn the shield right side out, matching the curved underarm portion.

3.   Lightly press the folded edges.

Directions for its placement will be given at the time the lining is applied. *Note:* To protect the sleeve lining also, insert two shields, and turn one into the sleeve and one into the garment.

A *removable shield* that can be removed for laundering may be constructed by covering a commercially made shield with your lining fabric. Use the purchased shield as a pattern and construct a covering for each section of the shield. If the addition of your lining fabric makes the shield too heavy, remove the original covering and insert the shield into the lining covers you have made. Attach to your completed garment by basting or by pinning inconspicuously with tiny safety pins.

A *hidden pocket* in the lining of women's garments is an excellent way of providing pocket space in garments (particularly jackets) where there are no pockets or where fake pockets and/or flaps have been utilized. The hidden pocket should be placed on the right-hand side of the jacket and slightly below the right breast.

To make a pattern and construct the hidden pocket:

1.   Place a sheet of tissue or soft paper under your right breast and lay your left hand on it, letting your hand dip downward.

2. Roughly draw a pencil line around the shape of your hand.

3. True the edges, draw a 1-cm (3/8'') seam allowance all around, and cut out two layers of fabric with the straight edge being on the lengthwise grain.

4. Press back the seam allowances on the straight edges.

5. Stitch the two layers together with the pressed straight edges to the outside.

6. Stitch around the curved portion and press again (Figure 20–1). The explanation for its insertion will be given with the lining application later in this chapter.

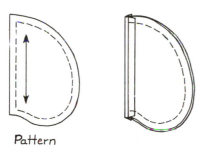

Pattern

FIGURE 20–1
Hidden Pocket.

Traditional Method of Applying the Lining

The combination method using hand and machine stitching is discussed in this section.

Equipment Needed:

1. A quantity of fine pins. In fabrics that tend to pin mark, use fine number 10 needles in place of pins.

2. Matching thread for permanent basting and stitching.

3. Basting thread of any color.

4. Several number 8 and number 9 hand-sewing needles. As a time saver have several needles threaded at one time, at least two with matching thread and two with other basting thread.

5. Seam gauge and scissors.

6. Thimble.

Applying Lining to the Body of the Garment

The same basic principles of lining application can be applied to garments with all types of sleeves, even though the major emphasis in this text is on the set-in sleeve.

1. With the seams pressed open, place the garment right side down on the table and lay the lining on it with the wrong sides together and with the underarm seams matching. Fold back the front section and pin the opened seams together. If there is an underarm panel section in the garment and no underarm seam, match the seams toward the back. (See Figure 20–2.)

Caution: Do not work over an outwardly curved area (i.e., dress form) when applying

FIGURE 20–2
Attaching Seams of Lining and Garment.

the lining at any time *except* when applying the sleeve and when fitting the lining across the neck and the shoulders. Try to avoid allowing too much ease within the body of the lining.

2. Check the armhole of the lining against that of the garment since frequently in fitting the underarm may have been lowered to increase the armhole or to increase the sleeve cap depth.

Place the armhole seam of the lining next to the garment seam and from the underarm carry it up the front to the shoulder and up the back to the shoulder seam. There should be ample shoulder seam, at least 2 cm (3/4'') at both front and back lining. If a shoulder pad is used, the lining will extend further over the shoulder since the pad decreases the *inside* circumference of the armhole.

In case there is not ample shoulder seam, unpin the underarm seam and raise the underarm seam of the lining along the garment seam, then clip the lining seam to fit the underarm of the garment.

3. With opened underarm seams lying on top of each other, stretch the seam slightly and pin in place along the two front edges of the seam allowance (Figure 20–2). Permanently baste the two seams together using a double strand of matching thread. (Always use a double strand for permanent basting.) Make very loose stitches at least 2.5 cm (1'') long and carry to within 7.5 cm (3'') of the top of the hem.

Repeat the entire front process for the second side.

4. Now fold the front lining sections into position on the garment and with the garment flat on the table, smooth the front lining from the underarm seams toward the facing. Keeping the lower edges parallel, slightly ease the lining to the garment the full length and pin in place through the middle of the front section (Figure 20–3). If a

FIGURE 20–3
Pinning Lining in Front.

waistline dart or tuck is needed, fold in the amount required and pin in place.

If the lining has been allowed to lie ''easy'' on the garment, no additional easing may be necessary since the lining assumes the inner part of a circle as it curves around the body. The lining must not be taut at any point.

5. Match the front armhole of the lining to the garment from the underarm to the shoulder. Pin and permanently baste the lining to the armhole seam of the garment, including the shoulder pad. Again refer to Figure 20–3.

6. If dart tucks are planned for the front shoulder, fold the dart into position, adjusting it so that it falls about halfway between the facing and the armhole. Pin in place for about 7.5 cm (3''). Using a small catchstitch (or another stitch of your choice) catch through all *three* layers of fabric to hold the tuck in place. Do not catch over the folded edge. Repeat for the second side. If the distance from the cut edge of the facing to the armhole is short (about 5 cm or 2''), it may be possible to eliminate the dart tuck,

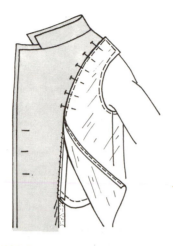

(A) Inserted with the Lining.

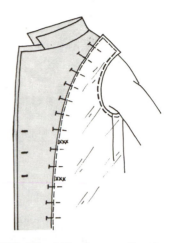

(B) Finished Pocket on Inside of Garment.

FIGURE 20–4
Applying Hidden Pocket.

thus allowing for a smooth fit across the front. Fold out (and trim off) any excess lining along the facing side.

7. Working inside the shoulder curve, overlap the stitching lines of the front lining to the garment across the shoulder. Pin and permanently baste the lining to the shoulder seam, placing the basting slightly back of the garment seamline (toward cut edge). Later, the back shoulder seam will lap over the front shoulder.

8. Turn under the front edge of the lining, keeping this edge as straight as possible, and allow an overlap of about 1.5 cm (5/8'') along the entire facing length. The lining should cover the tailor basting which holds the facing to the interfacing. If there is more than 1.5 cm (5/8'') turned under, baste through both layers of the folded edge and trim off any surplus fabric, maintaining the normal seam allowance (Figure 20–4, A).

9. If you plan to insert a pocket in the lining, it should be attached now before the lin-

ing is basted to the facing. To do this, place the open side of the pocket at the predetermined location on the right-hand side of the garment. Pin the lower, open edge to the facing 1.5 cm (5/8'') from the edge. This should be in line with the folded edge of the lining (Figure 20–4, A). Pin and baste the upper edge of the pocket to the lining. Incorporate the finish for this upper edge with the finish you will be using for the remainder of the lining.

10. Lay the lining over the facing edge and pin in place with pins at right angles to the lining edge and baste in position. Repeat for the second side. (See Figure 20–4, B.)

11. With the back of the garment right side down on the table, take hold of the two lower back armholes and pull gently, bringing the grains of the garment and lining into line. Pin the lining in place as shown in Figure 20–5 to keep the upper section of the lining grain straight with the garment while fitting the upper lining into position.

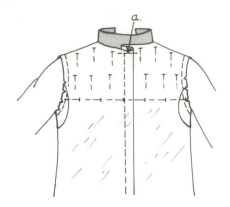

FIGURE 20–5
Adjusting Lining Across Back.

FIGURE 20–6
*Adjusting Lining at Neck and
Shoulders.*

12. If you are using the underarm wear shield, now pin it on the lower armhole area with the shield seam next to the lining.

13. Beginning at the underarm seam, match, pin, and baste the back armhole of the lining (including shield) to the garment armhole up to the shoulder seam, keeping the lining as smooth as possible.

14. Working inside the shoulder curve, fold the back shoulder seam over the front, covering the basted line on the shoulder. Then fit and pin the neckline seam to cover the back facing edge, or the neckline seam if there is no facing (Figure 20–6). Notice that in the illustration there is no back facing.

Note: If the center back lining ease pleat needs adjustment, it may be let out or taken up to fit the width across the back. The outer fold of the pleat is usually at center back and should turn toward the right-hand side of the garment as you face the lining. If your garment has a back vent, the ease pleat may be set to one side to line up with the

(A) Bar Tack Below Neck Facing.

(B) Catchstitch at Neckline.

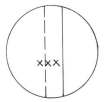

(C) Catchstitch Across Pleat at Waistline.

FIGURE 20–7
Location of Tacks at Back Ease Pleat.

edge of the underlap. Refer to "Lining the Vent" at the end of this chapter.

15. To prevent the inner fold of the center back pleat from falling loose inside the lining, permanently hand baste across the width of the pleat at the neck edge and within the seam allowance. (See a in Figure 20–5.) Now clip the neck seam allowance _only_ enough to allow it to lie flat as it is folded. Fold under the seam allowance and hand baste along the folded edge through both layers. Trim off any surplus lining on both neck and shoulders, leaving the normal 1.5-cm (5/8") seam allowance.

16. Lay the basted edges of the lining into position and pin in place, allowing some ease around the neck and across the shoulders. _Note:_ If there appears to be any strain across the back, either let out the center back pleat or remove the basting from the back armhole and allow the lining to shift slightly to allow more ease. Baste all edges of the lining to the facings with stitches about 1.3 cm (1/2") long.

17. Place a bar tack about 6 mm (1/4") in length on the fold of the pleat at the back neck facing (Figure 20–7, A). If the lining extends to the neckline, then catchstitch through _all_ thicknesses of lining about 2.5 cm to 3.8 cm (1" to 1 1/2") down the fold of the pleat (see B). _Do not catch over the fold_ since any strain across the back may pull holes in the fabric where the stitches are caught.

18. Hold the pleat in place at the waistline by catchstitching the lining across the width of the pleat, catching through the three layers of lining only (see C). Or, use the same decorative hand stitch used on the lining.

Critique #11 should be checked before permanently stitching around the lining.

The _lining stitch_ is a variation of the slipstitch and is used to permanently hold the lining in place (Figure 20–8). It differs from the slipstitch in that the needle is carried through the fashion fabric (facing) with only a tiny pick-up stitch into the lining fold. In contrast, for the slipstitch the needle is carried through a fold and then a small stitch is taken into the garment. The lining stitch is considered durable with the major portion of the thread buried into a firm fabric. It can become invisible since only a tiny stitch is caught into the lining edge. Use either matching polyester or mercerized thread to attach the lining to the facings. Silk thread is somewhat difficult to handle and unless _very securely_ fastened the ends may tend to slip and work free.

Use a small needle (#9 recommended) and fasten the thread end with a fastening stitch. Slip the needle into the facing (fashion fabric) and then barely catch into the edge of the lining fold. Start the next stitch by placing the needle into the facing directly opposite the place where the thread emerged through the lining. On the front facings where there is little strain, stitches may be about 6 mm (1/4") apart. Around curves of the neck, shoulder, and armhole take smaller stitches for more durability. All stitches should be taut but not pulled too tightly. Also use the lining stitch to attach the lining to the hems of sleeves and the lower edge of jackets.

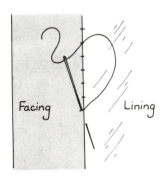

FIGURE 20–8
Lining Stitch.

Lining the Sleeves

The sleeves have been checked for the correct width, and the seams have been stitched and pressed open. Follow this procedure:

1. Fold the seam allowance of the cap toward the inside of the sleeve.

2. Beginning at the top of the cap, hand run a tiny ease line around the entire cap along the fold (Figure 20–9, A).

3. Clip the seam in the underarm area to allow the seam to lie flat. Notch out any excess folds which appear in the top of the cap as the ease line is drawn up.

Note: If the underarm seam is left standing, the sleeve lining must extend over the seam. If additional length was not allowed when the sleeve lining was cut, check to be sure that the lining will cover the seam. This seam allowance may be made smaller if necessary.

4. Insert the sleeve lining using one of two methods: (A) Permanently baste together the vertical underarm seam of the lining and the fashion fabric, or (B) leave the seams free. Method A has the advantage of preventing the lining from shifting within the sleeve and is especially helpful in men's sleeves and in large, loose sleeves found in some coat designs. A disadvantage is that unless care is taken, the lining directly below the armhole area in the sleeve may not have enough ease to allow the garment seam to lie perfectly flat. Method B requires less handling and since the sleeve is anchored around the armhole and the hem area, the lining is stabilized sufficiently for most jacket and coat sleeves.

Method A Procedure:

a. Turn garment and lining sleeves wrong side out.

b. Match the two opened underarm seams. If the sleeve is two piece, match the shorter inside seam.

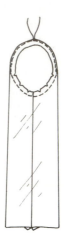

(A) Basting Ease Line Around Cap.

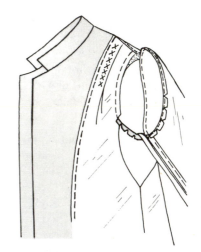

(B) Basting Sleeve Seams Together.

FIGURE 20–9
Applying Sleeve Lining.

Make sure that the sleeve lining extends far enough to cover the armhole seam of the garment. Pin the two underarm seams together from the armhole to about 7.5 cm (3'') above the turn of the hem (Figure 20–9, B).

c. Baste together very loosely as was done on the underarm seam in the body of the garment.

d. Slip the hand through the sleeve from the top, take hold of the lining and the garment at the wrist, and turn the sleeve right side out.

Method B Procedure:

Insert sleeve matching the seams. Be sure that the correct lining sleeve is in the correct garment sleeve.

5. For either Method A or B, at the underarm seam, overlap the lining sleeve over the garment armhole seam. Ease and pin in place around the entire cap, allowing more ease in the upper part of the cap than in the underarm. Place the pins at right angles to the seamline. The sleeve should hide the stitching line along the armhole seam of the garment (Figure 20–10).

6. Baste in place and closely stitch, using lining stitches about 3 mm (1/8'') apart. Small stitches are necessary for durability in this stress area.

FIGURE 20–11
Pinning Ease Pleat for Vent.

Lining the Vent

If you have a vent opening in the back of your jacket or coat, the lining must be anchored around it before hemming is done. The following procedure is different from that in the pattern guide sheet and is superior in its wearability and ease of construction. This method eliminates a slash at the top of the vent (as most patterns show) and thus is more durable. *Attention:* Unless your lining was cut on a fold at the center back, this method is not workable. (Refer to Chapter 5.)

Before attaching the back neckline lining to the garment, shift the location of the center back foldline as follows:

1. To hold the lining in place in the back, place a row of pins through the lining and garment and pin the entire length on each side of the pleat. Remove the original bastings from the pleat so it is free (Figure 20–11).

2. Measure from the center back seam of the garment over to the visible edge of the

FIGURE 20–10
Pinning Sleeve Seam.

vent underlap. On the lining, measure from its center back the exact width of the vent and place pins in a line to designate the new location of the pleat foldline (Figure 20–12).

3.   Transfer the foldline of the ease pleat to align with the row of pins (toward the right). The folded edge underneath *must* turn toward the center on the inside of the lining.

4.   To prevent the lining from being too short or too tight from the neck to the top of the vent, pull the garment taut between these two points, allowing the lining to be somewhat slack. Pin the lining and the garment together at the top of the vent opening.

5.   Pin the lining along both sides of the vent. Check to see that the foldline falls directly over the edge of the underlap.

6.   To determine the area to be cut away from under the pleat, baste a marking line (a) along the vent *beside* the foldline of the lining. Baste another line (b) exactly *on* the foldline (Figure 20–13).

7.   Open the pleat and mark 1.5-cm (5/8") seam allowances at each of the two long edges and the upper edge of the vent and cut away the section of the lining (Figure 20–14). The amount of the cut-away may be no more than 2.5 cm (1"), depending upon the width of the ease pleat.

8.   Check to see that there is adequate ease from the top of the vent to the neck. Clip the seam allowance at the top of the underlap to allow the seam to turn under (note x in Figure 20–14). Do not clip the opposite corner. Turn under the seam allowances along each edge and lay them in place covering the raw edges of the vent. The two folded edges of the lining along the vent should fall together when the vent is closed (Figure 20–15).

9.   Use the lining stitch to hold the lining in place.

10.   Place a short bar tack on the pleat fold at the top of the vent to hold the lining securely.

FIGURE 20–12
New Foldline Location.

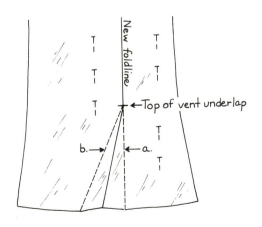

FIGURE 20–13
Marking Vent Opening in Lining.

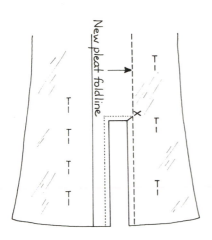

FIGURE 20–14
Removing Excess from Pleat.

FIGURE 20–15
Lining in Place over Vent.

Hemming the Lining

To determine the turn for the hem of the lining in both jackets and coats, try on your garment and have your assistant make the proper adjustments. Or place the garment on a dress form or on a shaped hanger if no

dress form or assistant is available. Adjust on your figure (or on a hanger) pulling the lining slightly so that it fits your body smoothly.

Jacket Lining Hem:

The lower edge of the lining in a jacket is usually attached to the top of the jacket hem. Proceed as follows:

1. From the outside, place pins parallel to the hem edge and about 12.5 cm (5'') above it through *both* the lining and the garment. Pin the sleeves in the same way (Figure 20–16).

2. Remove jacket and lay it full width on a table and fold up the lining to the inside so that the folded edge is 2 cm (3/4'') above the turn of the jacket hem. Pin along the fold.

3. Measure and mark the hem the same width as the jacket hem, pin and trim away any surplus. (The cut edge of the lining will extend above the cut edge of the jacket hem.)

4. Leave the ease pleat in the center back basted in place so that the lining and jacket

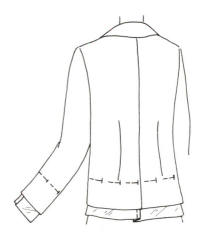

FIGURE 20–16
Pinning Lining and Jacket Together for Hemming Lining.

are the same size and will fit smoothly between the underarm seams. (The vent is handled separately.)

5. Baste the lining to the jacket 1.3 cm (1/2'') *above* the folded edge of the lining. This basting should follow along the finished edge of the hem.

6. Roll back the folded edge of the lining about 1.3 cm (1/2'') and stitch the lining hem closely to the top of the jacket hem. This permits the folded lower section of the hem to be free for ease from the hem edge of the jacket to the shoulders (Figure 20–17). Be sure the stitches do not catch through the outer layer of the lining or the ease will be negated.

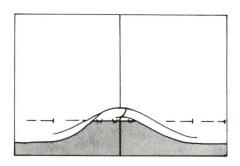

FIGURE 20–17
Attaching Lining Hem to Jacket.

Coat Lining Hem:

The lining hem in a coat is finished separately from the coat. Proceed as follows:

1. Follow the same procedure for pinning the lining to the lower coat edge as was done with the jacket. Place pins about 18 cm (7'') above the hem.

2. Then lay your coat full width on the table and turn up the lining to the inside so that the folded edge is 2 cm to 2.5 cm (3/4'' to 1'') from the turn of the hem. Pin along the fold.

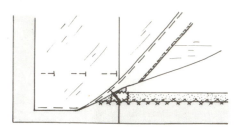

FIGURE 20–18
French Tacks to Hold Lining to Coat.

3. Release the basted ease pleat and measure the lining hem the same width as the coat hem, pin and trim off any excess width.

4. Hand baste through the folded edge of the hem or press along the fold.

5. Machine ease stitch a line about 1 cm (3/8'') from the cut edge. Ease in to fit the lining but be careful not to ease too much.

6. Finish the edge by stitching straight seam tape or lace along the eased line. Or if the fabric does not ravel excessively, pink the edge. Place pins parallel to the edge just below the eased line.

7. Hand hem by using the inside hemming stitch and then press with a dry iron after removing all bastings.

8. Use French tacks about 2.5 cm (1'') long to hold lining and coat hems together at the side seamlines (Figure 20–18). Place tack about 3.8 cm (1 1/2'') above the turn of the garment hem and attach to lining at the point directly opposite.

Sleeve Hem:

Handle the sleeve lining exactly as the jacket hem with this exception: Do not fold the lining so that it reaches within 2 cm (3/4'') of the turn of the sleeve hem (unless hem is narrow), but fold it back so that it covers the *top* edge of the hem by 1.6 cm (5/8''). Allowing the lining to extend toward the lower edge too far means that it becomes too visible as the garment is worn.

Lining the Raglan and Kimono Sleeved Garment

The raglan sleeve is handled similarly to the set-in sleeve. Lengthwise seams in the sleeves and garment are stitched and pressed open. The garment armhole seam is permanently basted to the raglan seam allowances, and the sleeve is applied like the set-in sleeve. Any adjustment to obtain a smooth fit can be made on the front and/or the back seams. Follow all other aspects of the lining as done in the traditional method.

With the kimono sleeve, stitch the shoulder seams together, leaving the seam open from the top of the shoulder to the neck facing—about 18 cm (7''). This will allow some space for adjusting the fit of the shoulder. Press the sleeve seam open. Fit the lining into the garment following the procedures for the traditional method. Adjust the shoulder ease, clip back shoulder seam allowance at top of the shoulder, turn toward front and permanently baste into position. Lap the back shoulder seam allowance over the front, pin and hand stitch in place. Follow all other aspects of the lining in the traditional manner.

Note: The contemporary method using the machine application can be utilized providing you did not attach the facing edges to the garment. Construct the lining in the same manner in which you constructed the main body of the garment.

the garment since the front and back facings must be free.

Stitch all sections of the lining together in the same manner the garment was stitched, including the insertion of the sleeve, and press open. If shoulder pads are used, decrease the armhole edge of the shoulder seam by the depth of the pad and taper to the neckline; that is, if a 6-mm (1/4'') thick pad is used, stitch the seam at the shoulder that much wider, then taper toward the neckline.

With the right sides together, fit and pin the lining to the facings (front and back), matching the shoulder seams and the center back and then stitch. *Option:* To anchor the armhole seam, loosely hand baste the underarm seams of the lining and the garment together by reaching up between the lining and garment. Or, from the lining side, hand stitch in the well of the seam, catching into the armhole seam of the garment. If the hem of the lining is to be treated like the jacket lining in the traditional manner, then stitch the lining to the facings to within about 5 cm (2'') of the lower edge. After hemming, hand catch this small area to the facing.

If the lining is to be loose at the lower edge (as for a coat in the traditional method), it can be hemmed before the lining is completely attached or it can be hemmed following the traditional technique.

The sleeve hem must be treated as in the traditional method.

Contemporary Method for Applying the Lining (Machine)

The machine method of lining may be preferred for loose fitting or casual garments and for children's coats where a durable and quick application is desired. The decision to use this method should have been made prior to the time the facings were attached to

Partial Linings

Partial linings are often used to reduce weight in lightweight garments and to cover visible areas of construction, such as interfacings and shoulder pads. Therefore, some lining must be used in the upper portion of the garment.

In Chapter 5 under "Adjustments for

the Unlined Jacket or Coat,'' a description for cutting the back of the unlined jacket was given. Continue as follows:

1.   Narrowly hem the lower edge of the back lining piece.

2.   For a lined sleeve garment, insert the lining in the sleeves following either method previously described.

3.   For an unlined sleeve garment, insert the lining and then bind all edges of the armhole seam, using as narrow a binding as possible for a tailored professional look. Use lining for a bias if lining fabric is not too heavy.

Any final pressing of the lining must be lightly done without flattening edges to any extent. Rounded surfaces are more attractive in lining fabrics than are sharp ones. The sleeve lining hems should be allowed to roll softly without any pressing.

The finishing touches are often the little things that make a garment special and give it the custom look. Before your garment is "finished," be sure that you have given it any of these touches that it needs. Try it on to see how it hangs on you. Are the button markings in the correct position? Does it need additional fasteners to keep it in place as you move? If the pattern did not show a belt, might you want one? Note areas that need some final pressing. Be critical.

Buttons

Attaching Buttons

Placement. Button placement was established when the buttonholes were marked, but recheck the placement before attaching the buttons. To recheck lap the fronts, matching the center front markings. For horizontal buttonholes place a pin through the end of the buttonhole closest to the edge or from the top for vertical buttonholes. Be sure the layers of fabric are smooth and flat. Carefully lift the buttonhole over the pin and then secure the pin at the marked location on the center front line.

Thread and Stitching. Use a single strand of buttonhole twist drawn through beeswax. A single waxed strand has less tendency to knot and will be less bulky to fasten. Choose a needle large enough to accommodate the thread but be sure the needle will pass easily through the holes in the button.

Anchor the thread with a fastening stitch on *right* side of fabric. *Note:* For slippery silk thread, insert the needle about 2.5 cm (1'') away from the button position and run the thread between layers of fabric, coming out at the button marking, then make the fastening stitch.

21
FINISHING

Attach the button through the interfacing but do not allow the stitches to show on the facing side. Catch a yarn of the facing fabric if back is not usually visible. If the collar is convertible, do not catch the facing *at all*. The needle is not carried through the facing side unless a backing button is used.

Shank. The shank, either attached to the button and/or made with thread as the button is sewed, must allow the button to enter the buttonhole easily and must not be tight or compress the buttonhole when it is buttoned. Bubbling around the buttonhole is caused by a shank that is too short.

1. The *length of the shank* should equal the thickness of the buttonhole plus 3 mm (1/8'') for ease. For *holed buttons,* this is the length of the threads between the button and the fabric. For *shank buttons,* subtract the length of the self-shank from the required length, and the difference is the length of the thread shank. Position the shank button so that the self-shank is aligned with the opening of the buttonhole, thus the shank will not spread the buttonhole.

2. The *thread shank* is made by stitching a number of times between the button (through the holes or self-shank) and the fabric, allowing the length of the shank between the button and fabric. Gauge the length of the shank by placing an object (i.e., matchstick, bobby pin) of the correct size (diameter = length of shank) between the button and the garment (Figure 21–1).

FIGURE 21–2
Wrapping the Thread Shank.

3. After taking a couple of stitches, insert the button through the buttonhole to determine the accuracy of the shank length. Take two or three additional stitches through the button, then hold button and fabric firmly apart and tightly wrap the thread around the threads of the shank (Figure 21–2). Secure with a fastening stitch on the right side under the button. Run thread ends between layers and clip at a distance from the button.

Suggestion: Attach buttons with large holes with a cord, braid, or yarns as follows:

a. Ravel heavy yarns from the fabric and use singly to attach button if very heavy, or braid the yarns to form a heavier yarn. Wrap shank with your sewing thread to reduce bulk.

b. Use commercial cord or make a small bias cording of lightweight fabric and place the cord through the holes in the button. End the cords under the button, sew ends together and attach the button with a thread shank.

Backing Buttons. For buttons that take strain through frequent buttoning and unbuttoning or pull during wear, a small button stitched behind the garment button will prevent the buttons from tearing out. Follow instructions for sewing on a button, but place flat, small, 2- or 4-holed button (preferably the same as the main button) inside of the garment behind the button. Sew through the backing button as the button is sewed on. Complete the shank and fasten

FIGURE 21–1
Establishing the Shank Length.

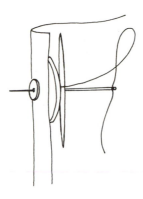

FIGURE 21–3
Sewing Button and Backing Button.

1. Mark a circle on your fabric twice the diameter plus the thickness of the ring.

2. Using a double strand of thread, place a small hand gathering stitch 3 mm (1/8'') inside the circle. Leave the needle attached (Figure 21–4, A). Cut out the circle.

3. Center the bone circle on wrong side of the fabric and pull up the gathering stitch until fabric is taut over the ring (B).

4. Secure the gathering with a fastening stitch.

5. Secure the ring and decorate the button by using buttonhole twist or a double strand of sewing thread. Take small backstitches

the thread as previously instructed (Figure 21–3).

Decorative Button Ideas

The selection of buttons (or at least determination of the diameter and thickness) is made before the buttonholes are constructed. The following discussion is meant to show some available options in the choice of buttons for your garment.

Good looking buttons are another hallmark of a fine garment. Buttons covered to match the garment may give a custom look, but beware of bulky, homemade-looking covered buttons. In addition to commercial kits and commercially covered buttons (some of which have unique shapes or combinations of fabric and metal), the following are some ideas for making your own buttons.

Ring Buttons. Fabric buttons can be easily made using bone or plastic rings available at notion counters. Purchase the rings in the diameter desired for the finished button unless your fabric is very heavy; then use a size smaller ring. Follow this procedure:

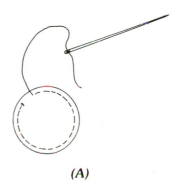

(A)

(B)

(C)

FIGURE 21–4
Making Ring Buttons.

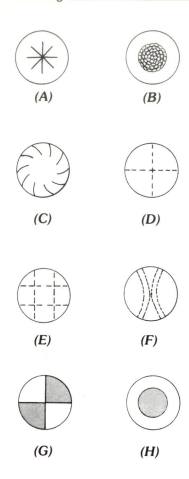

(A)   *(B)*

(C)   *(D)*

(E)   *(F)*

(G)   *(H)*

FIGURE 21–5
Decorative Ideas for Ring Buttons.

(even or half-backstitch) around the inside of the ring. Catch both layers of fabric (C).

Note: This stitching may be omitted if the fabric is very tightly secured around the ring, or the two layers of fabric may be secured at other points in the center of the button so the ring cannot shift.

Other decorative effects may be achieved by:

    a. Using other stitch configurations or embroidery stitches. For example:

    (1) Stitches form spokes (Figure 21–5, A).
    (2) Center is filled with a spiral of chain stitches (B).
    (3) Ring is overcast (C).

    b. Applying decoration *before* the ring is covered. Before cutting out the circle, stitch a design by machine or hand, using double-sewing thread or single-buttonhole twist. (This technique may also be used before covering commercial button forms, but centering the design on the button is difficult.) Attach front to back of button at points where lines cross. For example:

    (1) Sunburst effect (D); attach in center.
    (2) Double stitching (E); attach at four points in center.
    (3) Double-needle curves (F); attach loosely where stitching crosses ring.

    c. Combining two fabrics *before* covering the ring.

    (1) Stitch two fabrics together to form the desired design (G).
    (2) Applique a circle of a contrasting fabric on the circle (H) as follows:

Cut a circle twice the diameter of the inside of the ring, hand baste around the edge, then pull up as in Steps 1 and 2 for covering the ring. Slipstitch this circle to the background fabric. Cover the ring and secure by stitching around circle, as explained at the

FIGURE 21–6
Forming Shank on Ring Button.

beginning of Step 5. *Note:* If possible relate the design on the button to other design features on the garment. Two-fabric covered buttons are especially attractive when they utilize a fabric that has been used as a trim elsewhere on the garment (i.e., piping, cording, collar).

6. Stabilize the back of the button by taking several small stitches into the gathered area. It will be necessary to form a shank as the button is attached to the garment (Figure 21–6).

Chinese Knot Buttons. For each button to be made, have a piece of pliable cord or prepared tubing about 30.5 cm to 46 cm (12″ to 18″) long. The larger the tubing, the more length will be required. Mark one end in some manner to differentiate between the two ends x and y. To make the button:

1. Throw the center of the cord over the fingers of the left hand, with one end around the tip of the thumb as in Figure 21–7, A. Note the location of the marked end.

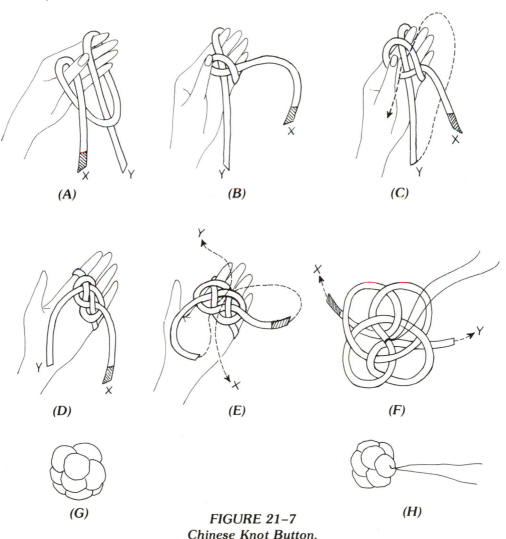

(A) (B) (C)

(D) (E) (F)

(G) (H)

FIGURE 21–7
Chinese Knot Button.

2. Next, slip the loop from the thumb to the palm of the hand and place the tip of the thumb against the loop of the cord, as in (B).

3. Take the end of the cord "y" around under the "x" end and continue to thread it over and under in the direction taken by the arrow, as in (C). It will then appear as in (D).

4. Next, bring both ends up through the center as shown by the arrows in (E). Then place the palm of your left hand on a table and withdraw your fingers without disturbing the position of the cord. Loosely tie a piece of string or cord around the large loop that was around the hand. By holding this cord, you will be able to maintain the shape of the button as the cords are tightened. This loop can easily disappear inside the button, but it must remain visible after the button has been shaped.

5. Carefully begin to pull the knot into shape. Pull a little here and a little there. Continue until the *loop that went over the hand* has been worked out entirely. It will then appear as in (F).

6. With the cord in this position, pull it into the finished shape, as shown in (G) and (H). When the knot is finished, there should be *nine convolutions* visible and it should appear ball shaped. Remove the string that was slipped through the large loop.

7. Cut off excess cord, leaving the under part of the button as flat as possible. Hand whip over the cut ends to give stability to the button. Do *not* leave cord or tubing for a shank because the buttonhole twist will make a smaller shank than the cord will when the button is applied to the garment.

Snaps, Hooks, and Eyes

Metal snaps or hooks can detract and cheapen an otherwise expensive looking garment if they are visible as the garment is worn or carried. The following alternatives are functional, yet will give your garment a finished look.

Covered Snaps

Commercially covered snaps available in limited, basic colors only may be purchased. A snap covered in lining or underlining fabric to match your fabric will be less conspicuous. Consider whether the snap will be placed against the fashion fabric or the lining and then match the covering color to the background. For tailored garments use a medium to large snap, size 1/0 to 1. To cover snaps:

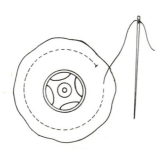

FIGURE 21–8
Covered Snap.

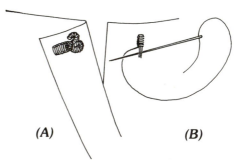

(A)   *(B)*

FIGURE 21–9
Covered Hook and Eye.

1. On the covering fabric, draw two circles about twice the diameter of the snap. Use the end of a spool as a guide for a circle.

2. With a double strand of matching thread make a tiny even hand basting stitch about 3 mm (1/8'') inside the circles. Do not cut the thread but leave it attached to the fabric (Figure 21–8).

3. Cut out the circles.

4. Place half of the snap face down on the circle and draw up the basting thread and fasten securely. Cover both the ball and the socket and then snap them together. This will create a hole in the socket and the ball will be exposed. Never cut a hole in either part of the covering; cut edges will easily fray. Worn edges will be more durable. To give greater durability to the covering touch the raw edges lightly with clear nail polish before attaching to your garment.

5. Use your regular sewing thread and with your needle ''feel'' the holes around the snap and sew to the garment. Fasten securely. *Note:* Large snaps often have a hole in the ball and socket, making it easy to correctly position one part to the other. Push a pin through the ball to the outside of the garment to determine the placement of the socket part of the snap.

Covered Hooks and Eyes

Large covered hooks are available in limited colors, or you may cover your own to match your garment. For coats and suits choose a medium (size 2) or larger hook. Using a double strand of matching sewing thread, blanket stitch very close together over the wire until the metal is covered. Use a single strand of buttonhole twist to cover large hooks (Figure 21–9, A).

Cover the metal eye in the same manner, or make a thread eye by making a bar tack (Chapter 7), overcast with blanket stitches (B).

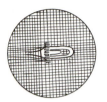

FIGURE 21–10
Hidden Hook.

Hidden Hook

In fabrics that are somewhat loosely woven, the ''bill'' of the hook may be brought to the right side between the yarns of the fashion fabric, leaving the remainder of the hook under the fabric; or from right side reverse the procedure by pushing the lower part of the hook through the fabric. Sew the loops of the hook through the outer layer of fabric and the interfacing (Figure 21–10). If the yarns of your fashion fabric are small enough to be threaded through a needle, use this to attach the loops of the hook to the outer layer and the interfacing. Otherwise, use your regular matching sewing thread. The hidden hook is often used with a thread eye. Raise the bill of the hook to allow space for the bill to hook over the eye.

Inside Ties

Belted garments that do not button, such as wrap coats and jackets, will stay in place better if they are secured before the belt is tied. They may be secured with snaps or hooks, but oftentimes a tie will be more satisfactory.

Using lining fabric, construct a tie about 90 cm (36'') long by 2 cm (3/4'') wide with both ends enclosed. Securely hand stitch the middle of the tie length to the underarm seam at the right armhole (Figure

21-11, A). At the waistline, slightly under the edge of the underlap, make a thread eye about 2.5 cm (1'') long (B). To use, insert one tie end through the thread eye, adjust the garment so that the underlap does not drop below the overlap and tie. The armhole seam gives support to the tie without any distortion in the side seam.

Belts

Since belts are relatively simple to make, the discussion in this section will include tips which may not be found in your pattern guide sheet.

(A)

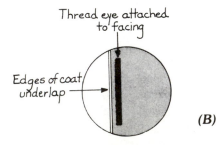

Thread eye attached to facing

Edges of coat underlap

(B)

FIGURE 21–11
Inside Ties.

Tie Belts

Tie belts are most satisfactory in light to medium weight fabrics. Fabrics such as heavy fleece are often too bulky to stay tied. Belt patterns usually have a seam on one or both edges which creates bulk in many fabrics. To reduce bulk, the seam may be pressed open and centered on the underside of the belt. This construction has the disadvantage of a seam appearing on one side of the belt.

For a belt with only one seam, cut it on the straight lengthwise grain, twice the finished width plus two seam allowances. The length is determined by adding the amount needed to tie, a minimum of 61 cm (24''), to the waist circumference.

If the interfacing is needed for body, interface only the section that encompasses the waist, not the ends. A fusible interfacing is especially satisfactory used in this way. Cut the interfacing 3 mm or 1/8'' (6 mm or 1/4'' for heavy fabrics) less than the finished width of the belt. For a belt with the seam centered on the underside, center the interfacing on the wrong side of the fabric, then fuse; or for a nonfusible interfacing, catchstitch along the edges to hold the interfacing in place. Stitch the edges together, leaving an opening about middle way in the length of the belt. Also leave the ends open. Press the seam open (Chapter 8). Center the seam in the under section. Now stitch across the ends of the belt (Figure 21–12, A). Trim and grade as necessary. Turn the belt, slipstitch the opening and press.

Since a tie belt is seen from both sides, use buttonhole twist or topstitching thread on the bobbin as well as the top for a topstitched belt.

Self-Belt with Buckle

For a belt with a buckle, commercial belting or a firm interfacing the width of the finished belt is usually needed for body. The

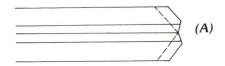

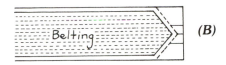

FIGURE 21–12
Belt with One Seam.

belt may be made by machine, by hand, or by fusing.

Machine Method (Using commercial belting):

1. Trim the end of the belting to give a good point.

2. Fold fabric, wrong side out, over the commercial belting. With zipper foot, stitch close to the belting.

3. Center the seam so it lies directly over the pointed end of belting and press the seam open. Stitch end of belt close to belting (Figure 21–12, B). Trim the seam.

4. Turn the stitched belt and insert the belting.

Hand Method (Using commercial belting or heavy interfacing):

1. Cut the garment fabric with one long edge on the selvage.

2. To form a point, fold the fabric in half lengthwise and machine stitch across one end. Trim to 6 mm (1/4'') and press seam open (Figure 21–13, A).

3. Turn the seamed end right side out to form a point; slip the point of the belting (cut on same angle) into the point of belt; center belt on the fabric. Fold raw edge over the belt. Pin, or use glue stick if pinning is difficult. (Fuse if fusible interfacing is used and omit Step 4.)

4. Remove belting from the point and lay it flat as shown in Figure 21–13, B. Machine stitch the raw edge to the belting being sure the fabric is not caught on the right side.

5. Fold the selvage edge over the raw edge on the wrong side and slipstitch in place (C).

Fused Method:

A piece of fusible web may be cut like the belting, and the raw edges of the belt butted together on the back and fused. This method will reduce bulk in heavy fabrics since the seam does not require lapping; however, it is not recommended for ravelly fabrics or for belts that will receive heavy use.

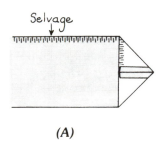

(A)

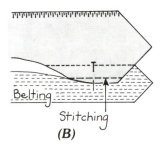

(B)

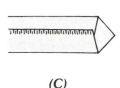

(C)

FIGURE 21–13
Constructing Belt by Hand Method.

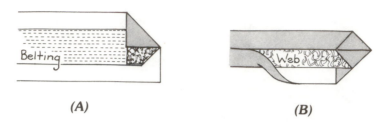

(A)   (B)

FIGURE 21–14
Constructing Belt by Fusing.

1. Cut fabric twice the finished width. Cut one length of commercial belting and an identical piece of fusible web.

2. Center belting on fabric.

3. Cut a triangular piece of web; lay on the point. Fold fabric over the point and fuse (Figure 21–14, A).

4. Fold the fabric over belt and press. Cut edges should meet.

5. Lay strip of fusible web on top of belting (Figure 21–14, B). Trim away any web not covered by fabric at the point. Fold fabric over the web and fuse in place, being sure to follow exactly the manufacturer's instructions.

Attaching Buckles. Buckles with a prong require an eyelet or slot for the prong to pass through. The prong will move more freely, especially in heavy fabrics, if a rectangular opening is made.

Center the opening over the center front marking on the belt as follows:

1. Mark a rectangle that is twice as long as the size of the loop at the end of the prong and the width of the prong.

2. Stitch just outside this rectangle (not necessary for fused belt).

3. Cut away the marked rectangle. Overcast if fabric ravels.

4. Place prong through the rectangle and adjust so the prong is centered in the rectangle. Blanket stitch the end in place (Figure 21–15).

Note: For a custom finish, make hand eyelets like the keyhole of a handworked buttonhole (Chapter 12).

Belt Carriers. Belts on jackets and coats may be kept in place by the use of fabric or thread carriers. Those made of strips of self-fabric are the most durable, but are often too bulky. Matching thread loops are less conspicuous. Carriers are usually placed at the side seams unless other seams cross the waistline and the carriers relate to these structural seams.

Cut and construct all *fabric* carriers in one long strip. To reduce bulk, cut on the selvage, if the selvage is not wider than the finished carrier, and fold in thirds. Allow carriers to have enough ease so the garment will lie flat when the belt is in place.

Thread carriers may be made like a large bar tack (or thread eye, Figure 21–9) or a thread chain (see Chapter 7). The bar tack method is the most secure and durable. The carrier should be 6 mm to 1.3 cm (1/4'' to 1/2'') longer than the width of the belt to allow for ease.

To attach a belt invisibly, make a chain about 3.8 cm (1 1/2'') long, attaching one end to the side seam and one end to the belt.

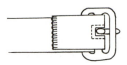

FIGURE 21–15
Rectangular Opening for Prong of Buckle.

Final Pressing

The last step in the construction of your jacket or coat is to give it any needed final pressing. Since it was last checked for needed pressing before the lining was inserted, no further pressing should be needed at this point. However, if it has become slightly mussed, hang it at eye level in a good light and carefully examine it to determine any areas that are not smooth, edges that ripple or are not sharp, or any other imperfections that can be improved by careful touch-up pressing.

Slight wrinkling may be removed holding the steam iron over the garment to let steam penetrate the fabric. Lightly brush, if necessary, to raise the nap or smooth the fabric.

Lightly press all lining edges including center back pleat with a dry iron, but do not flatten. Use a cloth between iron and lining. When all touch-up pressing is complete, hang your garment on a padded hanger and let the air circulate freely around it until it is completely dry. Always hang it on a padded or shaped hanger to help retain the shoulder shape.

Use Critique #12 for the final check on your garment.

Your custom-made jacket or coat is now complete and should be worn with pride for many years!

The skirt or pants may be constructed before the jacket to gain experience in handling the fabric, but since many of the techniques are similar to those discussed in the previous chapters, the specific instructions for these two types of garments have been placed in the last chapter.

This chapter is planned primarily to give you suggestions for changes you may wish to make in the directions from your regular pattern guide sheet. Consequently, it is not planned to provide a step-by-step procedure but to supplement material you may already have available. You will be referred to specific parts of previous chapters where this information is pertinent to the particular construction process in which you are involved.

Before you begin, you may wish to review Chapter 2, "Selection of Garment Components"; Chapter 7, "Stitching and Seam Construction"; and Chapter 8, "Pressing."

Preliminary Steps

Have clearly in mind the procedure you wish to use if it differs from your pattern guide sheet. Make your own procedural outline, if your sequence will vary from the pattern guide sheet. It may be more beneficial to you to plan your own, particularly if you have had a considerable amount of experience. At any rate, you should know your plan of work.

Locate specific information for the fitting and construction of skirts and pants in the following chapters. They are listed in the sequence that you will most likely follow.

Chapter 3 —Body and pattern measurements and pattern adjustment.
Skirts—Fit the paper pattern. (*Use Critique #1.*)

22
SKIRTS
AND PANTS

Pockets

Pockets in skirts and pants are similar to those for jackets and coats in that they may be applied, inseam, or slashed. Follow the detailed instructions in Chapter 13 for each specific type of pocket.

Note: Men's pants often have double-welt pockets in the back. The five-line double-welt pocket is recommended for this location. For stability the pocket bag should be cut long enough so that it will extend to the waistband.

Inseam pockets and pockets inset in a design line are common in skirts and in both men's and women's pants. Follow the instructions in Chapter 13 to construct these. The following hints may also be helpful:

1. Pockets placed into the side seam will lie flatter when you sit down if the seamline is closed (or if the pocket opening is top-stitched closed) 2.5 cm to 5 cm (1'' to 2'') below the waistband.

2. Topstitch the edge of the pocket opening to help it lie flat. Understitch if topstitching is not desired.

3. Always pin or baste pockets shut while fitting. A garment with inseam pockets should be fit a bit loosely to prevent pull on the pockets.

A front (pocket) stay may be placed between the pockets to keep them from pulling and gaping. Cut this as an extension on the under pocket or add a separate piece across the front between the vertical edges of the pocket bags.

Measure and cut the stay as follows (Figure 22-1):

1. Lay the under pocket section on the front pattern.

2. From the lining fabric cut two pieces as indicated in the shaded area, allowing a seam allowance beyond the stitching line of the pocket and ending at the lower end of pocket opening or of front zipper. Mark the dart if one is present. For a skirt with pleats

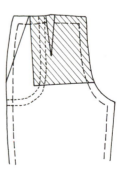

FIGURE 22–1
Stay for Pocket.

in the front, fold out the pleats along the foldlines before cutting the stay. For pleated pants, the front pleat usually will fold out straight down the front and the second pleat may form a dart that may be folded out if it extends to the bottom of the stay. Or mark the dart if it is shorter.

Construct the stay. After the pockets are completed and before inserting a front zipper:

1. Clean finish (turn under and stitch on the fold) the bottom of the stay and stitch darts, if present.

2. Stitch stay to pocket, placing right side of stay against underside of pocket bag, raw edges matching (refer to Figure 22–1). Stitch and press the seam allowances toward the stay and topstitch to hold them flat.

3. For pants with a front opening, baste the stay to the waistline seam and to the front crotch seam. Check the fit of the stay before inserting the zipper. For a garment without a front opening, baste the front edges of the stay together, check the fit, then stitch the seam and press it open. Baste the stay and garment together at the waistline.

Pleats

Pleats may be loose, stitched as tucks, or topstitched. Follow your guide sheet for specific instructions. Stitched pleats may incorporate fitting, so baste these pleats in place and fit before stitching.

The inner fold of pleats must be supported to hang properly. This may be accomplished by extending the pleat to the waistline (always for nonstitched pleats). For a skirt with stitched pleats bulk in the waist and hip area may be reduced by cutting away the underlay of the pleat through the stitched area. Use one of the following methods to support the pleat:

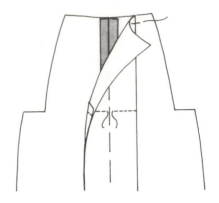

FIGURE 22–2
Self-Stay.

Self-Stay:

1. Stitch the pleat along the stitching line and baste the remainder closed.

2. At the end of the stitching, stitch the underlay from the fold edge to the seam (center to outside of the seam for an inverted pleat).

3. Cut along the fold from waist to the second stitching line and along the seams, leaving 1.5-cm (5/8'') seam allowance (Figure 22–2).

Lining Stay:

1. Fold pleats in skirt pattern and allow to spread at waistline if they do not lie flat. Make a dart to decrease the spread.

2. Cut a stay from lightweight lining fabric the length of the stitched area plus a seam allowance.

3. Baste to wrong side of the pleated skirt at waistline.

4. Turn under the lower edge and slipstitch to the top of the pleats that have been basted and stitched in place (Figure 22–3).

Note: The stay may extend to the side seams or may end at the last pleat. The ver-

FIGURE 22–3
Lining Stay.

tical edge is then turned under and slip-stitched to the seam of the pleat or turned under and stitched if it ends at the fold of a pleat.

Pleat Attached to Underlining. The underlining acts as the stay with the top of the pleat being slipstitched to it.

Topstitched Pleat. Pleats that open at the lower portion of a straight skirt often have diagonal topstitching across the top to secure the pleat. If the topstitching is not desired, use the self-stay or attach the pleat to the underlining.

Handling the Crotch Seam

To fit properly, a crotch seam must conform to the body configuration. To accomplish this, the crotch seam must be stitched after the inseams to allow the pant legs to form a sharp reversed V in the lower crotch area. When the front and back crotch seams are stitched first and then the inseam, a rounded effect or a reversed U is formed at the lowest crotch point. Since that is not the body configuration, a poor fit results. Stitching the

crotch seam as the final seam is also more durable. It should be handled as follows:

1. After stitching the seam, place a second row of stitching 3 mm (1/8'') inside the crotch seam allowance on the lower curve of the crotch, then trim close to this stitching so about a 6 mm (1/4'') seam remains in the curved area.

2. Allow this seam to remain standing. *Do not clip.* Finish the cut edges with a machine or hand stitch that encases the raw edges. The seam above the crotch curve may be pressed open and finished as other garment seams.

Zippers and Other Closures

Zippers are the most common closures for skirts and pants. In women's garments the zipper may be placed in the center back, center front, left side seam, or in a design-line seam, depending on fashion and personal preference.

For heavy fabrics that will receive wear, a heavyweight metal pant zipper will be more durable than a regular skirt zipper. Purchase a longer length if the exact length is not available. The excess teeth and tape can be cut off the upper end after the waistband is stitched, eliminating the need to shorten the zipper from the lower end. In order to shorten the zipper in this manner, the slider must lock at any point on the zipper where it is pressed down.

Lapped and Centered Zippers

The *lapped* zipper application gives better coverage of the zipper teeth and tape than the centered or slot zipper and thus is usually used for front and side plackets. The *centered* application (as well as the lapped) may be used for the center back placket. The *fly-front* zipper application is a variation of the lapped zipper and hides the zipper better than the other two methods.

Instructions for the basic zipper insertion will not be included here; follow instructions included with the zipper or use some other satisfactory method. The following suggestions may be helpful:

1.   If the seam allowances are less than 2 cm (3/4''), especially on the front or overlap side, stitch woven seam tape close to the cut edge to enlarge the seam allowance. Also use on heavy fabrics to reduce bulk.

2.   Use clear plastic tape or topstitching tape to provide a guideline for topstitching. Be cautious about using this method on fabrics that may be damaged by the tape.

3.   For an invisible couture finish, use a hand pick-stitch instead of machine topstitching. This may be accomplished in two ways:

   a.   Use the hand stitches to attach the zipper in the same manner as machine topstitching.

   b.   Do the hand pick-stitch through the outer layer and the seam allowance only. Then position the zipper and baste on top of the pick-stitch. From the wrong side, turn the garment back as close as possible to the hand stitching; leave the seam allowance lying on top of the zipper. Machine stitch as close as possible to the fold using a zipper foot (Figure 22-4).

4.   A *simulated hand pick-stitch* can be done as follows:

   a.   Baste the zipper in place. From the wrong side, turn the garment back as close as possible to the basting with the zipper under the seam allowance.

   b.   Machine blind stitch beside the fold to simulate the hand pick-stitch (Figure 22-5).

5.   When a zipper is placed in a curved seam, such as the side seam, staystitch the overlap 3 mm (1/8'') from the stitching line and the underlap 6 mm (1/4'') from the stitching line. Ease the fabric slightly as the zipper is pinned to the fabric. Check smoothness by laying the seam right side up over a curved pressing ham.

6.   Use a hand or machine bar tack to reinforce the lower end of the front lapped zipper in pants for increased durability.

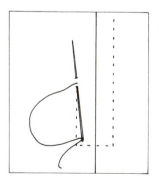
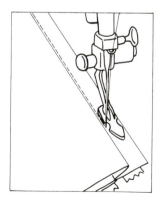

FIGURE 22-4
Hand Pick-Stitched Zipper with
Machine Stitching.

Zipper in a Pocket

A garment with inseam pockets that begin at the waistline may have the zipper placed invisibly inside the left pocket. The zipper will be placed about 5 cm (2'') in from the side seam on the under pocket section that is cut from the garment fabric. The upper pocket section is cut of lining. (If desired the under section may be seamed with lining fabric used for the inside part of the bag. The zipper is inserted into the seam.) The waistband must have at least a 5-cm (2'') extension (underlap) which will be stitched to the top of the pocket nearest the seam. The remainder of the underpocket will be stitched into the waistband with the garment front. Proceed as follows:

1. On the underpocket section baste a lengthwise grainline the length of the zipper tape beginning 5 cm (2'') from the top of the side seamline.

2. Cut a strip of lightweight lining or underlining fabric (preferably matching in color) about 3.8 cm (1 1/2'') wide and 2.5 cm (1'') longer than the zipper. Or, if the garment fabric is firm, use a small piece of lining fabric to reinforce only the end of the

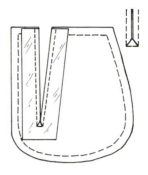

(A) Facing the Zipper Opening.

(B) Zipper Inserted in Under Pocket.

FIGURE 22–6

rectangle. Fold the strip in half lengthwise wrong sides together and lightly press a creased line.

3. With the underpocket section right side up place the strip with the crease line matching the basted grainline. Pin in place.

4. Start at the top of the strip and stitch a rectangle that is 3 mm (1/8'') from each side of the creased line. Slash along the line and diagonally into the corners as in Figure 22–6, A.

5. Fold the facing strip back against the stitched lines and press from the faced side.

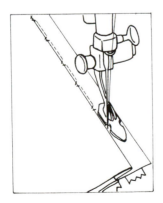

FIGURE 22–5
Simulated Pick-Stitched Zipper
(Machine).

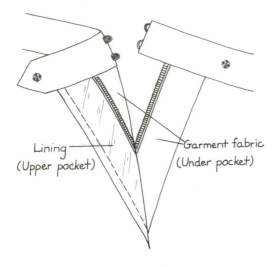

Lining
(Upper pocket)

Garment fabric
(Under pocket)

FIGURE 22-7
Completed Zipper in a Pocket.

6. Place the zipper under the opening and pin in place. Stitch around the zipper keeping close to the edge of the rectangle (Figure 22-6, B). A second row of stitching may be placed at the edge of the tape to hold it flat.

7. Complete the pocket as described in your pattern guide sheet. When applying the waistband, attach the under pocket section to the underlap. The remaining part of the under pocket is attached to the overlap section (Figure 22-7). When the zipper is closed, the pocket must be smooth.

Zipper in a Pleat

The placement of the zipper should be planned when the garment is cut out. It should be as inconspicuous as possible and not distort the pleat. It may be at the side front or side back as well as the usual center front or back or side location.

For *box or inverted pleats* (two folds meet), make a seam in the center where the folds meet and place the zipper here. If the pleat is topstitched, this stitching may also secure the zipper. If the pleat is not stitched down, the zipper will lie under the folds.

For *one-way pleats* (knife pleats), place a seam and the zipper on the inside fold of the pleat (Figure 22-8, A). Insert the zipper as follows:

1. Stitch the seam below the zipper. Press as stitched. Clip left seam allowance (layer next to body) at top stitching and press (Figure 22-8, B).

2. Turn garment right side out and place zipper under the folded edge with the fold next to the zipper teeth and stitch close to the edge.

3. Fold pleat in place and pin along the outside fold. Close the zipper and from the wrong side, stitch the loose side of the zipper tape to the seam allowance (C).

Note: In a fitted garment if the pleat is wide and/or lies over a body curve and it gaps, place snaps or hooks and thread eyes under the outside fold of the pleat to hold it flat.

Fly-Front Zipper

The fly-front zipper, traditional for men's pants, has also become commonly used in women's pants and occasionally in skirts. In men's pants the fly laps left over right and is usually reversed in women's garments. Instructions for a woman's garment with a fly that laps right over left follow. Also included are step-by-step instructions and illustrations because complete directions may not be included in your pattern guide sheet.

The facing for the overlap may be cut as one with the right front or as a separate facing that will be attached.

A pattern with a fly front zipper will include all of the needed pieces, except perhaps the fly shield. The fly shield is optional for women but is usually included for men.

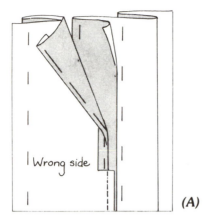

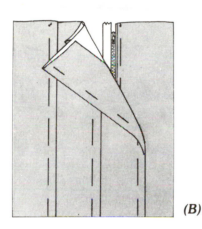

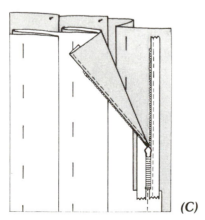

FIGURE 22–8
Zipper with Knife Pleats.

To Construct the Shield:

1. Cut two additional pieces (usually one of the fashion fabric and one of the lining) from the fly facing pattern and duplicate all markings.

Note: The shield in men's pants may be cut long enough to cover the entire front crotch seam. After the fly is completed, the lower end of the shield is stitched to the open seam allowances of the front crotch seam with small hand backstitches.

2. Place the two cut pieces (lining plus fashion fabric) with right sides together and stitch the long curved edge. Grade, notch, and turn. The long raw edge may be finished as other seams, *or* trim 6 mm (1/4'') from the top or fashion fabric side and turn the lining to finish the edge.

To Construct the Fly-Front Opening:

1. After cutting your fabric, duplicate all markings and transfer the topstitching line so that it is visible on the right side.

2. For the *cut-on facing*, staystitch for 2.5 cm (1'') across the dot that marks the lower end of the placket. Clip to the staystitching at this point. Fold back the facing on the center front and press.

3. Beginning about 3.8 cm (1 1/2'') from the crotch point, stitch the front crotch seam to the point where the zipper will end and backstitch 3–4 stitches (Figure 22–9).

4. For a *faced placket* join the facing to the edge of the right front from the point marking the end of the zipper to the waist. Backstitch at this point being sure the crotch seam and the facing seam end at the same place. Grade the seam, clip if curved, and press the seam toward the facing (Figure 22–10).

5. Place the closed zipper face down on the right side of the facing with the edge of tape on the foldline or seamline. Place zipper stop about 3 mm (1/8'') above the end of zipper

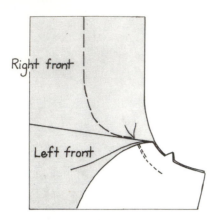

FIGURE 22-9
Stitching Crotch Seam.

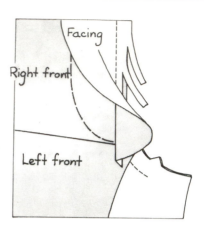

FIGURE 22-10
Join Fly Facing.

marking. Top of zipper may extend above the waistline. Stitch the right zipper tape (toward cut edge of facing) to the facing close to the zipper teeth, then stitch close to the edge of the tape (Figure 22-11). Be sure to fold zipper tape up even with zipper stop.

6. Fold the fly facing into position. From right side, topstitch along the marked fly line beginning at the bottom of the fly (Figure 22-12).

Note: Since the zipper tape is stitched to the facing it is not necessary to catch it in the topstitching.

7. Close the zipper. Lay the overlap over the underlap, matching center front at the waistline. Turn under the edge of the

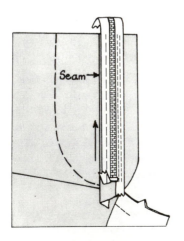

FIGURE 22-11
Stitch Zipper to Facing.

FIGURE 22-12
Topstitch Marked Fly Line.

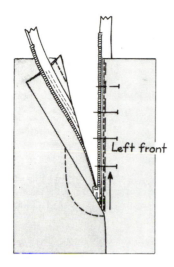

FIGURE 22–13
Stitch Underlap Edge of Zipper.

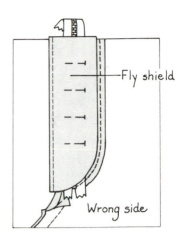

FIGURE 22–14
Placement for Fly Shield.

underlap along the zipper teeth (about 6 mm or 1/4'' from the center front). Note the amount to turn under at the waistline, then open the zipper and turn under the same amount the length of the opening. Close zipper to check the placement, then open and stitch close to the edge (Figure 22–13).

8. *Attach the fly shield.* Place right side of the shield on the wrong side of garment, matching the curved edge of the shield to the curved line of topstitching. Pin in place (Figure 22–14). Open the zipper and from the right side, stitch on top of the previous stitching (Step 7) that attaches the zipper to the underlap (Figure 22–15). *Or,* fold back the garment and stitch the zipper tape to the fly.

9. Make a bar tack by hand or machine across the lower end of the placket. Catch through all layers, including the shield.

10. With the zipper *open,* staystitch across both ends of the tape at the waistline, then trim off excess zipper and tape (Figure 22–15).

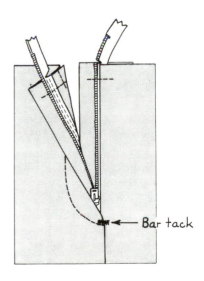

FIGURE 22–15
Completion of Fly Front Zipper.

Other Closures

Buttons and buttonholes are often used on skirts and pants for a decorative closure. Refer to Chapter 12 and note the following suggestions:

1. Check the pattern to be sure the underlap is wide enough to extend under the entire length of the buttonhole.

2. Do not use vertical buttonholes on fitted pants or skirts because stress will "unbutton" the buttons.

3. If the garment is fitted, be sure buttons are placed close enough together and garment has enough ease to prevent "gaposis."

4. The distance between the bottom button and the hemline of a skirt should be *no less* than the distance between the buttons; usually the space is larger.

Linings

Linings are optional in most skirts and pants. Maximum stability is given by underlining, but lining will help prevent stretching in areas of stress. A skirt may be fully lined or may have a partial lining in the back that is usually handled as an underlining. This lining is cut exactly like the skirt back but extends far enough below the hipline to prevent "seat sag." For the fully lined straight skirt, seat sag will be reduced by attaching the side seams of the lining and skirt.

For unlined, narrow-legged pants, the knees are susceptible to stress. The front knee area may be reinforced with a piece of lining fabric the width of the front pant leg and about 20 cm (8'') long. Locate the position of your knee on the pants when seated and center the reinforcement over this area. Stitch it into the inseam and outseam. *Do not* attach upper and lower edges.

Skirt and pant linings are generally attached only at the waistline and around the zipper which results in a garment with no exposed raw edges on the inside. For this method the lower crotch curve should be double stitched with a 1-cm (3/8'') seam, clipped, and pressed back on itself. This allows additional length for the seam to set over the standing crotch seam of the garment.

An *alternate method for lining pants* is to complete the lining for each leg, insert it into the garment, and then stitch the crotch seam incorporating the lining with the garment. An advantage of this method is that it provides strength to the crotch seam and often fits better than the lining that is stitched separately.

For the fully lined skirt or pants cut lining as instructed in Chapter 5. Stitch the darts and major seams of the lining in the same manner as the garment, leaving the zipper area open. Press seams open and darts in the opposite direction from the corresponding ones in the garment. The lining should be a bit smaller than the garment to fit smoothly inside and protect the fashion fabric from strain. This may be accomplished by taking *slightly* larger seams than in the garment.

Place lining and garment wrong sides together and with darts and seams matched at waistline, baste along the waistline seam. Turn the edges of the lining under along the zipper. Check fit to be sure lining lies smoothly inside the garment before slipstitching edges to the zipper tape.

Note: For gathered areas, apply the lining, then gather through both layers of fabric. This will allow both fabrics to gather as one and be less bulky than if they were gathered separately. However, gathers may fall more smoothly if the lining is gathered as a separate piece. Or darts may be incorporated in the lining to reduce bulk. Test your fabric to determine the better procedure.

Waistbands

Waistbands for Women's Skirts and Pants

A straight waistband, 2.5 cm to 5 cm (1'' to 2'') wide, is the most common way to finish the waist of skirts and pants. A contoured, or shaped, waistband that rests above or below the waistline, or a ''no waistband'' faced waistline may also be used. You can easily change the type or width of waistband included with your pattern.

Suggestions for Standard Waistbands.
Specific instructions are not given for standard waistbands since they are included in patterns and you undoubtedly have the required experience. However, these tips may be helpful for your tailored pants or skirt.

Cutting the waistband. Your waist measurement, the width of the waistband, and your body configuration will determine the length needed for the band. Wide waistbands generally require more length than narrow ones. If you are using a 5-cm (2'') waistband in width, measure your body circumference 5 cm (2'') above your waistline. To this measurement add a minimum of 1.3 cm (1/2'') for ease. If you plan to tuck in anything heavier than a lightweight blouse or shirt, add more ease.

The end of the waistband is usually placed flush with the overlap of the placket. The underlap must extend a minimum of 2.5 cm (1'') to allow for a fastener. A 5-cm (2'') underlap is preferred by many to allow for letting out if the waist measurement increases. If a pointed end is desired on the overlap, allow extra length by adding 1.3 cm (1/2'') plus one-half the width of the waistband for a point with a 90° angle.

To reduce bulk place the facing edge of the waistband on the selvage and omit one seam allowance. The band may be cut on the crosswise grain if it is to be firmly interfaced.

Interfacing. Choose an interfacing that is strong and has enough body to keep the waistband firm. For added stability machine stitch the interfacing to the facing side of the waistband. A commercial nonroll stiffener is available for those who have problems with waistbands rolling.

Fusible interfacings generally are also very satisfactory. Fuse to the top layer of the band if feasible. Fuse to both the top and the facing for added stability. Cut a firm fusible the finished width of the band so it will not be fused to the seam allowance.

Application. For a waistband without topstitching, apply it to the right side of the garment, fold over and finish the back by hand; *or* allow the waistband facing to extend 3 mm (1/8'') below the seamline, baste in place, and from the right side machine stitch in the well of the waistline seam.

For a topstitched waistband, apply the waistband to the *wrong* side of garment, turn under the seam allowance on the right side, and topstitch close to the folded edge.

To reduce bulk, remember to grade the seam allowances and clip away the top of darts and seams within the seam allowance of the garment.

Stitch ends of the waistband from the fold at the upper edge of the waistband to 3 mm (1/8'') *beyond seamline* and backstitch so the bulk can be trimmed out of the corner without clipping the stitching. This also applies when stitching the waistline seam.

The Grosgrain-Backed Waistband.
Fashion fabric is often too bulky to use for the facing of the waistband. The use of a grosgrain backing usually eliminates the need for interfacing (unless more body is desired) and replaces two layers of fashion fabric at the lower waistline seam. Complete

instructions for its preparation and application follow. Purchase grosgrain that matches the fashion fabric, and is the width of the finished waistband and at least 10 cm (4'') longer than the waist measurement.

Preparation of Waistband:

1.   Shrink the grosgrain by placing it in hot water, allowing it to remain there until the water is cool. Remove and let dry.

2.   Steam press the grosgrain, pulling on it as you press to eliminate any stretch it may have.

3.   Cut *exactly on grain* a crosswise (or lengthwise) strip of skirt fabric twice the width of the grosgrain plus 6 mm (1/4'').

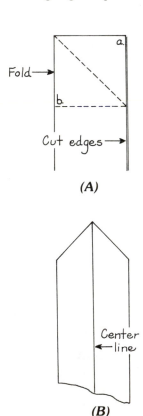

(A)

(B)

FIGURE 22–16
Making Template for Waistband.

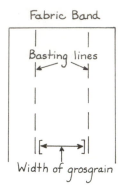

FIGURE 22–17
Lines for Pressing Band.

For length allow the waist measurement plus about 12.5 cm (5'').

4.   Press the fashion fabric band as follows:

   a.   *Method I (using a template)*. Cut a strip of paper about 2 mm (1/16'') narrower than the finished band width. For a pointed end fold in half lengthwise (Figure 22–16, A) and then fold down (a) at right angles to the lengthwise edge (b). Trim on the creased line, leaving a well-shaped point.

   Cut a strip of firm tagboard the same shape and about 30.5 cm (12'') long. Draw a line down the center length (Figure 22–16, B). Place the template in the center of the fabric band and fold the cut edges to meet the center line on the template. Press both edges of the band. For a straight end, press seam allowance over the template. Follow instructions in Step 7 for the pointed end.

   b.   *Method II (use basting as marking lines)*. On the fabric, baste two parallel lines *on exact grain* the entire length of the band (Figure 22–17). The width between the basting lines should be the grosgrain width plus 3 mm (1/8''). Fold on the basting lines and press. The two cut edges should meet.

5. Make a pointed end on the *grosgrain* by folding it lengthwise (selvage edges even) and stitching across the end about 3 mm (1/8'') from cut edge (Figure 22–18, see A). Trim off the folded corner close to the stitched line to remove excess bulk. Finger press the seam open and turn so that the seam is on the inside; the stitched seam forms an even point. Press (Figure 22–18, see B).

6. Hand baste the angled sides of point (b).

7. Make a pointed end on the fashion fabric band in the same manner as was done for the grosgrain. Be sure that the right sides are together. Press. Trim away excess bulk as indicated by dotted line (Figure 22–19).

Option: The pointed end may be made before the lengthwise pressing is done.

8. Join the grosgrain and fabric by lapping the grosgrain onto the fabric 3 mm (1/8'') below the foldline. *Stitch* on the grosgrain side *close* to the edge, starting about 1 cm (3/8'') away from the end (a, Figure 22–20).

9. Transfer the waistline measurements from the fitting band to the grosgrain, and to the fabric starting 1.3 cm (1/2'') from the base of the pointed end. (For a band that is flush with the zipper overlap, start at the

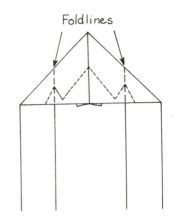

FIGURE 22–19
Trimming Waistband Point.

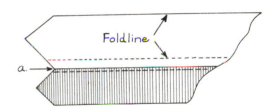

FIGURE 22–20
Grosgrain Stitched to Fabric Band.

end.) Use hand basting to mark the right side, center front, center back, and the left side. Double lines at center front and center back are useful as an aid in quick identification of these locations. Allow at least a 5-cm (2'') underlap (extension beyond the waist measurement). (See Figure 22–21.)

10. Press and shape the band to conform to the curve of the skirt top. Stretch lower edge slightly (Figure 22–22).

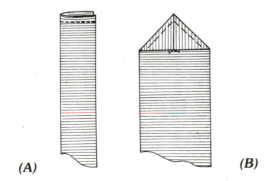

(A)   **(B)**

FIGURE 22–18
Making Point on Grosgrain.

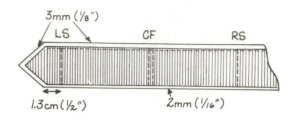

FIGURE 22-21
Grosgrain Marked for Applying to Skirt.

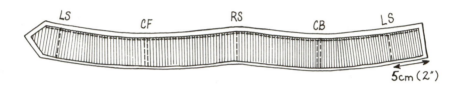

FIGURE 22-22
*Pressed Band Ready for Application
to Skirt.*

Application of Waistband to Skirt (or Pants):

Two methods are presented for attaching the waistband. Both involve a combination of machine and hand stitching, but differ in the side of the waistband that is hand and machine stitched. In Method I the fashion fabric is machine stitched to the garment and the grosgrain stitched by hand. Method II reverses the procedure. Method I is appropriate for firm fabrics and/or waistbands cut on lengthwise grain. For the inexperienced this method may be easier than Method II. Method II is especially advantageous for unstable fabrics and waistbands cut on the crosswise grain, but may be used for any fabric. This method requires the ability to do inconspicuous hand stitching.

Method I (fashion fabric side of band stitched to right side of skirt):

1.   Open fabric band and pin to skirt, *exactly* matching side seam markings of band to side seams of skirt, as well as center front to center front, and center back to center back. The folded line of the band should lie on the seamline of the skirt. Ease waist fullness on side hip area, front and back. *Hand baste* (Figure 22-23). Check fit.

2.   Machine stitch along the basted line.

3.   Grade skirt side of seam allowance and trim tops of darts and seams to reduce bulk. Press.

4.   Allow grosgrain to lie in place, covering the fabric seam. Match center front, center back, and side seam locations. Pin in place

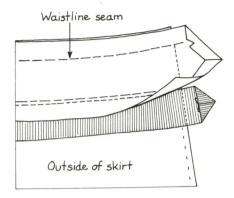

FIGURE 22–23
Fabric Side of Band Stitched to Skirt.

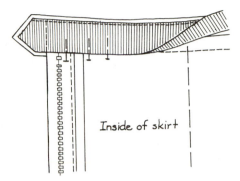

FIGURE 22–24
Grosgrain Pinned for Hand Stitching.

with pins at right angles to the seamline. Grain must remain straight (Figure 22–24).

5. On wrong side of skirt, use the lining stitch to attach the grosgrain to the stitched line on the skirt.

Note: Commercially made stiffeners are available and may be inserted inside the waistband before the final hand stitching is done. If it has a slight concave curve, be sure to insert it in the band so that the curved portion is next to the outside of the band. You must also consider the curve of your body when inserting the stiffener. In other words, do not make the insertion with the waistband flat on the table.

Method II (grosgrain stitched on wrong side of skirt):

1. Pin the grosgrain to wrong side of skirt matching the side seams, center front, and center back (Figure 22–25). Ease fullness evenly at center front and center back and side hip seams or wherever needed to fit body contours. Place the grosgrain so that the lower edge barely covers the stitching line of the skirt.

2. Hand baste close to the lower edge of the grosgrain and machine stitch as close to the edge as possible.

3. Grade skirt side of seam allowance and trim tops of darts and seams to reduce bulk. Press.

4. Allow the fabric side of the band to lie in place covering the waistline seam. Match center front, center back, and side seams location. Pin in place with pins at right angles to the seamline (Figure 22–26). *Grain must remain straight* at all matching points.

5. Slipstitch the band carefully to the outside of the skirt so that the band does not look "held down." Hand stitching must be invisible on the right side of the waistband.

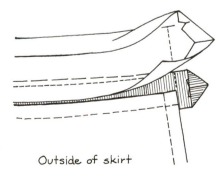

FIGURE 22–25
Grosgrain Side of Band Stitched to Skirt.

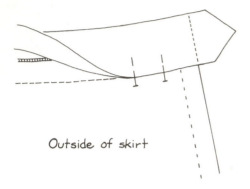

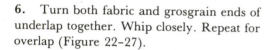

Outside of skirt

FIGURE 22–26
Fabric Side of Band Pinned for
Hand Stitching.

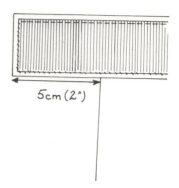

5cm (2")

FIGURE 22–27
Hand-Stitched Underlap.

6.   Turn both fabric and grosgrain ends of underlap together. Whip closely. Repeat for overlap (Figure 22–27).

Application of Fasteners:

1.   Snap. The purpose of the snap is to hold the pointed end of the band in place.

> **a.**   With the placket closed, sew the ball part of the snap on the pointed end of the band. Do not place too close to the point. (See Figure 22–28.)
>
> **b.**   Attach socket part of snap to fabric layer, making sure that the band is placed so that the placket line will remain in a straight line when the band is fastened.

2.   Hooks and eyes (regulation style). The hook supports the strain of the waistband.

> **a.**   Sew round eyes on grosgrain end of the underlap, allowing the eye to extend beyond end of band.
>
> **b.**   To determine placement of hooks, fasten the snap and allow band to roll slightly over your thumb to simulate

the curved position the band assumes when worn. Mark location for hooks from the place where the eyes extend. Sew in place. This allows hooks to be

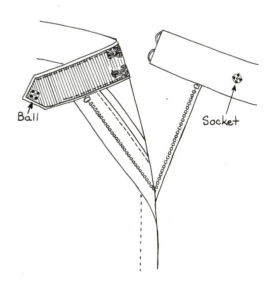

Ball

Socket

FIGURE 22–28
Placement of Snap and Hook and Eyes.

flush with squared underlap and prevents "bumps" where hooks are sewed.

3.   Hooks and eyes (wide style).

a.   Follow same procedure as above except sew the hook on the grosgrain side of the underlap with the hook facing away from body as it is worn.

b.   Follow procedure as in Step 2b to determine placement for the long eye. *Note:* If desired, a wide hook and eye may be used at pointed end of band instead of a snap. A regulation hook and straight eye (or thread eye) may be used if preferred.

Contoured Waistbands

The contoured waistband is either wide and flares out above the waist or the top rests at the waistline (or below) and the band flares out over the hips. If you do not have a pattern for a contoured band, make one as follows:

Above-the-Waistline Band. Determine the desired width and measure the body circumference at the top of the band. Cut a straight piece of paper the desired width and the length of the waist measurement, plus ease. Slash strip at even intervals (about 5 cm [2''] apart), cutting to, but not through one edge. Allow slashed edge to spread evenly until it measures the circumference (plus ease) previously determined (Figure 22–29). Tape the slashes in place and check the pattern on your body. If one area of the body is flat and the band stands away at the top, close slashes as these points and allow the others to open more. Add overlap to end of band and add seam allowance on all four sides.

Below-the-Waistline Band. Follow the procedure just outlined, except measure and fit below the waist. *Or,* if you have fitted your garment to the waistline, use the top

FIGURE 22–29
Pattern for Contoured Waistband.

edge of your pattern (or garment if it was adjusted) to make the band. Fold in the darts and lap the side seams at the top (so that the pattern lies flat.) Trace the waistline, center front and center back, then measure down the desired width of band. Mark new seamline on pattern and/or garment. Proceed as above.

Suggestions for Contructing the Contoured Band. The previous general suggestions on waistbands also apply to contoured bands. Other suggestions are as follows:

1.   Wide bands need to be firmer than narrow ones. To increase firmness use a fusible interfacing, or machine pad stitch, and/or use more than one layer of interfacing.

2.   Stay the top and bottom seamlines with narrow tape.

3.   Always recheck the fit of the waistband before applying it to the garment.

Suggestions for Faced Waistlines

1.   If no facing pattern is available, make one by following the procedure given for making a pattern for a below-the-waistline band.

2.   Apply interfacing to garment while the garment is right side out to allow it to take the inside curve.

3. Stay the waistline seam with tape to prevent stretch.

4. Understitch the waistline seam to prevent the seam from rolling outward.

5. Tack the facing only at darts and seams and along edges of the zipper.

6. Grosgrain ribbon 1.3 cm to 2.5 cm (1/2'' to 1'') wide may be used as a facing and the interfacing omitted.

 a. Shape the grosgrain with a steam iron by stretching one side and easing in the other.

 b. Place eased edge on the waistline seam on the right side of the garment and topstitch close to the edge of grosgrain. Be sure it will fit smoothly to the curve of the skirt. Tape the seamline to prevent the grosgrain from stretching back to its original straightness.

 c. Tack the lower edge of grosgrain at darts and seams.

7. Place a hook and eye at the waistline.

Waistbands for Men's Pants

The waistband on men's pants is usually cut in two pieces with a large seam at the center back. Each section is stitched to the pants prior to stitching the center back seam to allow for easy adjustment in the waist size.

Note: Although not standard construction for women's pants, this method is also advantageous for women who may change waist dimensions.

The facing on men's tailored waistbands is frequently a cotton twill pocket fabric and often extends below the outer waistband, allowing the waistband seam to be pressed open. This facing material is available preassembled with a stiffener and is stitched to the top of the waistband,

turned to the inside, and attached to the pocket extensions and seams. Follow your pattern guide sheet for additional instructions.

Belt Carriers

Belt carriers for pants are constructed in the same manner as those for jackets and coats (Chapter 21) and are about 6 mm to 1 cm (1/4'' to 3/8'') in width, or may be wider for men's pants. Personal preference dictates the carrier placement, but usually they are positioned 5 cm to 7.5 cm (2'' to 3'') from the center front, at the side seams, and either center back or on each side of the back (both locations for men). Carriers may be attached by the following methods:

 Method I. Position carriers on the waistline seam before attaching the waistband, then stitch with waistline seam. Fold under the seam allowance on the loose end and machine stitch to the top of the band.

 Method II. Before attaching waistband, stitch one end of the carrier to the top foldline of the waistband, fold it down, and stitch the other end when the waistband is attached. No topstitching is necessary in this method.

 Method III. Traditionally, men's belt carriers are attached after the waistband is completed. Stitch the top of the carriers 3 mm (1/8'') below the top of the waistband and the lower end 3 mm (1/8'') below the waistband (more if a wider belt is to be used). The lower end is stitched through the extension of the waistband facing.

Hems

Follow the instructions in Chapter 19 for marking and handling hems. Linings are usually hemmed separately from the garment and may have swing tacks at the lower edge similar to the long coat. Refer to Chapter 20 for measuring and hemming the lining for coats. For ease of pressing the swing tacks may be omitted so that the lining may be pulled free from the skirt or pant leg.

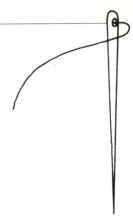

APPENDICES

	#1 Body Measurements	#2 Minimum Allowances for Ease*		#3 Total	#4 Pattern Measurement	#5 Difference + or -
WIDTH: Upper Body						
1. Neck circumference		0				
a. Back neck		0				
2. Shoulder width		j: 1 cm	(3/8'')			
		c: 1.3 cm	(1/2'')			
3. Shoulder length:		j: 6 mm	(1/4'')			
a. Left		c: 1 cm	(3/8'')			
b. Right						
4. Back width		j: 2.5 cm	(1'')			
		c: 3.8 cm	(1½'')			
5. Extended back width		0				
6. Chest width		j: 6 mm	(1/4'')			
		c: 1 cm	(3/8'')			
** 7. Bust (or chest for men) circumference		j: 7.5 cm	(3'')			
		c: 10 cm	(4'')			
a. Front bust or chest width		j: 2.5 cm	(1'')			
		c: 3.8 cm	(1½'')			
b. Back bust or chest width (7 minus 7a)		j: 5 cm	(2'')			
		c: 6.5 cm	(2½'')			
8. Waist circumference		s: 1.3 cm	(1/2'')			
		j: 6.5 cm	(2½'')			
		c: 10 cm	(4'')			
a. Front waist width		(half of total)				
b. Back waist width						
WIDTH: Lower Body						
9. Hip circumference		s: 2.5 cm	(1'')			
		j: 7.5 cm	(3'')			
		c: 12.5 cm	(5'')			

Large figures will usually require more ease than small ones. When ease allowances vary for different garments, the following letters are used:

j—indicates ease for jacket or coat to be worn over lightweight blouse and suit weight skirt.

c—indicates ease for coat to be worn over a medium weight sweater or jacket (more ease will be required to wear over very bulky garments).

s—indicates ease for skirt or pants.

Allow additional ease if jacket or coat is to be interlined or if fabric is extremely thick and bulky.

* Allowances for ease are the *minimum* for ease of movement and appearance.

**Key areas for measuring.

	#1 Body Measurements	#2 Minimum Allowances for ease*		#3 Total	#4 Pattern Measurement	#5 Difference + or -
WIDTH: Lower Body (Cont.)						
a. Front hip width		s: 1.3 cm	(1/2'')			
		j: 3.8 cm	(1½'')			
		c: 6.5 cm	(2½'')			
b. Back hip width (9 minus 9a)		s: 1.3 cm	(1/2'')			
		j: 3.8 cm	(1½'')			
		c: 6.5 cm	(2½'')			
10. Hip depth						
** 11. High hip circumference		s: 2.5 cm	(1'')			
		j: 6.5 cm	(2½'')			
		c: 10 cm	(4'')			
a. Front high hip width		(one half total)				
b. Back high hip width (11 minus 11a)						
LENGTH: Upper body						
** 12. Back waist length		j: 6 mm	(1/4'')			
		c: 1.3 cm	(1/2'')			
13. Front waist length		j: 1.3 cm	(1/2'')			
		c: 2 cm	(3/4'')			
14. Bust depth		j: 6 mm	(1/4'')			
		c: 1.3 cm	(1/2'')			
15. Upper back side length		j: 6 mm	(1/4'')			
		c: 1.3 cm	(1/2'')			
a. Left						
b. Right						
LENGTH: Lower Body						
16. Floor to waist:						
a. Left side						
b. Right side						
c. Front						
d. Back						

(Continued on following page)

	#1 Body Measure- ments	#2 Minimum Allowances for ease*		#3 Total	#4 Pattern Measure- ment	#5 Differ- ence + or -
LENGTH: Lower Body (Cont.)						
17. Skirt length						
SLEEVE						
**18. Upper arm circum- ference		j: 7 cm c: 10 cm	(2 3/4'') (4'')			
19. Elbow circumference		j: 7 cm c: 10 cm	(2 3/4'') (4'')			
20. Wrist circumference		(style)				
21. Shoulder to wrist length		2.5 cm	(1'')			
a. Shoulder to elbow length		1.3 cm	(1/2'')			
b. Elbow to wrist length (21 minus 21a)						
PANTS						
22. Crotch depth		1.3 cm	(1/2'')			
23. Crotch length (total)		3.8 cm	(1½'')			
a. Front crotch length		1.3 cm	(1/2'')			
b. Back crotch length (23 minus 23a)		2.5 cm	(1'')			
24. Thigh circumference		7.5 cm	(3'')			
25. Distance below widest hip						
26. Front width across thighs		s: 2.5 cm j: 5 cm c: 7.5 cm	(1'') (2'') (3'')			

Appendix B
PROCEDURAL OUTLINE FOR CONSTRUCTION OF JACKET OR COAT

Chapter		Date
2	Select pattern, fabric, and findings.	_____
3	Check fit:	
	Take and compare body and pattern measurements.	_____
	Make major adjustments.	_____
	Check fit of paper pattern.*	_____
4	Construct and fit test garment (optional).*	_____
5	Prepare fabric and pattern.	_____
6	Lay out, cut, mark, and staystitch	_____
	Garment fronts: follow selected outline in Chapter 9 (record steps below).	_____

_____

_____

_____

_____

_____

_____

_____

_____

	Stitch shoulder seams	_____
16	Construct collar.*	_____
17	Apply front facings and collar.*	_____
18	Apply sleeves and shoulder shaping.*	_____
	Complete front facings.	_____
19	Hem lower edge and sleeves.	_____
20	Prepare and apply lining.*	_____
21	Attach fasteners and complete details.*	_____

---

*Critiques are available in the Appendices for each of these steps.

Appendix C
FITTING AND CONSTRUCTION CRITIQUES

Critiques are included so you can check your garment fit and construction at crucial points. Failure to check at these points may result in problems later and a more difficult correction.

To gain experience in evaluating your work by professional standards, use the following scale and write the number in the space after each point on the critique. The space may also be used for comments.

1. perfect, or close to it

2. not perfect, but passable

3. passable only

4. needs help badly

The critique titles and the chapter(s) in which you will find reference to them are as follows:

Critique #1

Checking the Paper Pattern

JACKET OR COAT (Body of Garment):		
Neckline seam conforms to neck (or sets away equal distance for design)		
Shoulder seam bisects shoulder		
Back shoulder darts or ease point to body bulge		
Adequate ease for reaching at mid-armhole		
Chest or bustline: Adequate circumference (minimum 7.5 cm or 3''); not excessive		
No strain over bust or chest		
Darts or seams impart fullness to largest area (point of bust)		
Armhole: Positioned for desired shoulder width		
Adequate circumference (min. 2.5 cm or 1'' below underarm); not excessive		
Front waist length coincides with pattern		
Back waist length coincides with pattern		
Center front perpendicular to floor		
Waist circumference adequate for style		
Hip circumference adequate for style		
Side seams bisect body, perpendicular to floor		
Length appropriate to body and design		
Hemline level		
Button and pocket placement as desired		
JACKET OR COAT (Sleeves matched to garment underarm):		
Ease in upper arm, minimum of 7 cm (1 3/4'')		

(Continued on following page)

Sleeve cap height adequate for fitted, set-in sleeve		
Elbow fullness centered at elbow		
Length as desired		
SKIRT (pinned to fitting band):		
Ease adequate at hipline		
Ease adequate at waistline		
Center front and back, side seams perpendicular to floor		
Side seam bisects body		
Darts or fullness point toward body bulge		
Hemline parallel to floor		

Critique #2

Fitting the Test Garment

JACKET OR COAT (Body of Garment):		
Grain is parallel to floor at: Bustline		
Arm break at front and back		
Ease Back shoulder—adequate to reach		
Bustline—7.5 cm to 15 cm (3'' to 6'')		
No strain lines		
No vertical or horizontal folds		
Balance—evenly balanced on body Front view		
Side view		
Line and Set Neckline:		
Seamline follows base of neck or as needed for design		
Neither too large nor too small		
Shoulders smooth—no wrinkles, hollows, or too tight areas:		
Front		
Back		
Seams bisect the body and are straight:		
Shoulder		
Side (also perpendicular to floor)		
Back		
Front opening:		
Perpendicular to floor		
Does not pull when fastened		
Adequate overlap for size of button		
Button placement correct for body and design		

(Continued on following page)

Front darts point to point of bust or seams place fullness in correct area		
Back shoulder darts point to body bulge		
Armhole (with shoulder shape in place):		
Neither too small or too large (minimum 2.5 cm or 1'' below underarm)		
Seamline in correct position for shoulder width and fashion		
Smooth curve to arm break		
Fitted garment:		
Midriff correct circumference for body and design		
Waistline—correct circumference		
Hipline—correct circumference		
Fits smoothly, no drag lines		
Waistline seam (if present):		
Appears parallel to the floor		
Side seams match		
Correct placement for body and design		
Length correct for body and design		
Pocket size and placement correct		

JACKET OR COAT (Sleeve)

Grain Parallel to floor at lower armhole		
Perpendicular to floor from shoulder to elbow		
Ease (minimum 5 cm or 2'' or more for a coat)		
Balance—equidistant from front and back of arm		
Line and Set Sleeve cap:		
No excess fullness or strain lines		
Even distribution of ease		

Darts—centered on elbow		
Length as desired for style		

JACKET OR COAT (Collar)

Fits smoothly around neckline		
Sets in correct position for style		
Neck hugging collar has adequate ease		
Outer seamline covers neckline seam		

SKIRT OR PANTS:

Grain

Parallel to floor at hipline		
Perpendicular to floor from waistline		

Ease

Adequate at hipline, minimum 2.5 cm (1'')		
Adequate at waistline, minimum 1.3 cm (1/2'')		
Crotch length adequate for sitting and movement		

Balance—evenly balanced on body

Front view		
Side view		

Line and Set

Vertical seams and/or creases or pleats perpendicular to the floor		
Side seam bisects body		
Darts or fullness:		
Front—point toward body bulge		
Back—point toward body bulge		
Smooth fit, no drag lines, wrinkles, or tight areas		
Hemline is parallel to floor		
Pockets do not pull; lie flat if so intended		

First Fitting

JACKET OR COAT (Body of Garment):		
Grain is parallel to floor at: Bustline		
Arm break at front and back		
Ease Back shoulder—adequate to reach		
Bustline—7.5 cm to 15 cm (3'' to 6'')		
No strain lines		
No vertical or horizontal folds		
Balance—evenly balanced on body Front view		
Side view		
Line and Set · Neckline:		
Seamline follows base of neck or as needed for design		
Neither too large nor too small		
Shoulders smooth—no wrinkles, hollows, or too tight areas:		
Front		
Back		
Seams bisect the body and are straight:		
Shoulder		
Side (also perpendicular to floor)		
Back		
Front opening:		
Perpendicular to floor		
Does not pull when fastened		
Adequate overlap for size of button		
Button placement correct for body and design		

Front darts point to point of bust or seams place fullness in correct area		
Back shoulder darts point to body bulge		
Armhole (with shoulder shape in place):		
Neither too small or too large (minimum 2.5 cm or 1'' below underarm)		
Seamline in correct position for shoulder width and fashion		
Smooth curve to arm break		
Fitted garment:		
Midriff correct circumference for body and design		
Waistline—correct circumference		
Hipline—correct circumference		
Fits smoothly, no drag lines		
Waistline seam (if present):		
Appears parallel to the floor		
Side seams match		
Correct placement for body and design		
Length correct for body and design		
Pocket size and placement correct		

JACKET OR COAT (Sleeve)

Grain Parallel to floor at lower armhole		
Perpendicular to floor from shoulder to elbow		
Ease (minimum 5 cm or 2'' or more for a coat)		
Balance—equidistant from front and back of arm		
Line and Set Sleeve cap:		
No excess fullness or strain lines		

(Continued on following page)

Even distribution of ease		
Darts—centered on elbow		
Length as desired for style		

JACKET OR COAT (Collar)

Fits smoothly around neckline		
Sets in correct position for style		
Neck hugging collar has adequate ease		
Outer seamline covers neckline seam		

SKIRT OR PANTS:

Grain

Parallel to floor at hipline		
Perpendicular to floor from waistline		

Ease

Adequate at hipline, minimum 2.5 cm (1'')		
Adequate at waistline, minimum 1.3 cm (1/2'')		
Crotch length adequate for sitting and movement		
Balance—evenly balanced on body		
Front view		
Side view		

Line and Set

Vertical seams and/or creases or pleats perpendicular to the floor		
Side seam bisects body		
Darts or fullness:		
Front—point toward body bulge		
Back—point toward body bulge		
Smooth fit, no drag lines, wrinkles, or tight areas		
Hemline is parallel to floor		
Pockets do not pull; lie flat if so intended		

Critique #3

Sample Buttonholes

Fabric:		
Rectangle on grain		
Lips on grain, unless on bias		
Lips narrow as feasible for fabric, even width, firm		
Lips lie parallel and close together		
Corners square and secure, no puckers		
No interfacing visible on right side		
Bulk reduced as much as possible		
Correct length for button		
Hand worked:		
Opening straight and on grain		
Keyhole symmetrical and open		
Stitches closely and evenly spaced		
Stitches even depth (max. 3 mm or 1/8'')		
Edges flat and firm		
Purl stitches even along opening		
Thread appropriate for fabric (weight and color)		

Completed Buttonholes

Fabric:		
Rectangle on grain		
Lips on grain, unless on bias		
Lips narrow as feasible for fabric, even width, firm		
Lips lie parallel and close together		
Corners square and secure, no puckers		
No interfacing visible on right side		
Bulk reduced as much as possible		
Correct length for button		
Hand worked:		
Opening straight and on grain		
Keyhole symmetrical and open		
Stitches closely and evenly spaced		
Stitches even depth (max. 3 mm or 1/8'')		
Edges flat and firm		
Purl stitches even along opening		
Thread appropriate for fabric (weight and color)		

Critique #4

Pockets and Flaps

Applied pockets and flaps:		
On grain or as designated		
Pairs identical in size, shape, and placement		
Curves smooth, lines straight, corners square		
Bulk reduced as much as possible		
Layers lie smoothly together		
Topstitching even and suitable		
Lie smoothly over body curve		
Seams not obvious on edges		
Slashed (welt) pockets (check above also):		
Welts firm, straight, even width		
Welts lie parallel and close together		
Corners square and firm		
Inseam pocket:		
Seamline and topstitching appear continuous		
Pocket opening firm		
Pocket and opening lie flat		
Position is functional		

Critique #5

Shaped and Taped Fronts

Shaped Lapel Lapel rolls on roll line		
Degree of roll correct for type of collar		
Corners of lapel roll slightly under		
Interfacing smooth, no bubbles or roughness		
Layers lie smoothly together (firmly fused if fusible interfacing)		
Nonfusible interfacing free at shoulder		
Interfacing extends into neckline seam allowance (3 mm or 1/8'' for fusibles)		

Taping
    Tape lies flat and smooth (curves
       notched, corners mitered)		

Edge of tape placed on garment side of seamline		
Straight edges straight, curves smooth		
Seam allowances accurate and even		
Front edge (below lapel or to neckline if no lapel):		
Fabric lies flat		
No stretch to edge when pulled		
Tape eased along lapel edges but lies smoothly		
Bridle stay (for garment with lapel) Will not stretch when pulled		

Firmly attached to interfacing (and to
       fashion fabric when fusible interfac-
       ing is used)		

Fabric is eased slightly to stay		
Stitching not visible from fashion fabric side when lapel is rolled		

Attached no closer than 3.8 cm (1 1/2'')
       to shoulder seam with nonfusible
       interfacing		

Critique #6

Shaped Undercollar

Stand is firm		
Corners roll slightly under		
Interfacing smooth, no bubbles or rough- ness		
Degree of roll correct for type of collar		
Interfacing seam smooth at center back neck		
Collar conforms to neckline shape		

Critique #7

Completed Collar

Outer seam graded to prevent ridging		
All possible bulk reduced on corners and curves		
Edges as sharp as feasible		
Seam rolls under on all outer edges		
Layers of collar lie smoothly together when collar curved to final shape		
Ends are equal length and same shape		
With collar rolled, neckline stitching lines lie on top of each other		
Markings for matching to garment are visible at neckline seam of upper- and undercollars		

Critique #8

Completed Collar and Facing

Collar:		
Fits smoothly around neckline		
Rolls smoothly at roll line		
Covers neckline seam in back of neck		
Corners (ends) roll under slightly (do *not* curl up)		
Ends are equal in length		
Seam around outer edge not visible when garment is worn		
Layers lie together smoothly		
Firm enough to hold desired shape		
Edges sharp—bulk controlled as much as possible		
Lapel:		
Rolls smoothly at roll line		
Lies flat at gorgeline where lapel attaches to collar—seams graded so seam next to neck widest		
Gorgeline forms smooth, continuous lines or correct angle with top edge of lapel		
Corners roll under slightly		
Corners are equal length, same shape		
Seams around outer edge not obvious when garment is worn		
Roll line conforms to body, does not stand away		
Layers lie together smoothly		
Edges sharp—bulk controlled as much as possible		

(Continued on following page)

Front edge (below lapel):

Edge does not give when stretched		
Lies flat, smooth, and straight		
Seam on edge not obvious		
Angles or curves at lower edge smooth, identical in shape		
Layers lie together smoothly		
Edge of interfacing or facing not visible		

Critique #9

Sleeves Basted

SHOULDER: *Grain* is parallel to floor at front and back arm break		
Ease—back shoulder: Adequate to reach		
Under fabric takes stress when arms are flexed		
Line and Set Shoulder seam is straight, bisects shoulder		
Shoulder seam is not obvious from front view		
Armhole seam in correct position for shoulder width and fashion		
Front shoulder is smooth, no wrinkles or hollows		
Armhole seam creates smooth vertical line		
Back shoulder area is smooth, no hollows, wrinkles, or too tight areas		
SLEEVE: *Grain* Parallel to floor at lower armhole		
Perpendicular to floor from shoulder to elbow		
Ease Elbow circumference adequate for movement		
Armhole large enough for easy movement		
Upper arm at least 5 cm (2'') or more for a coat		
Balance—equidistant from front and back of arm		

(Continued on following page)

Line and Set

Sleeve hangs in straight alignment, no drag lines		
Sleeve cap is smooth, no ripples or flattened areas		
Slight roll is created at upper cap of sleeve (unless design indicates flatness)		
Elbow fullness in correct position		
Length as desired for design		

Critique #10

Prelining Check

Shoulders and sleeve (see Critique #9):		
Bottom edge of sleeve appears parallel to floor		
Bottom edge of sleeve is firm at foldline		
Hem is not visible		
Hem lies smoothly inside sleeve		
Lower portion of armhole seam double stitched and trimmed, or clipped and pressed open		
Shoulder shape firmly basted to interfacing Smooth armhole seam (no dimpling from tight basting)		
Collar, lapels, and front (see Critique #8):		
Fabric buttonholes (see Critique #3):		
Back neatly finished		
Pockets (see Critique #4):		
Hems: Stitches and hem edge not visible from right side		
Seams lie flat (graded), not bulky		
Layers of fabric lie smoothly together		
Width appropriate and uniform		
Lower edge even and parallel to floor		
Pressing: Edges as sharp as feasible (except soft hems)		
No over pressing (shine, flattened nap, etc)		
Bulk reduced wherever possible		
Seams flat and smooth		
Fabric smooth, no wrinkles, bubbles		
Overall well-pressed appearance		

(Continued on following page)

Topstitching:		
Appropriate length stitch (heavier thread, longer stitch)		
Straight and even distance from edge		
Grain not distorted by stitching		
Stitches uniform in length		

Critique #11

Lining Pinned (Body only)

Adequate ease across back shoulders		
Fits smoothly to inside of garment		
Underarm seams very loosely basted to seams in fashion fabric (pin only if to be removed for decorative detail or machine application)		
Lower edge of lining equal distance from lower edge of garment		
Covers facing with adequate seam allowance		
Seams lie on top of each other		

Critique #12

Completed Jacket or Coat

Details not previously critiqued:

Lining Securely sewn at armhole		
Adequate ease across shoulders		
Unpressed ease fold at sleeve hem		
Lower edge even distance from lower edge of fashion fabric		
Lightly pressed ease fold at jacket hem		
Swing tacks to control loose hem		
Fits smoothly to inside of garment		
Facing—lining seam straight and/or smooth curves		
Decorative treatment of lining:		
Appropriate to garment		
Does not add bulk		
Smooth and evenly applied		
Technique correctly executed		
Buttons Shank length adequate		
Buttonholes lie flat when being used		
Thread shank is firm		
Stitches not visible on facing		
Snaps or hooks Inconspicuous		
Neatly attached		
Belt Even in width		
Adequate firmness for method of closing		
Bulk reduced as much as possible		

Carriers:

Neatly constructed		
Lie flat over belt		
Selection of design, fabric, and notions:		
Suited to wearer (design and fabric)		
Supporting fabrics compatible		
Lining compatible		
Notions and trim appropriate		
Decorative treatments add to professional appearance		
Overall professional appearance: Patterned fabric:		
Pattern matched at center front and all vertical seams, sleeves, center back of collar, detail areas		
Pleasing placement of dominant pattern		
General appearance of continuity		
Buttonholes (Critique #3)		
Pockets and flaps (Critique #4)		
Collar and lapels (Critique #8)		
Sleeves (Critique #9)		
Hems (Critique #10)		
Lining (Critique #12)		
Well pressed (Critique #12)		
Special details		

Critique #13

Completed Skirts and Pants

Fit:
Grain—parallel to floor at hipline

Ease Adequate for movement and comfort		
Appropriate for garment design		
Balance Equidistant from each side of the body		
Equidistant from front and back of body		

Line and Set
    Vertical seams and/or creases or pleats
        perpendicular to floor		

Lower edge parallel to floor		
Smooth fit, no drag lines, wrinkles, or tight areas		

Zipper placket:
Top of zipper close to waistband

Zipper teeth not visible		
Stitching straight and even		
Lies flat and smooth		
Zipper operates easily and smoothly		

Waistband:
Even width

Corners square		
Adequate firmness to hold shape with minimum bulk		
Securely and neatly fastened		
Layers lie flat and smooth		
Neatly finished on back		
Fits figure		

Hem:
Stitches and hem edge not visible from
    right side

Seams lie flat, not bulky (graded)		
Layers of fabric lie smoothly together		
Width appropriate and even		
Even and parallel to floor		

Pressing:
Edges as sharp as feasible		
Creases or pleats sharply pressed		
No over pressing (shine, flattened nap)		
Bulk reduced wherever possible		
Overall well-pressed appearance		

Pockets (refer to Critique #4 for specifics)
Correctly placed for use and visual relationship to garment		
Lie smooth when worn		
Straight lines straight, and/or curves smooth		
Bulk reduced as much as possible		

Buttonholes (refer to Critique #3)

Fabric:
Correct placement for size of button		
Lips narrow as feasible for fabric		
Lips even in width, firm		
Corners square and secure		
Back neatly and evenly finished		
Bulk reduced as much as possible		

Hand worked:
Opening straight, keyhole symmetrical		
Stitches closely and evenly spaced		
Stitches even depth		
Edges flat and firm		
Purl stitches even along opening		

TOPSTITCHING:
Appropriate length stitch (heavier thread, longer stitch)		

(_Continued on following page_)

Straight and/or even distance from edge		
Grain not distorted by stitching		
Stitches uniform in length		
PATTERNED FABRIC: Pattern matched at center front, vertical seams, center back, detail areas		
Pleasing placement of dominant pattern		
General appearance of continuity		
Darts—tapered and smooth		
LINING: Fits smoothly inside the garment		
Lining and garment seamlines are aligned		
Attached with garment at waistband		
Neatly finished at zipper and hem		
PANTS CROTCH AREA: Crotch seam stitching continuous from front to back		
Lower crotch curve double stitched, trimmed, and overedged		
Lining fits smoothly in crotch		
SELECTION OF FABRICS AND NOTIONS: Garment design and fabrics compatible		
Fabric will not stretch at knees and/or seat		
Notions compatible to fabric and design		
Suited to wearer (design and fabric)		
Decorative treatments add to professional appearance		
OVERALL PROFESSIONAL APPEARANCE: Neat—no visible markings or bastings		
Well pressed		

Appendix D
CONSTRUCTION OF SHOULDER SHAPES (PADS)

1. Make a tissue pattern using as your guide the front and back pattern pieces pinned together at the shoulder (Step 1). Use the armhole curve from notch to notch, extending the line 1.3 cm (1/2'') beyond the seams at the shoulder. Draw another curve about 2.5 cm (1'') from the neck edge extending to the front and back notches. *Note:* The pad extends 1.3 cm (1/2'') into the sleeve at the shoulder to prevent drooping.

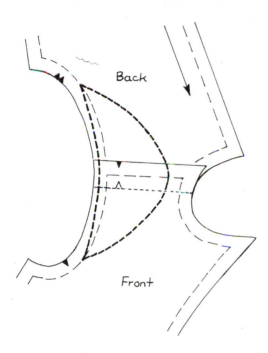

Back

Front

STEP 1
Pattern for Shoulder Shapes.

2. From this pattern, cut graduated layers of polyester fleece (or use cotton felt or nonwoven interfacing), making as many layers as needed to give the desired firmness, height, and shape (Step 2). Maintain same curve at armhole edge for all layers.

STEP 2
Layers for Shoulder Shape.

(Continued on following page)

3.   Cut a layer of hair cloth or other firm interfacing the full size of the pattern to give firm support across the top.

4.   Stack all layers with armhole edges even, largest layer uppermost.

5.   Curve layers over your hand and beginning at top center, stab stitch the entire pad to hold a curved shape (Step 3). Repeat for other shoulder.

Note: Shapes can be made for raglan or kimono sleeves following the same procedure. The difference is that you allow the pattern to extend over the curved portion of shoulder. Darting or notching the edge will be required to give the pad its curved shape (Step 4). Draw the cut edges together by carrying the threaded needle under and over the notched edges (Step 5).

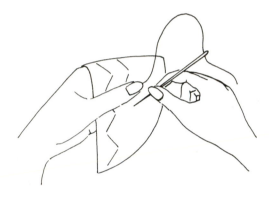

STEP 3
Shaping the Shoulder Shape.

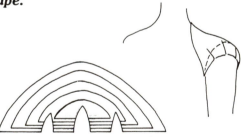

STEP 4
Shoulder Shape for Raglan
and Kimono Sleeves.

STEP 5
Joining Cut Edges.

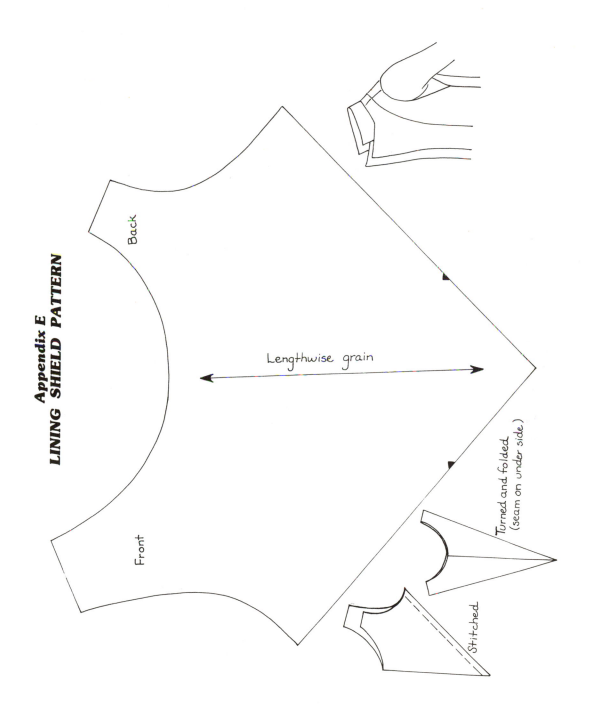

Appendix E
LINING SHIELD PATTERN

Back

Front

Lengthwise grain

Turned and folded
(seam on under side)

Stitched

365

Appendix F
TAILORED PLACKET PATTERNS

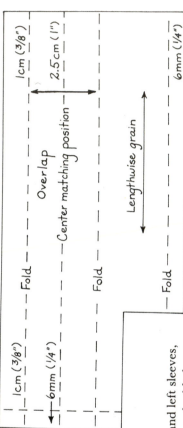
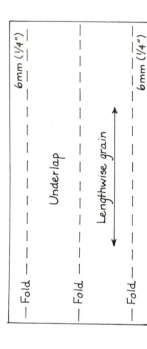

To cut plackets for the right and left sleeves, the pattern should be laid on a double layer of fabric with right or wrong sides of the fabric together.

Appendix G
REFERENCES FOR ADDITIONAL INFORMATION

General Construction Techniques

Musheno, Elizabeth J. (editor). *The Vogue Sewing Book,* 2nd edition. New York: Butterick Fashion Marketing Company, 1973.

Colton, Virginia (editor). *Reader's Digest Complete Guide to Sewing.* Pleasantville, NY: The Reader's Digest Association, Inc., 1976.

Pattern Adjustment and Fitting

Minott, J. *Fitting Commercial Patterns.* Minneapolis, MN: Burgess Publishing Company, 1978.

Minott, J. *Pants and Skirts to Fit Your Shape,* 2nd edition. Minneapolis, MN: Burgess Publishing Company, 1974.

Perry, P. (editor). *The Vogue Sewing Book of Fitting, Adjustments, and Alterations.* New York: Butterick Fashion Marketing Company, 1972.

Men's Tailoring (traditional techniques)

Poulin, C. *Tailoring Suits the Professional Way,* 3rd edition. Peoria, IL: Chas. A. Bennett Company, Inc., 1973.

Smith, Bev and Hurd, Maxi. *Men's Tailoring for the Home Sewer.* Portland, OR: Irwin-Hodson Company, 1975. (Address for ordering: 1057 Landaro Drive, Escondido, CA 92027.)

NOTES

NOTES

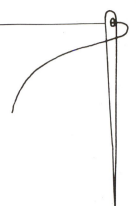

INDEX